VICTORY AT HONSHU

Now with the starlit sea as a background, we could make her out, a large patrol, anchored two miles from Kuki Saki and asking for it!

The outer doors were open aft as I conned *Tang* for a zero gyro angle shot.

"Fire!" The torpedo left with the characteristic whine. A loud rumble occurred when the torpedo should have been halfway to the gunboat . . . it had hit bottom! The enemy had been alerted!

"Fire!" and a Mark 23 steam torpedo, set to run on the surface, left with a zing directly for the enemy's middle. The explosion was the most spectacular we had seen, topped by a pillar of fire and tremendous explosions about 500 feet in the air. There was absolutely nothing left of the gunboat.

THE BANTAM WAR BOOK SERIES

This is a series of books about a world on fire.

These carefully chosen volumes cover the full dramatic sweep of World War II. Many are eyewitness accounts by the men who fought in this global conflict in which the future of the civilized world hung in balance. Fighter pilots, tank commanders and infantry commanders, among others, recount exploits of individual courage in the midst of the large-scale terrors of war. They present portraits of brave men and true stories of gallantry and cowardice in action, moving sagas of survival and tragedies of untimely death. Some of the stories are told from the enemy viewpoint to give the reader an immediate sense of the incredible life and death struggle of both sides of the battle.

Through these books we begin to discover what it was like to be there, a participant in an epic war for freedom.

Each of the books in the Bantam War Book series contains a dramatic color painting and illustrations specially commissioned for each title to give the reader a deeper understanding of the roles played by the men and machines of World War II.

CLEAR THE BRIDGE!

The War Patrols of the U.S.S. Tang

RICHARD H. O'KANE
Rear Admiral, U.S.N. (Ret.)

BANTAM BOOKS
TORONTO · NEW YORK · LONDON · SYDNEY

*This low-priced Bantam Book
has been completely reset in a type face
designed for easy reading, and was printed
from new plates. It contains the complete
text of the original hard-cover edition.*
NOT ONE WORD HAS BEEN OMITTED.

CLEAR THE BRIDGE!
*A Bantam Book / published by arrangement with
Rand McNally & Company*

PRINTING HISTORY
*Rand McNally edition published July 1977
4 printings through May 1979
Bantam edition / May 1981*

*Illustrations by Greg Beecham.
Maps by Alan McKnight.*

ACKNOWLEDGMENTS

I take this opportunity to express my thanks to the individuals within the Department of the Navy and the submarine forces who supplied documents and records. To Mare Island Naval Shipyard, Lawrence Savadkin, and William Leibold, I am indebted for assistance in obtaining the photographs; to artist Fred Freeman for the basic cutaway submarine drawing; and to the National Geographic Society for confirming prewar names on the charts.

In verifying the operations of other submarines, I relied on the authority of Theodore Roscoe's *United States Submarine Operations in World War II* and W. J. Holmes's *Undersea Victory*. For details of surface ship operations, Samuel Eliot Morison's impeccable *History of United States Naval Operations in World War II* answered all questions.

For *Tang*'s operations, I thank Murray B. Frazee, Jr., who saved my file of expanded patrol reports, sailing lists, and detailed recommendations for awards to members of the ship's company; and Floyd Caverly, who supplied additional information. For reviewing the manuscript, I will always be grateful to Mrs. Peggy Grey, author Paul Schubert, and Mrs. Henry Bothfeld.

Finally, I am deeply indebted to my wife, Ernestine G. O'Kane, for assisting me at many times, and without whose help the completion of this book would have been impossible.

R. H. O'K.

Forgive me for writing here to the relatives of all men who served in Tang *and especially to the kin of those who sailed on her last patrol:*

As you may know, I attempted to reach some parents and relatives after repatriation and later following final survey to duty in 1946. It was too early and perhaps will ever be so, for no matter how one views the loss of *Tang,* a thought of *Titanic* will always be present in a situation wherein the captain returns and shipmates are left behind.

Believe me, on that fateful night I became physically exhausted in trying to reach my ship and men, then so close ahead. Whence came the strength for the following eight hours to take me to within a stone's throw of China's shore will always remain a matter of wonder.

If your kin's name is not mentioned in this chronicle, it in no way means that he was not just as important to *Tang*'s operations as were shipmates whose billets were nearby and whose names thus came to mind. In fact, many of the more remote battle stations require the more resourceful and reliable men, for they are on their own, with no one to advise them or correct a mistake.

For the following page, therefore, I have compiled a combined sailing list that includes every submariner who served in *Tang* but who had been detached prior to her last patrol. In the next few pages, I have prepared the final sailing list of old hands and new who fought her through the typhoon and in the Formosa Strait, and who understandably will always have a special place in my thoughts. In later pages you will find the citations from our presidents, one or both of which were awarded to each shipmate who patrolled and were so dearly won by so many.

As I wrote this chronicle and replotted the courses, all of the time knowing the actual fate awaiting my crew and ship, it became necessary time and again to saddle up my buckskin and ride into the hills so that, upon my return, I might continue with a clear eye. Nothing could compensate for the loss that so many of you have borne. It is my hope, however, that when you have read this true account and perhaps in spirit patrolled with us, you will always think of your kin and *Tang* with utmost pride, as do I.

Our *Tang*'s two Presidential Unit Citations have been passed to her successor, the U.S.S. *Tang* (SS563), now operating in the Pacific. God willing, may her commission and those to follow continue to guard the peace.

Respectfully,

Richard H. O'Kane

Sebastopol, California
June, 1977

Served in U.S.S. *Tang* Prior to Fifth War Patrol

Arne I. Anderson	MoMM2c	Albert L. Kohlstrom	CMoMM
Bruce H. Anderson	Lt	Charles Kormanik	MoMM1c
Ralph C. Anderson	S2c	James W. Laird	EM2c
Raymond J. Aquisti	BM2c	Euclid H. Lambert	TM3c
Norman F. Aufdenkamp	S1c	Robert C. Ludy	QM2c
Wilburn Barnett	S1c	Morton H. Lytle	LtCdr
Calvin G. Barrick	QM3c	Robert B. MacDonald	CMoMM
Dallas G. Bowden	EM1c	Myron O. Mack, Jr.	S1c
Marvin E. Breedlove	CCS	Lester Madison	St3c
Emil W. Brincken	FCS1c	Arden E. Markham	RT3c
Cleon Bussey	Ck2c	James F. Marnell	TM2c
Dante N. Cacciola	S1c	Frank Maselli	SC2c
Frank G. Carrisalez	S1c	Dalton E. Mathis	CMoMM
James D. Cazola	MoMM1c	Raymond D. McNally	Y3c
Paul C. Collins	MoMM2c	Roy J. Miletta	RM3c
Charles R. Conder	EM3c	Jessie R. Miller	TM1c
Ardery J. Cooper	EM3c	James H. Montgomery	TM1c
James F. Cross	TM3c	Franklin Nielsen	RT3c
Roy H. Crotty	CMoMM	Earl W. Ogden	CSM
Hal A. Davis	EM1c	Guy Overby, Jr.	MoMM2c
Henry W. Dardinski	FCS2c	Charles O. Pucket	Ltjg
Carl T. Dilley	TM1c	Rudolph K. Reidenbach	S1c
Clyde R. Dotson, Jr.	F3c	Leroy C. Rowell	CPhM
James Flemming	S1c	Edward A. Russel	CMoMM
Murray B. Frazee, Jr.	LtCdr	Fred Schroeder, Jr.	RM1c
Thomas P. Gannon	RM3c	James W. Scott	QM3c
Robert B. Gorin	TM3c	John J. Sertich	S1c
Walter H. Hallfarth	CEM	Donald R. Sharp	TM2c
George H. Hanskat	EM3c	Everett Shearer, Jr.	EM3c
Robert L. Harding	MoMM2c	James G. Smiley	MoMM1c
Raymond R. Hardon	MoMM2c	Joseph L. Sutton	StM1c
Edward E. Hinson	RM1c	Robert Taylor, Jr.	StM1c
Calvin G. Jancik	SC2c	William C. Walsh	Lt
James R. Johnston	SC2c	Alvin K. Warren	SC3c
Wm. F. Keenan, Jr.	MoMM1c	Don W. Watje	TM2c
Herman Kendrick	StM2c	Clement O. Wilson	TME2c
Clifford M. Kirkelie	CRM	Frederick D. Wixon	SC1c
Joseph D. Kivlen	CEM	Harvie E. Young	CEM

Sailing List of U.S.S. *Tang* for Fifth War Patrol

John G. Accardy	SM3c	Sidney W. Jones	CQM
Ralph F. Adams	StM1c	Louis C. Kaiser	MoMM3c
Dwayne D. Allen	MoMM2c	John T. Kanagy	EM1c
Phillip E. Anderson	TM3c	John T. Kassube	Cox
Chares Andriolo	RM2c	John A. Key	SC3c
Homer Anthony	F1c	Ralph B. Knapp	FC3c
William F. Ballinger	CTM	Richard J. Kroth	Ltjg
Edwin C. Bauer	Y3c	Leroy R. Lane	EM1c
Edward H. Beaumont	Lt	Paul L. Larson	CPhM
Edwin F. Bergman	RM1c	Robert P. Lee	RM3c
Frederick N. Bisogno	TM3c	William R. Leibold	CBM
Wilfred J. Boucher	TM3c	Lindley H. Llewellyn	RM2c
Bernard V. Bresette	QM3c	Charles W. London	F1c
John Bush	EM2c	Chester Loveless	EM1c
Floyd M. Caverly	RT1c	Ellroy Lytton	MoMM1c
Benjamin Chiavetta	Y3c	Robert V. McMorrow	MoMM1c
Walter J. Clark	QM3c	John J. McNabb	F1c
Robert J. Coffin	EM3c	Pete Narowanski	TM3c
James H. Culp	CEM	Richard H. O'Kane	Cowdr
Arthur J. Darienzo	EM2c	John J. Parker	CCS
Jesse B. Dasilva	MoMM2c	Basil C. Pearce, Jr.	Ens
Clayton O. Decker	MoMM3c	Rubin M. Raiford	Ck2c
Marvin V. De Lapp	CMoMM	Francis J. Reabuck	F1c
William E. Dorsey	MoMM1c	Darrell D. Rector	GM3c
Fred M. Enos, Jr.	Ltjg	Ernest Reinhardt	F1c
Lawrence H. Ericksen	F1c	James L. Roberts	SC3c
Daniel C. Fellicetty	Y3c	George L. Robertson	MoMM2c
Bruce H. Finckbone	EM2c	Lawrence Savadkin	Lt
Henry J. Flanagan	Ltjg	Seymour G. Smith, Jr.	QM3c
John W. Fluker	TM1c	Frank H. Springer	Lt
John M. Foster	TM1c	Edward F. Stepien	F1c
William C. Galloway	TM2c	Fred L. Sunday	EM3c
Thomas E. Gentle	F1c	Hayes O. Trukke	TM2c
George J. Gorab, Jr.	EM3c	Paul B. Vaughn, Jr.	Cox
Osmer D. Gregg	Cox	Charles W. Wadsworth	TM3c
Howard W. Hainline	QM3c	Howard M. Walker	StM1c
Frank G. Harms	MoMM2c	Leland S. Weekley	CTM
Glen O. Haws	MoMM2c	Robert E. Welch	QM2c
John F. Henry	F1c	James M. White	GM1c
John H. Heubeck	Ltjg	Walter H. Williams	Y2c
Albert L. Hudson	CMoMM	Paul T. Wines	Ltjg
Homer W. Ijames	RM3c	George Wukovich	MoMM1c
Stewart S. Imwold	MoMM3c	George Zofcin	MoMM1c
Donald M. Jenkins	Y3c		

CONTENTS

The Commandant
requests the honor of your presence
at the
Launching of The United States Ship Tang
at the
Navy Yard, Mare Island, California

Tuesday, August 17, 1943

Ceremonies three thirty-nine p. m.   Launch at three fifty-nine p. m.

Mrs. Antonio S. Pitre, Sponsor

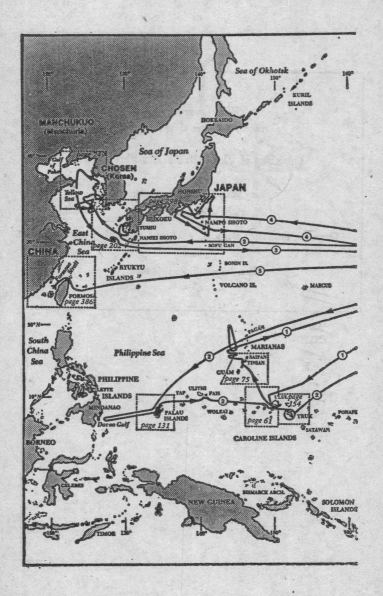

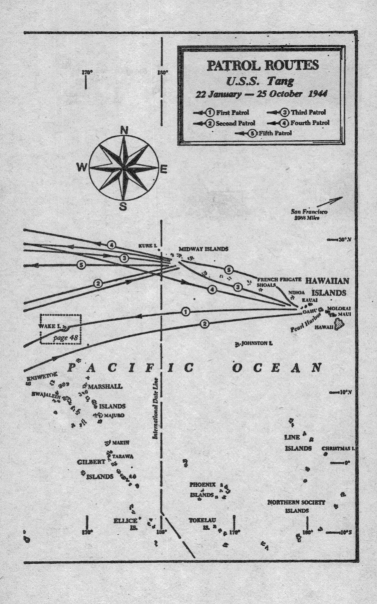

PATROL ROUTES
U.S.S. Tang
22 January — 25 October 1944

◄—① First Patrol   ◄—③ Third Patrol
◄—② Second Patrol   ◄—④ Fourth Patrol
              ◄—⑤ Fifth Patrol

San Francisco
2068 Miles

—30° N

KURE I.   MIDWAY ISLANDS

④

⑤

③   FRENCH FRIGATE HAWAIIAN
              SHOALS   ISLANDS
②   NIHOA
                          KAUAI
              ①   OAHU   MOLOKAI
                                  MAUI
              ②   Pearl Harbor
                                  HAWAII

WAKE I.

page 48

⊃–JOHNSTON I.

P A C I F I C   O C E A N

ENIWETOK
        ♦ MARSHALL
KWAJALEIN
        ISLANDS
        ♦ MAJURO

                          LINE
                          ISLANDS   CHRISTMAS I.

        MAKIN
        TARAWA   —0°
GILBERT
ISLANDS

                  PHOENIX
                  ISLANDS

                          NORTHERN SOCIETY
                          ISLANDS

ELLICE   TOKELAU
IS.   IS.   —10° S

170°   170°   180°   170°   160°

PROLOGUE

She stood tall and proud, her bullnose a good 30 feet above the ground. Dignitaries had assembled on the christening platform, and launching awaited only the moments of slack between flood and ebb tide. Below, a few of us who would fight and command her mingled with the masters and leading men who had brought the submarine to this moment; all of us would have an active hand in her completion. The shipyard's whistle sounded; the encased bottle of champagne burst on her stem, drenching the bow, and the sponsor's voice was firm and clear: "I christen thee *Tang*."

Tang accelerated down the ways, and her deep, streamlined hull entered the water with little more than a ripple. With snubbing anchors controlling the cradle, our submarine floated clear handsomely.

Her mission had been established on December 7, 1941, the afternoon of the Japanese attack on Pearl Harbor, by directive of the Chief of Naval Operations:

> EXECUTE UNRESTRICTED AIR AND
> SUBMARINE WARFARE AGAINST JAPAN

Over a million tons of Japanese shipping had been sent to Davy Jones's locker since then, but that was only a prelude to the task ahead. Another 5 million tons must follow, or better yet, the enemy must be convinced that sending his ships to sea was futile. It was August 17, 1943, and *Tang*, now coming alongside the dock, would be the 70th new American submarine to join in the battle.

She would be my first command, culminating nine consecutive years in combatant ships, for Japanese conquests in East Asia, the sinking of the U.S.S. *Panay* in China, and early rumblings in Europe had kept me and my contemporaries from the U.S. Naval Academy on continuous sea duty. Mine had commenced with a year in the taut cruiser *Chester*,

1

followed by over two years under mild and wild skippers in the destroyer *Pruitt,* the last of the World War I four-pipers. She served as a demanding school in communications, commissary, gunnery, torpedoes, tactics, and in true seamanship. *Pruitt* also introduced navy life and the separations it can impose to my boyhood chum, Ernestine Groves, who became my wife on June 1, 1936. With the required surface ship duty well behind me, my request brought orders to U.S. Naval Submarine School in January of 1938. Together again and with our infant daughter, Marsha, Ernestine and I were off to New London, Connecticut, and from there, five months later, to Pearl Harbor, where I reported aboard the navy's largest submarine, *Argonaut.*

Argonaut was a monster, a continuous challenge, with 12 torpedoes forward, 78 mines aft, and mounting two 6-inch guns that could hurl hundred-pound projectiles nearly 20 miles. Fortunately, my billets closely paralleled those in *Pruitt,* and knowing my way in their requirements gave me that much more time to learn my ship for qualification in submarines. The required year passed, and the board of two skippers put me through my paces during a grueling day in port and another at sea; but they signed the certification, and I wore the submariner's twin dolphins.

In September, 1939, all operations at Pearl took on a most serious air with President Franklin D. Roosevelt's proclamation of Limited Emergency. Our son, James, was born the same month. Major units of the Pacific Fleet arrived in 1940, and commencing in the fall of 1941, available submarines quietly departed on patrol with their torpedo tube outer doors open for firing. My qualification for command was approved, and my promotion to lieutenant came by dispatch prior to Thanksgiving, when *Argonaut* departed Pearl to patrol south of Midway. A skirmish with two Japanese destroyers on the night of Pearl Harbor was our only action with the enemy; but *Argonaut*'s lack of air conidtioning coupled with our required all-day dives resulted in ever increasing humidity and attendant electrical grounds, and fighting the ensuing small fires became almost routine. Nearly half her major machinery became inoperative, but that did not stop *Argonaut* from carrying out her mission to defend Midway. Little did we know, until reaching Pearl Harbor on January 22, 1942, that she had been the only ship available to oppose an expected assault. We found our families fine but all waiting on two hours' notice for evacuation from the Islands. Waiting also were my orders to report as executive officer of *Wahoo*, under construction at Mare Island Navy Yard, up the bay from San Francisco, which was *Argonaut*'s destination for some modernization. Most fortunately, this provided me the opportunity to settle my family nearby.

I had loved my last ship, but it did not take long to transfer my affections. Of half the displacement and with twice the power, *Wahoo* would have twice *Argonaut*'s speed and maneuverability. Further, she would carry 24 instead of 12 torpedoes and had ten instead of four tubes to launch them. To me, the living spaces seemed more like a streamlined train's than a submarine's. The control room and the conning tower each sported a radar, and in the conning tower was a torpedo data computer, too; all this equipment was new to me. Needed only was a ship's company to match, but already a sharp nucleus of officers and petty officers who were qualified in submarines had assembled, and a few of them had patrol experience. Together we instructed the new hands. Our captain was meticulous and enjoyed an excellent reputation in torpedo fire control. He trained his ship thoroughly, and all seemed to augur well for *Wahoo*.

But on a 55-day patrol of Truk Atoll, only two of our many contacts resulted in attacks, and only one freighter was sunk. For the second patrol, which would take *Wahoo* to the Solomons and then on to Australia, the chief of staff privately arranged for Lieutenant Commander Dudley W. (Mush) Morton to accompany us as a PCO, or prospective commanding officer for another boat. I hoped his presence would turn the key for us, but with enemy ships about, only a freighter and a submarine were sunk. Our skipper was exhausted, and when we reached Brisbane it appeared likely that he would stay in port, at least for a patrol's time.

In our apartment in Brisbane, Mush Morton and I analyzed the patrol and aired our views about situations in *Wahoo*. Our complete agreement concerning actions that might have been taken and on many possible shipboard improvements enhanced the rapport we had established on patrol. Six days later, I addressed him as Captain. As we discussed my role as his exec, Mush related his experience at PCO school in New London. While he made periscope observations and tactical decisions, two senior instructors recorded their own recommendations. Unencumbered by the mechanics of making the observations, the instructors were able to record quicker and better decisions.

"So you will be my co-approach officer," he said. "You'll make all observations and fire all torpedoes, but I'll con *Wahoo* to the best attack position." And then with a chuckle Mush added, "This way I'll never get scared."

This was a responsibility and an opportunity unique in our submarine forces, and I spent the following fortnight calling angles on the bow, that is, the angle formed by the longitudinal axis of an approaching ship and my line of sight intersecting her. My estimates of these angles would soon be used in determining enemy ships' courses. This task helped in keeping my mind off the deep sorrow I felt when I learned that a returning U.S. Army bomber had observed the destruction of my dear *Argonaut* by two enemy destroyers southeast of New Britain.

But all my thoughts were ahead on January 16, 1943, when *Wahoo* departed to patrol the Palau Islands. The destroyer *Patterson*, who had performed so notably in the terrible Battle of Savo Island, joined us for two days of mutual target services en route. Our skipper put his ship through her paces; I called angles on the bow, the quartermaster read my stadimeter ranges, and all three of us were satisfied. When *Patterson* turned back, sending Godspeed by signal searchlight, *Wahoo* was already 400 miles on her way.

One week later, deep inside New Guinea's Wewak Harbor, I was to fire my first six warshots, the final two down the throat of an attacking destroyer. The last torpedo in our forward tubes broke her back, but since we were already starting for the bottom we thought for a moment that the detonation was her first depth charge. Two days later, the firing was spread over 12 hours as *Wahoo*'s remaining 18 torpedoes put down a convoy of four ships. On the fourth patrol, to the East China and Yellow seas, our 24 torpedoes sank six ships and damaged another, while our deck gun sank two more. During her fifth patrol, to the Kuril Islands and down the east coast of Japan, *Wahoo* sank three more ships and damaged two others.

Wahoo was leading the pack in ships sunk. I had been promoted to lieutenant commander. The ship's company had all shared in a Presidential Unit Citation, and our skipper recommended awards for his subordinates each time he was decorated. Understandably, men were in line hoping for a billet in our ship. But *Wahoo*'s storage batteries, of experimental design, had been failing rapidly; on the last patrol they had had less than half their original capacity, a severe and dangerous handicap, and their replacement had already been scheduled at Mare Island. My waiting orders to command *Tang*, then building at the same shipyard and only 20 miles from my family, could not have been more welcome.

And so, after five patrols in *Wahoo*, I had left her with a bit of a lump in my throat and walked toward the building ways. Ernestine was at my side, Marsha and Jim scampered ahead, and in my hand was an invitation to witness the launching of the submarine I would command. I could accept that challenge with absolute confidence, for I had already fired more warshots than all but a few of our submarine commanders.

Tang would spend her entire life in war, on missions that took her twice the distance around the earth. According to postwar findings by the Joint Army-Navy Assessment Committee, her leading patrols in number of ships sunk ranked first, third, and tied for sixth in the 1,560 war patrols by our submarines. One of her devastating torpedo salvos brought results unparalleled in all navies, while her rescue of naval airmen made headlines across the nation. In total number of ships sunk during the war, *Tang* placed second and in total tonnage fourth. All of this she accomplished in a period of nine months from the date of departure on her first patrol, her sinkings averaging one ship every 11 days, twice the rate of her nearest rival. Sadly, as *Tang*'s story testifies, in war there can be an inverse moral: The greater the performance, the harsher the consequence.

PART I

Shakedown
MARE ISLAND TO PEARL HARBOR

1

To the casual eye, *Tang* had appeared ready for sea upon launching, but she was now securely moored abreast our shipbuilding office. Electrical cables had been snaked below, and already shipyard workmen had resumed the tasks that had been interrupted by the christening. According to the schedule, their work would continue for nearly two months. During the first few weeks, our ship's company assembled. Some men arrived from submarine school or schools pertinent to their particular rate. Many came directly from other submarines or after extended periods with one of the manufacturers of *Tang*'s major machinery. A few reported from bases or ships and had no submarine experience, but there was a place for each of them as well.

The senior officers and petty officers brought with them, perhaps, more varied patrol experience than had ever before been assembled for fitting out and fighting a submarine. Those men who had served in some of the 29 Asiatic Fleet submarines had experienced the general Japanese onslaught that coincided with the attack on Pearl Harbor. During the retreat from the Philippines, their submarines had been assigned trying and sometimes impossible missions in the delaying actions. Then, from bases in Australia, their boats ranged the Southwest Pacific and adjacent seas after enemy ships. At the outset, the men from Pacific Fleet submarines had had an easier time of it. Only the five submarines undergoing repair were at Pearl Harbor on December 7, 1941. Neither they nor the submarine base was damaged. Another five were out on patrol, with torpedo tube outer doors open for firing. The remaining 12 were at sea or on the West Coast. Offensive action against enemy shipping started immediately. Their patrols ranged from the Solomons to the Kurils, through the Pacific islands to the Japanese Empire, and on to the Yellow Sea.

For those members of *Tang*'s crew who had not yet

patrolled in submarines, these officers and petty officers formed an experienced nucleus to point the way. They would make it their business to instruct the new hands, for in submarines perhaps more than in any other fighting unit, the survival of all could depend on the performance of any individual.

If our ship's company brought something unique to *Tang*, she more than matched it. Great sections for other boats of her class were now moving from shop to ways, and they appeared identical to sections of previous submarines. A close end-on look at the cylindrical pressure hull, however, showed steel plating of twice the former thickness. The external frames, welded to the pressure hull, seemed to be rolled T-bar and had dimensions you might expect to see in the girders of a steel bridge. In the torpedo rooms, where the ballast tanks and framing were inside the pressure hull to permit streamlining, the frames remained visible; they were massive, both in depth and thickness of plate. Thus *Tang* would be the first deep-hulled submarine in the Pacific, with tactical capabilities due to her superior depth still unknown.

Lieutenant Murray B. Frazee, Jr., from Gettysburg, had reported early as executive officer and navigator. Fraz was of medium height, and his firm features bore the touch of a smile, evidence of the sense of humor he'd surely need. Seven patrols in *Grayback* had given him confidence, and with this came enthusiasm for the task ahead. Though he and I had served in boats of different temperaments, their basic organization was the same, and I liked what I heard and saw.

Fraz's assistant in many of the administrative tasks, and a key figure in the ship's company, would be our chief of the boat, Chief Torpedoman's Mate William Ballinger. Fraz handed me Ballinger's file. His home was Rosemead, California, but he came to *Tang* from patrols in *Tunny*, and with an outstanding record. At my nod, the exec sent for him. It was some minutes before Ballinger reached our shipbuilding office, having come from witnessing tests of *Tang*'s torpedo tubes. He was a bit taller than Fraz, and his dark hair, strong features, and military countenance took my eyes from his greasy dungarees. It was evident that he already understood his dual responsibilities, for much of his prestige as chief of the boat rested upon his billet as our leading torpedoman. We spoke of his skipper in *Tunny*, Commander John Scott, whom we both admired, and I congratulated him on his new billet.

Already, some of the men were assembling spare parts in the storerooms provided ashore for each ship's department. Those not engaged in this or the necessary fire watches incident to the welding aboard were attending specialized schools. All hands were busy. Now when you have someone who is carrying the ball, don't stand in his way. I took my own advice, leaving Fraz in charge, and proceeded to the shipyard's design section to investigate the true strength of *Tang*'s pressure hull. As I hoped, it could probably take twice the pressure of the stipulated 438 feet. Various hull fittings, however, were considered to be of lesser strength. We would look into that later.

At a naval shipyard, where construction does not follow a strict production line, it is possible to include new equipment not shown in the original plans and to make other innovations that have proven desirable in actual combat. We stretched this a bit to include items that would improve our habitability, though generally this was just a matter of installing a particular piece of equipment in a more convenient location. One item that did not fall into either category was a Taylor ice cream machine. Such a luxury was unheard of for submarines but was authorized for the wardroom of capital ships. That didn't really mean much, for where could even a battlewagon find one? Well, *Tang*'s chiefs had—and apparently only an hour ahead of the wardroom on the just-modernized *Tennessee*. If I did not take immediate action the battleship would get the machine by default, my forged signature on the chit notwithstanding.

"Why, only the Chief of the Bureau of Ships could authorize such an installation!" It was the answer I had expected from the shipyard commander, but the key was in the way he'd worded his negative reply. My phone call reached the acting chief, who was at first lukewarm but became quite receptive when I pointed out that the installation would be entirely independent of our own refrigeration system and so could not cause its failure. He simply said, "Get it." With the whole conversation on a green transcribing disk, we did just that, though I'm not sure who or even if anyone paid for it.

Ensign Fred Melvin Enos, Jr., from across the causeway in Vallejo, took on a somewhat simpler task. Mel was fresh-caught; a Naval Reserve Officer Training Corps graduate of the University of California and submarine school, he had yet to go to sea. But much of what he lacked in experience he made up for in eagerness. His project involved a useless warming oven built between the frames of wardroom country's forward bulkhead. I wanted it converted to a thermostatically controlled baking oven for our stewards, as it was right there in the pantry. If a steward became adept at making pies and pastries he could very nearly write his own ticket in the navy, and I'd never been averse to sampling their experiments. It seemed that I'd barely turned my back when the installation was complete, and on this one I don't know if a pound of butter or half a ham did the trick.

These were typical of the fun projects. There were others much more serious, which affected our ship and her fighting ability. One of these involved the target bearing transmitters (TBTs). Our periscopes did not transmit sufficient light for any dark night use, so on all but moonlit nights, attacks had to be carried out with our boat on the surface, and bearings taken from the bridge were transmitted to the conning tower by the TBTs. The brackets holding the TBTs were often welded onto the bridge structure in any convenient place, though the shipyard had seen the light in locating *Tang*'s after TBT on a centerline pedestal. We took care of the forward one ourselves. Down came the gimbal-mounted gyrocompass repeater, which was rarely used for taking bearings from the bridge. The repeater was rigidly reinstalled flush through the bridge cowl, with its face still in plain sight. In its place on the centerline, where alignment could be checked by a sighting on the bullnose, went our forward TBT. The V-shaped receptacle of the TBT would take the center hinge pin of a pair of binoculars to transmit bearings, including my firing bearings, below.

Our diesels, generators, and main motors were aligned, a task that must be done after a ship is waterborne. The 300 tons of batteries were installed, bringing *Tang* close to her surface trim, and one after another our major pieces of machinery were being tested. Participating, or just observing all of this was the best possible way for our ship's company to learn the boat. If there were building yards where workmen loafed on the job, Mare Island was not among them. On the contrary, it was not at all unusual to see an electrician or a machinist continue at his task well into the next shift so that others' work would not be delayed. With this type of effort, *Tang*'s completion stayed right on schedule.

Commissioning is not given the fanfare of a christening, for it is not as spectacular as a launching. In many ways, however, it is more solemn and significant to the participants.

It marks the state of a ship's completion, when the responsibility and authority pass to the prospective commanding officer. *Tang*'s commissioning ceremony was short and to the point. With her crew and officers assembled, the shipyard commander read his directive. I read my order to take command and nodded to Sidney Jones, our chief quartermaster; the jack and colors were hoisted smartly as the commission pennant was broken from our main. The first watch was set. *Tang* was now a part of the United States Navy and I was in command. I took this occasion to read to all hands my charge from Secretary of the Navy Frank Knox:

> Immediately after her shaking down period the U.S.S. *Tang* will be assigned to duty wherever she is then most needed. It is entirely possible that you will proceed directly into combat. Your first action may be by day or night, against any type of vessel or aircraft possessed by our able and ruthless enemies.
>
> Your future Fleet, Force, and Unit Commanders must rely on the U.S.S. *Tang* as an effective fighting unit from the hour when she reports to them for duty. It is your task to justify their confidence.

If there was any doubt in the mind of anyone concerning the seriousness of the coming weeks, this letter would square them away, for a charge to me was a charge to every member of the crew.

The ceremony was not completely serious since as of that day, October 15, all hands commenced drawing submarine pay, with time before the shakedown to spend it in San Francisco. I believe that some of the men's smiles, however, were occasioned by the assistant shipyard commander, who produced a receipt for me to sign—for one submarine. I could read their minds; the crew had been signing their lives away in drawing our equipage, and now a chit had even caught up with the captain.

We had six weeks before our shakedown. These began with dockside trials of all engines and systems, the majority coming under Lieutenant William Walsh and his engineers. Then came our first underway trials. I thought of my *Wahoo* experience in this, when the bridge gyrocompass repeater had been 180 degrees out of phase and my captain wanted it fixed right then. We ended up with no compass at all. I would not make that kind of mistake, but as it turned out I was not called upon, for *Tang* had no bugs. She performed as if she'd been at sea a year, and it was rather up to us to catch up to her.

Between the firing of dummy torpedoes to check the proper operation of *Tang*'s ten torpedo tubes and our initial dives, all spares for our machinery came aboard. The dives themselves were normal, not stationary ones in the bay as had previously been the practice. Our first dive differed from one on patrol in only two respects. First we waited for the "Christmas tree," the bank of indicator lights showing the status of all hull openings, to change from red and green to all green, signaling that they were closed. Then a slight air pressure was built up in the boat; it held constant, showing that the boat was tight. The vents were opened, allowing the sea to flood the ballast tanks, and down we went. The engineering officer is customarily a submarine's battle stations diving officer, and Bill Walsh took her down on this occasion. Having come to *Tang* from two war patrols in *Tautog*, he found this strictly routine and trimmed the boat precisely with a minimum of pumping.

Our deep dive, to 438 feet, required more preparations. Vertical and horizontal battens, each made of two overlapping pieces that could slide one upon the other, were installed by the shipyard. Micrometer gauges were attached to permit accurate measurements of the hull's compression at various depths. Compared to that of earlier submarines, our deflection at 438 feet was negligible. I was sure the shipyard would use the accurate figures they had obtained to improve the design, but for us they spelled a confidence no submarine could have had before.

We had agreed to help in the training of a floating dry dock on our way back to Mare Island from our deep dive, so we rolled through the Golden Gate with three engines on propulsion. Our fears of the usual drawn-out procedure were allayed when *Tang* rounded Tiburon Island. The floating dry dock was already flooded down, with just the sides and bow a few feet above water, and swinging to the tide. We made a wide sweep so as to approach her open end on a steady course and had slowed only to 10 knots, hoping to get our bow across the sill before the dock could yaw again with the swirling tide. With 50 yards to go, it did not look good. I ordered, "All back emergency," for another try, but before the screws bit in, the dock swung back and aligned herself perfectly. We stopped, and *Tang*'s bow coasted over the sill at a good 7 knots. "All back two-thirds" settled her in handsomely, and no one outside our ship's company knew that luck was the major factor.

Tests could go on forever, but as with significant figures in mathematics, there comes a point where carrying anything beyond a certain degree is meaningless. Lieutenant Frank Springer, whose primary duties included our torpedo fire control, brought such a case to my attention when he showed me the final test data on the torpedo data computer (TDC). It was solving firing angles to the quarter of a degree, while our torpedoes would follow a course no closer than half a degree. *Tang*'s other systems were performing normally, too, and what we now needed were independent operations, in which each watch section could go through its paces and all hands at battle stations could acquire the necessary coordination. *Tang* had only her high-speed endurance test remaining, so we reported ready for our shakedown. Our departure for San Diego was set up with the stipulation that we take along the shipyard representatives of Fairbanks Morse and General Electric so they could observe the endurance tests of our diesels, generators, and main motors, which would be run en route. This was no concession on our part, for we would gladly have taken both of them right on to patrol. *Tang* would get under way at midmorning on the following day, December 1, 1943.

2

The special sea detail had been stationed and the mooring lines singled up when I came aboard. In a minute we were under way. The passage through San Pablo Bay, on between The Brothers, and past Angel Island, with San Francisco looking like she'd been transplanted from the Mediterranean, would intrigue anyone, but our business lay off to starboard, in the main ship channel. The bay had been as clear and smooth as a lake, but mist and rolling swells greeted us as we passed under the bridge and through the Golden Gate. *Tang* seemed to come alive.

"Ship dead ahead. It's her stern." The report was from the starboard forward lookout, and the stern of the *Patterson* was now distinguishable through the mist. The destroyer would escort us down the coast and was, by coincidence, the same one that had accompanied *Wahoo* to sea from Australia. With the sea buoy now astern, we both changed course to south, directly into the trough of the seas.

Tang's present complement was 79 and included seven officers. Motor machinist's mates, electrician's mates, and firemen accounted for nearly half the enlisted men; torpedomen, gunner's mates, and seamen made up another quarter; the rest included cooks, steward's mates, quartermasters or signalmen, radiomen, fire controlmen, yeomen, a radio technician, a boatswain's mate, and a chief pharmacist's mate. All hands except the executive officer, his assistant navigator—a chief petty officer (CPO)—and me would stand watches either in their specialties, or manning the radar, as steersman, lookouts, soundman, planesmen, or as duty chief in the control room. Watch duties for the other officers would be diving officer, officer of the deck (OOD), or assistant OOD. The OOD would be responsible for carrying out my instructions, initiating dives, and everything else that affected *Tang*'s safety or her routine. He would also initiate action to close the enemy until either Fraz or I assumed the con. Of all the men in our ship, Fraz would spend the most time on his feet, but his availability would insure that exhaustion would never interfere with my carrying out my duty to put the enemy on the bottom.

As is customary, our ship's company had been divided into three watch sections. When we were through with our shakedown, any one of the sections would be able to carry out all normal evolutions, surfaced or submerged, including diving and surfacing. In *Tang,* we carried this a bit further, with a cook or messcook and steward always on watch so there would never be an excuse for stale or cold coffee. At battle stations, every man would have a specific job. All assignments, including those for emergencies, were posted on the Watch, Quarter, and Station Bill for everyone to see.

Up to this moment, our surface operations had been in waters where a mistake could mean a grounding or possible collision. The special sea detail, consisting of our more experienced men, had been on watch. Now, for the first time, we stationed the regular sea detail. The first section took over the watch. Until we next entered port, the special sea detail would be members of the regular watch sections.

At two-engine speed, *Tang* was riding fairly comfortably through the swells, though some of her crew might not have agreed. Our ever increasing speed as we worked up to full power did not improve matters, however. Rather, it imposed an unpredictable circular motion on top of our roll, as though the ship were following a giant corkscrew. It was coming up noon, and the odor of frying chicken permeated the boat, reaching even the bridge through the hull ventilation. A fried meal should not have been served on our first day at sea, but there was the menu over my signature, posted in the crew's messroom. Untouched on the tables remained enough fried chicken for three-quarters of the ship's company. The cooks stowed it in the freezer room.

If we were having trouble with cooking oil, *Patterson* was having a worse time with lube oil. She was rolling half again the degrees of our boat, especially to port, and snapping back as destroyers are wont to do. Lube oil was building up in her port sumps, leaving too little to starboard and forcing her to slow. Since *Tang* was well into her endurance run, we informed Commander Western Sea Frontier, who controlled shipping along the Pacific Coast, that *Tang* was proceeding independently. He would tell us if he didn't like it, but stealing the jump with a logical plan usually brings agreement and avoids further dispatches. There were none.

Tang had proceeded a hundred miles down the California coast by late afternoon, on a track to the west of the Channel Islands. The seas were moderating, and those hands who had forgone the noon meal commenced collecting in the crew's mess. The evening meal had been changed to steak, potatoes, and vegetables, and the tone of the conversation in the messroom told that all was well within our ship.

Frank Springer was in the wardroom, already working on his qualification notebook, and he handed me the drawing of the compensation system that he had just finished. It included *Tang*'s variable ballast tanks and the associated pipelines to the trim manifold. Forward and aft, occupying the space surrounding the torpedo tubes, were the trim tanks, properly shown as being partially filled with seawater. The amount of water in these tanks would be varied to adjust *Tang*'s weight and tilting moment.

Amidships, the space between the pump room deck and the

pressure hull was divided into five sections. Three of them were designated as auxiliary tanks, and on one of these Frank had put the legend "fresh water." The other two auxiliary tanks were shown partially filled with seawater and would be used for adjusting *Tang*'s overall weight to obtain neutral buoyancy. In compensating, the trim pump would shift ballast between these tanks or pump to sea through the manifold. To increase ballast, the tanks could be flooded from sea.

Forward in the same space and extending to the keel, negative tank was shown filled with seawater. This 14,000 pounds of negative ballast would give *Tang* an initial down-angle and speed her dive till the ballast was blown to sea and the flood valve closed. The largest tank of the group, located just aft of negative, was labeled "safety." Normally kept flooded, it could be blown partially or completely dry to compensate for serious flooding inside the pressure hull.

It was a neat and complete diagram, and I initialed it in the space Frank had provided. It was good to see him so far along, for he would have to qualify ahead of his juniors.

The navigator's evening stars showed us within a mile of the track he had laid down before our departure and a bit ahead of our estimated position. The hours of darkness are those a submarine likes best, for her low silhouette blends into the sea and her lookouts can always spot a surface ship first. It was not a time to let down our guard; at sea there was no such time as that. But those not on watch could relax a bit in the increased security. The night passed quietly, and morning stars showed that we would reach San Diego by midafternoon. At midmorning the endurance trial was successfully completed.

Tang moored at the naval base on schedule, and two senior friends greeted me at the dock. Commander E. R. Swinburne, whom I had known since submarine school, had already procured a destroyer escort to act as target for us in the morning. Commodore Byron McCandless I had known since I served in *Pruitt;* he was now the base commander, and fortunately for us, anyone who had ever served in four-stack destroyers could do no wrong. Over a cup of coffee that evening I did ask a favor: Could we borrow a wire recorder? One came aboard after midnight.

Tang was under way at dawn, with an hour's run to the northern edge of our operating area. The destroyer would start up from the south for the first of three preliminary tracking and simulated firing runs; we would not fire exercise torpedoes until late morning. Below, Ensign Henry Flanagan was supervising the final adjustments on 12 exercise torpedoes. Hank, who hailed from New London, had fleeted up from chief torpedoman's mate and would soon be promoted again. Tall and rugged, he had come to *Tang* from seven war patrols in *Tambor* and another in *Thresher*. *Tang*'s torpedo department was in the best of hands.

At school and during drills aboard, the ship's company had been put through its paces. It was now coming up my turn, for no matter how well the torpedo fire control party could solve the problem, the result would be no better than the periscope dope—ranges and especially the angles on the bow—that I provided. And that was but part of my task, for unless I conned our ship to a good attack position, even a fine solution for enemy course and speed could result in torpedo misses. My reputation in torpedo attacks had probably preceded me from *Wahoo*, where Mush Morton had conned the boat while I made the periscope observations and fired the torpedoes. The number of escorts accompanying Japan's merchant ships had been increasing steadily, however, and it became very difficult to convey to my captain in a few words the ship formations that I could see at a glance. Now, more than six months later, that difficulty would have further increased, so I would follow the normal procedure of both manning the scope and conning the ship. *Tang* would use *Wahoo*'s unique firing method, however. This consisted of firing a series of single shots, each directed by a separate periscope bearing to hit a selected point along the side of the enemy ship. The method used by most submarines required only one firing bearing. Then, to obtain the desired coverage, they used the TDC's spread knob to direct their torpedoes along slightly divergent tracks.

Lieutenant Bruce (Scotty) Anderson had the deck as we entered the operating area. He hailed from San Francisco and had reported from the merchant marine. In his billet as first lieutenant, he was responsible for deck and auxiliary maintenance not assigned to other departments. As of the moment Scotty had other things on his mind. This would be his first dive as OOD. Well, he had to start sometime, though the experience is a bit like being pushed into cold water. Scotty had his instructions, so Fraz and I went below and waited. A loud "Clear the bridge!" from topside told us that the destroyer's tops had come over the horizon. The lookouts were tumbling below simultaneously with the two blasts on the

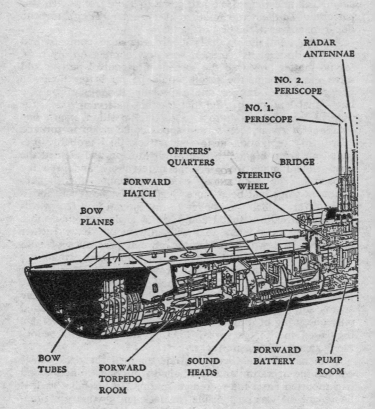

RADAR
ANTENNAE

NO. 2.
PERISCOPE

NO. 1.
PERISCOPE

OFFICERS'
QUARTERS

BRIDGE

STEERING
WHEEL

FORWARD
HATCH

BOW
PLANES

BOW
TUBES

FORWARD
TORPEDO
ROOM

SOUND
HEADS

FORWARD
BATTERY

PUMP
ROOM

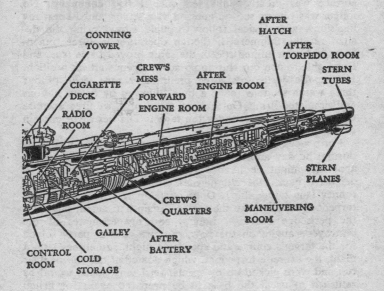

CONNING
TOWER

AFTER
HATCH

AFTER
TORPEDO ROOM

CIGARETTE
DECK

CREW'S
MESS

AFTER
ENGINE ROOM

STERN
TUBES

RADIO
ROOM

FORWARD
ENGINE ROOM

STERN
PLANES

CREW'S
QUARTERS

MANEUVERING
ROOM

GALLEY

AFTER
BATTERY

CONTROL
ROOM

COLD
STORAGE

diving alarm. I counted all four lookouts and watched Scotty, with the quartermaster, close the hatch and then man the periscope. Frank Springer, the assistant OOD in the conning tower, had grabbed a periscope bearing of the target ship and then had practically dropped to the control room to take over the dive, which had been initiated by the duty chief. *Tang* slid under the waves quite normally. These two officers, yet to qualify in submarines, had taken us down and had us right on course to intercept the target.

I had already found that maneuvering a submarine on the surface was greatly simplified once I had command. No longer was I being second-guessed by a senior, and I knew my decisions, with logical follow-through, would bring the desired results. Submerged, though operating in three dimensions and with limited speed, the same proved to be true, and I was able to con our ship to an advantageous attack position. During the destroyer's three preliminary runs, each of our three watch sections made a dive followed by battle stations and simulated firing. On the final three runs, we fired exercise torpedoes, set to run under the target. The destroyer captain called them hits.

For a week, except for three afternoons, we fired torpedoes during the day and made night approaches after dark. Each approach might be likened to a slow-motion version of a defensive back (the submarine) heading off a broken-field runner (the target ship). Once our ship was in position, our torpedoes would make the tackle. Again and again, based on the periscope bearings, ranges, and my estimates of the destroyer's angles on the bow, our fire control party solved for the target's course and speed. At night, sometimes late at night, the exercise torpedoes, which floated at the end of their run and were picked up by special retrieving boats, would be returned to us at the base to be prepared again for firing. These were days of concentration on the skill in which *Tang* must excel, making her torpedoes hit. Every drill, every evolution was pointed to this end, and even the wire recorder that Commodore McCandless had supplied played its part. It had eight channels that could record for a half hour, or it could be switched to four channels for one hour, and so forth, on up to one channel for four hours. There were microphones by the attack periscope, by the TDC, next to plot, and in the control room. Everywhere we turned, it seemed, a microphone was staring us in the face. Everything we said during an approach was recorded. Between runs, we would play it back, first in its entirety and then after erasing all of the unnecessary orders, exclamations, and extraneous conversation. The result was amazing—a crisp order, the acknowledgment, and then quiet. Three-quarters of everything we had said could be erased. We all learned to think before we spoke and to limit what we said to the problem at hand.

During the afternoons when our destroyer escort had other commitments, we got to the business of finding what hull fittings might limit the depth to which we could dive. In time of peace I might have accepted the stipulated test depth of 438 feet, but knowing that there would be destroyers overhead dropping depth charges and that extra depth could mean survival, establishing a maximum depth closer to the hull's true capability seemed in order. The dive was slow and deliberate, with battle telephones manned in each compartment, and with officers and senior petty officers stationed throughout the submarine. At any sign of trouble, *Tang* would start up again immediately. Bill pumped from auxiliary to sea periodically on the way down to compensate for the loss in buoyancy as *Tang*'s hull was squeezed in by the increasing pressure. With the submarine swimming down with neutral buoyancy or against some positive buoyancy, a change to ascent would require only that the planes be shifted to put an up-angle on the boat. We passed our test depth, but at 450 feet a gauge line came apart and one of the hoses to our Bendix speed log ruptured. A raw potato, jammed over the gauge line, plugged it until its stop valve was located and shut off; the speed log's valves were in plain sight and quickly secured. We started down again. At 525 feet, the rollers that held the sound heads in the lowered position against sea pressure cracked. The heads housed themselves with a swoosh, and *Tang* made a steady climb to the surface.

Commodore McCandless greeted us as usual, apparently taking a personal interest in our submarine. His shipfitters went to work installing engine cam-type rollers on the sound gear. Our spindle-type rollers were not designed for external pressure and should not have been used in the first place. While this was going on, our machinist silver-soldered a new fitting on the gauge line and substituted welding hose on the Bendix log. With hose clamps from Western Auto and new insides, our speed log should now be the best installation under the sea.

On the next free afternoon, *Tang* rolled down past 525

feet, on past 550; everything remained tight. We were on our way to 600, but just 20 feet shy the flanged joints in the vent risers took off like road sprinklers, with 300 pounds per square inch pressure behind them, rather drenching the area but with little volume. We started up and the leaking stopped, but we kept right on going up. These nine-inch diameter pipes connected the tops of the inside ballast tanks in the torpedo rooms to vent valves located in the superstructure. They were built in flanged sections to follow the circular contour of the hull and were bolted together. Since both ends opened to sea pressure, there was thought to be no way to test the installation; but *Tang* had. The trouble probably lay in improperly tightened bolts next to the frames and pressure hull, which were almost impossible to reach. Again the destroyer base came to our rescue. Commodore McCandless had his shipfitters up half the night making special crowfoot wrenches to reach the nuts and bolts. The butt end of each wrench was fashioned to fit into one of our torque wrenches so that with the combination each bolt could be tightened exactly the same.

Before dawn we were ready to try again, but our final torpedo firing came first. The target practice went well in all respects, and then *Tang* started down. No one batted an eye till we passed 575 feet, but the very fact that 600 feet was the last figure on the depth gauge did cause some uneasiness, like coming to the edge of the ocean. The pointer moved to the 600-foot mark and then to the pin three-quarters of an inch beyond. There were no leaks. We came back up to 600 and maneuvered at various speeds over the ocean floor. Then, just to convince ourselves of what we really had, we topped things off with a maneuver we'd been practicing. Bill gave her an up-angle by the stern, and we went through the maneuvers backward. *Tang*'s actual test depth was 612 feet.

The climb back up to the surface was a long one. We timed it for future use. The sea and setting sun did look pretty good, and we headed for the base. So far we had been concentrating on torpedo firing and materiel. A total of 43 exercise torpedoes had been fired at actual moving targets, our engineering plant was performing beautifully, and *Tang* had depth capabilities no American submarine had known before. Now we needed to concentrate on personnel, on the routine that would get our submarine to her patrol area and get her there undetected. We'd do something about that starting the next day, when *Tang* would leave on a week's independent operation, which I had requseted as a part of our shakedown.

After supper, over a game of cribbage, Fraz and I worked out the general plan for the coming week. There were no southern boundaries shown for our 50-mile-wide operating area. We did not ask for clarification, but rather would take advantage of this for a patrol down Mexico's coast. Everything except firing torpedoes would be done exactly as if we were on patrol off Japan—reconnaissance, approaches, the works. There should be just enough spice to keep it interesting, and so that the experience of the older hands would rub off on others, we would shuffle the officers' watch list.

Fraz took the con when we got under way, and Frank brought us alongside a week later. There was not much that a submarine does that we hadn't tried out during that short period, though Mexican fishing boats had substituted for Japanese *marus*. I had a last cup of coffee with the commodore, and he nodded approval of our patrol, though of course he was not responsible for our operations. We had done well not to inquire about the missing area boundary beforehand, for Commander Swinburne was quite aghast when I told him what we'd been doing.

"Why, you could have caused an international incident if you'd been sighted!"

"Sir, if *Tang* can't avoid the Mexican fishing fleet she doesn't have any business going on patrol," I replied. He seemed to come around to my way of thinking, or perhaps he'd just remembered that tomorrow *Tang* would start back for San Francisco, and we'd be out of his hair.

There was no escort and we were given an outside route back up the coast. This permitted extending our patrol a bit, though it soon became evident that the troops were thinking of the city and Christmas. We settled down to a routine that would approximate that of a submarine returning from patrol. In two days, *Tang* moored at Mare Island shined up so that leave and liberty could commence immediately.,

The yuletide days were full, though business proceeded at a modest pace. Among other things, this included the required reading to the ship's company from *Articles for the Government of the Navy*. These regulations left little in doubt, especially the first 70 articles. Informally known as "Rocks and Shoals," they spelled out the conduct required of all members of the naval service in peace and war, stating the penalty that would be imposed for any breach. By way of emphasis, the severity of the punishment preceded the listed offenses.

I stepped into the crew's mess as Frank was reading to the duty section and found myself standing as stiffly at attention as I had when I first heard the articles under John Paul Jones's flag. The first three articles covered conduct and morals, divine services, and irreverent behavior, but with Article 4 came the blood and thunder: "The punishment of death, or such other punishment as a court-martial may adjudge, may be inflicted on any person in the naval service found guilty of. . . ." The offenses included mutiny, disobedience, intercourse with an enemy, desertion in time of war, sleeping on watch, striking the flag or attending to an enemy or rebel, or when engaged in battle treacherously yielding or pusillanimously crying for quarter.

In submarines, most of these offenses were extremely unlikely if not physically impossible once the hatch was closed. But fully applicable was Article 19, pertaining specifically to the duties and obligations of a commanding officer: "Or does not do his utmost to overtake and capture or destroy any vessel which it is his duty to encounter."

If there were any doubt about the proper action to be taken, this article would point the way in *Tang*. No other words were necessary; we all knew our mutual responsibilities. But just in case someone needed reminding, all 70 articles were posted, as the *Articles* themselves required.

The reading of the *Articles* seemed a bit incongruous with the spirit of Christmas, but our fellow submariners were firing torpedoes that very day, and being in every way prepared was a part of my charge. Adding to *Tang*'s preparedness, Fraz had somehow stolen the senior instructor from the radar school. Lieutenant Edward Beaumont, from Paxton, Massachusetts, reported on board with bona fide orders and would fill two important niches. He would be our radar and assistant engineering officer and he would round out the watch list, making it possible for *Tang* to have an OOD and assistant OOD on watch at all times when under way.

Another development, not too unexpected, was nonetheless disturbing: We had several reluctant sailors. Our deep-deep dive, the knowledge that I was dead serious concerning the *Articles*, *Tang*'s pending departure from stateside—any or all of these might have led several of our hands to request transfers. I did not ask who the specific individuals were, though I did suspect a few. Fraz and Ballinger would handle this under my instructions: First, in fairness to men at Pearl who deserved some time stateside, there would be no exchanges or transfers before we reached the Islands. Any hands who still wanted to leave *Tang* at that time would be transferred without aspersion when a replacement volunteered. More and more were the outstanding qualities of both Fraz and Ballinger becoming evident, for I heard nothing more about the matter.

A change in schedule was greeted by cheers from the bachelors and jeers from the family men, for *Tang* would proceed to San Francisco, or more specifically to Hunter's Point Naval Shipyard, right after Christmas. With gas rationing, commuting would be difficult if not impossible for many of the family men, but the reason for the change was most urgent. *Tang* would dock to receive newly designed low-cavitating propellers. We already knew we would be able to dive deep enough to find a temperature gradient should one exist in the seas we patrolled. An abrupt change in the water's temperature, a temperature gradient meant a change in the water's density as well and would bend the wave front of the enemy's echo range back toward the surface, clear of any submarine below the gradient. With the new, quieter propellers and reasonable ocean depth to dive in, we would likewise be able to avoid detection by passive means—listening—and still run at most any speed.

Our high-speed run to Hunter's Point—only two hours from under way till our bow crossed the sill—left the signalmen on Treasure Island still challenging as we disappeared down the bay. Early liberty and late quarters took care of the family men, and San Francisco showed our bachelors how to truly ring in a New Year.

3

Her bow sliced through the crests of the winter seas and then eased down through the troughs. As the diesels drove her

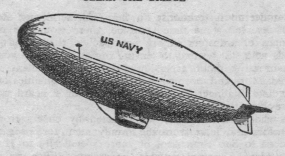

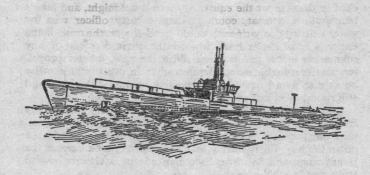

steadily on, there was none of the hesitancy or shudder that would be felt in a surface ship of her tonnage. Down the dual lines of her wake, the Golden Gate was fading in the mist; but ahead lay the whole Pacific and the seas beyond, where *Tang* would seek out the enemy.

The navigator took his departure with a range and bearing on the Farallon Islands and recommended the course to our assigned corridor. This was a moving rectangle that would follow us on to the Hawaiian Islands. If we maintained the speed prescribed, there would be no ships within 100 miles ahead or astern of us, nor inside 50 miles on either beam.

Our escort, a blimp from Sunnyvale, came up from the south and took station ahead. It would remain with us until late afternoon, primarily to help in identifying *Tang* as friendly so that we would not be driven down by our own planes. The responsibility for our safety, as always, was our own, and with two blasts on the diving alarm, we would be out of sight before a plane could reach our position.

Frank relieved me of the con and I went below. He could handle anything that was likely to take place. If the situation was changing or in doubt he would inform me or call me to the bridge, but if it seemed prudent, he would dive without hesitation. Tall and serious, Frank had my complete confidence.

Fraz had completed his immediate duties as navigator, so he joined me in the wardroom. Over a cup of coffee, we planned the coming hours, deciding to keep them simple. A trim dive after the blimp was released and regular underway routine would complete our day. This did not mean that we would be idle, for everyone would have four or more hours of watch or the equivalent before midnight, and routine school of the boat, conducted by a petty officer who was qualified in submarines, would continue for the men in the duty section during the short periods when they were not on watch. In a patrol or so, this training and individual study would lead to their qualification and the right to wear silver twin dolphins.

My own school started immediately, for waiting in my desk was a stack of recent submarine patrol reports. Though the reports were brief, the method of operation of each boat and the data contained in each report could provide the key to remaining one jump ahead of the enemy. My immediate task was to know more about him than anyone in Pearl's training command, our next hurdle before going on patrol.

We still had a low overcast at midafternoon, and at the latitude of San Francisco dusk would come at about 1630. That would give the blimp just time enough for a daylight mooring. It had carried out its escort mission well, for though we had planes on the SD (our air-search radar), none had approached us. We released the blimp with thanks for a good job and received the pilot's Godspeed.

Scotty sounded two blasts as soon as the escort had disappeared, and we slid under the waves for our scheduled trim dive. I assumed the con and Bill took the dive, for these were our battle stations and the trim must be satisfactory to both of us.

"Level off at sixty-four feet, Bill," was my order, and I

received prompt acknowledgment. Bill blew negative to the mark previously established on the gauge as we passed 48 feet, leveled us off at 60, and eased *Tang* down to the ordered depth. He had calculated and compensated accurately for the weight and placement of the fuel, stores, and torpedoes that had come aboard, and was able to request speed reductions promptly as the final pumping of trim and auxiliary tanks was completed.

"Satisfied with the trim," came over the intercom in Bill's usual calm voice. We were at 64 feet with a one-degree down-angle, and the Bendix log showed 3 knots. That down-angle was exactly the aspect I wanted, for now just a touch of speed would swim *Tang* down against a tendency to broach in heavy seas. In minutes we were back on the surface and again at three-engine speed.

Dusk came on and there were no evening stars. Secretly, I suspected that the navigator was just as happy in using dead reckoning instead of working up a star fix. During the second dog watch we entered our corridor and steadied on the new course of 225.

It had been a long day, though the relaxation that comes with good meals and accompanying conversation had made the time slip by quickly. I picked up my Night Order Book from the holder just inside my cabin door. Fraz had thoughtfully inserted a slip of paper with essential figures I might need. I wrote briefly.

Under way on course 225° true, en route Submarine Base, Pearl Harbor. Three main engines are on the line, speed 17 knots.

There should be no shipping sighted, but do not let this in any way relax your vigilance. I expect the entire watch to be as intent and serious as if we were in a patrol area.

Report any changes in weather or other circumstances.

If in doubt, call me to the bridge. If in doubt about being in doubt, call me immediately or dive.

Remember, no officer will ever be reprimanded for diving, even though it prove unnecessary.

In the control room and along the forward and after passageways, the nighttime red lights to hasten our eyes' adaptation to night vision seemed to impose a general quiet throughout the living spaces, though no such instruction was given. Men going on watch moved quietly, speaking softly. I put my ear close to the pressure hull; the seas beyond the void ballast tanks were just audible. This was as near as one could come to a peaceful moment in a wartime submarine.

During the midwatch, the OOD reported the wind backing to starboard, and later, the stars breaking through overhead. We were pulling clear of the stormy low pressure area, also confirmed by a rising barometer. If a star fix showed us to be in the leading half of our moving rectangle, as we expected, we could delay our advance while conducting a simulated submerged approach and firing.

The navigator and Chief Quartermaster Jones were already taking sights when I started for the bridge. I let them come below to work out their position lines before I went on up. A half hour later Fraz's voice came up the hatch. "It looks good, Captain." I dropped to the conning tower to see the chart. Things looked good indeed, for we were 15 miles ahead of the midpoint of the rectangle and could now spend an hour or more submerged. If we dived during the forenoon watch, another section would take her down; then we could go to battle stations.

At first thought, a simulated approach and attack might seem too nebulous to have real training value. However, the same section of the TDC used to determine enemy course and speed could also generate a complete, realistic problem. To have all the elements for a sonar approach required only the recording of the enemy ship's speed as well as its range and bearing for each minute of the exercise. To introduce the sound bearings realistically, we developed our own device, consisting of my shaving brush and a dynamic microphone. The microphone was plugged into the receptacle in the forward torpedo room that normally received the output from one of our sound heads so that the noises created with our device could be heard on the conning tower receivers.

Two men, armed with the recorded problem, a stopwatch, and *Tang*'s "super sound device," conducted the enemy's maneuvers. An experienced soundman, wearing an earphone so that he could hear what he was doing, could generate any type of propeller noise by repeatedly pushing the bristles of the brush against the microphone—the *thump-thump-thump* of a freighter or, with a faster circular motion, the *swish-swish-swish* of a destroyer. Further, he could control the volume by the pressure he applied and so indicate the range, and could make the sounds in the cadence of a propeller's revolutions per minute to give an indication of speed.

The operator's assistant, with the problem data and the stopwatch, would indicate the correct bearing for each minute on the azimuth scale atop the sound head's housing. In the conning tower, the sonarman would train the sound head in searching; when he came close to the correct bearing he would be given faint screw noises, which would peak as he crossed the bearing. With a series of these bearings, the propeller revolutions per minute, and estimated ranges, the TDC operator could solve for enemy course and speed, arriving at a fairly close solution as the apparent ship passed by. With experience, we could also introduce our own maneuvers and those of enemy escorts into the problem. However, since I would never base my firing on sonar information alone, all simulated firings would follow periscope observations as a drill in my procedure, though of course in these exercises I would make my periscope data agree with the information provided by the sonarman and the TDC operator.

Mel Enos took *Tang* down, and as he leveled the boat off handsomely, I reflected that a short two years before, an officer with his time in service would likely be just observing, not diving. Since that time, the necessity for filling new-construction crews and qualifying replacements had shaken a little realism into even the most conservative naval officers. After all, Mel was surrounded by experienced men who would prevent any serious errors. Right now, our trust in Mel seemed reflected by his self-confidence. He made no mistakes.

The bonging of the general alarm and the order "Battle stations torpedo" came over the 1MC, *Tang*'s announcing system. All stations reported manned over their battle telephones, and the practice approach proceeded right up to the firing point. Then came my firing command, "Constant bearing—mark! . . . Fire!" a separate command on a new periscope bearing for each torpedo. On each "Fire!" the plunger that would send the torpedo on its way was pushed smartly home. Had the torpedo tubes themselves been readied for firing, four Mark 14 torpedoes, each with a 500-pound warhead, would have been speeding at 46 knots into the Pacific.

It was a good exercise, even though it did not seem that our firing data, when compared with the recorded problem, would substantiate a hit. Of more importance was the participation by all hands, who had carried out their tasks splendidly. We could discuss the apparent miss later in the wardroom while on our way again.

"Prepare to surface. Lookouts to the conning tower," I called. I made a careful sweep around with the periscope, then ordered, "Sound three blasts. All ahead two-thirds." A minute later, now standing on the dripping bridge, I ordered the turbo blowers started and the lookouts topside. The bow was riding well with the seas nearly abeam to port so I ordered, "All ahead standard, three main engines." The exhausts sputtered as the diesels fired, while the turbo blowers forced the remaining water from the ballast tanks, slowly raising us from an awash to a fully surfaced condition. By the time the ballast tanks were dry, as evidenced by huge bubbles rising along our sides, we had regained our cruising speed.

After the navigator had obtained a morning sun line, he joined Frank and me in the wardroom to discuss our simulated attack. Over a cup of coffee, we compared our solution of enemy course and speed at the moment of firing with those that had been recorded for the problem. We had the ship going too fast and on a more divergent course. These were cumulative errors, and the TDC's angle solver had directed the torpedoes to intercept at a point ahead of the enemy.

"But we fired a spread of four," commented Fraz. He started figuring out loud, "Nine knots equals three hundred yards a minute . . . . The torpedo you fired under her stern would have blown her whole bow off!"

"Well, you don't sink ships with hits in the bow," was my response. But I conceded that the crew might feel better about their efforts if they knew we wouldn't have missed completely. So word of a ghost ship with a missing bow was passed along by the chief of the boat.

Though wartime cruising was a full-time task in itself, we continued our efforts to perfect those drills and evolutions that would likely be required during the training period still ahead of us at Pearl. One after another we were able to put these scheduled drills on the shelf and move steadily into the routine we would follow when en route to a patrol area. If we now heard the words "Fire in the after engine room!" it would be no drill.

Each night, shortly after the evening meal, a movie would start in the forward torpedo room, though it had to vie with a good library and acey-deucey. Toward midnight, the unmistakable aroma of fresh-baked bread would permeate the boat, and the on-going watch section would pass through the messroom, where a pile of hot rolls awaited.

Walker, the steward on watch, brought a dozen or so to the wardroom. They were worth rolling out of my bunk for, and I joined Fraz, who couldn't resist them either. I'm sure the navy's doctors knew what constituted a balanced diet, but they had misjudged what a submariner would eat by a mile. On patrol it had turned out to be about twice the quantity of baked goods, in part because baking had to be done at night when the galley was available, so enough extra had to be baked for the watch sections.

Our progress had been good even though we had to take one of the main engines off propulsion for a short time when charging batteries. During these periods, the auxiliary diesel made up some of the difference, and our overall speed suffered little. Thus, on the fourth night out of San Francisco, we crossed the 500-mile circle from Pearl Harbor; we reported as required to Commander Submarine force, Pacific (ComSubPac) and requested a rendezvous point and escort for early morning two days from then.

Molokai was in sight at dawn on January 8, and before 0800 we had our escort in sight a point on our port bow. Our passage through the Kaiwi Channel, between Molokai and Oahu, was fast and uneventful. Diamond Head was abeam to starboard when the chop of the channel suddenly stopped, and our ship steadied, as if entering a lake.

"Rig ship for surface" and "Make all preparations for entering port" came over the 1MC just minutes apart. In the channel, the deck detail came topside and fell in at quarters on the forecastle. For many of our ship's company, this was their first view of Pearl Harbor. They could see only the remnants of the December 7 disaster, for the seemingly impossible salvage was nearing completion. A right turn around ten-ten dock and a wide left turn around Sparrow Point brought *Tang* to her berth at the submarine base. While the troops were busy with the dozens of tasks incident to arrival in port and making preparations for sailing the next day, I left the ship to make various courtesy calls.

Courtesy calls are more than just the exercise of naval protocol, for they renew acquaintances and offer the senior, and sometimes the junior, the opportunity to speak what is on his mind in private. After a brief but cordial conversation with Vice Admiral Charles A. Lockwood, ComSubPac, I proceeded to the training command. The command had apparently been upgraded, for to my surprise, Captain John H. Brown, a practical, senior submariner greeted me.

"Now what would the *Tang* like to do, and does she need anything?" were his first questions after we'd gotten around to business. Things were looking up for our ship and the training command, too, since formerly boats were just told what to do. Fortunately, I had brought with me a proposed eight-day schedule, which also included a brief of our shakedown. It omitted any reference to our deep-deep dive and other maneuvers that were *Tang*'s concern, but did show our many day and night approaches and the firing of over 40 exercise torpedoes.

Captain Brown looked over the proposed operations, which were basic; our approaches were designed to cover the situations a boat would be most likely to encounter on patrol.

"That looks good to me. Will you have Frazee work it up with operations?" said the captain. I was surprised that he knew the name of *Tang*'s executive officer, but I shouldn't have been. Knowing men was one of Captain Brown's long suits and had undoubtedly played a part in his pending promotion to rear admiral.

Sad news, especially for me, was confirmation of a rumor we had heard stateside. My beloved *Wahoo* was indeed "overdue and presumed lost." This would add an extra note of seriousness and determination to our final training.

The training period off Pearl Harbor provided good exercise in the mechanics of approach and attack. The target ship, a destroyer escort (DE), would come over the horizon zigzagging on a base course laid down so as to pass in *Tang*'s general area. If our submerged approach was aggressive, we would be able to close to an attack position. That is, if we were not sighted or picked up by the DE's echo-ranging, for she would then avoid. Some realism was lacking since enemy ships would not be so conveniently routed, and if they made contact, the escorts would attack us.

After nearly a week of day and night operations, we had a breather in port. About midmorning, I left the ship for the training command.

"Well, how's it going?" asked Captain Brown, as if he'd received no reports on our boat.

"Just fine, as far as the mechanics of approach and attack

are concerned, sir. What we really need are some end-arounds and uncanned situations," I replied. Captain Brown started to speak of the space limitation of the submarine sanctuary and the time such exercises would take. Then he stopped.

"What you're really saying is that you're ready to go on patrol," he said. I answered with a simple "Yes, that's correct, sir."

"I've had some interesting reports on *Tang*," he said. "Also, I've been checking, and no submarine has left here on her first patrol with less than three weeks of training."

Captain Brown had obviously been anticipating my statement or he wouldn't have been checking on past policy. I didn't want to push him into a position of having to say no; with a time precedent established, though by a former commander, my insistence might do just that. The next move was obvious: I invited the captain to sail with us the following afternoon for our late day and night operations.

Our ship performed splendidly while Captain Brown was aboard. I knew it and he knew it, though at first he did seem a little taken aback when I continued with my cup of coffee after the OOD reported the target in sight.

"This is the time I'll be spending getting my shoes and jacket on," I volunteered. "And besides, trying to get to the conning tower now might be a bit treacherous."

Two blasts and the thump of lookouts' feet hitting the control room deck punctuated my statement. The OOD had obtained the original true bearing prior to diving; on my first periscope observation, with a generous amount of scope, we had a second true bearing. With a single order, *Tang* was off to intercept.

After the night exercises were completed and while we were en route to port, Captain Brown stepped into my cabin and sat down on the bunk. I buzzed for a couple of cups of coffee.

"Well, I'm going to let you go," he said. But then he added, "I would caution that you are way ahead of much of your crew, and you'll do well to temper some of your tactics for a time."

This was undoubtedly good advice—my actions and decisions did sometimes leave the troops a step behind—and I would keep it in mind. On the other hand, *Tang*'s deep-deep dive was one thing our crew had already done that no other U.S. submarine crew had even considered.

Our pending patrol operations took Fraz and me to headquarters the next day. While awaiting the admiral and from his vantage point, we had time to observe our boat and the others down on the waterfront. Except for the revamped bridge fairwater and periscope shears, *Tang*'s superstructure followed the traditional design adopted during the year of Limited Emergency preceding the war. This gave all of our boats their excellent seakeeping ability. Like the tip of an iceberg, what we could see belied the ship below: A 312-foot hull with 28-foot beam and a surfaced keel depth of 16 feet displaced over 1,500 tons. Four diesels, most conservatively rated at 1,600 horsepower each, could drive the submarine on the surface at well over 20 knots. When she was submerged, 252 battery cells, totaling more than 300 tons, could move her in for attack at over 10 knots when necessary, or at dead slow speed for three days. But *Tang*'s most significant feature was one she shared with all submarines—the ability to reach the enemy's most remote supply lines and to patrol there.

Like other boats at the finger piers, in fact all U.S. submarines since the lettered boats of World War I design, our submarine bore the name of a fish. The tang is an elongated flat species from the Indies that carries spines protruding aft on each side of its tail: So in the tradition of her christened name and in surface ability our submarine matched any of the others; submerged she had depth capabilities beyond any of them. Within weeks, possibly days, we would be putting all of this and ourselves to test and would perhaps justify the spines that our troops had added to a sketch of *Tang*'s namesake to represent the forward torpedo tubes, giving the fish a most ferocious appearance.

Our four-day readiness for sea period remained busy but not hectic. Reloading torpedoes, fueling, taking aboard stores, attending briefings, and squaring away dozens of smaller items kept two sections busy, but one section got ashore each day. With this schedule, all departments were ready for sea by late afternoon of the fourth day.

In the quiet of my cabin on the last evening at Pearl, I thought of some of the factors that had brought *Tang* to this moment. Of her completion and underway trials, right on schedule and without a hitch. They were a tribute to the men of Mare Island and gave us our initial confidence. So a bit of each workman remained with our ship and crew. Of Commodore McCandless, whose assistance had made our deep dive successful. Of the dive and our realistic shakedown, which had demonstrated our capability. Of the friends and loved ones who had gathered at the Golden Gate Bridge to see us off and whose prayers we knew were with us. And of *Tang* herself, a vibrant ship, performing without flaw under the most critical eye. She surely would not be found lacking during our coming endeavors against the enemy.

The sound of men moving along the passageway on returning from the movies at the base was followed shortly by a quiet knock. Fraz entered and reported, "All hands are aboard and *Tang*'s ready for patrol, Captain."

PART II

First Patrol
IN THE
CAROLINES AND
MARIANAS

1

January 22, 1944, had come quickly. At noon *Tang* sounded a prolonged blast and backed smartly out of her slip. The port screw went ahead two-thirds, and she commenced a rapid twist in an almost stationary position; then all ahead two-thirds, and she was on her way. As we cleared the harbor, our friend the destroyer escort took station ahead. We proceeded down the prescribed lane, then headed west.

Consolidated PB2Y Coronado

Our destination was Wake Island, which had been in Japanese hands since mid-December, 1941. Staging planes through this atoll would be one way the enemy might counter Operation Flintlock, the pending U.S. assault on Kwajalein, the Japanese stronghold in the Marshalls, 600 miles to the south. In a low-level attack on Wake, our flying boats could very likely destroy any fuel dumps and prevent an enemy counterattack from this quarter. Thus two such strikes, coming about six days apart, were planned for Commander Thomas P. Connally's squadron of Coronado seaplane bombers, then based at Kaneohe, Oahu.

Originally, *Tang*'s small part was to provide lifeguard

service should any bomber come down. During the readiness for sea period, Fraz and I had driven over to Kaneohe, on the windward side of Oahu, to work out details with the squadron commander. Tom Connally was as lean and wiry as he had been when I knew him at the Naval Academy, where he was an Olympic gymnast. As we discussed plans for the strikes, his enthusiasm and confidence were contagious, and *Tang* was soon a participant. In addition to lifeguard during the strikes, we would conduct a pre-strike reconnoiter of Wake aircraft activity and possible resupply. If our findings warranted it, *Tang* would withdraw to report to the commander, whose squadron would be in readiness at Midway. For the strikes themselves, *Tang* would serve as a beacon for the Coronados, stationing herself on the selected path for the bombing runs and ten miles from the center of Wake's facilities.

Following her lifeguard duty, *Tang* was to proceed to an area in the northern Carolines and from there to Truk. This prospect of several patrol areas meant at least an extra thousand miles in transit and called for two things. One was the conservative use of diesel oil whenever it was compatible with the patrol. The other was extra fuel. We had already prepared for this latter requirement while our boat was still on the ways. Meat was dear and rationed, so for the consideration of one smoked ham, the shipyard's night shift had seen to the installation of oilproof neoprene gaskets in negative and safety tank floods and vents. *Wahoo* hadn't minded donating the ham, since the whole ship's company, except for the few of us who were going to new boats, was on leave while she received new batteries.

For this patrol, we had filled safety with fuel, enough to take us nearly to Wake Island at an economical speed. We would be light on diving, for safety would normally flood with salt water, about 20 percent heavier than oil. Bill would compensate for that by blowing negative only part way dry when we dived. The situation of being light would last only until we had used enough fuel from our normal system. Then the oil in safety would be transferred to the regular fuel tanks, and safety would resume its normal function. If this worked well, the increased cruising range might let us find an extra ship sometime, and all for the price of a ham.

This then was *Tang*'s situation as our escort turned back for Pearl Harbor and we proceeded west at one-engine speed. Our objective was to reach Wake Island and, if possible, to do so undetected. Since there would be no possibility of enemy planes for some days, we would concentrate our search on submarines. To this end, each lookout, with 7 × 50 binoculars, was searching the water to the horizon in two careful sweeps, one with the top of his binocular field just above the horizon, and the next three-quarters of a field lower. Between sweeps, he would lower his glasses in order to give his sector a rapid search with the unaided eye. Though contact with an enemy submarine was very unlikely, the lookouts were aware that at this speed we were vulnerable. I watched their concentration. The Japanese skipper whose periscope went unsighted would be good indeed. With pride and confidence, I went below.

Yeoman McNally was right on, perhaps prompted by the executive officer, and had laid the stack of new patrol reports on my desk. I started to pick one up, but a quick turn through the boat took precedence. I had encouraged the oncoming OOD to do this. The firsthand information he gained and a quick glance at any orders would then permit him to assume the watch with a simple "I relieve you, sir." The momentary inattention possible were this information to be conveyed orally would thus be avoided. If I believed it good for them, then it was good for me, too. These were not inspections, just informal turns, and nothing more than the normal courtesies shipmates would show to one another was expected.

In the galley, just aft of the control room, Wixon was supervising the preparation of the evening meal, but the tables in the crew's mess were still occupied by men playing acey-deucey or reading books that had been supplied by the Red Cross. Already, trash and garbage had accumulated and would have to be put in weighted sacks for disposal after dark. In the living spaces, aft of the messroom, some men were reading, but all was quiet. The crew's washroom was crowded as hands scrubbed up for supper. The pinging rumble of No. 1 main engine greeted me as I went through the door to the forward engine room. Chief MacDonald, our leading motor machinist's mate, was overseeing the watch. His brown hair, ruddy complexion, and pleasant smile bespoke his name, but gave no hint of the engineering skills he brought to *Tang* from patrols in *Halibut*. A standby watch was conducting general maintenance in the after engine room. First Class Electrician's Mate Kivlen, from eight patrols in *Thresher,* was overseeing two strikers on the control levers in the maneuvering room. There the electrical output from the diesel generators or the batteries was directed to the four main motors, or from the generators to the batteries when on charge. On occasion, the frightening figure of 5 million watts would pass through this control cubicle. Someone else might have been surprised to see crates of oranges lashed in out-of-the-way places. But this was a trick I had brought from *Wahoo;* our crew was sure to snitch them, and that was the reason for stashing them equally throughout the boat. Satisfied, I went forward. Walker had just brought me a cup of freshly brewed coffee when a messenger came forward from the control room.

"The officer of the deck reports that the sun has set, Captain," he said, pronouncing each word carefully, as if he had memorized the report. This was probably the case, for he held a small slip of paper at his side. The important thing was the conciseness of the report. He would soon be at ease and would need no prompter. To help this along, I thanked him for his report and sent back word to man the SJ (surface-search) radar now, and to secure the SD radar and high periscope search at dark.

Blessed darkness would follow sunset in less than a half hour at this latitude, and then a submarine could feel almost as secure as when submerged. We would follow the night cruising routine we had used along the Mexican coast. The evening meal, movies, and other activities would most likely continue uninterrupted.

About 2000, the OOD requested permission to open the messroom hatch to dump trash and garbage. It was a good opportunity for me to go topside into the cool night air and judge for myself if the hatch should be opened. Though the seas were from the starboard quarter, they were barely rolling into our superstructure, and I nodded to Ed Beaumont, who had the deck. The hatch was opened, the weighted sacks went up and over the side, and everything was secured again in seconds. Somewhat envious of Ed with his topside watch, I went below for a game of cribbage with Fraz and then my stack of reports.,

On the second day out, we checked Bill's compensation with a midmorning dive. He held the boat up at periscope depth with negative still flooded by keeping an up-angle on the submarine. Then he blew negative slowly until we were leveled off at one-third speed and thus established a new mark on the gauge, which would serve as a guide to whoever dived during the next few days. Our routine would now include daily dives, though at no scheduled time.

When two days from Wake Island, we were within possible range of enemy search planes, so our lookouts had to cover the sky as well as the water to the horizon. This they did in horizontal sweeps above the horizon, then searching a triangular area to overhead. As before, after each sweep the glasses were lowered to permit a rapid view of the whole area with the unaided eye. We thus expected to sight any plane while it was still many miles away, before it saw us. Should a plane get by the field of the binoculars, the rapid search with the unaided eye must spot it in time for us to dive before it could attack.

Instead of the formal position slips that had been required when I was in the navigator's shoes, I had requested that Fraz bring his chart to the wardroom after supper. At other times I would see it on the chart desk. On the evening of January 26, the exact 2000 position, run ahead from his evening star fix, showed that we were 20 miles ahead of the position laid down on our track. We had gained a little each day in spite of our recent dives. This fitted in well with converting safety tank back to its normal function, for the diesels had now used somewhat more fuel from our regular tanks than safety held. The oil was transferred without incident, but before flushing safety we changed course to north. Any oil slicks that we might leave while flooding and blowing safety to rinse it out would lie on a north-south line and would not disclose our track. After an hour's run and half a dozen blows, *Tang* came back to the course for Wake.

Taking a tip from the "remarks" section of two patrol reports that discussed radar detection, we kept our SJ radar trained clear of the bearing of Wake Island as we moved in on the night of the 27th. Frazee's navigation was exact and we needed no range to the atoll, so why take the chance of advertising our approach with radar signals? At the crack of dawn, *Tang* dived five miles northeast of Wake.

Frank took the dive as we slid under the sea and leveled the boat off at 64 feet. He soon requested one-third speed and reported a satisfactory trim. On the first periscope observation it was still too dark to distinguish any details. Then, just as darkness had come quickly, so did daylight. I made a fast sweep in low optical power, with its wide field, for a submarine never knew what might have moved in during darkness. All was clear. Then I flipped the handle to high power and made a slow search. The tops of structures on Peale Island popped above the horizon, as if coming up out of the sea. Everyone was quiet. "Bearing—mark. Down scope," I called. "Zero zero six," said Jones, as he read the relative bearing from the azimuth scale on the scope housing and lowered the scope simultaneously.

Fraz had already converted the relative bearing to true and was laying down the line as I stepped over to the chart desk. The line bisected the high point of the island, the northernmost part of Wake Atoll. I sketched in very lightly the track we would follow past the islands. It would keep us three miles off the reef but still close enough for the reconnaissance we wanted. Fraz smoothed out my sketching with sharp, straight lines and entered the course to be steered on each leg. I brought *Tang* to the first leg.

"Will you take the con and call me when we reach here," I said, indicating a point where we would change course in about a half hour, and then gave search instructions. We would expose no more than three feet of periscope and would take looks every five minutes. In this manner we would not be surprised by a plane that might take off and be overhead were the interval much longer.

I went below, for I had a reason for wanting my executive officer to close the island. It hearkened back to an experience I had had in *Wahoo* as Mush Morton's exec. We were both on the bridge closing a promontory at dawn and dived a little too early. Before we could do anything about it, a fine ship whipped around the point and was gone. I remember Mush's exact words when we discussed our failure later. "With two of us up there we're just too cautious. From now on you'll take her in, dive, and call me when you've got a ship in sight." I might not go quite that far, but there were bound to be many times when Fraz would have to carry the ball, and a good place to start was right here.

Fraz and I took turns on the periscope that morning, changing at about two-hour intervals. First came Peale Island, which had once held the Pan American Hotel in the China Clipper days of the mid-1930s. It had apparently burned during the Japanese assault; at least we could not see it. Continuing our clockwise course around the atoll, we then passed the northern arm of Wake Island, which is shaped like a big V, open to the northwest. Before the Japanese had taken the island from us, most of the facilities and landing strips were located near the apex of the V. We saw the buildings but no signs of activity. Finally came Wilkes Island, originally an extension of Wake's southern arm but now separated from it by a dredged small-boat channel.

By midafternoon *Tang* had examined all of the atoll except where the lagoon opened to the sea at the mouth of the V. From three miles out we had not seen any activity, but neither was there anything that would warrant altering the strike date. We moved off to the southwest, where we would surface at dark. This seemed to be the most likely place to intercept any ship or submarine supplying Wake from the Empire and a secure spot for us to charge batteries.

It had been a long dive, and since the seas were calm we took a suction through the boat shortly after surfacing and as soon as the charge was started. Opening the forward torpedo room hatch and the doors to the engine room brought a true gale through the ship to feed those diesels. In three or four minutes, the air in the boat was completely changed, and any slight headaches disappeared instantly. The hatch was closed, and we commenced our night surface routine, changing it in one respect. We had no place to go, so we remained stopped for most of the night. This had two advantages: Our sound gear was effective now that it was not blanked out by our own screw noises, and we saved fuel.

On the following day we moved in submerged toward the open roadstead off the boat channel between Wilkes and Wake. That was the only anchorage, and should any ship have slipped by us, she might be there for our torpedoes. This was not our luck, so we proceeded submerged to our designated position for the first strike by the Coronado bombers.

In the forward engine room, the troops had a project with a deadline this very evening. *Tang* had to supply a suitable beacon light, but since we would be on the horizon as viewed from Wake, the light had to be screened from the atoll. Our signal searchlight was ideal, but rigging a suitable light-tight screen from the materials at hand was something else. That is, until someone thought of the yeoman's circular fiber wastebasket. The diameter of the bottom happened to be the same as that of the searchlight. With the bottom out, the fiber cone made a perfect screen, secured neatly with a band of the pharmacist's mate's wide adhesive tape.

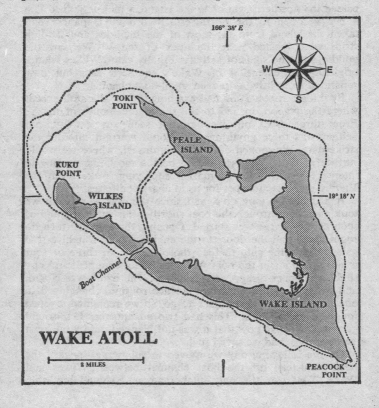

We surfaced during midevening twilight, while there was still a sharp horizon for the navigator's star sights. Fraz's position lines lay neatly through a needle point, and *Tang* had to move but a short distance to be right on station. The navigator continued to get good star sights from our stationary position, and on a horizon that would have been deemed fuzzy and worthless in peacetime. Our position remained good.

"Radar contact, bearing zero three eight, range thirty-six thousand." Ed's voice came over the bridge speaker. The contact could only be the Coronados, for planes had to be flying low to be picked up by our SJ.

"What's that relative?"

"One eight five."

Jones trained the searchlight just off our stern on *Tang*'s port quarter and gave the signal agreed upon, in the cadence of a gun salute: "If I wasn't a gunner I wouldn't be here, right gun fire," with Jones giving a long dash with the word "fire" at the five-second intervals.

And then the great flying boats were there, looming out of the darkness just above the horizon. Seconds later they were passing over our periscope shears, only a hundred feet above, their blue exhaust flaming at us and marking a line toward Wake.

It was perhaps just as well that I had to give no orders, for I felt my teeth clench and my eyes mist up as I wished those men Godspeed.

Flashes and flames on the atoll showed that their bombs were hitting, but there was no way for us to estimate the damage. *Tang* remained on station for 20 minutes so that any damaged plane would know where to find her and then headed down past Wake for possible rescue. About an hour after the strike, two enemy planes commenced dropping flares and searching the area, but neither came close to us.

It was not until after midnight that we received the good news that none of the bombers had come down and only one was damaged. To our surprise, the message further read:

TANG RELEASED FROM LIFEGUARD
PROCEED TO NEXT AREA

Apparently the second Coronado strike was off, so we presumed Operation Flintlock had been a success. Three engines went on the line for propulsion, one on charge, and we were on our way. Our elation was short-lived, however; three hours and 60 miles later, the second part of the message was cancelled, and *Tang* was ordered back to Wake. The second strike, scheduled for February 5, was still on; someone on the staff at Pearl had just goofed.

During the following days, *Tang* patrolled southwest of Wake during the night and closed the island each day. There were planes in the air during daylight, but no ships came to the atoll. We could not complain in one respect, for the air activity kept us on our toes and provided good periscope training, while the fish all about the reef gave our inexperienced sound operators conniptions with their grunting, whistling, and pseudo echo-ranging.

The repeat performance by the Coronados was uneventful and lacked some of the zest of the first strike, partly because it was a duplicate, but mostly because the planes came over at high atltitude this time. Though our reconnaissance did not disclose specific damage by either strike, Japanese planes were in the air daily, so they must have been shaken up.

Finally, shortly after midnight, our call sign preceded a coded message received on the Fox, the nightly schedule of broadcasts from ComSubPac to his submarines. Before Mel Enos could decode it, a second diesel had fired and *Tang* was on her way. As expected, all planes were safe and we were released from lifeguard duties. This was no false start, and though the Fox hadn't told us, this time we were sure that all had gone well with Flintlock.

3

It was now February 7, for we had crossed the date line, and our course was southwesterly, toward the Caroline Islands. This archipelago, located south of the Marianas, stretches from the Marshalls in the east and includes the Palau Islands in the west. Consisting mostly of small islands, reefs, and atolls, the Carolines would not have been of great importance except for one large island atoll in about the center of the chain. Made up of several nearly sunken mountains, surrounded by distant reefs, and with deep anchorages, it was frequently called Japan's Gibraltar of the Pacific; on the charts it is called Truk.

The progress of the U.S. offensive in the Central Pacific, through the Gilberts and Marshalls, had been too costly in its initial stages; it was still unacceptably slow. To speed this up through bypassing the Carolines and moving directly on the Marianas would still require neutralizing Truk. *Tang* and other submarines would participate for the present by stepping up the attrition of shipping in nearby areas, and would later be positioned to intercept fleeing ships during Operation Hailstone, a carrier air strike on Truk.

Pending final decisions concerning the strike, *Tang* did have a patrol area. About the size of the state of Connecticut, it was located north of the central Carolines and was essentially a holding area until just before the strike. No logical shipping lanes passed through it, but much in war is illogical and the unexpected frequently happens. At least we were on our own, and the problem was ours.

Tang would operate in such a manner that fuel would not be a limiting factor terminating this patrol. This very minute she was proceeding to her area at two-engine speed instead of three to make up for the diesel oil she had consumed during the false start. In the following days, when in our patrol area, *Tang*'s routine would also be patterned accordingly. Our first priority, however, was to reach the Carolines. Just before 0400, I was awakened by a slightly more severe voice than usual coming through the control room door. Some have called it submarine ears, but any change in the normal sounds wakens you instantly, especially if you're in a position of responsibility. You can then either get up immediately or, if you are cool, lie there and await developments. I had a better solution for such occasions—an eavesdropping switch on the commercial Voycall intercom, which served the bridge, conning tower, control room, and my cabin. I flicked the switch at the head of my bunk and listened to Chief Ballinger. He was lecturing the on-going lookouts concerning their responsibilities and the added dangers with coming dawn, when an enemy submarine tracking us could have dived ahead.

I sent for my Night Order Book and checked the time of morning twilight, then entered: *Make trim dive at 0520.*

Tang was on the surface again at a quarter of the hour, moving over a calm sea with a crisp horizon all around. On such a day, a single light puff of smoke or the rising haze from diesel engines of any ship would be visible even though the ship herself might be many miles beyond the horizon. Such visibility was a two-way affair, however, and called for a sun lookout. His sole duty was to examine the sun through protective lenses and the area in its vicinity with clear binoculars. Only from this area could a plane have a chance of attacking, but with an alert sun lookout even that was minimal.

The morning was uneventful, the noon meal satisfying, and then came the shout, "Clear the bridge! Clear the bridge!" punctuated with two blasts on the diving alarm. The other sounds of diving were normal, but the excitement in the OOD's voice had told half the story; the starboard lookout told the rest: There was a distant plane a point on our bow. *Tang* was passing 60 feet when we blew negative to level off at 80. That was a comfortable depth, giving some room to steady down should our trim not be too good or our planesmen a bit excited. We then went up to 64 feet for a periscope observation, cautious as always, for we could never know what might have transpired on the surface.

The executive officer gave the relative bearing, and I had the plane in sight on the first high-power observation. A Japanese patrol, probably a Betty, heading to the southeast. A few true bearings till the plane finally disappeared confirmed the direction in which it was heading, perhaps to Ponape, about 300 miles east of Truk. After another ten minutes, with the horizon clear all around, *Tang* surfaced and proceeded toward her area. The remainder of the day was uneventful, though possibly a bit more taut, and darkness was welcome.

The evening Fox schedule contained another message with our call sign, and Mel completed the decoding in a hurry. The submarine *Guardfish* would be passing close to our track and might be sighted the following day. Fraz suspected that the crew had a sighting pool, which was all right with both of us. In fact we would have liked a chance ourselves. If there was a pool, the crew member with the 15-minute slip won, for at 1315 on February 8, *Guardfish*'s periscope shears came over the horizon. We continued to close, and then unexpectedly *Guardfish* dived.

Was it *Guardfish*? Had she received the message? Though the answer was very probably yes in each case, a submerged submarine, friendly or not, was nothing to fool around with. *Tang* cranked on two more engines and gave the diving

"Betty"

position a wide berth, well beyond any possible approach and
torpedo range.

At midafternoon *Tang* entered her patrol area. The seas
looked the same, but there was one important difference; they
were now exclusively ours. No one would be telling us what
we could do here, or how we should conduct our patrol. We
had achieved our first objective, the next was to find the
enemy. The first move was obvious. With U.S. naval operations probably still in progress some 500 miles to the southeast, there would be no Japanese shipping in that direction, so
Tang headed west. Two-engine speed would take us far
enough by 0300. There we would conduct our search on the

following day. I wrote in my night orders: *Proceeding on course 254° true at 14 knots, 80/90* [80 percent load, 90 percent speed] *on two main engines, en route to our patrol station for tomorrow. The battery charge should be completed by about midnight. At 0300 stop, lie to, and man sound. If rolling becomes excessive, maneuver on the battery as necessary. Search our vicinity thoroughly, continuously, and diligently.*

The night was quiet, especially after we had stopped. Men coming on watch moved silently and talked in low voices and whispers. It was really not necessary, but I certainly would do nothing to alter their seriousness. Dawn came and we continued our search, now augmented by the search periscope, with *Tang* still on the surface, lying to and maintaining quiet.

This was a far cry from accepted submarine doctrine, which dictated having way on the boat, but what is doctrine anyway? I believe it is a set of procedures, established through experience, that provides a guide. But doctrine should be flexible, never rigid, for circumstances often dictate complete departures. Our situation that day was an example of such circumstances.

In order for us to utilize speed in searching, it was first necessary to know the general direction of the enemy's movement. We could then proceed on a very wide zigzag ahead and thus cover a broader front as the enemy overtook. But we were presently in an open-sea area, and enemy ships might be on any track, though the northwest-southeast courses passing through the western part seemed more likely. No amount of running around at our available speeds would increase the probability of sighting the enemy. In fact, to do so would only make us a target for a submerged enemy submarine and would blank out our sound gear with our own screw noises.

Tang was lying to in the center of a circle some 20 miles in diameter that we had searched by radar and sound during the three hours before daylight. It was clear of any enemy. The only planes that could reach our position were patrol bombers. We could sight them and dive before they sighted us, for our diving time when lying to was only five seconds longer than when proceeding at 15 knots. The only real danger was from a submarine, but she would first have to come into the area undetected by our sound, radar, scopes, and lookouts. Then she would have to conduct a many-mile submerged approach. This would call for considerable submerged speed.

Our soundman, with no interference from our own propeller noises or from other machinery, would detect her screws before she reached an attack position. The foregoing was not just conjecture or we would not be staking our lives on it.

In addition, lying to while in this open-sea area would use only the diesel fuel necessary for normal living, just a fraction of that consumed when cruising at one-engine speed. The oil we saved would be available when it might really be needed in pursuing the enemy.

There were, of course, the alternatives of a submerged patrol with high periscope searches or of periodic surfacing. Neither of these would insure the coverage we wanted, nor would they save the fuel, as we would then be charging batteries nightly.

We shifted our patrol station about 20 miles each evening so that if we were detected, shipping could not just be routed clear of a single spot. At the same time we were working south near the western boundary of our assigned area. During the forenoon of the third day, February 11, we dived for an unidentified plane, which I strongly suspect had feathers. At least a lazy gooney, its wings just touching the crests of the small waves, was the only thing in sight when we returned to periscope depth. *Tang* remained down the usual extra few minutes and then in general support of the lookout headed south, away from the reported plane.

At about 1130, "Fire in the galley!" came over the 1MC. The fire party from forward arrived immediately, but extinguishing the flames was another matter. The culprit was the large commercial deep-fat fryer, now loaded with salt but still blazing since the heating element could not be turned off. Fire parties from aft were called when the paint and cork on the bulkheads burst into flames. Fortunately, the spike on an old-fashioned fire ax ripped the armored electrical cable out of its junction box, effectively turning the machine off. The fire was on its way out until someone opened the hull ventilation clapper valves to get rid of the smoke. The rush of fresh air rekindled the flames, and acrid smoke filled every compartment. It took freshwater hoses and fire fighters wearing air-supplied diving masks to get the flames out. All hands except those with masks had been forced topside by the smoke, and they carried with them every available weapon as defense against a possible enemy plane.

On my next turn below to control, however, I found Fireman Anthony still manning the SD radar, with the thick glasses he always wore practically glued to the screen. We switched off the SD and I followed his heels topside. An SD contact would only add to our problems, for we couldn't dive anyway.

With the last ember out, our diesels gobbled up the smoke with a suction through both torpedo room hatches. In minutes *Tang* was again buttoned up and heading south, but with a blackened galley and messroom to remind Fraz and me to work over our Fire Bill. After an extra hour's run to put bad memories and the slight pall of smoke well over the horizon, we stopped and continued our search.

Before the usual cribbage and acey-deucey games when the evening meal was finished, Fraz brought in the Fire Bill. Ballinger joined us, for it was he who saw to its posting in each compartment and to the corrections, too. The changes were obvious. A simple sentence added to the bill for each compartment directed that ventilation clappers be kept closed until orders to the contrary were given.

Ballinger went aft, and Fraz was talking about an improved installation of the fryer. It was designed for operation on AC but had been installed on DC with its thermostat operating a separate relay. This should have been entirely satisfactory, but the relay, which was no part of the machine itself, had fused, leaving no way to turn off the fryer. None of our ideas seemed to offer any solutions, perhaps because our hearts were not in it. This conversation was brought to a happy conclusion by the reappearance of Ballinger, who had been discussing the same thing with some of the ship's company. The crew's solution was quite simple, and the chief of the boat explained it straight from the shoulder.

"Captain, the troops would like to get rid of the goddamned thing." This was not a profane ship, but the wish could not have been expressed more succinctly.

When it was pitch-black topside, following the weighted bags of garbage, the deep-fat fryer went to Davy Jones's locker.

Time had not dragged, but we had been 20 days on patrol without even a puff of enemy smoke to reward the hours of concentration. It is difficult to inject any levity into such a deadly serious business, but neither is it possible to maintain such a taut routine without some break. Now, one of the executive officer's fine qualities was a good sense of humor. I listened and went along with Fraz's plan.

While Mel Enos was on watch topside, Fraz encoded a message in the radio room addressed to *Tang*, *Sunfish*, and *Skate*. The other two submarines had preceded us on patrol, and our crew knew they were at Truk. With the connivance of the radiomen, the message was copied into the incoming Fox from Pearl, complete with call signs, identifiers, and the Ultra prefix, signifying that the message was based on information from a decoded Japanese operations message.

At the appropriate time, after Mel had come off watch, he was called to the radio room just as he had been for previous encoded messages. Word came forward shortly that we had something hot. Fraz raced aft, gathered up the tape as it came out of the machine, and headed for the wardroom; but he dropped the message portion on the control room deck on his way through. After giving the duty chief just enough time to thumb it through, Fraz retrieved it and came back to officers' country. Now for the first time I saw the completed message:

TANG WILL JOIN SKATE AND SUNFISH AS A
WOLF PACK TO ATTACK CONVOY CONSISTING OF SIX
TANKERS AND ESCORTED BY SIXTEEN DESTROYERS
TANG IT WILL BE YOUR MISSION TO EXPOSE
YOURSELF AHEAD OF THE CONVOY TO DRAW OFF
THE ESCORTS AND THEN EVADE AT YOUR
SUPERIOR DEPTH WHILE SKATE AND SUNFISH
WIPE OUT THE TANKERS GOOD LUCK

It was just corny enough to ring true, but what surprised Fraz and me was the speed with which the dope went through the boat. Muffled comment of "Jesus Christ, we're going to take all the bastards' depth charges!" and "How the hell are we going to get a combat pin if we don't even get to fire our torpedoes!" could already be heard from the forward torpedo room.

I knew that the submarine combat pin, awarded only if an enemy ship was sunk, was a prestige item, but I had not realized until this moment that it was of such importance to the troops. It appeared that we might have gone a little far, but the truth soon leaked out and a message the following evening solidified things. It was a true Ultra, addressed for action to *Skate* and *Sunfish* but only for information to *Tang*. A convoy would leave Gray Feather Bank at 0800 the following day, heading for Truk. Three more engines went on the line, telling all hands that *Tang* meant to get there first.

4

Our Operation Order specified 2400 of February 15 as the time we could depart from our patrol area to head for Truk and then to our assigned position for Hailstone, the carrier air strike. With the Ultra developments, we saw fit to modify this. While the navigator was plotting, we were making knots. The extra distance we could travel before midnight could be critical in reaching a position ahead of the convoy. Fraz completed the true plot shortly and called his recommendations up the conning tower hatch, "Course one six five at eighteen knots, Captain." We came left 15 degrees.

I dropped down the hatch to look things over with Fraz. His track showed we would have Ulul Island on our beam at 0300, which was fine, as the patrols from its airfield would not be out before dawn. With everything looking good, we gave one engine back to Bill Walsh for his battery charge. Frank Springer had the deck and was followed by Hank Flanagan. This fitted in well, too, for each was an extremely capable OOD. We could not afford the delay of a dive, and it took only a word to insure that they would call me if at all possible before sounding two blasts.

Before midnight, Frank reported a falling barometer, with seas pulling around to the south. Shortly, *Tang*'s bow started rising and falling slowly. With some misgivings, which a cup of coffee failed to allay, I went topside. Fraz was already there. We looked at the seas, which were building up fast, with whitecaps as far as we could see, till they blended into the darkness. They had already knocked our speed down almost 2 knots and promised to do better. Another engine would do little to make it up, most of the energy going into battering the seas. We went below to the wardroom where Walker, who had the steward's duty, had just completed an experiment in making peach turnovers. Hot ones, right out of the oven, were impossible to resist, so with the excuse that we probably wouldn't sleep much anyway, we scoffed a couple of them.

"We'll read it in the morning, Fraz. If we can't get to our spot, then we'll come left and head 'em off. It could be a bit woolly!"

"We can dive faster than a Zeke, Captain," Fraz replied. He was reading me five by five. We'd both be topside at dawn.

Mitsubishi A6M2 "Zeke"

Before getting some shut-eye, I took one of my frequent turns through the boat. In the forward torpedo room, Hank and his torpedomen were just completing a recheck of the final adjustments on their last torpedo. Aft, the watch standers were intent at their duties, though a note of excitement was evident. They already knew that the situation was taut but did not let that affect their confidence. In the engine rooms, where the roar of the diesels prevented the usual courteous exchange, the thumb and index finger sign conveyed their support. It was with men like these that the seeds of a fighting submarine germinated. How could any captain not do his damnedest to live up to his trust and their expectations?

Dawn broke on a dusty sea, perfect for a submerged approach, but the navigator's star fix showed *Tang* just passing Ulul. The convoy's projected track still lay 40 miles ahead. We came left 20 degrees to head for a new point ahead of the enemy, one that we still might be able to reach. With seas moderating, perhaps due to the shoals to starboard, the fourth main engine went back on the line. The SD radar was used sparingly until we were beyond its detection range from Ulul. Even so, on many of these short observations there were distant planes. These might be near the island or they might be patrolling ahead of the convoy. We had no way of knowing, for the SD was not directional; it gave only a pip to indicate a plane and the range.

At about 0930, a pip that had been hanging out around 18 miles commenced closing steadily. The reports came up from the control room—16 miles . . . 14 miles . . . 12 miles! Fraz was by his chart desk, next to the conning tower hatch, watching me. I turned my thumb down. "Take her down, Scotty!" he called, and the sounds of diving drowned out the next report.

Tang slid on down to 80 feet, then slowed and listened, but there were no distant propeller noises. Back at periscope depth, all was clear. However, we had a full can and could now make a submerged run in. For the next ten miles we slowed periodically for sound and periscope searches without results. With everything clear and no contacts on the raised SD, *Tang* surfaced to sweep the dusty horizon with the SJ radar and to search with the periscope lens 50 feet above the sea. Then came Ed's chilling cry, "Clear the bridge! Clear the bridge!" and two blasts of the diving alarm, and we were on our way down again. A Zeke had come out of nowhere, heading in on our port bow. *Tang* continued on down to 300 feet, just in case, but nothing was dropped.

We came back up to periscope depth; again all was clear. We had crossed the convoy's projected track, but now that we had been sighted, there would be no ships along that course— and most probably along any other course for Truk—on this day. Unintentionally, we may have convinced the Japanese that there were two submarines lurking out here. Maybe more, for *Sunfish* or *Skate*, perhaps even both of them, could be here, too. We'd worry about that some other time.

At my request, the exec brought the crew up to date over the 1MC. *Tang* would be waiting for the convoy whenever it dared to leave Gray Feather or Mogami Bank.

We remained submerged until dusk, searching on to the south on the chance that the Japanese convoy commander might make a run for it, skirting our known position. Certainly he would consider the area to the north contaminated. Our periscope exposures were cautious for the first hour, with quick sweeps followed by short high-power searches. With no more planes sighted, we commenced continuous searching, coming up to 50-foot keel depth periodically for looks with

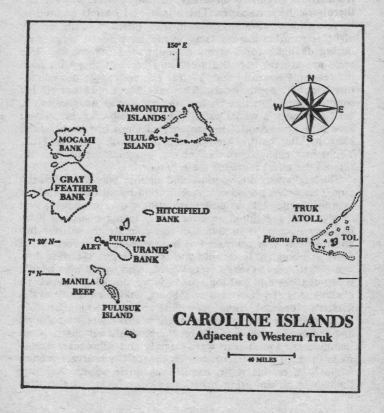

CAROLINE ISLANDS
Adjacent to Western Truk

40 MILES

17 feet of scope. These high searches would more than double the distance to the horizon and increase the range at which we might spot a freighter's tops accordingly. Nothing was moving, and we could only hope that the convoy had returned to the banks.

We waited until it was pitch dark before surfacing. The situation was quite different from that in our last area, in which the enemy might have been moving along any track, for we now knew that the convoy, if it were indeed on the banks, would move east. This permitted increasing the frontage of our radar search by running on north-south legs. It was necessary to complete each leg before a convoy, previously undetected, could finish its transit of our radar's northerly or southerly coverage. During the night we could search on the surface, and our speed of 15 knots assured us of covering a 45-mile front in this manner. With nearby airfields sporting Zeros, Tang would have to be submerged during daylight, for a sighting would send the convoy on a wide arc around her. But we would be searching with both periscopes, frequently with 17 feet exposed, while our soundmen listened continuously. The area we would search lay southeast of Ulul; this choice was not based on guesswork, for I had spent a whole patrol between the banks and Piaanu Pass into Truk Atoll. The majority of ships had then passed close to Ulul before heading across the open sea to Truk. Times had changed much, but not geography, and this still offered the safest route for the enemy.

The night was not routine, and neither was the following day. This was a period of concentration by all hands, and we manned battle stations quietly to review our procedures and to give each individual an opportunity to ask questions if he had any doubts whatsoever. In the conning tower, our fire control party was compact but not crowded. The rest of the party surrounded Jones and me on the scope. Starting forward of us, on the wheel, was Welch, who would also handle speed changes and call log speeds as we slowed for periscope observations. To starboard was Scott, who kept the Quartermaster's Notebook, Tang's complete and detailed log. Starting aft came Ogden at the chart desk, where he plotted Tang's and the enemy's movements on the navigational chart. Next, manning our sound gear, were Caverly and Schroeder. Across from them to port, Frank was on the TDC's analyzer section while Mel, on his right, handled its angle solver. Assisting them, and on the firing panel, was Ed, who could also man the SJ with Bergman should I stick the shears out for a radar range. Fraz remained in general supervision, coordinating plot with the TDC, taking care of such details as getting the torpedo tubes ready, and informing me of the degrees to go till firing on the track I had chosen. Fraz's supervisory role meant that the transition to night surface firing, when I manned the TBTs on the bridge, would entail minimal change in our procedures.

The questions that arose in the conning tower led to a general discussion in the wardroom that appeared to help each individual fully understand the relationship between his own and others' responsibilities. The next night we got the chance to put all this to test, for while we searched with two engines on the line and another still charging batteries, word came over the 1MC, "Secure the charge. SJ contact, bearing three zero five true, range thirty-one thousand yards." It was 0025 of February 17.

5

We would not go to battle stations yet, but the tracking party's task commenced immediately. It would solve for the enemy's base course and the zigzag plan while *Tang* headed for the convoy. At the first indication of the convoy's course, our boat would move to intercept it at a point about seven miles ahead. From that position we could counter any maneuver the enemy might make. Ranges and bearings were fed into the TDC and to the navigational plot. Frank did the analyzing on the TDC, but the navigator came down with the first good estimate of the base course. We came northeast to intercept. Continued tracking showed the convoy's base course to be 100 degrees true, its speed 8½ knots, and that it was zigging up to 40 degrees every ten to 14 minutes.

We were now close enough for a distinct presentation on the PPI-scope (plan position indicator) of the SJ. There were two good-sized ships; a somewhat smaller one, perhaps a destroyer; a small escort close ahead; an escort on either beam; and two wide flanking patrols. It looked more like a small task force than a convoy, and the high ratio of escorts to merchantmen showed what had been happening: Japan's merchant fleet was being sunk at three times the rate of its escorts.

Tang went to battle stations, the Bells of St. Mary's from the 1MC chiming throughout the ship. Compartments reported in record time since all stations had long since been manned voluntarily. This was not purely a case of dedication on the part of the troops, for it was at their stations that their own telephone talkers could provide a running account of everything that was going on—almost everything anyway, for at this moment a call came from radio. We had an Ultra from ComSubPac. This one was addressed for action to *Tang* and just for information to *Skate* and *Sunfish*. Fraz sent Mel on down since he would not be needed at the angle solver of the TDC for some time yet. Shortly, his voice came over the speaker:

> CONVOY WILL DEPART GRAY FEATHER BANK AT
> TWENTY TWO HUNDRED FEBRUARY SIXTEEN FOR TRUK
> NOTE SKATE SND SUNFISH THIS IS THE CONVOY
> YOU WERE TO HAVE ATTACKED BUT ONE OF YOU
> WAS SIGHTED AND CONVOY ORDERED TO RETURN
> ONTO GRAY FEATHER BANK

Well, this was our convoy all right, but we did not regret our search, for otherwise we might well be playing catch-up instead of being in position out ahead. I did not like the part about being sighted. Not so much because it was quite obviously referring to *Tang,* but because the somewhat slurring statement had been written behind a calm desk ashore. Sometimes a submarine did get sighted when doing its damnedest to make contact or press home an attack, but not through any sloppiness on the submarine's part. After all, bullets, bombs, or depth charges were the usual result.

The thoughts had taken only seconds, but they were an unnecessary distraction. I put them aside, for we had a man-sized task right astern of us.

I wondered why the convoy commander had chosen night-time to make this dangerous passage, especially in sufficient moonlight for a submerged submarine attack. I was to have the answer within the next few minutes. It was 0219, nearly two hours after our initial contact. The range to the convoy was 15,000 yards, and we were about to move in for the attack. Suddenly, a dark, narrow shape appeared astern and seemed to be crawling up our wake. I dropped down to the conning tower for a moment. There she was on the SJ at 7,000 yards, her pip neatly blending in with the luminous cursor line, which was trained like the hand of a clock on the convoy's center. Back topside, in spite of our flank speed, the enemy ship was still closing. She was a radar-equipped destroyer or fast escort, for she would not have been able to see a submarine at that range on any night. The convoy commander was apparently counting on her to take care of us.

Our business was certainly not with her; two blasts slid us down. We paused at scope depth to see if she would give us even a slight port or starboard angle on the bow. That would tell us which way to turn so as to be farthest from her track. Her silhouette remained sharp, however, and now her bow wave made a perfect V. It was no time to dally. We turned left toward the convoy and went deep. The bathythermograph showed a 6-degree gradient at 375 feet, and depth charges commenced as we were passing 450. There were only five of them, and though their whack was disturbing, we were not shaken up. The fact that we were busy leveling off at 500 feet and getting on with the approach had its compensations.

Tang was now in the enviable position of being immune to echo-ranging because of the gradient and able to use any submerged speed without fear of detection. Propeller noises come from cavitation, the partial vacuum that normally forms around the blades and then collapses; under the sea pressure at this depth, 250 pounds per square inch, the props could not cavitate.

After some minutes to put a little more distance between us and the destroyer, we slowed so our soundmen could get bearings. The convoy was drawing to our right; it had changed the base course to its left. A right turn and full speed would intercept. Unlike previous submarines, our boat did not throb at high submerged speeds; only the increased water noise and the Bendix log told those of us in the conning tower that *Tang* was making knots. Then came the long climb toward the surface, slowing on approaching cruising depth. A periscope sweep, and the ascent was resumed to expose the SJ's reflector. A moment was all the operator needed, for the range of 9,000 yards fitted our solution. *Tang* was again ahead of the convoy, and we would now concentrate on individual ships.

At 4,000 yards the leading freighter was giving us a starboard angle on the bow. We would fire from forward if she did not zig. At 3,000 the angle was 20 port; she had come right and would cross our stern. "Open the outer doors aft." The leading escort, which was patrolling back and fourth, conveniently crossed to the freighter's starboard bow, clear of us. With water lapping the scope, I watched the port escort cross our bow about 100 yards ahead. We were on the inside; nothing could stop us! The freighter came on, less than two ship's lengths from crossing our stern. I swung the scope's wire ahead of the point of aim, her after deckhouse.

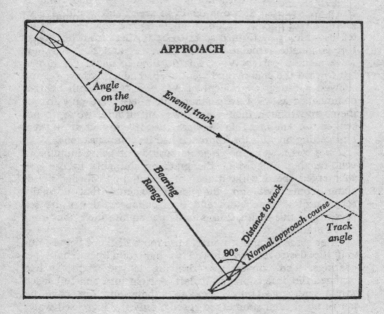

"Constant bearing—mark!" I said, now leaving the scope absolutely stationary. Jones read the bearing.

"Set!" called Frank as he held that bearing constant on the TDC; both its analyzer section and angle solver were now static, as were the gyro angles on the torpedoes. The freighter was continuing across the field.

"Fire!" I barked the instant her after deckhouse touched

the wire. Fraz hit the firing plunger simultaneously, usurping Ed's job.

There followed a slight shudder, the momentary zing of the torpedo's propellers, and the slight pressure on our ears as the poppet valve vented the residual air in the torpedo tube back into the boat.

The second torpedo went to the after edge of her midships superstructure, aimed and fired with exactly the same procedure. Another was sent to the forward edge of the superstructure, and the fourth to hit under a king post about 50 feet inside her bow. The whole firing, four individual shots, had taken 20 seconds.

"All hot, straight, and normal," called Caverly on sound.

"What's the time of run?"

"Fifty-eight seconds, Captain," Fraz replied, checking the table he had prepared against the range of 1,500 yards. Chief Jones was calling off the seconds as the torpedoes raced at 46 knots to intercept the enemy. "Thirty-five . . . forty. . . ." I raised the scope at 45; the seconds dragged. "Fifty-one, fifty-two, fifty-three, fifty-four, fifty—" *WHACK!* The exact sound of a depth charge. Her stern disappeared. Six seconds

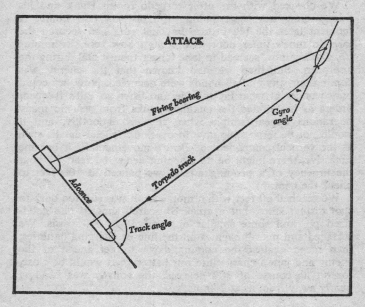

ATTACK

Firing bearing

Gyro angle

Advance

Torpedo track

Track angle

brought another whack; seven seconds later there came a third. The rest of the freighter practically disintegrated. While escorts milled around, she seemed to capsize toward us and sank stern first.

Again we did not dally. *Tang* went deep, leveling off at 575, and slithered away to the northeast. There were three reasons for this depth: the same security from detection that we had enjoyed on the approach; a reasonable working area on the depth gauge, which hit the pin at 612; and the unlikelihood of getting any close depth charges. Depth-charging is three-dimensional bombing. If the Japanese even possessed a depth charge with a hydrostatic exploder capable of operating at this depth, the chance of getting one close enough was extremely remote.

Distant depth-charging continued as I tried to relax over a cup of coffee. Before the first cup was finished, Fraz reported another contact. In the conning tower, Caverly, who was still at his station, flipped on the small speaker that carried the same sounds he had in his earphones. The faint *thump-thump-thump* of heavy screws came through the background noises.

· We checked with the after torpedo room. Hank and his reload crew were just pulling the last torpedo home. A moment later the big bronze bayonet ring had secured the torpedo tube's inner door, and *Tang*'s bow rose. Swimming up, like a guppy, seemed to take longer than it had during the approach. But then we had known that the enemy was coming our way and all hands were occupied. Now, we could only wonder at what lay topside and listen to Bill's frequent orders as he flooded the auxiliary tanks from sea. So many operations appear simple when they go smoothly, and it would not be impossible now to overlook crucial details such as the vertical component of *Tang*'s movement. If it became excessive, there might be no stopping her at 60 feet. Without the urgency of a pending attack, we paused at 100 feet to check the trim.

We reached 60 feet within moments; it was still too dark to spot distant ships, but a quick SJ search showed one good-sized pip and some smaller ones off at 14,000 yards. We surfaced and put all engines on the line or charging batteries, then raced against the coming dawn to get ahead of the enemy and jam a charge into our batteries. It would be close, for on its course of 300 degrees, the convoy was heading nearly away from us at 7 knots.

Like all diesels, our main engines had mean effective cylinder pressures, called MEPs, that could not be exceeded for long without inviting trouble, even piston seizures and wrecking an engine. Battery charging was guided by temperature voltage gravity curves, called TVGs. If the TVGs were exceeded, our batteries would gas and could quickly generate enough hydrogen for a devastating explosion. To prevent the accumulation of gas, a separate ventilation system was provided, fitted with blowers, flow meters, hydrogen meters, and alarms.

To reach an approach position, *Tang* would have to exceed the MEPs and push the TVGs. As captain, I viewed a possible engine casualty as one of the lesser risks in going after a million-dollar enemy ship. I didn't blame the engineers for not agreeing with me, for those diesels were their babies, but they fell in line admirably.

A fortunate characteristic of a storage battery is its ability to store enormous amounts of energy during the first part of the charging cycle and still remain well below maximum TVG curves. The engines on charge carried their share. All of them laid down a trail of smoke, indicative of overload, but *Tang*'s engines were Fairbanks Morse, and if anything could get us there with enough battery capacity for an approach, it would be these rock-crushers. They did; 40 minutes after surfacing we dived well ahead of the enemy.

The morning twilight was short here, close to the equator, and we had good details on the first periscope look. They were disappointing, however, for the ship had zigged away and was showing a 50-degree starboard angle on the bow. We knew where to go but, fortunately for the enemy ship, she didn't. During the next six hours she presented angles around through her stern to 150 port. Our best sustained speed closed to 6,000 yards at one time, but then she drew slowly away to the south and disappeared toward an area that should now be occupied by our submarine *Burrfish*. An *Asashio* type destroyer, a *Chidori* torpedo boat, a PC (patrol craft), and continuous air cover kept us from trying an end-around on the surface.

Reluctantly, we turned west for our assigned position during the first carrier task force strike on Truk. How I wished we knew a little bit about Operation Hailstone. A few details might let me judge the importance of our being on station, but we had apparently departed on patrol before the plans were firmed up. The freighter that had gone over the hill, though in ballast, was a valuable ship, and turned loose we could find and sink her.

Tang reached her assigned position after dark of February 17. It was right back south of Ulul Island, 12 miles bearing 194 degrees true to be exact. The island is 85 feet high, so we moved south a little to try out our SJ. It gave a fair pip at 16 miles, so we settled on that as a better position. No ship would pass between us and Ulul undetected, and we could not be seen from the island, even with radar, for it was very doubtful that the enemy could get a radar reflection from the tops of our shears, which would be the only part of us above the horizon.

Our mission was still to intercept ships fleeing the strike, and it would be novel to have ships driven to us. Fraz had plotted the positions of the other eight participating boats. *Aspro, Burrfish, Dace,* and *Gato* lay staggered to the south, at an average interval of 45 miles. Directly across Namonuito Atoll from *Tang* was *Skate,* and halfway between *Skate* and Truk lay *Sunfish.* In addition, *Searaven* and *Darter* were to the north and south of Truk as lifeguards. This disposition might let *Sunfish* and *Skate* or *Aspro* and *Tang* attack a single group of fleeing ships, but elsewhere only a single submarine attack would be possible. Considering the three boats who had come all of the way from patrols out of Brisbane, roughly 150 submarine days were going into this effort; but we wouldn't complain, for *Tang* occupied the best spot.

In the morning, numerous planes began showing up on the SD, most of them at the same range as our distance to the island. We tracked some out and others in. There was either increased patrol activity over anything we had seen before, or Japanese planes were being staged through Ulul in an attempt to counter our planes, which could now be striking Truk. Perhaps both actions were taking place. It was exciting enough to keep us on our toes, but those men off watch seemed to take it all in stride and caught up on some much needed sleep. In midafternoon a contact on the SD commenced closing. As prearranged, Scotty dived when it reached 14 miles. A half hour later all was clear on the SD and there was nothing in sight on the periscope, so we surfaced and continued our search until dark.

Able to establish our position by radar, the navigator needed no stars this night. Neither he nor I had quite calmed down from our first attack, but cribbage always seemed a good antidote. It was competitive but not so serious as to interfere with conversation. There was just one subject, however, the details of the attack. Frank joined in, and we came to some quick conclusions: We had underestimated the enemy, for he obviously had radar. It could have been on the destroyer or another ship of the convoy that was vectoring the destroyer to us. In either case, we had assisted the destroyer by keeping our SJ's cursor line right over her pip. We had brought this about by making too many bearing demands on our radar operator, disrupting his normal all-around search. The cursor would otherwise have been moving. The convoy commander might have been successful in thwarting attack by a shallow submarine, which would not have been able to reach the gradient at 375 feet, and possibly a deep boat if she had had to run at greater than cavitation speed for her depth on the approach. There was one other area of complete agreement: The crew had performed splendidly.

Having squared that away, we sent for the *Merchant Ship Identification Manual,* ONI-208J, for another attempt at classifying the ship we had sunk. The publication was not all-inclusive, nor was it a bible, but some tended to treat it so. *Wahoo* had brought back pictures, house flags, and life rings painted with both Japanese characters and the English equivalent, NITU MARU, in large block letters. This older freighter was not listed in ONI-208J, so the staff substituted the *Nitsii Maru,* whose pictures in the book didn't even jibe with sharp enlargements of the real ship. At a minimum, however, the manual did help in making an educated guess. On a daytime approach and attack, I would expect to provide our identification party with details that might help them narrow down the choices to a particular class, though rarely to a specific ship. In any case, the determination would be better than just "Unknown *Maru.*" All sinking reports required visual confirmation, and these would normally be modified by the reporting senior, who would affix an (EU) or an (EC) depending on whether, with the total information available, he considered the estimate of the class to be uncertain or certain, respectively. The tonnage listed would be from ONI-208J for that class.

With good help from the Quartermaster's Notebook, and my memory of fleeting silhouettes, Frank and Mel settled on a *Mansei Maru* class freighter, with a listed tonnage of 7,770, and it looked about right to me. With the latitude of 8° 04′ north and the longitude of 149° 28′ east handy in the notebook, I copied it all into my Night Order Book.

The freighter that had gotten away still occupied my mind. I found myself practically brooding over her probable meandering around to the south of us while we sat here twiddling our thumbs. Confusing dispatches on the night of the 17th did not help. One of them directed a submerged patrol. The other simply said, CRABAPPLES CRABAPPLES. There was obviously something missing from our Operation Order due to our early departure. After a dawn dive, with not even a plane in sight, we surfaced to find out what was going on. The area was clear, but not the ether waves. There was a message on the morning Fox that we normally would not have received until surfacing after dark, since our boats could not receive Fox frequencies submerged. The tape came out of the machine and *Tang* was on her way for Saipan, still wondering what "crabapples" was all about.

6

The complete dispatch had disclosed that Task Force 58, the fast carrier force that had just hit Truk, would conduct an air strike on Saipan the following week. Five of the submarines that had been at Truk, including *Tang*, were ordered on for this attack, with specific assignments to follow later. We had started off at one-engine speed, as that would put us there handily. The navigator laid down our track on the new chart and brought it down to the wardroom, where we could look over the situation.

With the Marianas in front of us, the possibilities for independent hunting unfolded. I picked up the phone from its receptacle to my left and ordered 18 knots. In minutes we felt the surge of two more diesels. Fraz stepped off our new four-hour positions along the track, and we were just starting our short-range planning when Chief Jones came to the wardroom's after door. He had heard the engine bells from

CPO quarters, located next to the control room, and surmised he'd be affected.

"Make it eighteen knots, Jones," said Fraz. He received a ready "Aye, aye, sir." This was a change no one objected to! Jones left for the crew's mess to correct the positions on their chart.

We might not know what ComSubPac wanted, except ships on the bottom, and ComSubPac was unaware of just what we were doing. Within a submarine, however, pending operations became common knowledge. At the initial one-engine speed, *Tang* was just going, but with three engines the crew knew that something was brewing. We hoped they were not wrong, for this was the situation: All submarines within some hundreds of miles had been pulled down to Truk for the air strike, very probably leaving the Marianas uncovered. This chain of mountainous islands, lying on a northeasterly-southwesterly line, provided a protected path for shipping from Japan to the South Pacific, especially since to the north lay the Bonins, then the Nampo Shoto, then Tokyo. Unless the other boats had surfaced also, which seemed unlikely, *Tang* was the only submarine to receive the morning message, and it had not been repeated. The others would not get it until after surfacing, probably on the 2100 Fox. By that time we could be 250 miles on our way and should reach a patrol station by the following night. There had to be ships, and with luck *Tang* would have the Marianas all to herself, at least for a time.

We rolled along smoothly, although numerous SD contacts kept us from relaxing. These planes ranged from 20 to 28 miles, and certainly suggested a patrol for a convoy. We changed course 30 degrees to the right until we had moved ten miles from our track, and then 60 degrees to the left, crossing our track and proceeding until we were ten miles to the left. The zigzagging considerably increased the frontage of our search, and our ship was still making 90 percent good in the direction we wanted to go. But our side excursions uncovered nothing visually or on the surface-search SJ radar. The planes were not behind us; we had been there. They had not come in from either beam. If they were ahead we'd find them soon enough!

Finally, about noon, the pips just disappeared. Maybe the Japanese pilots had gone back to Ulul and were sitting down to lunch too. There was, of course, no reason why the acey-deucey game or the casual reading should not have continued, though it was a little bit difficult to concentrate elsewhere when diving was imminent. For the rest of the day *Tang* had straightaway cruising. The ninth movie in our repertoire was shown for the second time, and then the quiet movement of men coming on and going off watch gave assurance to all hands below.

The navigator had a good morning star fix to go with his positions of the day before. In spite of our side excursions, we were making good over 17 knots; this would put us reasonably close to Saipan by dark. Our trim dive at 0830 might more properly be called a wetting. It was just to assure us that our submarine would dive smartly. After we leveled off at 60 feet, three blasts started us back up with our speed dropping momentarily to only 10 knots on the maneuver. Back up to cruising speed, *Tang* was slicing through the tropical seas with a purpose.

Blaat! Blaat! Down we went. A Japanese Betty was coming in from low on the horizon to starboard. We did not stop at periscope depth, for though these versatile planes were usually called torpedo bombers, they could carry depth charges equally well. We moved a couple of miles from the diving spot before returning to periscope depth. The Betty was still in sight, though just a dot above the horizon off to the north. We called the lookouts to the conning tower but waited another ten minutes before surfacing. This established our routine for nearly half of the day. Very close to the half hour a Betty would arrive; *Tang* would dive. The Betty would search for a few minutes and then depart. On each occasion, the executive officer or I questioned the lookout, and they were true sightings. We were wasting a lot of time, so when the fifth Betty showed up and hung out on the horizon, *Tang* continued on the surface.

The bridge speaker was always on, its cone acting as a microphone as well. For diving, the area on either side of the cone was free-flooding. Bridge noises were transmitted below quietly, but a voice directed toward the speaker came down loud and clear. The next "Clear the bridge! Clear the bridge!" though directed to the lookouts, made us jump below. Bill Walsh didn't raise his voice, but this command had more authority than had it been punctuated with profanity. In there somewhere were two blasts, but *Tang* was diving anyway. This time we kept right on going down, blowing negative at 80 feet and leveling off at 250. When Fraz proceeded to question the lookouts in the control room, three stepped

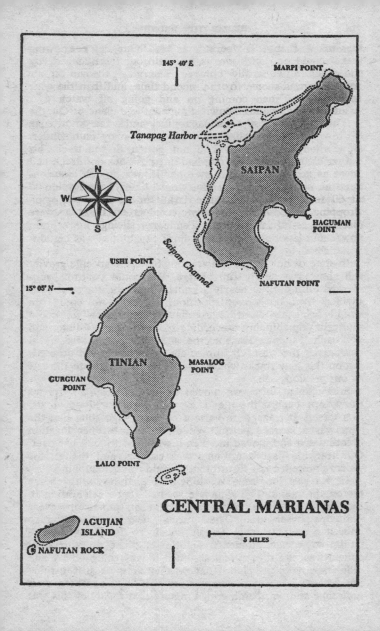

145° 40' E

MARPI POINT

Tanapag Harbor

SAIPAN

N
W   E
S

HAGUMAN
POINT

USHI POINT

Saipan Channel

15° 05' N

NAFUTAN POINT

TINIAN

MASALOG
POINT

GURGUAN
POINT

LALO POINT

CENTRAL MARIANAS

5 MILES

AGUIJAN
ISLAND

NAFUTAN ROCK

forward with the SD operator as well. Our Betty, knowing that it could not get in on us, had lain out there as a decoy and called in two smaller bombers, one out of the sun on our port quarter, the other from a high, small cloud cover on our port bow.

Twice now we had underestimated the Japanese. On the first attack, *Tang*'s superior capabilities and a fair knowledge of how to use them had thwarted the convoy commander. Now, though the enemy had not gotten in to attack, his master chart in Saipan surely had our positions and track laid down as accurately as our own navigator's. Should we continue as planned, the Japanese would likely have additional surprises waiting, even after dark. Further, any shipping would be routed clear of our projected positions. If we were to be successful in our present endeavor, a little more brain power and less reliance on our ship's capabilities was certainly indicated.

In spite of our frequent dives, our batteries' specific gravity still showed a nearly full charge. We could continue submerged until dark at nearly 9 knots. The navigator swung his dividers from our present position. The miles we could run would bring us close to Aguijan. From there we could intercept any shipping proceeding from Saipan to Guam, and approach Tanapag Harbor, the site of the Japanese naval base, from the west. Of immediate importance was proceeding on this new track, which lay nearly 30 degrees to the left of our previous one.

Surfacing at dusk, we moved on toward Aguijan. As we slowly approached the island, a small pip showed up on the SJ's screen. It tracked on various courses, suggesting that the ship was a surface patrol. We dived clear of her location before dawn and moved in when it was light to look her over. Our tracking party's estimate was correct, and though the patrol's presence was disturbing, it could foretell shipping.

It was east longitude Washington's Birthday, with cherry pie on the menu. The Japanese seemed to be celebrating it, too, for there were bombers in sight on practically every periscope observation. They turned near our position to approach their fields on Tinian, and in so doing gave *Tang*'s OODs some bad moments. Sighting a plane on a straight course was one thing. You assumed it was going on by and didn't see you. A plane that was circling or just turning immediately created the impression that it had sighted your periscope and was coming in. I'm sure that a part of this was psychological, a part due to the scope's monocular vision; on the other hand, it was impossible to know how sharply a pilot might turn, and prudence frequently dictated a fairly deep dive. *Tang* acted much like a yo-yo until she had cleared to the northeast, then proceeded slowly along Tinian's west coast.

With bombers still passing overhead occasionally, a Washington's Birthday dinner might seem a bit incongruous and likewise our holiday routine. However, the latter entailed merely the cancellation of our school of the boat and the usual short period of tricing up bunks for clamping down the decks in the living spaces. Just the fact that a man could sleep on through, whether he wanted to or not, was what really counted.

Since we had moved into the tropics, the Taylor ice cream machine had more than taken over the load of our late deep-fat fryer. I had to shake my head, however, as I watched the beautiful wedges of pie being smothered with globs of ice cream, but all hands seemed to like it that way. In fact, it had taken my mind off the enemy who was still in the skies overhead, at least for a moment anyway. The report of squalls and the noise of heavy rain on the surface of the sea called me to the conning tower. Dusk was coming, so we prepared for surfacing. The lookouts were ordered to the conning tower with rain clothes, and the wardroom steward brought additional suits. On this occasion I went to the bridge first, but I was able to call the lookouts and OOD up immediately. The weather was not nearly as forbidding as it had appeared through the periscope, the rain having beaten the seas flat about us. But that aspect was pushed aside, for off in the vicinity of Tanapag Harbor enemy searchlights could be seen between the passing squalls. The apparent signaling could mean ships, and since ComSubPac still had not given us a specific assignment for Task Force 58's air strike we meant to find out. *Tang* started off at two-engine speed, charging batteries with the others, and again pushing the MEPs. For the moment, the only wind came from our own speed.

This night could offer departures from our previous tactics, for it was overcast and further blackened by the passing squalls, which were, in truth, invigorating after our long dive. Already, our tracking party was busy identifying blops on the PPI-scope. Though the blops appeared sharp enough to be ships or groups of ships, one after another their course and speed corresponded to that of the prevailing wind, and they were declassified to squalls. The old-fashioned A-scope seemed to help. On its horizontal grassy line, the contacts showed up as vertical lines or pips, bouncing up when the bearing was on. Perhaps this was my personal preference for this situation, for it seemed to give the operator a horizon to search and a sharp elusive pip rather than the blop retained by the material of the PPI screen.

The painstaking search continued until a large dense squall that our tracking party was investigating suddenly developed a momentary tall pip. The normal performance of the SJ had been just about halved by the weather, for the range was 14,000 yards. The time was 2200, still February 22.

We moved in quickly with little fear of being sighted while outside of an attack position. The original pip soon developed into a total of five, with another group of ships now sometimes showing up to the north.

There were two ways we could attack under these low visibility circumstances. One would be to barge in, spread the torpedoes across the major ships, and retire. It was the method apparently used successfully by German submarines against our large North Atlantic convoys, especially in 1943. It could be efficient when there were many big ships, their ratio to escorts was large, and when replacement torpedoes were not too many hundreds of miles away. Ours was a different type of war. We had brought our torpedoes over 5,000 miles already, and getting replacements by the shortest route would require a round trip of 6,000 more. The Japanese convoys generally had no more than two or three ships, and the ratio of escorts to ships was large and getting larger. Therefore we would hunt out each enemy ship—cargomen of any sort or sizable warships, first come first served—and make every torpedo count. The one extravagance, at least as I viewed it, would be the firing of four torpedoes into each ship on this, *Tang*'s first patrol.

Selecting suitable targets under these circumstances would require a little more than just sneaking in for a look. We would have to be ready to shoot, withdraw quietly, evade the enemy's maneuvers, or perhaps dive. Before we had moved in too far, Hank Flanagan came to the bridge just to ask for a bow shot if it was in any way possible. I gave him my assurance, for we were in perfect agreement, though for different reasons. Hank was hoping to keep peace between his two torpedo rooms. The men from aft would be a little hard to live with if they unloaded their last torpedoes before the forward room fired a shot. I, on the other hand, did not want to end up with a one-ended boat. Imagine the last-minute maneuvering on our first attack if suddenly we could not have fired from aft! Hank went below to his forward torpedo room. We gave Bill time to secure the battery charge and get his final gravity readings, and then *Tang* went to battle stations.

Once again the chimes were just a formality. All compartments, from forward to aft, reported immediately after the general alarm had stopped, and we started in on the surface to gain an attack position on the nearest ship. Her base course was 275, essentially the same as that which had already been determined for the entire group. I say group, for as viewed on the PPI-scope, the ships were not in the formation I would expect of a convoy. At 4,000 yards we could not see her, but we knew her ability to spot us had been reduced accordingly. We stopped to assist our soundmen and twisted ship slowly to keep our bow on her bearing as relayed up from the conning tower. She came on with a small zig towards, detected by plot, and would now pass 1,200 yards ahead. The routine orders preparatory to firing commenced.

"Open the outer doors on tubes three, four, five, and six."

"I've got her," whispered Jones, standing just to my left. "She's a patrol boat." The almost simultaneous report of fast screws from Caverly confirmed the sighting.

"All ahead standard, right full rudder" would bring us to a

retirement course. We spoke in hushed voices while the range continued to close slowly. For a minute we had to present our broadside silhouette, but then we were in the clear undetected. This was no suitable ship for us; if we missed she could force us down and all the ships might get away. We would try again.

Tang went after the next nearest pip. There was no long run in this time, but gaining a position on her bow involved passing her up. A stern, or overtaking, chase was always an extended one, for we gained by only the difference in the two speeds. In a half hour, however, Fraz's plot showed us 30 degrees on the next ship's bow. The radar range was 3,800, and she would pass inside of 2,000 yards. This time we did not have to wait; her low, chunky silhouette marked her as a patrol or possibly a minesweeper. Our soundman's report of a slower, heavier propeller seemed to favor the latter estimate. Again we turned and pulled clear.

We did not secure from battle stations, as the crew would not have left anyway, but all hands not actively involved did stand easy. As understood, the senior officer or petty officer could send a few men at a time to get coffee and the snacks that had been laid out in the messroom. Perhaps it was just this short period of catching our breath that was needed. At least the time was a factor, for the major immediate squalls had now blown beyond us, and the unmistakable pip of a good-sized ship showed up to the north. She became clearly visible at 7,000 yards, but only with the aid of 7 × 50 binoculars. I blessed the patriotic family that had donated the binoculars I held, and Mr. Rogers and his optical shop at Mare Island, who had coated their lenses and affixed the vertical reticle. With the center hinge wedged in the slightly tapered slot of our forward TBT, I was marking bearings on the ship, a freighter, and calling down estimates of her angle on the bow. The base course was 255, her speed 9 knots, and now two escorts were in sight, strangely patrolling most of the time on her starboard bow and quarter, on the other side of her. We did not object.

A large zig away concerned us, so we moved quickly onto her track, and all hands went back to their battle stations. We were now keeping pace with the freighter 4,000 yards from the bow escort and waiting for the next zig. Zig she did, seemingly nearly at us, but then the slight port angle on the bow commenced to open. Not fast enough, however, and we made a dipsy doodle, a turn and short run away followed by a turn back, to open our distance to her track. *Tang* stopped, the steersman holding her head on course 270, practically perpendicular to that of the enemy. Fraz, in the conning tower, ordered the outer doors on tubes 3, 4, 5, and 6 opened as I continued to mark bearings and call her angle on the bow. Jones had his binoculars on the bow escort and would interrupt me only should she give us a zero angle on the bow, which would indicate that she had sighted us and was closing to attack.

"Ten degrees to go," said Fraz over the speaker system. The submarine and target dials of the TDC were now continuously presenting the respective aspects of *Tang* and the enemy, identical to what was seen topside. From these dials Fraz was reading the lead angle for a zero gyro angle shot and giving me advance warning of the degrees till the target reached the optimum firing bearing.

"Stand by for constant bearings," I warned and then swung the TBT until the reticle was on her stack.

"Constant bearing—mark!" The TBT remained motionless as the freighter crossed the field. Her after superstructure was coming on the reticle. Frank's "Set!" came in the nick of time.

"Fire!" I barked in an explosive voice, for like those about me I had been holding my breath. The next three torpedoes followed, fired in exactly the same manner to hit specific points along her port side. The torpedoes were on their way, and so was *Tang* at full speed and with right full rudder. The explosions commenced while we were but a quarter of the way into our turn. The freighter disintegrated under four hits; there could be no survivors. She was gone before we reached our retirement course, but not her bow escort. She put up a brave chase, closing inside of 3,000 yards, undoubtedly knowing that we could fire stern torpedoes down her throat. There was no signal on the maneuvering room telegraphs for the speed we wanted, but chiefs Culp and MacDonald knew. The Fairbanks Morse diesels whirled their massive generators, pumping 5 million watts through *Tang*'s four main motors, and we pulled steadily away, losing the patrol in the spume and smoke astern. The extra 3 knots the maneuvering room had conjured up in our boat could prove doubly important, for had we been forced down, getting up on the surface again could have been difficult as long as the escort remained in the area.

Though interrupted during the attack, the navigator's plot

continued to show the track of the other ships. Overtaking them in due course would offer no problem. The seas had been building up, however, so we slowed to give the forward torpedo room a steadier deck for their reload. For the time being *Tang* secured from battle stations. Our regular section watch could handle anything in the interim, and our tracking party needed a break, even a short one. I took a much delayed trip to the head, in the starboard after corner of the forward torpedo room, but paused a moment to watch the reload. Were I to make any adverse judgment, it would be that there were too many men involved, extra volunteers I would suspect, but the torpedoes were sliding home smartly. I nodded approval.

After a welcome cup of coffee in the wardroom, I went back to the conning tower, stopping off for a minute in the control room. By tradition a commanding officer is expected to instill confidence in his men, but after a few words with Chief Ballinger I realized that this could be a two-way proposition. I went up to the conning tower perfectly confident that we'd close in and sink the next ship just like the last.

Fraz took his turn below, Hank reported his reload complete, and *Tang* set off to seek out the next ship. I glanced at the Quartermaster's Notebook; a half hour had passed since our torpedoes had detonated. We changed course 30 degrees to starboard and went ahead standard to move from our position on the port beam of this group to a position sharp on its bow. At range 4,000 we went back to battle stations, but with a new set of lookouts. Chief Ballinger would regulate this so that more men could share this vantage point.

The ship we were seeking was now singled out and we stopped to let her come on. Sound reported an encouraging 120 propeller count, reasonable for a merchantman at the determined speed, but at 3,500 yards the dark shape developed into a destroyer with *Tang* 1,200 yards from her track. We had practiced running backward submerged, and I figured we could dive going astern, too, if need be. In any case, backing down offered the only way to pull clear without giving her a beam silhouette. Back we did, our propeller wash rolling down our sides, and she passed at 2,900 yards.

There was more than one reason for not shooting. With the increasing seas, I had ordered the torpedoes set to run at ten feet for the last attack. This was four feet deeper than we had set them at Truk and was necessary lest they broach and run erratic in our present seas. At this depth they would likely run under the destroyer. Further, with her lookouts close to the sea, like ours, she might very well spot us before we could shoot if we closed to a proper range on the surface. But since there was not enough light for any periscope use whatsoever, diving would mean a shot by sound bearings alone, not sufficiently accurate, especially against a destroyer. If these reasons had not been enough to convince me, the fact that we already had another ship picked out would have.

Tang went ahead. There was a boil of water around the screws until we gained headway, then the propellers bit in and our ship picked up speed. As we passed the next contact abeam, we found her with our 7 × 50s. Her low, tapered silhouette was unmistakable; she was a submarine, probably enemy, but we could not be sure. The decision was not ours to make, for except in certain Empire areas we could not fire upon another submarine unless it was positively identified as enemy. Our experience with *Guardfish* in broad daylight showed the impossibility of any identification here.

Tang's divergent course to get clear of the submarine put additional pips abeam. One of these promised to be a suitable ship with two escorts, one well ahead and one astern. We converged to find a fine freighter's silhouette at 5,000 yards, and shortly afterward the low shape of an astern escort. The bow escort remained just a pip, for some reason scouting nearly 8,000 yards ahead.

The visibility in our vicinity was improving. This permitted calling down details of the ship's profile, her raked bow, composite superstructure, and gun mounts on her bow and stern. From the control room, where there was time to use the identification books, came the first estimate of this ship's type. She was classified as an *Arimasan Maru*, and with gun mounts, very likely a naval auxiliary. The tonnage of this class was 8,663.

Her angle on the bow was now sharpening as we moved ahead into position for attack, and the details became less discernible. We had the immediate problems of attack facing us and were momentarily startled by a flicker of light at the ship's forward gun mount. It was not repeated, however, and the bearings with angles on the bow were called down for each visible change.

"We've got her on course two seven zero, speed eight, Captain." It was Fraz's voice. "Range twenty-eight hundred, we're twelve hundred yards from her track. It looks good from here." It looked good from the bridge, too, but a bit scarier perhaps, for at this stage her angle on the bow looked very sharp, and a slight change of enemy course would put us underfoot. That was always the case if you were really right in there, and there were invariably anxious moments until the rate of change of her angle became pronounced with the decreasing range. Perhaps it was well that I was busy twisting our boat for a minimal silhouette, marking bearings, and then settling her on the heading for near zero gyro shots. A black squall in back of us gave us further security from detection, but I more than welcomed Fraz's call, "Ten degrees to go, Captain."

"She's turned back, but she'll never make it." It was Jones, just in back of me, keeping track of the bow escort. I knew exactly what he saw: The escort ahead was coming toward us. It was like having another pair of eyes and the judgment to go with them.

"Constant bearing—mark!"

"Set!" from the conning tower.

"Fire!"

The next three torpedoes, each fired to hit a specific point, zinged out at eight-second intervals. From the instant of firing it was impossible for the enemy to maneuver his 600-foot ship to clear the divergent torpedo tracks. The whacks of the first two detonations resounded from below instantly, a second before we felt the explosions topside. The third torpedo hit forward of her bridge, causing a tremendous explosion. The marine life, suddenly phosphorescent, made the seas go white. *Tang* was hit from all sides by a monstrous shock wave, which seemed like the instantaneous detonation of a hundred torpedoes, but there was just that one heart-stopping crack. The naval auxiliary twisted, raised from the sea as you would flip a spoon on end, then plunged by the stern, engulfed in a mass of flames.

"Are you all right below?" I called. There was no answer.

"All ahead full, right full rudder." I gave the order automatically, still not knowing the situation below. When I saw the luminous pointer of the rudder angle indicator swing right, I took a half breath. Then Fraz's reassuring voice came from the conning tower.

"We're OK—checking the compartments." He paused and then, "What the hell was it?"

Tang was gathering way, so not too much was wrong. It

had seemed minutes before I had heard from below, but it was really only seconds; just time enough for the crew to feel themselves to be sure they were still there and to get their jaws off their chests. We were in the clear; the ship was gone, and again there could have been no survivors.

We cruised along abeam of the three pips remaining on our SJ while four more torpedoes were pulled from their skids into the empty tubes. The only possible damage from the explosion was found at this time, for the outer door of No. 5 torpedo tube was leaking slightly. It would undoubtedly seat tightly with sea pressure on diving. With the reload complete, and after time for those who wanted coffee to finish a cup or two, we turned our attention to business.

The visibility had further improved, and we were able to investigate the three remaining ships with but one approach. They were all patrol types, so we set off to find the northerly group of ships that had shown up intermittently back at 2230. The navigator laid down an overtaking search plan that would cover their likely positions. With our regular sections now on watch, *Tang* followed the wide zigzag track to the northwest, cruising at three-engine speed to insure a rate of advance that would catch up with the enemy.

I checked the Quartermaster's Notebook prior to writing up my brief orders for the rest of the night. On the first ship this night we had fired at 2349; the latitude was 14° 47′ north, and the longitude was 144° 50′ east. On this last attack we had fired at 0120. The latitude was 14° 45′ north, and the longtitude 144° 32′ east. I wrote them carefully in the back of my Night Order Book so this would remain a part of my personal record.

It was now a quarter of three on the morning of February 23, and I was ready for some shut-eye; but some of the men still wondered about the mighty shock. To me the answer was now plain: When a torpedo explodes, the initial detonation wave of its warhead—the whack—is felt instantaneously, for the sea acts as a solid and transmits this just as if it were a rigid iron rod. The explosion of our third torpedo had caused the detonation of the whole naval auxiliary's cargo, the equivalent of hundreds of warheads, with a shock wave of stupefying proportion.

I went to my cabin to try out my bunk.

8

Sleeping or even resting during the predawn hours proved impossible. Low voices from the wardroom indicated that others were having the same problem. I started across the passageway.

"But we could have sunk each of them with three torpedoes," Mel was saying as I entered the wardroom. Fraz and Frank were there, too. The exec's eyes were as wide and bright as one would expect at noonday, but I could not tell about the other two, for they were wearing red masks to start night-adapting their eyes prior to going on watch. It would take some hours, perhaps even a day to completely calm down from the excitement of this night.

"You're right, Mel, about firing a spread of three," I injected at the first appropriate moment, "but they're on the bottom, and that's what counts!" I would see what we could do about a better rotation of the OODs when we were attacking on the surface, for they would have to see it to believe it. That would be far better than any explanation. Actually I had now been tempted on three occasions to withhold that last torpedo and was sure that in the conning tower, with everything checking, it seemed the logical thing to do. But an exact plot, the visual presentation on the TDC, and the blops on the radar screen could not compete with but a single glance of the eyes and the judgment the good Lord had given us, even though we saw only shapes on a dark night. In each case, the fourth torpedo had insured destruction of the enemy, thus permitting me to concentrate on evasion immediately after firing. I regretted not one of them.

Frank and Mel had gone topside. Our system, which I had brought from *Wahoo*, with an OOD on the bridge and an assistant OOD in the conning tower, was paying extra dividends, especially when we were expecting contact with the enemy. The assistant OOD, acting as assistant navigator, interpreting radar contacts, supervising the conning tower watch, and always ready to initiate tracking, allowed the OOD to concentrate fully from the bridge. There were additional advantages; armed with all of the essential information, the assistant could relieve the OOD on a moment's notice for the latter to don rain clothes or get a cup of coffee, or they could change positions at any time, such as halfway through the four-hour watch. It was, of course, the addition of Ed to our complement that made this possible.

There was time for a game of cribbage before the navigator went topside for his morning stars. Fraz counted first and pegged out. We sat back for a moment, a little more relaxed.

"Tenacity, Fraz. Stay with 'em till they're on the bottom!" Fraz answered with a smile and a nod. We felt good about the way this patrol was progressing. Ships weren't falling in our lap, but we were finding them and the torpedoes were hitting.

By Fraz's star fix we were 150 miles west of Saipan, beyond the reach of our carrier planes should they even search in this direction. The Japanese would probably not send their ships farther west. We changed course to north. An Ultra from Pearl raised our hope by reporting the coming noon position of an enemy convoy, and we went to three-engine speed with only a 20-degree course change necessary. Nothing materialized, but having come this far a further search of this vast area seemed our best bet before returning toward Saipan. Perhaps it was our plan, maybe the Ultra was a factor, or just plain luck was staying with us, for a single faint puff of smoke rose off to the north and then blended into the clouds. It was distant, far beyond the horizon, spotted by Scotty on the tall search periscope. The enemy had made one mistake, for one bearing was all we needed. *Tang* was on course 015, heading for the enemy by the time I reached the bridge. It was 1109 on the morning of February 23.

Two pips on the SJ a little to the left of the original periscope contact gave the first course indication. We came left to parallel the enemy on a tentative westerly heading. The range to the two ships of 23,000 and 24,000 yards was close enough until we could find out more about them and how we might best attack. Our searching had been with normal lookouts, the raised search periscope, and when the horizon was fuzzy, the SJ radar. Now we had Jones atop the shears with one arm hooked through the last rung to keep him from falling and at the same time helping support his 7 × 50s. There was good reason for this. The binoculars had nearly half again the power and a much wider field than the periscope, and they could be kept much steadier on the horizon.

"I've got 'em," he called. "A big tanker, a freighter, and a destroyer. They're gone now." I motioned Jones down and he did not hesitate, for it was a lonely place a long way from the hatch. With Chief Jones at hand where we could talk without shouting, our tactics became obvious. His estimate of a 90-degree port angle on the bow checked with our tracking, and we came left to 225 degrees and went to three-engine speed.

Our first move was to preclude their sighting us by opening the range to where our radar could just maintain contact. This could be considerably farther out than the range at which we first had the pip, for once the contact was made the operator knew exactly where to search. *Tang*'s speed of nearly 18 knots would keep us abeam of the enemy, and then we would gain position ahead for a submerged approach and attack. This would be the last half of an end-around in which *Tang* would follow the arc of a quarter of a circle, but a circle whose center was moving at about 8 knots. The navigator worked out the details, probably more accurately than the enemy ships would maintain their course, if indeed they did not change the base course before our maneuver was completed. Fraz then plotted our track. It would take nearly three hours, with *Tang* moving along short segments of the arc, but that would leave plenty of time for a submerged attack during daylight.

The end-around proceeded quite exactly. We gained position well out on the enemy's bow and were moving toward the spot where we could submerge and run in for the attack. The problem as being run on the TDC and the navigator's plot looked good. This could be the exact type of submerged approach we had been hoping for, possibly firing a split salvo, or torpedoes from both ends, one salvo at the tanker, the other at the freighter, maybe even including the destroyer.

"Lost radar contact!" called Caverly. When information from sound was not required, Caverly was our battle stations radar operator. He was our radar repairman as well, so when he said lost, it was just that, not a faulty radar; the enemy had gone over the hill.

A serious mistake in any military operation is to base your tactics on your enemy's intentions unless you possess the capability of countering. This *Tang* possessed in speed, and we lit it out at full power right down the last true bearing line. We would reach the enemy's last known position before he could move beyond radar range from it. Any other course might add to this range, letting the enemy spring our trap. It was a hairy run, with Jones, Fraz, or me hanging onto the shears as we moved into gathering squalls, but then came the welcome call from the OOD, "Radar contact, bearing one three five degrees true."

"Head for it," I called.

"We are, Captain," answered Fraz, who had just dropped down to the bridge.

It soon became more than apparent that we would do well to maintain contact with the enemy for a night attack. Even this became an increasing problem as the convoy entered squall after squall. Sometimes the ships would emerge on he same course, sometimes on another, but more and more frequently it became necessary to go in after them and then to retire when they showed up suddenly closer than expected. It was no longer a question of remaining undetected; the enemy obviously knew we were there. The forays into reduced and sometimes zero visibility were a bit unnerving, for with our radar nearly blanked out there was always the chance of coming face to face with the destroyer. Delaying behind the convoy would have been a good destroyer tactic, but the enemy did not know the squalls were interfering with our radar; only we knew that. Finally the hour of sunset came and then welcome dusk, and at the same time we emerged from the squally area. *Tang* stopped.

If there was any doubt in anyone's mind that we had been detected, it was dispelled at this moment. The convoy was in a clear area, with the last twilight beyond to silhouette the ships. Several searchlight signals were sent from the destroyer to the other ships. They then lined up heading west with the tanker astern, and the destroyer took position ahead. While we could still see them, they steamed off to the west. With the dark clouds for a background, we watched from atop the shears with 7 × 50s until they had disappeared. Bill Walsh's men poured on the oil and cut down on the main motor fields so maximum current would flow. *Tang* was off on another full-power run down that last true bearing.

Instead of to the southwest, where the convoy's course at

dark would have taken it, the ships turned up on our port bow to the southeast. Had the convoy commander not left his most valuable ship out naked astern and so betrayed his probable intention to circle and lead his ships east, we might not have followed the last true bearing. But that was neither here nor there. He had them—destroyer, tanker, and freighter, in column and heading for Saipan—and it was just a matter of how and when to shoot.

Much of the day's excitement had been experienced by the individuals topside in the watch sections, but in a submarine it was impossible not to be involved. All hands were keyed up, perhaps too excited. To unwind a bit, at least physically, we resumed our regular underway routine, leaving tracking and similar activities to the watch section. Fraz and I took turns when there was doubt but for the most part were able to relax, too. The evening meal was served, and then the ship identification books were sent to the messroom, where all the lookouts could hash them over. If their conclusions concerning the ships we were chasing should coincide with those of the regular identification party, the information could be of use this night.

At 1930, the battle stations tracking party took over. Another hour or so would be required before *Tang* would be in all respects ready to move in, for the convoy's zigs were of the wildest sort, sometimes even backtracking, making determination of the base course difficult. Against this thoroughly alerted enemy, with the destroyer now patrolling at high speed on a large arc across the bow of the tanker, attacks like those of last night would be nearly impossible. We had three things going for us, however: the dark night, the very wildness of the zigzagging, and a peculiarity of all but highly trained lookouts.

When a person walks down a street or rides on a bus, he habitually looks where he is going. This habit is so ingrained that an after lookout tends to look where his ship is going. Only when the vital importance of his particular responsibility is thoroughly explained can you count on his complete concentration aft. *Tang* would take advantage of this, the dark night, and the wild zigzagging. She would attack from astern. Though this would mean taking on the much less valuable freighter first, we would not be subjected to the slicing bow of the destroyer. During the whole remainder of the night, and if need be till dawn, we could work on the tanker.

The duty chief had received the report of the lookouts. They had agreed, though I suspect with some dissenters, that the freighter was a *Tatutaki Maru* class ship. Perhaps not unsurprisingly, this agreed with the regular identification party's second choice. I was inclined to go along with the lookouts on this occasion, for they had made their determination by what they had seen, not by what they had been told. During the day we had been too busy to send many details down to our party, and no ship comparable to the tanker had been found by either group, but the information on the freighter was encouraging. She was long enough to hit easily and had boilers amidships to help her blow up.

It was 2030 and we went to battle stations in all respects ready. Our tactics would be to move up astern. When the freighter zigged, *Tang* would cross her stern and move up on the opposite quarter. The next zig back would put us near her beam, and we would shoot on a large track with the torpedoes angling in from her quarter.

Things never seem to work out quite as nicely in practice as they appear on paper, and this was no exception. On our first approach, the *Tatutaki Maru* zigged twice to the right, leaving *Tang* off in left field. On the next approach, her zig was less than hoped for, leaving us with too large a track for our torpedoes; they would be almost paralleling her course. The third approach was to our liking. *Tang* had worked well up on her port quarter about 1,000 yards off; her zig left would quickly bring her across our bow, and the torpedoes would hit on an average track of 130 degrees. Fraz ordered the outer doors opened. I was marking bearings and calling the angles on the bow, and then we were blinded and choking topside in the freighter's smoke.

These three approaches set a pattern. Sometimes we didn't reach an attack position; once she zigged away three times, spoiling our setup; and smoke from that coal-burning freighter, which had caused the original sighting, saved her again. True, we could have fired on the generated bearing of the TDC and she would probably have sunk with one or more hits, but we expected to hit with all torpedoes and see her go. An unexpected super right zig headed the *Tatutaki Maru* across our bow. The forward room raced to open the doors. I marked a single bearing and angle on the bow, then called, "Constant bearing—mark!" Her stern was crossing the wire, but there was no "Set!" She was nearly to our bow. Another "Constant bearing—mark!" and then came Frank's "Set!"

"Fire!" sent the first torpedo on its way. The next three followed in an eight-second cadence to hit along her starboard side. The freighter came to pieces under three hits. The tanker opened up with big guns from forward and aft almost immediately, while the destroyer closed in firing a barrage, seemingly in all directions. During the initial flurry some tracer shells seemed to land a thousand yards or so away from us, but this was just by chance. *Tang* was leaving the scene well astern when the destroyer crisscrossed through the area where the freighter had been, laying down 12 depth charges. We were quite happy to have the enemy think we were submerged back there as we headed for a position 10,000 yards, five miles, on the tanker's beam.

The firing time had been 2230, still on February 23, though I felt that days must have gone by. The position from the dead reckoning indicator (DRI) was 15° 16' north and 143° 12' east. The navigator would have to take a position from the DRI, too, for running up a position with our antics of the night would be impossible. Strangely, however, *Tang*'s firing setup had turned out nearly ideal—a range of 1,400 yards and a 105-degree average track, the torpedoes coming in from 15 degrees abaft her starboard beam.

I wrote in my brief night orders: *Cruising on base course 090° true, maintaining position between 8,000 and 12,000 yards on the port beam of the enemy. He is shooting every few minutes and dropping depth charges occasionally. The range will vary with his zigzagging, but be alert to note any continued change indicating a change in base course. If you lose contact, head down the last true bearing at full power and call the navigator. At 0300 go to three-engine speed and follow courses the navigator will recommend to place* Tang *on the enemy's base course, 10,000 yards dead ahead of him by one hour before morning twilight. We will dive before dawn and attack submerged.*

I left the usual space for the OOD's initials, a line for Jones to insert the time of morning twilight, and my call for one half hour ahead of that time, and then handed the orders to the executive officer.

"It's all in here, Fraz. Forget any stars and have Jones fill in on the four-to-eight. One of us has to be bright-eyed at dawn, and that means me."

Fraz glanced through the night orders and gave a cheery "Aye, aye, Captain," more than welcoming the opportunity to carry the ball. It was past midnight when I hit my sack.

9

The dawn attack we were anticipating held many advantages. The hours of tracking would let us make an accurate determination of the enemy's speed and zigzag plan. Having gone some hours unmolested, the enemy would probably have calmed down and, with the assurance that comes with daylight, might relax his vigilance. We would be able to dive in the most advantageous position and press home the attack with the accuracy and surprise of a true, submerged, submarine.

These thoughts, my confidence in Fraz and the whole ship's company, and even the occasional rumble of a depth charge confirming that the enemy was in our grasp, one or all of these kicked me off to sleep. Except for three reports of an extra ship, each diagnosed as simultaneous gunfire from the destroyer and both ends of the long tanker, my first consciousness was of holding a piping hot mug of coffee. It was not a wardroom cup, with a sissy handle, which one could contemplate or set aside. This was a GI cup, so hot I had to pass it from hand to hand. It was the sure way of getting the individual called onto his feet.

"It is one-half hour before morning twilight, Captain." I thanked the messenger, who undoubtedly went aft to tell of my balancing the mug while rolling out of my bunk. After a few years, I'm sure most submariners become quite good at this. After another cup in the wardroom, from the steward's freshly brewed pot, it was time to go topside. The few words I exchanged with the troops on the way revealed our mutual confidence. The hopes and expectations were evident, and I had never felt more sure of having the enemy in my fist than at this moment.

"Where are they, Fraz?" was my first question after taking a sweep with the 7 × 50s.

"Right back there ten thousand yards, where they're supposed to be," was his reply and the one I expected. It was not a curt answer, just a concise report reflecting some pride, for several times during the night, full power down the last true bearing had regained contact on a wildly maneuvering enemy.

No matter how careful we were to night-adapt our eyes with red masks and dim ruby-red lighting below, a few minutes in the existing darkness were still required for good vision. Even then it helped to know what to look for. Shortly a slight, fuzzy bump on the horizon was visible. Then it took the more defined shape of a "blurp," right over our stern. *Tang* was on course 090 and so was the enemy, though now zigging mildly.

"All stop." We would let the convoy, or what was left of it, come in to about 7,000 yards, and by remaining on our original course, we would be able to maneuver with it if necessary without presenting a broadside silhouette. The enemy closed, and Venus, now a morning star, came up dead ahead, nearly as bright as a quarter moon. You are always in the light path of the moon or a planet when you view it from your ship, but in this case *Tang* was also on the same light streak being viewed by the enemy. He was now taking on a distinct shape as he neared. I had to grit my teeth and tell myself, almost audibly, that he could not see us. The slight gray of morning twilight did not help, but we were putting together the best elements of a night approach and a daylight attack. This was no time for wavering.

"Ultra from SubPac!" came over the bridge speaker. It was Mel's voice, a bit excited. He read the message:

THE CONVOY YOU ARE APPARENTLY
ATTACKING HAS BEEN ORDERED TO CHANGE
BASE COURSE TO NORTH AT DAWN

"Christ!" It was more of a supplication than a profanity. The broken Japanese dispatch could well have been a ruse to get us off their back. I rejected the information in the Ultra. This was not a difficult decision, for we could not reach a position north of the convoy anyway. *Tang* went ahead on the battery to avoid a chance puff of smoke on restarting the diesels and then slid down to radar depth. The time was 0548 on February 24; we went to battle stations.

Bill held her neatly at 40 feet as we turned left to close the enemy. In a few minutes it would be light enough to see through the periscope. In the meantime radar ranges and bearings flowed to plot and the TDC.

"He's zigged left, Captain."

"Shift the rudder. Steady on north. All ahead standard."

If the enemy was coming to north, as the Ultra said, this would parallel him for a later attack should he head back for Saipan. If this was just a normal zig, we would be closing the track and gaining position for attack. The seconds dragged.

"Enemy course zero six zero," called Fraz, with a note of relief that we both felt equally. The enemy had zigged just 30 degrees, and *Tang* could reach him handily with a good high-speed run. We dropped to 100 feet and went ahead full. Till the scope went under, I watched the blurp, now almost a shape, but the vibration precluded a valid estimate of the angle on the bow. A course normal, or perpendicular, to the enemy's track would hasten the attack; we came left to 330.

The high-speed run would require 20 minutes. It would be interrupted only as we stopped the screws temporarily so our soundmen could obtain bearings on the tanker. This was the time to make all tubes ready for firing. There was no need to specify which ones—we had only eight torpedoes left, four forward and four aft. We would fire the last torpedoes from one end or the other, maybe both, since the loss of this tanker could hurt the enemy more than the loss of the other four ships put together.

Fifteen minutes into the run, plot showed we were getting close to the enemy's track. Bill brought *Tang* up to 64 feet as we slowed to 3 knots. A quick sound check, a quicker periscope sweep in low power, and I breathed normally.

"We're right on," I reported by way of assurance to all hands, as well as to myself. "Now stand by for a setup." The sea was like glass; the scope would barely break the surface and be down again. I glanced at our keel depth; Bill was right on. My hands indicated the desired height. Jones brought the scope up smartly.

"Bearing—mark! Range—mark!" I flipped the handles up and the scope was down. Jones called the bearing and then read the stadimeter range from the dial, now just above the periscope well. I had called the angle 25 starboard; the range was 2,600 yards. *Tang* was 1,200 yards from the enemy's track. Our 3 knots would take us too close by firing time, so we came right to parallel the tanker. It was 0609.

Subsequent periscope observations were short and frequent, each now for just one piece of information. A water-lapping look at the tanker's tops for a bearing, the next on the destroyer's mast, a range using deck level to tanker's tops as the stadimeter height, and an angle on the bow using the separation of the masts. The lens of the attack scope was never exposed for more than three or four seconds, nor more than inches above the surface, then back to the destroyer again.

"Down scope!" It was an unnecessary order, for Jones had it lowered as I flipped the handles. It served just to punctuate.

"Open all outer doors." The destroyer had crossed the tanker's bow and was heading directly at us, about 800 yards away. This was my problem; I would not disrupt our setup on the tanker until the last instant, and that was approximately one minute away. I had faced this situation before, in *Wahoo*, a much more taut one with the destroyer coming at nearly 30 knots at my raised periscope and with but one torpedo left that we could fire. By comparison this was nothing, except that this time I was in command. I counted to ten in a one-second cadence. Jones kept the scope at my eye as I raised my body from a crouching position.

"Bearing—mark!" The scope was down. "That's on the tanker. The destroyer has turned right and she's going down the tanker's side." The destroyer was absolutely dwarfed by the length of the loaded oiler.

The whole fire control party and, through the talkers, the whole ship knew what had just transpired. I believe they all breathed more easily with me, for everyone wanted that tanker.

We were not quite out of the woods. Between the second and third subsequent looks, the oiler had zigged 20 degrees toward us. This put us too close to the track, for the steam torpedoes in our forward tubes required a run of over 400 yards to arm their warheads. We could have fired angle shots to use up the extra yards in their turn, but fortunately *Tang* was already turning away for a stern shot. Continuing would just squeak us out for the straight shots we desired.

The angle on the bow was opening fast as she came on, giving the impression that we were on her beam until I lined up details known to be athwartship. She was looking for us, all right: From bow to stern, her rail was manned by white-uniformed sailors, an estimated 150 men on our side alone. Others were atop the bridge and after superstructure. She was a naval tanker, shown nowhere in ONI-208J nor in the book of enemy naval ships, but was comparable to our *Cimarron* and with estimated 6-inch guns. But why so many men? Had she taken them to sea on fleeing Saipan?

"Ten degrees to go, generated range five hundred." It was Fraz's report for near zero torpedo gyros and the range from the TDC.

"Stand by for constant bearings. Up scope." This time there was no special effort to conceal the periscope. What we needed were quick, accurate bearings, for at this range the angular change would be high. If we were sighted, the tanker could not possibly do anything about it; her last hope, the destroyer, was just passing under her stern heading away.

"Constant bearing—mark!"

"Set!" Frank was holding the bearing constant on the TDC. The big, squat stack was coming on the stationary periscope reticle.

"Fire!" Fraz hit the plunger, and the first torpedo zinged on its way. The next three followed, each to hit a specific point along her starboard side.

On the tanker, the lookouts saw the torpedo wakes and were pointing and waving right up to the explosions. I saw not one of them leave his post. It was quick; the torpedo run was only 23 seconds. Debris went into the air, and the entire ship was enveloped in a mass of billowing flame and grayish-brown smoke. She started down immediately. Fraz took the scope and watched her go in just four minutes. The time was 0643.

Tang went deep, too, and the depth charges started one minute later, but they were not close.

10

Tang was swimming down with a generous angle. There was no rush, for the destroyer had been on the other side of the holocaust and had no torpedo wakes to disclose our firing position. Her present depth charges were several hundred yards away, maybe even a thousand. As long as she was dropping depth charges she could not conduct a sound search for us without blasting her own soundmen's ears. Each moment counted, however, for we were moving farther away just by continuing on our firing course as we went deeper toward that hoped-for gradient. We needed to get there before she settled down to an orderly search.

Bill pumped from auxiliary to sea for brief periods to keep the boat's neutral buoyancy as her hull was squeezed by the increasing sea pressure. We passed 450 feet, and then the needle of the bathythermograph moved sharply, tracing a 5-degree water temperature change on the lamp-blacked card. It was exactly the gradient we wanted, at 475 feet. We would cruise below it.

"Level off at five hundred, Bill." Bill's acknowledgment was interrupted by an unexcited though disturbing report from Lieutenant Flanagan.

"We're taking some water in the forward torpedo room but can hold it for a while," were Hank's matter-of-fact words. It was the type of report I expected. More than one ship, including the *Graf Spee*, had become an ineffective fighting unit because too many damage reports, not the damage itself, had convinced her commander to withdraw. We had discussed this early in our shakedown. But situations can change quickly, especially in submarines.

Instead of leveling off, *Tang* passed 500 feet as if she were going on down to 600. I dropped down to the control room. Bill was doing what he could with planes and pumps and had called for speed. But speed alone, with our down-angle, would only drive us deeper. I ordered him to blow safety, but with Bill's calm order, De Lapp on the manifold gave only a shot of high-pressure air, as he would on surfacing, and *Tang* continued to drop. Twenty times that amount would be needed down here.

The responsibility for our ship was mine; I hooked them up in series and ordered, "Blow safety! Blow bow buoyancy!"

De Lapp blew and blew. The 3,000-pound air roared, and with speed to help the planes, *Tang* slowly took an up-angle. She should be swimming up, but the hand of the depth gauge still rested against the pin at 612. Were we climbing or still losing depth? We could blow main ballast and undoubtedly get back on the gauge, but great bubbles would accompany the inevitable venting, most certainly betraying our position to the enemy. We could not risk that unless it became absolutely necessary. On the occasions when we had tested *Tang*'s depth capability, some relatively minor mechanical failures had accompanied our increasing depths. The same should be true now if we were still sinking. We held on, waiting and listening. The minutes dragged, but they continued without incident, and I became ever more confident that *Tang* was indeed rising slowly.

"We've got her," called Bill as the hand on the depth gauge fluttered for a second and then moved off the pin. These had been the nine longest minutes of my life, and I daresay all hands felt the same.

The ship was under control and all pumps were on the torpedo room bilges. I went forward, ducked through the torpedo room door, and gasped. The scene was not as Hollywood would picture it, with men in water up to their armpits, struggling and sputtering. Nonetheless, Hank's crew was going about its serious business knee-deep in water. It looked like a lake, no less, half submerging the culprit, our leaky No. 5 torpedo tube. Water was spraying out of the gaps in the inner door bayonet locking ring, drenching everything forward.

In order to accomplish any repairs, and before the pumps could get ahead, we must have less sea pressure. Back in the control room, Bill was bringing *Tang* up steadily, now at 500 feet, with Fraz filling my shoes while I had been forward. We passed through the gradient, whose loss was the least of our worries. Now, instead of flooding auxiliary from sea to slow our ascent, we vented bow buoyancy a bit at a time. The bubbles would be small as they rose from the vent valve and, we hoped, would not become too large as they expanded on their way up. They might well be sighted, but we would change course as soon as bow buoyancy was full of water again. We had little choice in any case, for air in bow buoyancy would expand whenever we lost depth, forcing water out the holes in its bottom and making our bow light. The opposite would be true each time we sank a little. A galloping motion would be inevitable, and broaching from periscope depth likely.

Our safety tank was a different matter. It was as strong as the pressure hull and fitted with great mushroom flood valves that closed hydraulically and sealed with sea pressure. Right now it was nearly dry and completely sealed off from the sea.

It was safety, located a bit forward of our center of gravity, that was giving us the buoyancy to compensate for the water in the torpedo room.

We breathed a little more easily as Bill leveled off at 100 feet, for the pumps were gaining on the flooding.

"Light screws bearing three five zero degrees true." Caverly's report was not unexpected, but it certainly was not one that we wanted to hear. I squatted down next to him, and he flipped one of his earphones over for me. It held little resemblance to a combat information center, but we were faster and decisions could be made just that much more quickly. The true bearing remained constant; the destroyer would pass over us just as surely as constant bearings bring collisions at sea or at highway intersections.

"Stop pumping."

We were now completely quiet except for our slowly turning screws, and they were below any possible cavitation. Almost immediately we lost the destroyer's propeller noise. She had stopped or slowed to listen but at a minimum was coasting down the last true bearing she held on us. If we just waited, the next sounds could be her fast screws as she rushed overhead in a depth-charge attack. We had to look!

"Bring her up to eighty feet. Open the outer doors forward." Unless forced, we would not fire, for I already knew what firing on an alerted destroyer could entail, and that from a submarine with all of her capabilities. Ours would have to be a desperation shot, but just that situation could greet us at periscope depth.

Bill eased her up, using a minimum angle, for the free surface of water in the torpedo room would tend to accentuate any movement. It was like trying to balance an ice tray full of water. Under the precarious circumstances, *Tang* eased into 80 feet in a laudable manner. If Bill could do it at 80 without galloping, he could repeat it at 64. He had to. We started up. Jones brought the scope up exactly the same as when we had last squeaked a look at this destroyer before the attack. Fraz called out our depth. At 65 feet Jones followed my eye with the scope. The bright green surface was just above the lens; a flash of daylight and the scope was down.

"Ten starboard," I called.

"Range seven hundred," Jones read, and then the bearing. It checked with sound.

"Ease her down to eighty, Bill; we're coming left with fifteen degrees rudder." The additional information went to

Bill before the order to the steersman because any appreciable rudder tends to make a submerged submarine squat by the stern, and in our situation the diving officer deserved any advance warning possible.

Tang steadied on the reciprocal of a normal course, one that would add our travel to the component of the enemy's. We slithered away. Each of us was waiting for the other to make a move that would create a sound. It was *Tang*'s turn first, for the water had risen nearly a foot in the torpedo room since we had stopped pumping. Much more water would increase the likelihood of flooding out our sound training motors, located next to the torpedo room's after bulkhead, and we needed them as we never had before. When a submarine is truly quiet, any internal noise seems amplified; our multistage rotary drain pump was not bad, but the dual-piston trim pump sounded like two small pile drivers.

"Light screws bearing zero eight zero." It apparently sounded like two small pile drivers to the destroyer, too. We continued to pump, we had to, and sneaked up for a look. This time I informed the troops that we would fire only in defense, for word had drifted back that readying the tubes had added to their apprehensions on our first look. The destroyer was off at about 3,000 yards, which was good, but her angle on the bow was zero. The propeller count was low, probably so her soundmen could hear us above their screw noise. Our pumps did their best until the estimated range was down to 1,500; then we gave them a rest and went through another slithering evasion.

The destroyer did not seem hurried and gave us the impression that she was just waiting for the correct setup. Her tactics seemed disquietingly akin to our own when we were on the offensive. We had made some derisive remarks when she had had two ships and then one in her charge. Now that she had been relieved of them and could concentrate on us, there was nothing funny about her.

The pumping, evading, and waiting became a trying cycle, made the more so since at all times we had to be ready to shoot. Reload crews were no longer necessary and there was only one torpedo room to man, so there were extra hands to temporarily relieve many of those at battle stations. But others chose to stick it out, and I was especially proud of them. Meanwhile, our repairmen had not been idle. With rags and lead for backing, they were caulking the open segments of the bayonet locking ring, literally squeezing the extruding rubber gasket back toward its groove. At first this seemed to have little effect, just redirecting the water behind the ring, but by noontime the flow had diminished noticeably. An hour went by without pumping, and the enemy's approaches were reduced accordingly. Compared to the forenoon, we seemed to have the situation in hand, and I decided that we should leave well enough alone. Further caulking could distort and crack the ring, and then all would be lost.

An axiom of antisubmarine warfare is to stay with the enemy, for one never knows the extent of the troubles that may exist below. The Japanese captain had read the book, and the destroyer remained on top of us throughout the afternoon, sometimes so close we were sure she would drop. Perhaps it was wishful thinking, but we concluded that the 12 depth charges where the freighter sank, the occasional drops during the night, and the numerous charges after the tanker's sinking had left her with but one good salvo, which she was saving just for us. We were curious, though not distressed, at the lack of echo-ranging. Perhaps the destroyer had come out of Saipan directly from an upkeep period, with her gear in overhaul. Maybe the explosions on the tanker had put it out of commission. Or the ease with which she made contact with passive sound, just listening, made echo-ranging, which would advertise her presence, unnecessary. The enemy's error, I believe, was to assume that we were deep, where any sane submarine ought to be. How could he guess that we were watching him so as to counter every move? It was undoubtedly baffling to hear us, start a run, and then lose contact time after time.

Sunset was coming, and the following hours, until we could get on the surface, could be our toughest. We would have difficulty in seeing the destroyer through the periscope starting a few minutes into evening twilight. The first test came. I could not call an angle, and Caverly had her bearing constant. I listened with him and agreed with his guess at a slight drift to the left. We came right with crossed fingers. The destroyer passed clear, but this could not continue!

The time was now 2000, the calculated end of evening twilight; it was pitch-black through the periscope. The destroyer would be getting nervous, too, now knowing that we might be on the surface. We delayed pumping, hoping to add to her anxiety, and thoroughly expecting a high-speed depth-charge run. At 2040 the screws came in, speeding up, their fast *swish-swish-swish* roaring through our hull.

The bearing remained steady and then drifted just a hair to the right, but that was enough. We came left to parallel her on an opposite course, and she raced by close aboard. Her depth charges might detonate nearby, but not close enough. We waited, looking to starboard as if we could see through our hull. And then the sound of the destroyer's screws, now well past us, was smothered by eight tooth-shakers. To our surprise, when the detonations faded her screws could no longer be heard through the hull or on the JK sound gear. Plot showed her last course as nearly east. We could only conclude that this last run had come close by chance and that she had now slowed below cavitation to prevent our tracking until she was clear of us. There remained a segment of the ship's company, however, who were convinced that, humiliated at having lost both her ships, the destroyer had blown herself up. In either case, it was, as far as we were concerned, a highly agreeable parting.

11

I believe the whole ship's company breathed out in unison, though we were not hanging on the ropes below. True, the air conditioning had been off all day, and most fans as well. The heat from the night's battery charge had nowhere to go but up into the living spaces above the batteries, and we were hot and sweaty. Some would have given a buck for a cigarette, but in spite of our CO_2 absorbent they would not have lighted anyway. A healthy "submarine smell" was undoubtedly present, but since we were all in the same boat none of us noticed it. We had all been too busy to become over apprehensive, but as of this moment there was never a happier submarine crew.

The air compressors were now running, for venting safety into the boat and other normal uses of compressed air had raised our pressure several inches above atmosphere. It would blow a man topside should the hatch be opened normally. Even if the hatch were kept on the dogs with the latch as a backup, the time required for this tremendous volume of air to escape past the gasket and equalize the pressure, while we wallowed blind on the surface, would be unacceptable. We waited impatiently. The pressure in the boat was finally down. Sound made a careful sweep, and a mild cheer followed the three blasts. *Tang* surfaced on an even keel so as not to flood our sound training motors; the remaining air rushed past the hatch gasket and we were topside. The sea was all ours, under a black though star-filled sky, but best of all was the aroma of God's fresh air.

We headed north to put the scene of the day's activities behind. Preparations commenced for the repairs to No. 5 torpedo tube, and the aroma of frying steaks filtered to the bridge from the hull ventilation. They had not been on the menu, but our acting commissary steward, Wixon, probably with the connivance of the executive officer, had had them thawing since regular mealtime. Certainly, no one would object.

After we had made an hour's run, blessed with a calm sea, our divers went over the bow. Tended from on deck with the forward torpedo room hatch open nearby, they would not take long to get below again in an emergency. Just the same, the moments were always anxious when anything could disrupt a submarine's normal diving ability. Replacing the outer door gasket, working in the dark essentially by feel and mostly under water, could be difficult indeed. If I was concerned about our present nakedness, how did our men diving at the bow feel? I kicked myself.

ComSubPac's staff always picked the dandiest times to send us messages, and now another one came in on the Fox. *Tang* was assigned a new area; we'd consider it later, for we weren't going anywhere until this job was done. What I feared might take most of the night was finished in an hour, however. The outer door gasket was back in its dovetailed groove, the door closed, and the tube drained. We could take care of the inner door gasket while we were on our way. *Tang* was off at four bells and a jingle, heading north until we considered our new area. The important thing was to put a day's run behind us. There would be no ships to torpedo back there, and now that Saipan had been given a chance to settle down, enemy patrols would be out for sure. We bent on three engines; with but four torpedoes left, we were sure fuel would not be a factor in terminating this patrol.

I joined Fraz in the wardroom for a very late supper, if one could call steak, potatoes, and ice cream with fresh-frozen strawberries a supper. Our most recent message from Com-SubPac was on the dispatch board, somewhat conciliatory in comparison to the others. It read simply:

TANG ASSIGNED AREA OF SOUTHERN BONINS
BELIEVE WE CAN FIND YOU A SHIP THERE

Fraz and I chuckled. Intelligence was good at breaking Japanese operational messages, real or pseudo, but not one of the five ships *Tang* had put on the bottom could have pressed a radio key, much less completed a dispatch. So apparently the force commander thought we were having a dry run and had noted the manner in which we had been pushed around, more than 3,000 miles just in our areas if we included Wake.

Jones brought down the chart that included the Marianas and the Bonins. The navigator stepped off the distance to the Volcano Islands, for there were no southern Bonins as such. We had another 500 miles to go from our present dead reckoning position, more if we were supposed to pass Iwo and go on to Chichi Jima.

"We'll never get there anyway," commented Fraz, implying, I hoped, that the torpedoes wouldn't last that long. We seemed to be finding ships 50 miles off the Marianas right now, so why change on our route north? The navigator laid down the course I wanted, which would leave Pagan Island about that distance abeam. Jones took the chart back to the conning tower, with my orders to steer 345 degrees true. Fraz hit the hay, for he would have to be up at morning twilight to get his stars, and I went forward to the torpedo room. Hank's men were just completing repairs on the inner door of No. 5 tube. I picked up one of the lead-backed fillings and asked how we happened to have the lead available.

"We've got a pack rat aboard," Hank explained. "It's from a piece of toilet plumbing that was lying in the officers' head next to our storerooms at Mare Island." In a sense it had served its intended purpose such as no lead elbow ever had before. The night was too far gone for formal night orders. On the page for the previous day I copied down the position of our last attack, latitude 15° 50′ north and longitude 144° 21′ east, then turned to the current date and wrote: *Stay alert*.

Dawn came on bright and clear, a good day for planes scouting ahead of shipping. The navigator's morning star fix showed us abreast of Pagan, so planes from any sector were possible. A sun lookout went topside, and we manned the search periscope; if the Japanese continued running their ships along this island chain, one place was just as likely as another. If they didn't, then the war in the Central Pacific would be as good as over. The morning progressed uneventfully, and so did the afternoon except for increasing seas. All hands were slowly calming down, and *Tang* was resuming a normal patrol routine. It included plenty of sack time and, in view of the last few days, no drills whatsoever. Except for a late morning clampdown of the decks below, any man not on watch could spend his time flaked out with a good book or getting ahead on his shut-eye, and most were doing exactly that. The watch standing was something different. If there had been any laxity in the past, and I had reason to believe that in the case of two or three men there had been, the events of the last ten days had made Christians of them. Not just the respect of their shipmates was involved, but their very own hides.

"Smoke on the starboard bow!" The cry carried on into wardroom country.

"Here we go again!" said Fraz, sliding out from the inboard seats in the wardroom, and another cribbage game I might have won was declared no contest. There were no further puffs of smoke, but since they were first sighted on our bow, the enemy must be heading in a southerly direction. We came right until *Tang* would be converging slightly on his most probable track.

Though Caverly had torn down our SJ radar time after time on this patrol to replace tubes or capacitors or resistors, this was the first time it had been out when we had a contact. To get the thing into a submarine, it had been squeezed from all sides. Now, though the major units could be removed, replacing a part required considerable dismantling. Stepping over parts spread around the conning tower deck and keeping an eye glued to the search scope at the same time was quite a trick. But we could sympathize with Caverly, who was trying to solder parts between our feet.

Jones made the next sighting; just the tops of two ships stuck up over the horizon, but his true bearing was all that we needed at this time. The enemy had surprisingly drawn rapidly to the right, though that first single bearing on one puff of smoke could have been somewhat in error. The change in bearing did confirm the enemy's southerly heading, however, and now the very large distance between the masts of each ship showed that we were approximately on his beam. We would have to stay out at this range, about 20,000 yards, while moving ahead, for otherwise the enemy would have our silhouette against the late afternoon sun. Without the radar we would have little opportunity for accurate tracking, and from this range we could learn very little about the enemy we were to attack. The navigator consolidated my thoughts. His plot showed that we could not count on shooting before dark. Even the waxing moon would not provide enough light for a submerged periscope approach. We would find out what we had over the horizon first and then decide how to attack, perhaps this night on the surface after moonset, perhaps at dawn.

The following hours were cautious ones. We stayed abaft the enemy's beam and closed sufficiently to identify the two major ships by poking our search periscope up over the horizon periodically. *Tang*'s shears were always hull down for the enemy, even if he had lookouts in his highest tops. It was like submerged tracking, except we were on the surface. The ships' base course was 160 degrees, and they were zigging mildly with an overall speed of 8½ knots. What we had in sight was enough to make our hearts pound: The leading ship was a large four-goalpost freighter, a worthy ship in herself; but the other was the *Horai Maru*, a very large, coal-burning, two-stack transport. He picture was in our identification books. The thin tops of three other ships, probably escorts, were inconsequential. We would attack the transport.

Without the SJ, I decided, our best bet would be a crack of dawn submerged attack and I privately informed Fraz of my intention. His reaction should not have surprised me. By my tone I had elicited his opinion, and he gave it.

"Oh, Christ, Captain, then it's so damned long till dark!"

I believe Fraz was a little surprised at the language he had used, but he was closer to the troops than a captain can ever be and was undoubtedly reflecting more than his own feelings. Perhaps *Tang* was not up to another one of those hairy days of evasion so soon, but on the next one we wouldn't be leaking! Well, Fraz had spoken his piece, and I would not want my executive officer to feel that he couldn't. His was the major influence, but Lieutenant Beaumont's report of the SJ being back on the line was the clincher; we would attack tonight.

The sun set, and then came the end of evening twilight. We

moved in to 10,000 yards and tracked from the enemy's quarter. Now with accurate ranges from radar, it became evident that the convoy's zigs were imposed on a constantly changing base course, or worm turn, similar to a sine wave. At 2130 the moon had set. We started our approach but quickly found ourselves astern of the convoy as it made a column movement, each ship turning in the same water as the ship ahead, to course 090, due east. These were maneuvers one would expect of warships. It now became a case of searching out the *Horai Maru*. Ahead were shapes, blops on the radar totaling five, but we could not distinguish all of them with our 7 × 50s. The tracking party had them on a steady course as we started our approach.

Tang left the trailing ship—a small one that we had not seen before—3,000 yards abeam, and also her patrolling escort, noted only on radar. Then came our *Horai Maru*, steaming straight east. For an attack we had to pass her up and come nearly abreast of the freighter and astern of the freighter's starboard escort. *Tang* was essentially a part of the convoy's formation, still 3,000 yards abeam, and it remained only for us to turn left and move in for the attack. But the convoy turned first, another column movement, to the right, bringing the freighter close to our bow. We backed away, marking bearings and with the outer doors open. She rolled across our bow in the increasing seas, and I was sorely tempted to mark a constant bearing and let her have two torpedoes as her massive hulk crossed the reticle.

"She's turning," said Jones, who had his eye on the transport. "A little wide," he commented. He was right; the slick boil of the sea where the freighter had turned was just this side of the *Horai Maru*. This gave us more time for a setup, so we twisted for a straight shot and I commenced marking bearings. She came on quickly, a shower of sparks rolling out of her after stack.

"Range sixteen hundred, ten degrees to go, Captain."

"Watch the nearest escort, Jones." It was really an unnecessary reminder.

"Constant bearing—mark!"

"Set!" Her great stern came into the field and touched the reticle.

"Fire!" A slight shudder and our 21st torpedo was on its way.

"Constant bearing—mark!"

"Set!" Something was wrong! The wake of the first torpedo

was in my binocular field, heading for the middle of the ship. It should have been leading her bow. But any one torpedo could be erratic.

"Fire!" Her after stack had touched the vertical line.

"Constant bearing—mark!"

"Set!" There was no torpedo wake down my line of sight.

"Zero angle, Captain, but she's still two thousand yards off." It was Jones at my side, reporting that the escort was coming in. There was no reason to confirm it; he knew what he was looking at. The transport's forward stack came on.

"Fire!"

"Constant bearing—mark!" It would take but seconds to get this last torpedo streaking on its course.

"Set!" There was the third torpedo's wake in my 7 × 50s' field, barely leading my present point of aim.

"Constant bearing—mark!" Now sure that the TDC had enemy speed too slow, I gave a new bearing well forward on the transport's bow.

"Set!" Her stem came on. If the TDC's firing solution was correct, this one might miss ahead.

"Fire!"

"All ahead flank." We would cross the transport's stern. I crossed my fingers. The seconds went by. We steadied with the escort closing astern. We had missed.

12

Tang was not through with this convoy; only the shooting part was over. Operating on priorities as usual, our next task required no major decisions. The problem was dead astern, a narrow shape that was laying down a smoke screen better than our own. She was apparently steam powered, and the smoke was from lighting off more boilers. A minimum of 15 minutes would elapse before she could further increase her speed. The beauty of our Fairbanks Morse diesels was their ability to deliver full power immediately. Our smoke was due to overloading beyond the rated horsepower, but the extra horses were pulling us away. During the coming quarter of an hour (it seemed like more time if I didn't think in terms of minutes) we had to lose the patrol or she would likely close in and drive us down. In itself, that would only be an inconvenience, but it would surely make our one remaining task impossible.

Sometime I'll visit Beloit, Wisconsin, and tell them about their engines, for the range opened steadily to 3,000 yards. *Tang* slowed to full. The engines stopped smoking, and we came right, leaving a blotch of smoke for the escort to investigate. We closed the convoy again, not to attack with our deck gun—I had once been a party to such a futile effort—but we would do our best to bring a fellow submarine in to attack.

Mel had our message ready from the contact code. In but five, five-letter groups it gave the basic information of what, where, how many, and what doing. Really, plain language would do, for the enemy would guess its content on the first transmission. The radiomen broadcast it on 4155 KC, the basic submarine frequency, on 8310, and the higher harmonics, but Pearl did not answer. Topside, the mild sparking at our antenna insulator due to the increasing salt spray was disturbing. Nothing came of this until we opened up on the low area frequency, 450 KC. Then the insulator took off, blinking like a loosely screwed-in light bulb. We were a bit jumpy about this, and it proved not to be just our nerves. Out of the night came a signal searchlight. It was quite obviously a challenge, for we received an S-8, S-8, S-8, repeated several times. Perhaps we were thought to be the trailing patrol, which we never had seen through our binoculars, and it was a submarine.

Tang had been transmitting for more than two hours; if there was a friendly submarine within striking distance she would be on her way to intercept. No receipt or reply would be coming, for Japanese direction finders would then pinpoint her. Our answer to the challenge was a course change, putting the enemy dead astern, and just by chance heading us on 070, our initial leg toward Midway.

It was 0045 on February 27. I wrote in my night orders: *Proceeding on course 070° true at four-engine speed en route Midway Atoll. We have but one priority, to reach port safely. I will expect no relaxation on the part of any watch stander until we pass through the reef.* I left no morning call, but before proceeding below I copied down the firing data on our attack. We had fired at 2241 on the 26th. The latitude was 17° 48′ north and the longitude 143° 40′ east. Well, at least we'd scared them more than they'd scared us, I think.

I received my morning call anyway. It was a message from ComSubPac, addressed to all submarines, and stated:

SUBMARINE THAT FIRED ON THE HUSO MARU AT
TWENTY TWO FORTY TWO ON TWENTY FIVE FEBRUARY
REPORT THE CIRCUMSTANCES

Submarine warfare surely had changed during the months I'd been away. Now the staff was breaking the enemy's dispatches and looking down our throats if we missed. SubPac had the name of the ship wrong and had not converted to our east longitude date, but adding the time of our torpedo run to our firing time would put the time in the dispatch only a few seconds off. There had been a couple of flickers of light at the stern of the transport, I now recalled. Perhaps the enemy had a flashlight and stopwatch at hand. I did some quick calculations. We would not be at the 500-mile circle from Saipan, where we would report our departure from patrol, until after midnight. To open up with a radio signal now would provide the Japanese with our position. Another position when their direction finders locked onto our transmission early tomorrow would make it two. They already had one for last night. That would be enough for the enemy to plot our course and speed. SubPac would have to wait. I thanked the messenger and tried to get some more rest. This dispatch didn't help. It was no use; it would take a cribbage board to get everything back on an even keel.

As I might have expected, Fraz was waiting in the wardroom, having finished his morning stars and just as incapable of relaxing as was I.

"I wasn't going to show you that, not yet anyway, but I figured it would be a sure way of getting a cribbage partner," he commented, and then dealt. I cut a five, which was good for both of us, but the game was interspersed with talk of the previous day and night. Our pegs moved slowly around the board.

A submarine was never held accountable for every one of her misses, any more than a quarterback who now and then fails to connect. Most submarines frequently spread their torpedoes to give a greater coverage than the length of the ship, especially when the firing data was shaky. What counted was the end result, though of course the captain, like the quarterback, could be replaced, for the success or failure was on his shoulders. There was no use in our crying over spilled milk, nor in trying to affix any individual blame for missing the *Horai Maru*. However, if we didn't iron it out and find wherein we erred, I would be remiss indeed.

Frank and Mel had come down from the 4-to-8, so after breakfast those of us who were specifically involved in the firing setup reviewed the attack. Looking back calmly, we soon saw the causes for our misses. Except for the tanker, we had been firing on 8- to 9-knot ships, and our afternoon tracking had shown the convoy with a similar speed. Our radar had been out of commission then, and we had very probably missed a wormturning on top of the zigging. This would account for our speed solution being about 1½ knots too slow. On resumption of the wormturning, just before we fired, the transport had turned outside in the column movement, was behind and closing up. The shower of sparks from her stack was a clue that she was pouring on the coal, which could easily account for 3 more knots. We had, perhaps, been putting too much stress on seeking minimum gyro shots, twisting to get our bow ahead of the transport and steadying just before firing. During the twisting period, the bearings I marked would have been introduced into the TDC with an error equal to our ship's swing during the short period between the mark and the actual physical setting. It would be little, but enough to account for another knot or so of analysis error.

Sometimes errors cancel each other, but these tended in the same direction, resulting in an estimated enemy speed error at firing of up to 6 knots. Six knots is 200 yards a minute. Our torpedo run was approximately 70 seconds. The ship would have been 650 feet farther along when our torpedoes crossed her track, but the one aimed just forward of her bow must have barely missed her stern.

There was one other lesson. This was the first attack in which I had not known personally the solution for enemy speed at firing. I was frankly amazed when I learned we had her at 8½ knots. My seaman's eye had told me about 13. In the future I would keep myself completely informed and would impose my judgment if required, for the responsibility was always mine alone.

Now that we knew the reasons and could avoid the same errors in the future, we felt better about it, partly because all of us knew that no submarine had ever before put five ships down on her first patrol, nor had any that had unloaded all her torpedoes had anything like our percentage of hits.

Other than traveling as safely as possible, and that meant as fast as we could go, there were lesser things to be done while en route to base. Some were enjoyable, and some were not. Those men nearing qualification put in extra hours at their studies. The executive officer worked on the data sections of the patrol report, and I unlimbered my pencil hand for some précis writing of the patrol narrative. The content of the usual chapter had to be condensed to a paragraph, the paragraph to a line, and sometimes the line to a single word or figure.

Early in the morning of February 28, *Tang* crossed the 500-mile circle from Saipan, and we opened up with the required message, giving the dope on the *Horai Maru,* the expenditure of torpedoes, and the ships sunk. To avoid the usual extra exchange of messages for routing, we stated that we would follow the route the morning Fox had prescribed for *Halibut.* SubPac would next hear from us when we crossed the 1,000-mile circle from Midway.

To keep time from dragging, and for an ulterior motive, we commenced daily field days. Whenever a compartment was ready, I would inspect it that one time. With the responsible officer, petty officer, and chief of the boat present, I laid down the law. If anyone messed up their space they were to report it to Ballinger, and the culprit would clean it up. On the lighter and more enjoyable side, the cooks had a different type of field day, breaking out the best of our meats, which had been none too good—a surprising number of cartons marked "fry cuts" had contained stew meat instead—and splurging with stores that might otherwise be turned in at base. A ship's company never ate higher on the hog.

The 1,000-mile circle came quickly. The required message was sent requesting a rendezvous for two days later, at 1000 the morning of March 3. The last compartment had been checked off, and the navigator's position showed us right on at sunrise. The light-greenish sky characteristic of all coral atoll landfalls showed up dead ahead at 0930. The only escort available was the garbage scow. We rolled up to the reef, slowing as we passed the masts of a sunken rescue vessel. Warned by the hull of a submarine that had missed the entrance in a treacherous sea, *Tang* threaded the narrow channel through the reef. The harbor had changed since I had last been there. We twisted left, entering a new basin, and moored starboard side to a new pier.

The exuberant Gooneyville Band was good, the awaiting paymaster better, but what our troops really liked was the sight of their relief crew, who would stand all of their watches for the next two weeks.

PART III

Second Patrol
LIFEGUARD
AT TRUK

1

Midway Atoll was no Capri, but for a ship's company returning from patrol it had most of the essentials. No rolling decks, no watches, no tricing up bunks, and good chow when one wanted it were the things that counted most. There were other diversions, one not inexpensive, and to take care of that, payday proceeded briskly. All of the pay records had been forwarded from Pearl to the base disbursing officer. Individual chits had been made out, and it remained only for the crewmen to line up alphabetically to draw their money. *Tang*'s wardroom, with its two doorways, made an ideal walk-through disbursing office. Each man got to touch his money, put a ten-spot in his pocket, and witness Ensign Enos with Chief Ballinger seal the remainder in an envelope bearing his name. This had become a submarine way of countering the civilian contractors' workmen, some of whom would have been escorted to the city limits of Reno or Las Vegas. They were pros with dice or cards and always awaited the uninitiated submariner's first night ashore. Our lads could learn the truth by losing ten bucks, when it was all they had, just as well as by dropping $150 or so. For those who didn't learn, or did not want to learn, Mel would be breaking out the envelopes from the publications safe daily to make similar disbursements. If, however, a man wanted to send money home, his total was the limit, but he had to return from the post office with the receipt for the money order.

While this was going on, I walked up the dock with Commander Chester Smith, who had greeted us as we came alongside. He had been skipper of *Swordfish* in the Southwest Pacific, on patrol when the war started, and sank his first ship but a week after Pearl Harbor. Between patrols his sub had rescued American High Commissioner to the Philippines Francis B. Sayre, 12 of his party, and five enlisted men from Corregidor, taking them all in *Swordfish* on down to Fremantle. Considered among the best of submariners, he would be our division commander during our refit. We could not have asked for better.

Returning to *Tang*, for there was still business aboard, I saw my ship from a distance for the first time in six weeks. Gone was the former glossiness of her black paint. Salt water, wind-driven spray, and the tropic sun had bleached it to a slate gray, somewhat splotched, like the camouflaged freighters of World War I. No longer as if out of the showroom, she looked like she'd been places and done things, and indeed she had. I liked the way she looked and made a mental note that no one was to get loose with fresh paint. Coming up the dock was the ship's company except for the senior petty officers and officers. To a man they were grinning from ear to ear. At the moment I could not say whether the pride I felt was in our ship or these men; both, I guess, for they were inseparable.

Aboard, Fraz was checking the last corrections to the blue stencils of our patrol report. Officers and leading petty officers were going through their departments with their counterparts in the relief crew, and the officer in charge was awaiting me. We inspected *Tang* casually from torpedo room to torpedo room and then returned to the wardroom.

"What do you think of her?" I asked as soon as we each had a cup of coffee in hand.

"It's hard to believe you just came in from patrol, Captain. She looks ready for an old-time military inspection." He hesitated and then continued, "We'll keep her just this way." As a former warrant officer, he'd been brought up in the days of spit and polish and knew exactly what I wanted.

Fraz had the stencils ready for my signature with the crazy wire pen at hand. Jones was standing by with the inked tracings from our charts and would deliver the package to the division commander's office for his endorsement and that of the deputy force commander on the island. Next would come ComSubPac's endorsement and then distribution to all boats and to 18 interested commands, including the submarine school, all the way up to the Chief of Naval Operations and Commander-in-Chief, U.S. Fleet. So we had all checked our spelling, dotted our i's, and crossed the t's. The few repair requests had been discussed with the base repair officer and duly submitted, and I decided it was a good time to go ashore before something should come up to prevent it.

Midway was no longer the single low island with an additional sand spit, sometimes visible at low tide, that I had first seen in the mid-1930s. After the lonely cable station had come Pan Am's China Clipper facilities, and then shortly the naval and Marine installation. Now, the boat passage through the reef had become a ship channel and the sand spit an air station; low buildings, shops, and quarters dotted the two islands. Only the gooneybirds were unchanged; as before, they were everywhere.

Fraz joined me near the former Pan Am houses, occupied by the senior officers on the island.

"Have you ever seen the inside of one of these houses?" he asked, looking to the right and then down. There on the usual low sign was the name C. D. Edmunds, Captain USN. He was the deputy submarine force commander. The sun was now well over the yardarm; we could make our official call and mooch a drink or two all at the same time. We turned up the walk and were greeted by the captain's steward at the door. He immediately got each of us a drink, and only then did he tell us that Captain Edmunds was over at Eastern Island seeing Commander Peabody off on the plane for Pearl. He was referring to Eddie Peabody of banjo fame, a loyal reserve officer, who had been knocking himself out for two years now in getting around to see the troops. There was a bit more delay in the captain's return than his steward had anticipated, and during this time two things happened. Properly, we switched from his whiskey to beer, but in doing so we spotted a boned rib roast, the likes of which we hadn't seen since before the attack on Pearl Harbor. It had obviously been set out to be at room temperature for roasting.

"Are you thinking what I'm thinking, Fraz?" I asked, glancing at the wall clock.

"You mean that if we play our cards right we should get invited for dinner?"

Fraz understood perfectly. The captain and Eddie Peabody both returned, for the plane had engine trouble. To save time, the roast was cut into thick steaks. Eddie Peabody, a real all-around entertainer, kept us rolling with his banjo and stories, and to top it off agreed to stay an extra day for our crew.

Our days were not completely free, as the responsibility for our ship still rested with us. We would not have had it otherwise. Certain jobs *Tang*'s crew did themselves, such as the complete recementing of No. 5 torpedo tube's outer door gasket and the inspection of the other nine tubes. None of us would trust that to anyone who was not going on patrol with us. The base work required inspecting as each job was completed, but little of this caused any real inconvenience since our officers were never more than five minutes away. They could generally be found at the old Pan Am hotel, now popularly called the Gooneyville. A large corner room had long since been set aside as a wardroom or meeting place. Tables, some with and some without poker cloths, a bunch of chairs, and a large refrigerator loaded with beer were the sum total of the furnishings. With friends, what more could one want? It was here that we learned what really happened on submarine patrols, the things a submariner was perfectly at ease sharing with a contemporary but were too trivial or personal to be included in the patrol report. In toto, they made up the woolly narratives, and in them the staff seldom shared. The beer helped let down the bars between junior and senior officers, and should an evening's yarns have been wire recorded for airing on stateside radio, the term "silent service" would have been dropped forever.

We were seeing little of *Tang*'s crew, which was the way we both probably wanted it. However, our fishermen had a great day on March 7, returning with the bilges of their motor sailer loaded with mahi mahi. They gave away all they could and as sportsmen refused to let the rest go to waste. Thus started the fish fry. A small mountain of fish, cut up, rested in cold storage overnight, and the 8th started off with softball and beer. CPOs against officers, firemen against seamen, torpedomen against electricians, cooks and stewards against auxiliarymen. It was supposed to be a round robin, but by midafternoon just who was playing whom seemed in doubt. There was one thing clear, however: Whichever team had Fireman Anthony won. At first, they pitched him easy because of his thick glasses. Then it became apparent that he'd lay the ball out of reach and clear the bases if anyone was aboard. Eventually, Anthony ended up at the plate seemingly for all teams. The mahi mahi disappeared along with the beer, and the game folded when Anthony could no longer swing the bat.

The ease with which a slight alteration could be made to a submarine was directly proportional to the distance from the States, or more specifically from the Bureau of Ships, in Washington. The particular work request we had submitted was worded carefully, however, so as not to elicit too much inquiry. It said simply: "Install coaming to stiffen top plate between the periscope shears." It would certainly seem that this was to get rid of some periscope vibration. What it didn't say was that an oblong hole would have to be burned in the plate to receive the coaming, which would then be welded in place. Midway was the place to do this, and it was completed beautifully and without question. *Tang* now had a secure lookout platform in her tops, a crow's nest. Standing on the next lower horizontal stiffener plate, a lookout would have this coaming at chest height. He couldn't fall out and only had to raise his arms and duck to start down. He would not have time to use the rungs on "Clear the bridge!" so a padeye above and a cleat forward at bridge level were welded in place so that we could attach a clearing line with sister hooks, to be used whenever the station was manned. No longer would one of us have to hang precariously from the rungs as we had when chasing the tanker.

The second day after the softball game, Ballinger and Fraz came to see me. The troops had had their fill of gooneybirds and the night life and wanted to get on patrol while they were ahead. I presumed Ballinger was referring to the lack of trouble. He was a real chief of the boat, for there had been no mast cases for me to deal with. If anyone had been in trouble, he'd settled it, though perhaps with Fraz's support. I didn't know and wasn't expected to inquire.

I reported our readiness for March 16, with two days' and one night's training commencing on the 12th, and final loading the day before our departure. The training might not have seemed necessary, but we had some cobwebs to shake out and new crewmen to introduce to *Tang*'s method of operation. This could best be started during the controlled circumstances of a training period. Then too, we wanted practice in getting below from our new crow's nest.

While we continued preparations in an unhurried, orderly manner, *Sunfish* and *Skate* came in from patrol. Mostly by listening, Fraz and I learned that neither of them had been in a position to take advantage of the first Ultra down at Truk; and each had suspected that the second Ultra pointed the finger at the other for being sighted. But they shared my views in two respects: No remarks were necessary, and any submarine with a chance ought to go after every such possibility. *Skate* had sunk the cruiser *Agano* off Truk, and *Sunfish* had put down two fine ships at Saipan, arriving there the day after *Tang* had. We had practically run around each other, perhaps even routing ships into each others' laps. This certainly confirmed that two or more submarines could operate in a relatively small area as long as they adhered to the mandate of not firing on another submarine unless she was positively identified as enemy. We didn't consider at the time that this could become complicated if an enemy submarine showed up and didn't know about the rules, for a question of mine disrupted the conversation.

"What the hell is 'crabapples crabapples'?"

There was a look of some disbelief on the part of both skippers, and then they told us. It was the plain-language code word, specifically for Hailstone, directing all submarines to go to deep submergence while our surface forces steamed through an area. Well, sometimes it pays not to get the news, and those first two ships *Tang* had sunk near Saipan just didn't have a guiding star.

The brief training period was to the point and showed up one deficiency, related to the crow's nest: Our submariners' hands were not sufficiently callused to take the gaff of sliding down a clearing line. Leather gloves from the Marines' small stores took care of that. With our Operation Order was a personal letter to me from Captain E. W. (Joe) Grenfell, ComSubPac's chief of staff. It read in part: "I thought you might like to know what occasioned our dispatch of the 25th. Your answer gave intelligence additional evidence that the transport is being repainted as a hospital ship so that she can return singly immune from attack."

Well, at least our attack on the *Horai Maru* had not been completely meaningless. Of perhaps more importance to *Tang,* the staff was back in our good graces. It was late afternoon of March 15 when Fraz reported that all departments were ready for sea and patrol. In the privacy of my cabin, we spoke of the problem areas of *Tang's* first patrol and shared a confidence that these were indeed solved. Moving to our expectations for the coming foray, I found that we were speaking in positive terms, more frequently using the name of our ship. It was a natural change that accompanied our increased confidence and the attendant respect we held for *Tang.* All hands remained on board for the evening meal, and no one asked permission to leave the ship.

2

In spite of the early hour, Commander Smith had come down to see us off. With his Godspeed I went to the bridge.

"Ready for getting under way, Captain." Fraz's report was exact and concise. The joking and informalities ashore at Midway had ceased with our training period. It was necessary that it be this way, lest orders or the significance of formal conversations be misunderstood. Numbers 1 and 2 main engines were on the line, rumbling quietly as if impatient to get on with the work. A long task lay ahead for all four of them.

"Let go the spring lines. Slack the stern line. Take a strain on the bow line."

Hank watched as Boatswain's Mate Leibold took charge in carrying out my orders. This was the young man whom Hank had wanted to swap for a torpedoman's mate, any torpedoman's mate, but a few months earlier. *Tang*'s stern swung out from the dock.

"Let go all lines. All back two-thirds." *Tang* gathered sternway quickly.

"Port ahead two-thirds, starboard back one-third." She lost her sternway and twisted toward the basin entrance.

"All ahead two-thirds." We gathered headway, making the careful S-turn to line us up with the dredged channel and the narrow exit through the reef. The jagged coral heads seemed especially close in the morning light, but in minutes they were all astern, and *Tang* was once again in the deep Pacific.

Fraz and Jones had been plotting our progress using the after periscope and establishing our departure with bearings on the structures of Sand and Eastern islands.

"Recommend course two five four, Captain," said Fraz, coming to the bridge. We came right and went ahead standard, then steadied on the first leg of our voyage. It was the reciprocal of our course to Midway and indeed would take us right past Pagan Island, north of Saipan. We would not be patrolling there, however; we would continue for another 1,200 miles to the Palau Islands, generally called just Palau. In preparation for the extra thousands of miles, *Tang* was loaded to the gills with fuel and chow. The regular sea detail was assuming the watch, while below the ship was being rigged for dive. In minutes *Tang* would be able to carry out any operation demanded of a submarine. We were on patrol.

Our Operation Order was brief and written in the familiar manner. It said in part: "When in all respects ready for sea, proceed to area 10 W west of Palau. Stay beyond normal search in passing Ulithi and Yap, and regulate speed so as to reach position 60 miles bearing 255 from Toagel Mlungui Passage by 28 March for carrier task force strike."

The orders were specific and left little opportunity for a submarine to use her full capabilities. Neither Fraz nor I was particularly happy with them, for 3,500 miles was a long way to send a submarine for a one-shot, long-shot possibility. A fleeing ship, if any, would have to pass within 15 miles of our position if we were even to make contact. We had expected an Empire patrol, but in all fairness, no submarine could build a reputation in one patrol, and there were others awaiting an opportunity in Japan's coastal waters, too. We looked over the legs of our routing, which Fraz had laid down precisely on the charts. As it turned out, they made a pretty good compromise between a zigzag and a straight course. The daily course changes were sufficient to clear an enemy submarine that might be vectored ahead and at the same time added practically nothing to our overall distance. An average zigzag would add about ten percent, or an extra day's run, a day of transit in which we would be the prospective target. I would prefer our track anytime.

The days and nights went by quietly, for *Tang*'s crew was well shaken down. The lookouts were thoroughly briefed in the critical area for their search, the seas to the horizon and for submarine shears beyond. On March 19 and 20, however, patrol planes from Wake were possible, and we would cross the atoll's likely supply route from Marcus Island, so our lookouts would search the skies as well. The two diesels that had been driving us on had now consumed enough fuel to permit transfer of the extra oil to our normal system. Since the diesel oil floated on top of salt water in the tanks, the transfer merely pushed a like quantity of salt water out to sea. After a routine dive at dawn, we surfaced feeling that *Tang* was in fighting trim.

The 19th remained bright. There should be no trouble in spotting any plane that could reach our position. Seas from the northwest, however, were causing a roll that made the use of our periscope for spotting another submarine difficult at best. I took over the search scope for a few minutes. My left wrist was in constant motion, elevating and depressing the internal prism to keep the field on the horizon. This was the time to put *Tang*'s crow's nest to use, for with a slight body movement in rhythm with the roll, a lookout would be able to keep his 7 × 50s steady on. The manila clearing line went up in place and so did the lookout, complete with gloves and binoculars. His sole job was to spot any submarine ahead. I was more than satisfied. If a man in the tops had proven necessary over the centuries, who were we to decide otherwise because of on-again, off-again radar? To my surprise, my enthusiasm was not completely shared.

"It's just such a goddamned long way to the hatch, Captain!" Ballinger replied to my direct question. Well, I had asked, and the answer was short and to the point. That was the beauty of having a real chief of the boat. He had an ear to the crew, and his prestige permitted him to tell the captain. Both Fraz and I had tried out the crow's nest and it had seemed great. On our short training period, our lookout from the tops was among the first down the hatch. Perhaps he had one eye on the hatch, or maybe it was a bit different just in training next to Midway. Fraz went aloft for part of a watch and came down better understanding the lookout's apprehension. Hearing the "Clear the bridge" with the wind whistling around his ears was Fraz's main doubt. There seemed a partial solution, however, in making this a special billet that could be filled only by the extra agile. The select few from each section, all volunteers, were soon held in some esteem. But just to be sure, our OODs now yelled their first "Clear the bridge" direct to the tops whenever the crow's nest was manned.

There was no patrol from Wake, nor supply ship or submarine on the Wake-Marcus line. My night orders seemed repetitious, giving the routine items of course, speed, status of the battery charge, and sometimes a caution. On the 22d, however, I made the following entry: *Proceeding on course 245° true at 80/90 on numbers 3 and 4 main engines. The battery charge should be completed by 2200. Tang will be within 150 miles of Pagan Island by dawn. Ship contacts are possible tonight, and aircraft at daylight.* In the usual place at the bottom of the page, I requested a call for 0600.

"Ship broad on port bow!"

The answering bells from the maneuvering room telegraph had sounded, and *Tang* was listing to port with right full rudder by the time I passed through the control room. I checked my rush to the bridge, for Hank was already taking the correct action in putting the enemy astern. The time was 0512. I went on up to the conning tower and then topside.

The thin masts, visible with 7 × 50s, immediately suggested a patrol, but she was hull down from bridge height. We would remain on the surface, where we would be able to see her hull in full daylight with our raised search periscope. This would avoid the possibility of being held down, perhaps for hours, should we look her over submerged. The morning surface haze cleared. Our ship was a nice trawler. There had been occasions earlier in the war when some of our submarines attacked such ships and even smaller fishing boats. I recalled the endorsement to one of the patrol reports: "A small but valuable inroad into the vital Japanese fishing industry." A patrol or two in Empire waters would convince most anyone that such attacks were comparable to swatting mosquitoes on the Jersey Coast. Our business was in sinking merchantmen and warships. Even though the trawler appeared to have a lot of antennas and might be spotting as well as fishing, she was not a suitable target for *Tang*. We moved back to our track in a wide sweep, with Pagan Island still nearly 150 miles away.

The day went smoothly. Our dawn contact had brought home to all hands that we were in enemy waters. At lunch, two blasts took us down. A distant patrol plane continued on its course. *Tang* surfaced and did likewise. At 1700 the outlines of Pagan and Alamagan islands became distinct. Our navigator and Chief Jones checked our position with true bearings on the highest points of each. To avoid being sighted, we dived and continued submerged till near the end of evening twilight. The passage between the islands was uneventful. In the clear to the west, we stopped so Ed and Caverly could check our SJ radar on the islands, known targets at known ranges. Static from internal sources could closely resemble the reflections from the sea, called sea return. In the past, it had not been too unusual for a submarine to barge along fat, dumb, and happy, relying on a radar that was sick or even dead. Various checking devices had been furnished, generally called echo boxes. Even they were not foolproof. The skeptics, and *Tang* would continue to be among them, would still take advantage of an island or pinnacle for test and tuning. After one patrol, our expert, Ed, had joined the club, too.

Our short delay assured us of a peaked and tuned SJ. With some anticipation, we were now skirting the area of our major contacts of but a month before. A watch could not have been more alert and eager, but the night passed quietly.

"Ultra from ComSubPac!" It was Ed's voice, for now all watch officers had worked into the decoding board. It was not a true Ultra, based on broken enemy codes, but the information was just as good, maybe better:

BARB REPORTS CONVOY ONE NINE ZERO MILES
BEARING THREE TWO ZERO FROM PAGAN
LAST COURSE ONE THREE FIVE BE GUIDED BY
PROVISIONS OF YOUR OPERATION ORDER

The time was 0907, and *Tang* was off at four-engine speed to intercept at a point almost due north. Fraz and Jones plotted it out accurately. If 135 was the convoy's base course, not just a leg of its zigzag, and its speed was average, we could intercept in five hours. The search was intent. Noon passed and so did 1300. The tops of the convoy could come over the horizon at any moment. Another hour passed.

"Clear the bridge! Clear the bridge!" and two blasts sent us down with a sharp angle. Two lookouts confirmed a patrol plane on the horizon broad on our starboard bow. Back at periscope depth, we had a Betty in sight. It continued on to the north and disappeared. After 30 minutes down, we resumed our surface search. The first hour revealed nothing, but at 1608 two SD contacts sent us down. The ranges on the radar were ten and 11 miles, but on return to periscope depth neither was in sight. The plane activity indicated a convoy or something, but our search until dark up the reciprocal of the convoy's reported track disclosed nothing. We were disappointed but not surprised, for we had been trying to do in hours what had required days for our first ship. Somewhat reluctantly, we headed for our assigned station.

Ulithi and Yap were left well to the southeast of us without incident. We dived at 1651 on March 27 to avoid an unidenti-

fied plane and entered our assigned area, 10 W, west of
Palau, at 2000. The night was calm as we moved quietly to
our station, 60 miles bearing 255 from Toagel Mlungui Passage, and 3,500 miles from Midway.

3

Tang lay to in the relative safety of a dark night, made more
secure because she was making no noise that would hinder
her soundmen, and none at all that could be heard from
without her pressure hull. Sixty miles to the east was the
enemy. We could not lure him to us; we must search and
wait.

A private communication had accompanied our Operation
Order, probably because we were not available for a briefing
at Pearl, and it explained the coming strike. Prior to Hailstone, major Japanese naval units had withdrawn from Truk
and were now stationed at Palau. From this base they could
threaten our pending operations in the Marianas and the
campaign of General Douglas MacArthur to capture Hol-
landia on the north central coast of New Guinea. To remove
this obstacle, Task Force 58's aircraft would strike Palau.
The nucleus of the force would be coming from Majuro, a
major base in the Marshall Islands, 2,500 miles east of Palau.
Additional units now operating off the northeast coast of
New Guinea would join it en route.

We could only guess, but it looked like a dozen or so
carriers, together with all of the support ships, would be
involved in Operation Desecrate. Coming so close to the
Japanese fleet, surely our new fast battleships would be
included. Just how a task force of this size hoped to make the
passage undetected was beyond us. Perhaps, with a prepon-
derance of force, they did not consider surprise a critical
item. If so, they were overlooking its importance to participating submarines.

With *Tang,* on an arc 60 miles from Toagel Mlungui Pass,
were four other boats. *Archerfish* would lie to the south of us,

and to the north, clockwise along the arc, would be *Bashaw*, *Blackfish*, and *Tullibee*. They were probably already on station. Close in to the pass was *Tunny*; on the other side of the atoll, off Malakal Pass by Peleliu Island, lay *Gar*. These two would be lifeguarding during the strike on the 31st. In addition, *Pampanito* would be at Yap and *Harder* down at Woleai for subsequent small strikes.

We were all called fleet-type submarines, but this was just a between-the-wars designation. It had come about when the fleet was looking for eyes to scout ahead. But the task required more speed than could be built into submarines. Longer range aircraft came along and took over the job, but the designation fleet-type stuck and seemed to spark a continued effort to include submarines in offensive fleet operations. In their enthusiasm, the staff seemed to forget that submarines had stayed in business for three basic reasons: their ability to dive and thus avoid detection and operate independently; their long legs, which permitted them to reach the enemy's front door; the surprise that these first two made possible. Taking away or downgrading any of these reduced the submarines' potential or destroyed their effectiveness altogether. Our submarine disposition at Truk and now at Palau was not compatible with the preceding premise. For example, assuming that we had reached our station undetected, our chance of making contact with a fleeing ship depended on the ship's passing within 15 miles of us. Contacts by *Bashaw* or *Archerfish*, about 40 miles distant, would be well out of our reach should we even know of them. But just suppose *Tang* remained lucky, what would we have for a target? It would be a thoroughly alerted ship just leaving port, with echo-ranging escorts, zigzagging at top speed, and racing through our area or over us like an express train. There might be torpedoes fired, but it would not be the precise kind of attack that could coldcock the enemy. Even though the submarine was unsighted, it was expected. True surprise came days into a voyage, or when the enemy least expected attack, not in a situation like this.

I regretted that Fraz's and my ideas on improving exactly this situation had apparently not reached Pearl in time or perhaps were reposing with a routing slip while awaiting further staff comments. They were so simple, perhaps too simple to ring a bell. In them, the submarines were simply staggered at secure communication intervals along the legs of a V covering the probable path of fleeing enemy ships. The submarine closest in, at the apex, would send out the contact using a variation of a code I had learned in grammar school, "One if by land, two if by sea." In this case, a single echo-ranging ping would indicate the right leg, two pings the left. Relayed out, the message would let all submarines start moving for the attack, and the result could be a surprise indeed. At night, the distance between submarines could be greater, and the same signals could be sent by keyed SJ radar. Of course, lots of boats didn't have an Ed Beaumont and probably hadn't operated on their SJs so that the transmitter impulse could be hand-keyed, but switching the high voltage would do the same thing. We had done this to reduce the likelihood of the enemy's detecting our SJ, for he would hardly recognize a short impulse, but it also permitted using the SJ for simple communication.

Any fleet or task force commander would undoubtedly desire a plan that offered the maximum possibility of putting a Japanese capital ship on the bottom. It could be debated, no doubt, but I believed the "Paul Revere" disposition would do the job better and with half the submarines. One thing I could not argue with—we had considerably more information about Operation Desecrate than we had had for Hailstone at Truk. But with the knowledge came restrictions we had avoided previously, for at Truk *Tang* had been on her own most of the time. But again, we were on patrol, and like the other submarines with us, we had to make the best of the situation. I wrote in my night orders:

Lying to on patrol station, 60 miles bearing 255° true from Toagel Mlungui Pass. SJ, SD, and sound are manned, but do not in any way let this relax the vigilance of all lookouts. Allow up to three volunteer lookouts on the bridge as conditions permit. The duty chief will assure that they have their eyes night-adapted before sending them topside. Maneuver at low speed on the battery as is necessary to dampen out our roll.

A contact could come at any time from any direction, including up or down, so act accordingly. We've made it here; let's find a ship.

I reread the orders, crossing my fingers at the last line. The extra lookouts would be those lads, especially from the engineers, who wanted a smell of unused air and a look topside, even into the darkness. There were others who had gone below when we left our base and would take pride in

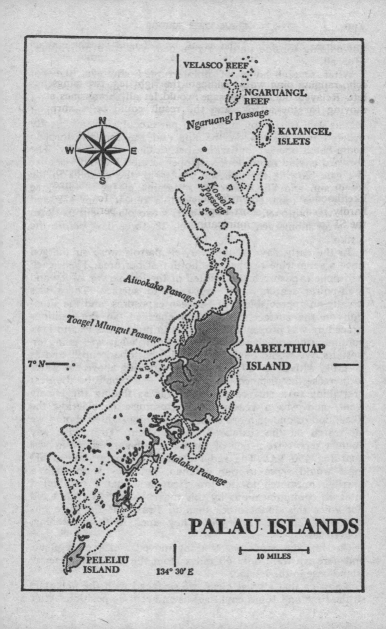

VELASCO REEF

NGARUANGL
REEF

Ngaruangl Passage

KAYANGEL
ISLETS

Kossol
Passage

Aiwokako Passage

Toagel Mlungui Passage

7° N

BABELTHUAP
ISLAND

Malakal Passage

PALAU ISLANDS

PELELIU
ISLAND

134° 30' E

10 MILES

not coming topside until we returned. We were individuals, after all.

After several hours of uninterrupted shut-eye, the hot coffee tasted particularly good, perhaps because I was sufficiently awake to enjoy it. Topside, the sky in the east had not yet started to gray. It would be a long dive, and *Tang* might just as well start it off filled with pure, cool night air. Scotty ordered two engines on the line and the forward torpedo room hatch opened, but with a petty officer standing by. The forward engine room door was opened, and I could visualize the gale blowing through the boat, with the curtains in the wardroom and CPO quarters streaming aft at a 45-degree angle. Five minutes from forward, a repeat from aft, and *Tang* was buttoned up again. Scotty's two blasts sent us down to patrol submerged on this March 28, three days before the strike.

In the early days of the war, all patrols were submerged once a submarine reached the border of her area. Then, each periscope exposure had consisted of the low-power sweep and high-power search, as if preparing to surface. There was usually an appreciable time between exposures, and the situation on the surface could have changed, so the cautious procedure was proper. A better way in most areas was to look continuously and therefore always know what was going on upstairs. We would be doing this with both periscopes, and as at Truk, with about 17 feet of scope sticking above the water to increase the distance we could see. This would be the next best thing to a surface search as far as finding the enemy went, and was a reasonable compromise considering the likelihood of one or more submarines being sighted should we all search on the surface during daylight. To receive any contact report from one of the other submarines, radio was guarding 450 KC. The radar elements atop our raised SD mast would serve as our antenna, but they were such a horrible mismatch to the low frequency that I considered intersub communications by this means very doubtful. I did not voice this doubt other than to Fraz, but I'm sure our radiomen felt the same way. They stuck to their listening, nonetheless.

Our first day wore on. Nothing moved, not even a plane, and here we were only 60 miles from the last major enemy island base in the Pacific.

Knowing that all was clear, we surfaced with the first stars so the Fraz and Jones could get us an accurate position. After the low-pressure blowers had brought us from an awash to a fully surfaced condition, we again took a suction through the boat. It would be unfair for those below not to share immediately the pure night air and for the smokers to still have their lighted cigarettes die out. Rather than roast the beef in a hot boat, we delayed the evening meal a half hour, and the roasts were turned into steaks for frying after we surfaced. The steaks for all hands were brothers to those Fraz and I had mooched that first night at Midway, and I looked inquiringly at Fraz. He just nodded, then cut me in later. He had personally checked the boxes of boned fry cuts, rejecting those that appeared to have been tampered with, so this time *Tang* got her share of good steaks, and very probably the staff at Midway got the boxes we had turned in, which said "fry cuts" on the outside but had pot roasts and stew meat inside.

The 2100 Fox had a message addressed to *Tunny* and *Gar*, and for information to us. Without explanation, it ordered them to be on their lifeguard stations on the 30th. To us this meant an advancement in the strike date, and considering the enormity of such a change with hundreds of units involved, an enemy sighting of Task Force 58 seemed the probable cause. Why else would they advance the date? There would be no change in our search. If the enemy moved this way, we would make contact. We made no announcement concerning our guess; the ship's company would then be keyed up in expectation, with a letdown should nothing move. Better that we maintain constant vigilance.

The battery charge was completed well before midnight, and all was quiet. *Tang* took another deep breath before daylight, and then Frank took her down, leveling off at the ordered 100 feet. We listened there until it would be light enough to see through the scopes and then came quickly to 64 feet. A quick sweep revealed nothing, and the high-power search showed only the crisp, clear seas, with small whitecaps cut off sharply at the horizon. No wonder ancient mariners feared the edge of the seas.

"Bring her up to fifty feet."

Tang rose like an elevator, then rolled forward to a slight down-angle at 53 feet, settling in to the ordered depth. Another quick sweep and all was clear. Thus commenced our all-out search for the day. Light clouds seemed low, but that was because they were so distant. Among them we would try to find a single puff from a smoky *maru*, or a light brown haze from a diesel motorship. I turned the search scope over to Scotty, who had the watch with Frank, and went on below.

A patrol plane at noon reminded us that airfields and lagoons for seaplanes were only three times as far away as the distant clouds. From 64 feet we watched it cruise by five miles to the east. We hoped its search might indicate the track of a convoy, so *Tang* moved over onto its path. Nothing developed except some threatening weather off to the northwest. Finally the sun set. Mel had the lookouts standing by when I came to the conning tower. We had been searching all day, but out of habit I went through the customary careful search before surfacing.

"Bearing—mark!" I glanced up and read the relative bearing, 70, of a thin mast, its pronounced rake indicating an approximate course.

"Take her down to sixty-four feet. All ahead standard." I estimated the angle on the bow, though I had not really seen it. Fraz gave the normal approach course, and the steersman steadied on it.

The one thing that every OOD tries to prevent, having the captain come to the conning tower and sight a ship, had happened to Mel. Sooner or later it happened to all of us, for the captain has a pretty good idea of where and when to look, and perhaps of more weight, of just what to look for. Maybe that's why he's in command. Mel was somewhat abashed, but he got over it quickly when I welcomed him to the club.

The ship was undoubtedly a patrol, but we'd move in to look her over and at the same time freshen up our tracking party. On additional thought, if you're approaching a patrol that's looking for you, be ready to shoot. *Tang* went to battle stations. The Bells of St. Mary's chimed out in earnest from our 1MC for the first time in a month. Even though they never could have the authority of the klonking prewar general alarm bell, the note still raised my heartbeat a bit, and I'm sure I was not alone in this.

Without going to full speed and seriously exhausting our battery, which was already low after our all-day dive, *Tang* could not reach the ship. In a few minutes it would be dark, however, so we waited and then moved ahead on the surface for submerged observation in the intermittent moonlight and possible firing. Not the moon but lightning flashes revealed our target after we had dived. It was a PC type patrol, now joined by a similar ship and six large planes in groups of two.

The boats had on their running lights and the planes their landing lights, bright ones, and proceeded with their search. It took us two hours at periscope depth and another two at 500 feet to get clear of the mess. No one could say, however, that we hadn't had a realistic drill, and we wondered if the Japanese anti-submarine commander was saying the same thing.

The first explosions of Desecrate came during lunch on the 30th, a good one followed 15 seconds later by another. That timed well for torpedoes, so we surfaced for a better look and found three planes to the east. They closed to seven miles and down *Tang* went, not asking questions, though they were probably friendly. Nothing else happened. The second day of Desecrate was all enemy—a close bomber for breakfast, a medium bomber for supper, and two planes after us at 2230. This pair milled around but came no closer than eight miles, so we remained on the surface, though with the OOD's thumb resting lightly on the diving alarm. Task Force 58 had made the Japanese awfully mad, and they seemed bent on taking it out on us. We hadn't even said boo!

I had hoped for a release from our patrol station so that *Tang* could close Palau, but none came. Probably ComSubPac knew nothing of the status of Task Force 58, and would not, for radio silence would be maintained during the force's withdrawal. So we twiddled our thumbs, sighting one large plane at dawn for April Fools' Day, a flash and loom of searchlights toward Palau to start the 2d—and then came an Ultra!

4

The course was west by south, 260 degrees true. Just under 500 miles ahead lay Mindanao, the southernmost large island of the Philippines. *Tang* could reach it in a day but for two factors, our dwindling fuel supply and a most unusual part of our Ultra instructions.

North of New Britain, on April 18, 1943, Admiral Yama-

Lockheed P-38 Lightning

moto, Commander-in-Chief Combined Fleet, had been shot
down by our P-38s. This had proved a severe blow to Japan's
fortunes. Now, less than a year later, the Divine Wind had
backed again, for according to our Ultra, the plane of
Admiral Koga, the new fleet commander, was down in a
small tropical storm. *Tang,* uninvited by the Japanese, was to
join in the search.

An hour after midnight, we passed into the areas controlled by Commander Submarines Southwest Pacific (Com-
SubSoWesPac); he would be our operational commander
even though we might not have occasion to communicate
with him at Fremantle. Marking a spot might confuse the
enemy's search, so we lay to and proceeded again with the
touchy business of converting our two reserve fuel oil tanks
to normal ballast. Having men and tools down in the superstructure while on patrol made all hands uncomfortable, but
the blanks bolted over the vent valve openings were quickly
removed. We rinsed out our new ballast tanks, blowing them
out with the turbos and flooding again till we were reasonably
sure the oil slick would not trail along after us. Surprisingly,
only 30 minutes had elapsed when we resumed our voyage.
That was but half the time required when we were north of
Truk, so there had been room for improvement.

Our search commenced at dawn and would continue all
day as *Tang* plodded along at one-engine speed through the
likely area. Only long-range bombers and submarines could
bother us, and the latter faced the problem of keeping their
scopes undetected on the glassy sea. Our regular watch could

handle them both, but to insure that their routine search was not interrupted, extra lookouts went topside and on aloft. Again our shears looked more like a porcupine than a periscope support, but as long as the men could all get below, the more eyes the better. Just to be sure, we decided on a trial dive after the morning watch had relieved.

At 0807 came the expected "Clear the bridge! Clear the bridge!" and not until we had slipped under the sea did those of us below know that a Japanese bomber had added a touch of realism to our drill. With this incentive, *Tang* had dived in the usual time and without any strain. The plane was searching in a lazy S off over the horizon on our port bow and remained in sight for a half hour before disappearing to the west. Since it was covering that area, we'd continue the track that Fraz had laid down on the chart. Not often does an enemy receive best wishes, but should that patrol bomber spot something, its report could bring out a ship for our torpedoes. We wished it luck. If eyes straining through 7 × 50s and periscopes could have had their way, Koga would have been found; but only the usual bits of flotsam, a coconut, and an oil drum added momentary excitement to our search.

The conversation in the crew's mess did not seem to carry on into the control room this evening, perhaps due to a general disappointment. It should not have been so, for this was just another day of patrol, except on this day the possibilities had been so great that we may have forgotten that our chances of finding the admiral were very small. Of one thing we were convinced: Koga had escaped to Davy Jones's locker.

Fraz brought his chart down to the wardroom with our projected 2000 position on the track, and we started thinking about the next day. We would enter our new area at midnight and patrol east of Davao City. From there we would commence the real operations that had brought us farther west and had been detailed in the second half of the Ultra. Four Japanese cruisers had been sighted by an Australian coast watcher as they proceeded up Davao Gulf, an enormous bay extending up from the southeast tip of Mindanao. *Tang* would join forces with available submarines from Fremantle to intercept them. ComSubSoWesPac was closer to the scenes of current action than the command at Pearl. Less hampered by surrounding commands and staffs, he could seize upon this opportunity and issue some broad, flexible orders. The submarines would do the rest, and sink all of them.

A single rock-crusher moved *Tang* quietly into her area at midnight and on to its western boundary, still 120 miles short of Mindanao, at 0300 on April 4. The OOD stopped our ship as directed in the night orders and instigated the all-out search that had now become routine when our boat was lying to. As soon as Fraz and Jones had their stars on morning twilight's first horizon, two blasts took us down.

Our trim dive was routine. We stayed down only till periscope visibility was good and then commenced our surface patrol. A good breakfast, another day, and new possibilities seemed to give us a lift. That apparently applied to everyone, for on his own, Jones came forward with our best chart of Davao Gulf. At my invitation, he joined us at the wardroom table; he had visited the gulf in S-boats before the war and was able to point out advantageous positions. That we did not have a large-scale chart did not bother us (I had navigated *Wahoo* into Wewak Harbor using a chart we had prepared from an Australian school geography). If we ran aground while traveling submerged, we could just back off the shallow spot; and if we proceeded slowly with decks awash while on the surface, we'd only have to start the turbos to be clear for backing.

The first plane of this area interrupted our speculation, providing the only topside activity for the day. Below, the troops were not idle. A general campaign for all hands to complete the course books for their next rate was under way. The executive officer had instigated the program when *Tang* reached her first patrol station, and the ball seemed to be rolling without coercion. The messroom looked like a schoolroom when I came forward from a midmorning turn through the boat. At only one table was an acey-deucey game going on. At the others, groups were working together, filling in the answers and getting ready for their tests. On patrol, this was something to see; at least these men were accomplishing something important.

We were concerned about our fuel, not that it wouldn't get us home, but the high-speed chases that had been the making of *Tang*'s first patrol would not be possible too much longer. My concern was not shared by all. I was in no position to avoid overhearing a torpedo room conversation. The crew had stepped off the distance to Fremantle on their messroom chart and figured, should fuel become critical, *Tang* could have her refit down under. The stories from Fremantle had pretty well permeated the submarine force, especially that of a cooperative venture by the enlisted men of the staff and boats. Pooling resources, they had purchased an excellent thoroughbred prospect, employed a trainer, and raced their horse just once. At the last minute all of their money went on his nose through the trackside bookies. The tales of submarine bluejackets with fists full of pound notes were still reverberating.

And then the real motive behind an Australian refit unfolded. In any ship's company there is always at least one adept gambler. *Tang*'s was Steward's Mate Walker, apparently equally at home with cards or bones. Members of the crew had pooled their $10 stipends at Midway, and with this Walker had taken the civilian workmen to the cleaners. So the crew's request for an early departure from Midway was not then purely flag waving or boredom with the gooneys, and had nothing to do with the lack of mast cases or trouble. It was just a sure way of getting the money off the island. What better place to spend it than Australia!

Fortunately, there is a regulation strictly forbidding financial dealings between officers and enlisted men. Certainly, interpreted broadly, this meant I should not become involved. It was my out, but I wondered just how much cash they had on board and where they'd stashed it away.

Another message finally came in on the Fox, an operational change, but not the one we anticipated or wanted. *Tang* was moved in to the 100-mile position, another 20 miles closer to Davao City. The boats from Fremantle were similarly stationed; we were back to the circular screen, net, trap, or whatever one wanted to call it. I had my own name for it, but we had agreed to save our profanity for the enemy.

The air patrol was a couple of hours late on April 5, apparently covering our new position on a later pass. The following day it didn't even show up. The 2100 Fox brought another message, directing us to return to area 10 W at Palau. Thoughts of continuing our patrol through the South China Sea and on to Australia were replaced by those of returning to a stagnant area over 450 miles to the east, not a happy exchange. More disturbing was the thought of four enemy cruisers probably steaming off to join their fleet, when they should have been attacked by the submarines assembled to do exactly that. The other participating submarines must surely have had identical sentiments.

Midway did not have all of the facilities necessary to convert *Tang*'s numbers 4A and 4B ballast tanks to additional reserve fuel oil tanks, as had recently been authorized. This would have added another 1,500 miles to the cruising range of the average boat and, the way we were operating, another 2,000 to *Tang*'s. Apparently SubPac's staff engineer did not have a list of the boats with this conversion, or if so, staff operations hadn't seen it. Already *Archerfish* had cried uncle and was creeping back to base low on fuel. *Tang* was still patrolling for four reasons: our early departure, which allowed a slower, more economical speed; our straight course, which saved a good ten percent over zigzagging; the extra fuel we had stowed wherever possible; and our singular method of patrolling when we didn't have anyplace to go, lying to day or night. Now we would add a fifth.

The 500 KW auxiliary engine, 670 horsepower, was carrying the electric load and pushing us along at 4½ knots, sometimes up to 5 when the electric ranges were off and the auxiliary load was light. It seemed and sounded like an outboard motor, kerring away, but at least if and when we made contact, we'd have the wherewithal to run the bastard down, though we felt a little naked passing through unknown waters at this speed. This was especially true during the second and third days, when the seas were scattered with oil drums, probably the deck cargoes of sunken ships, extending on out to the horizon in all directions. An enemy's scope would be difficult to spot, but we convinced ourselves that he would give us at least 6 knots in his angle solver, for no submarine traveled at 4½, and his torpedoes would miss ahead. Then too, our lookouts were thoroughly aware of the dangers and needed no prompting. There were always waiting volunteers, and sometimes I wondered if some of them just preferred to be topside when cruising like this.

We could look forward to more secure nights, with the advantage of our good SJ, but on the midafternoon test it went out of commission. Caverly's concise report contained all the necessary information and a bit of sentiment, too: "The SJ's just crapped out, Captain." Ed Beaumont, Caverly, and Bergman started round-the-clock repairs. One thing that never crapped out was the vision the good Lord gave our lads, and two more lookouts went to the forward 20-millimeter gun platform. In the event of a dive, they would clear into the gun access trunk, whose lower hatch was already closed. I didn't like it and they didn't like it, but that's the way things are sometimes.

Surely this short voyage was the modern wartime equivalent of a privateer caught in the doldrums, not knowing what might fetch up from where. Time did not drag, for the potential dangers and opportunities were so great, but keeping the adrenaline at a decent level must truly have tried nature's mechanisms.

Air patrols had kept our bow and stern planes limbered up on the odd days, and now one hour into the 10th, as we neared Palau, the Japanese changed their schedule. At dawn we were shielded by a nice overcast, but a steadily decreasing SD radar range was disturbing until it commenced opening up, at five miles. At breakfast, a plane that would spot us if it broke through the low clouds drove us down till its pip disappeared. The following hour passed routinely, and then a calm, loud "Clear the bridge! Clear the bridge!" and two precise blasts sent us down again. We knew by Hank's voice that this was no plane, but neither was it a ship for us. The single stick and deckhouse of a patrol boat poked over the horizon. We tried to close, but she was heading off to the northeast at over 15 knots and out of range. We wondered if she, too, had been searching day after day after day. *Tang* was now less than 50 miles from Palau. We would continue on submerged to close the island undetected. The navigator laid down our track to a point five miles off Toagel Mlungui Pass.

5

It was late afternoon when Bill reported the lower slopes of Babelthuap Mountain, our first landfall since Pagan Island, over three weeks earlier. The summit was obscured in the overcast, and nowhere on the green inclines were there sharp, known projections for bearings to fix our position. Seaman's eye agreed with our dead reckoning, however, and *Tang*'s position was good enough to intercept shipping headed for Toagel Mlungui Pass into Palau. After more than 2,000 miles since last sighting land, not knowing exactly where we were seemed excusable. This is but one of the advantages a submarine holds over aircraft; when there is doubt about her position, she can just stop. Besides, closing the reef submerged this day would entail turning right around before dark to reach a secure location for our battery charge. I decided to leave well enough alone. *Tang* poked along at periscope depth, with an occasional high search, and surfaced well into evening twilight.

The night would provide a new experience for a good part of our ship's company, for we would not be using radar. As far as the SJ went, we had no option, since its transmitter was still undergoing a rebuilding job. The SD would not be fired off because at this range from an enemy base its longer wavelength signal could be picked up by direction finders, and bombers would be vectored out along the bearing that the shore installation had obtained. Some might not come too close, as they would not know our distance from the island, but for others we would have to dive. In either case, our presence would be known, and any ships would be routed clear of us. Being without radar would take a little getting used to, even for those of us who were patrolling that way when the war started. There would be other differences and areas of emphasis. After we had surfaced, I included them in the night orders.

Lying to, approximately 15 miles west of Toagel Mlungui Pass, charging batteries. We will not be using radar, so be sure each lookout is completely night-adapted before assuming his watch and understands our status. Sound is manned and may be our major defense. Hold any maneuvering on the battery to lowest speeds and maintain quiet.

The duty chief will assure himself that all trash sacks are well secured and weighted, as we want no telltales in this area at dawn. Our low silhouette gives us the advantage, but only if all lookouts do their best. A patrol or ship can come from any direction.

Keep me completely informed. Call me at any time. If in doubt, dive!

We will dive early into morning twilight, and patrol submerged.

It had been a quiet, serious night, blessed by clearing skies. With *Tang* now submerged, Fraz and Jones were working up their morning stars, and the duty steward had just brought hot coffee to the conning tower. On the dispatch board was a message from *Trigger* to ComSubPac that radio had intercepted. She would be four days late in moving into the southern half of area 10 W due to a convoy encounter en route and some damage. Maybe with her help we could stir something up. There was definitely something to be said for this old-fashioned patrol routine, for the tension of the night was gone and we were in a secure position, ready to attack. Scotty was on the scope, and I had complete confidence in him as an OOD, but I wished he had more interest in the machinery that surrounded us. He would have to master it all before qualification.

The spot we had selected for the day's patrol was ten miles west of Ngaruangl Passage. From there we would be able to intercept any shipping that came through this pass or around Velasco Reef heading for Toagel Mlungui. Later, we could spot and trail for night attack any outbound ships. It looked like a natural, the first likely place to intercept the enemy in our entire four weeks and 5,000 miles of patrol. *Tang* moved in cautiously, for the enemy must come to her as he steamed through either pass or around the reef. Everything depended upon remaining undetected, even unsuspected. Each search would start with minimum scope, and only occasionally would we come up to examine the lagoon and the seas to the west.

The first call came during breakfast, distant echo-ranging. Bergman had just returned to his radar repairs and took the sound watch. Then he flipped on the speaker above the receivers so that the rest of us in the conning tower could hear. The report had been good, but the hollow pings lacked the cadence of an automatic man-made signal and contained a varying inflection. We had some distant porpoises, but even their talk was better than nothing, for it had served to liven things up a bit. The porpoises, the grinding of groupers' teeth, and the other varied noises near the reef were our only sound contacts. The periscope did no better. *Tang* should have joined the Audubon Society, however, for seabirds were in sight almost continuously. They seemed to delight in hanging around the scope, as if above a school of fish, which might just have been the case. We headed northwest an hour before sunset so as to surface farther at sea but still close enough to sight any ship through 7 × 50s. Nothing moved.

Since *Trigger* would not be entering her area until April 14, we moved south after our battery charge was completed. Our new position, off Toagel Mlungui, would cover both areas a little better, but just to be sure, our submerged track took us two miles off the channel entrance. This seemed a little cramped, so we spent most of the day two miles farther out. One four-motored flying boat, which landed in the lagoon, was our only sighting in two days. Time was not lost, however, for Frank and Mel completed the rigid requirements for qualification except for an exercise torpedo shoot. If our patrol should come by, we might just let Frank simulate a firing; but the Japanese did not oblige.

In midafternoon a mild cheer came down from the conning tower. Five days of struggle had put the radar back on its feet. The pile of useless condensers, resistors, and tubes would fill a couple of white hats, and that did not count two modulator units that had leaked their oil. We all liked this higher powered SJ when it was working, but would gladly have swapped it for the previous model, which the older boats had. Though that one didn't have the zip, the bugs had been taken out and it was more reliable. The present trouble seemed to be mostly a matter of heat, and better ways of dissipating it would have to be devised.

After looking over the channels and the reefs, it was apparent that they would not be used after dark. Quietly we withdrew farther to the northwest, where we could use our SJ, and resumed our usual night patrol routine.

"Radar interference bearing zero five zero, Captain." I thanked the messenger and gave my head a quick shake to chase away the cobwebs. I liked patrolling without emitting any radar or other signals but would have to admit that sleeping was better with the SJ in shape. Frank was in the wardroom putting the finishing touches on the drawings in his qualification notebook. It was 0155, so he would have been at it since coming off watch at midnight. I knew that some considered me a stickler in adhering to this peacetime requirement, but Frank's qualification for command would follow quickly. At that time he should know the boat more thoroughly than any of his juniors, and it looked as if he would. After a cup of coffee, we both went topside, pausing in the conning tower. Fraz was there ahead of us, now keying the radar transmitter. The reply was a simple short period of interference, a long one, and a short one again. It was an R, or Roger, and could only come from *Trigger*. Three-quarters of an hour went by before we had a pip at 18,000 yards. That augured well for future simple secure communications, probably out to 20 miles.

We closed rapidly, and our combined speeds brought *Trigger* and *Tang* together in less than a half hour. I had been dubious about the new camouflage submarine paint jobs—decks black, sides a light gray haze, and all voids in white—but this rendezvous convinced all of us topside. Without 7 × 50s we could not see *Trigger* lying to at 500 yards, and we would have missed her with binoculars except for the seas pouring out of the limber holes where the superstructure met the ballast tanks.

Trigger needed spare parts to repair her damaged equipment, but there wasn't time before dawn to put over a rubber boat. By blinker gun we settled on preliminary arrangements for covering the area and established communications by sound pings for possible future use. She was not in shape to patrol in close, so we headed in to Toagel Mlungui Pass, with another rendezvous set up for after dark. With *Trigger* to handle offshore shipping, we could move in closer. *Tang* dived and crept to a position two miles off the channel entrance. Nothing stirred inside the large lagoon during the long morning.

At lunch Hank sent down word of squalls moving in from the northwest. Fraz went up to take a look. Soon the sound of rain beating on the surface of the sea set up a dull roar below. By 1400 we were surrounded by heavy rain, with visibility no more than a mile. Should a ship appear, there would be insufficient distance to track her, and torpedo firing would be as from the hip. To prevent this, and lest a ship slip by in the reduced visibility after all these hours of waiting, we surfaced and took a new position, six miles from the channel. Here our SJ would make timely contact and *Tang* would have maneuvering room for attack. Still the enemy did not move, and at dark we headed out to find *Trigger*.

It was past midnight when we finally located her, for again our SJ was on the verge of giving up the ghost, and as luck would have it, so was *Trigger*'s. It had been the plan to transfer spare parts this night by rubber boat, but with the seas kicked up by heavy squalls, "'tweren't fittin' fer low'rin'." Instead we resorted to the line throwing gun—tin can method, and sent over the information about the area, our ideas for covering it with two submarines, and a list of simple tactics with signals. Fritz Harlfinger, commanding *Trigger*, sent back some compatible ideas. We all saw eye to eye and now needed only some moderate weather for transferring the spares and some enemy ships to work on.

The Japanese did not cooperate, but the weather did. After another full day off Toagel Mlungui, with a morning flying boat and an afternoon bomber as highlights, we found *Trigger* again. Through 7 × 50s we were watching as she got her rubber boat ready in the usual place forward of the conning tower. All of a sudden we heard the whoosh of air as she unexpectedly opened her forward group vents. Down went her bow, half under water, and the boat crew paddled off as if from a sloping beach.

It was not unusual to read in a patrol report, "Contacted the U.S.S. so-and-so to exchange information concerning shipping in the area." In submarine language that also meant that the boats exchanged movie programs. This night was no exception. The sopped cans were struck below, where willing hands used up a fair amount of Chief Pharmacist's Mate Rowell's gauze and cotton in wiping the salt water from the film. There was no record of the film having been damaged by this; in fact, the submariners claimed that the salt water just fixed the emulsion a little better.

On the return trip, *Trigger* took the required spares, compressor valves and cages, radar tubes, and our spare battery ventilation motor. Fortunately, this could replace her burned-up sound training motor. If they flushed the salt water out and dried it in one of the galley ovens, it should work fine. There was no need to tell *Trigger* this; her crew had been through these things before.

Though there had been no ships yet, the other activities of April 15 seemed to give all hands a lift. Maybe it was just the change, but of course the new movies were not to be overlooked. On the following day, *Tang* varied her routine with an all-day submerged search down along the reef to investigate the lower lagoon and the western entrance to Malakal Harbor. Staying in close to the reef without adequate charts kept Fraz and Jones on their toes. In this kind of situation an experienced soundman was indispensable as he noted changes in the intensity and bearing of the noise created by the seas passing over the reefs. The navigation was excellent, but the harbor was empty. Still, the Japanese would not likely leave their ships in exposed roadsteads when small fjords were at hand among the various steep islands. Like many a submarine on patrol, we clung to the hope that sooner or later the enemy would send his ships out. If he didn't, the war was essentially over.

The 17th brought one flying boat, but that night our board deciphered a message in which *Tang* and *Trigger* were information addressees. Fraz and I read it somewhat flabbergasted. *Sunfish* would be indefinitely delayed in reaching area 10 E. That was the eastern side of Palau, where *Gar* had been on lifeguard during Desecrate. She had long since departed. We could surmise only that it was *Archerfish* who had relieved *Gar,* but she, too, had left for lack of fuel while we were en route to Davao Gulf. No submarine was now off Malakal Pass, and the Japanese were probably running their ships through it and on to the Empire unmolested.

Because of the total lack of shipping, Fraz and I had become pretty well convinced that Toagel Mlungui and the lesser passes had been mined by our aircraft during Desecrate. But we still couldn't quite bring ourselves to believe that *Tang* would be left guarding mined channels, and the arrival of *Trigger* had somewhat allayed our apprehensions. Now, having two of us in essentially the same area to the west and no submarine to the east showed that lack of knowledge or confusion existed in ComSubPac's staff, maybe both. There had been a comparable situation at Wake soon after the war began. *Tambor* was put in *Triton*'s area to the north of the atoll instead of the vacant area to the south. *Triton* broke radio silence, announcing that there was an unidentified submarine in her area, and if it was there on the succeeding day she was going to torpedo it. The operational-urgent messages that hit the schedules that night were something to decode. But over two years had passed since then; by now we should have learned to put the round pegs in the round holes, and even the square ones in the square holes, too.

We decided to sit on the information until we made the next scheduled rendezvous with *Trigger* after our usual submerged patrol. Maybe the following Fox would contain a message to us clarifying the situation and with some area reassignments to properly cover the shipping lanes to these islands. Frank had the complete story of this side of the atoll and could present our views to Captain Harlfinger and come back with his. This was something that just couldn't be done by blinker gun or any of the secure means of communication.

At 2130, after another fruitless day with only the usual flying boat, Frank and Leibold paddled out toward *Trigger,* barely visible though but 400 yards away. Our rubber boat was quickly swallowed up in the darkness, but we could soon tell by the activity on *Trigger*'s deck that it had reached there safely. With them were more compressor parts and a spare radar modulation network for exchange. Maybe *Trigger's* would work for us and vice versa. It was worth a try.

The conference went on while we stood on one foot and then the other, expecting the rubber boat to heave in sight momentarily. Finally it was alongside, with Ed assisting from on deck. I believe he really just wanted to get his hands on the modulation network, but I did see him help pull Frank up. Frank's report was brief. Though *Trigger* was in full agreement that something had to be done, she wanted to stick together for another day or so while she completed repairs to the damage from her drubbing by the convoy's escorts.

Tang spent the next three days patrolling close in during the day and then withdrawing to charge the batteries and to give room for a radar run on any inbound convoy. A daily flying boat or bomber over the atoll was our only reward. On April 22, however, activity picked up with a flight of five bombers just before noon, a single at 1300, and five more at midafternoon. Though we saw no explosions, we believed the planes were ours, flying up from New Guinea. On the first Fox that night was a message addressed for action to *Tang*.

6

The sea was crisp, the kind that seems to kick the flying fish into their long glides. Two had landed on deck during the night, and a third had bashed into the conning tower, their whitish-blue shapes just visible in the dim predawn light. Mel sent for the duty steward, and in three shakes Adams was scurrying around on deck retrieving them. He was just as excited over the one large fish as if he'd caught it himself, and in a sense he had, for it was still flipping. A submarine is not a democracy, and I chose the large one for breakfast. They are bony things, but if you've been brought up on the New England coast handling that is no problem.

It was a new day, and *Tang* was heading for a new area with a new mission. Most of this we liked, but it was not without problems. The area west of Palau was dead and in

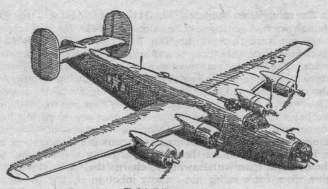

B-24 Liberator

our opinion would remain so indefinitely. Now heading east, we had a greater chance of intercepting the enemy. At this moment, 60 miles east of Palau, we could be crossing the track of a ship heading in from Yap. By morning our present speed would put us on a line connecting Yap with Woleai, and so it would go as *Tang* passed through the Carolines right back to Truk. Among the problems was the 1,200 miles to get there. If there had been any doubt before concerning the staff's lack of knowledge of fuel capacities, this dispelled it. It also accounted for our one-engine speed. If time were not a factor, we'd be back on the auxiliary now, and in all truth that little engine might have to go on propulsion yet. Still, this was a challenge of a sort. Unlike steam plants, a diesel's injectors measure an exact amount of fuel. There are no tricks such as running on back pressure; only reduced speed and auxiliary load will help. *Tang* would see what she could get along without and at the same time not get torpedoed. Another part of the dispatch that we did not like was the list of exact positions we were to occupy. Again, here were directives from Pearl to cover an operation 3,000 miles away. This time, however, *Tang* had an out, for she would be the only submarine at Truk for the continuing strikes by our Liberators from the Marshalls and for the second carrier air strike. We'd go to the assigned positions—we had to start from somewhere—and then we'd go wherever necessary and do whatever we had to in rescuing downed aviators. Lifeguard was our mission.

The complete operation would not be new to us, for though we had not been called upon at Wake for any rescue when we were there during our first patrol, all hands had given it considerable thought and some preparations had been made. The bridle for towing a floatplane clear was still aboard and might be used even if just in towing a raft. At Desecrate, we had been aghast when ComSubPac moved *Tunny* from close in to Toagel Mlungui Pass out to 30 miles for her lifeguard services. Presumably, that was to permit her to remain on the surface to receive reports of downed aviators and then to effect rescue. It was our expectation to move in as soon as our identification was established and to be off the reef, or at least at a close-in focal point. Involved with dive-bombers, fighters, and capital ships, the Japanese would surely not be diverting any of their air to attack a single submarine. But there could be opposition from shore batteries, so at midafternoon we would commence preparations to counter that.

I still did not feel that a deck gun, in this age, was of much value to an attack submarine. During construction I had argued to at least have our gun moved aft of the conning tower. If an enemy ship had comparable or greater speed, it was axiomatic that she'd be able to outgun us. Our own gun would be used for defense, shooting astern. With the gun mounted forward of the conning tower, we would have to change course in order to bring the gun to bear on a pursuer. That would not only present a broader target to the enemy but would also reduce the component of speed, not a nice situation when a sub couldn't dive. On the other hand, if we had more speed, we could pick our position, and a gun aft was essentially as good. I may have won the argument, but the gun stayed forward. Now, however, with the prospect of using the gun against land-based forces, I might have to review a part of my thinking, and Frank had pointer and trainer drill set up at 1500.

Fraz and I took turns on the bridge as Leibold pointed and Cacciola trained the 4-inch, 53-caliber deck gun. Their targets were obliging gooneys, skimming the waves. White, our gunner's mate and gun captain, was in charge, slamming the breech and calling a realistic "Ready one!" Leibold was elevating or depressing against our roll and kicking off the simulated rounds as *Tang* momentarily steadied, while his trainer was apparently staying on in azimuth. Though these three had fired as a team only during our shakedown, a knowledgeable glance would indicate they were no novices. Frank, on the spotting scope, an additional eyepiece of the pointer's scope, confirmed this. We secured until sunset, when a search plane would be unlikely to interrupt our further preparations.

On schedule the OOD called, "Battle stations—gun!" The gun crew would fire as many rounds as necessary to establish the correlation between the sight bar range on the gun and the actual radar range. The operation was simple, something we should have done on our shakedown. No target was necessary, just the sharp horizon. At 2,000-yard sight bar increments, the gun crew fired seven careful shots, kicked off with the cross hair exactly on the horizon. Ed and Caverly recorded the radar range of the splashes, and surprisingly, knowing the exact bearing, were able to record all of them. The pointer and trainer remained topside with Frank to determine the limiting point of evening twilight for accurate sighting and then they, too, went below.

The seas and night were quiet, but below decks things were buzzing a bit. We had altered course to the northeast, and the chart in the crew's mess told all hands that Fais Island lay ahead. *Tang* would dive short of the island about midmorning, then move in to reconnoiter. There was always the small chance of finding a freighter there, loading at the phosphorite plant, and it was no secret that failing this some target practice was assured.

Fraz and Jones had a good round of morning stars and *Tang* was right on the track at our dead reckoning position. Ten hundred came; Mel's unexcited "Clear the bridge" and two blasts sent us down to close the site of the refinery at a quiet 4 knots. First with high periscope and then with but two feet as we drew near, our search was careful and thorough. No ship was moored at the refinery, and to even things, new gun emplacements were plainly visible. They would be enough to keep any submarine that had ideas of bombarding the refinery off to seaward at a respectable distance.

Tang's plan was not original but contained refinements over a previous visit I had made in *Wahoo*. The first step had already been taken when Frank plotted the curve of radar versus sight bar ranges. Now we moved in cautiously to obtain the exact bearing line between the island's lookout tower and the refinery. It was 128 degrees true. With this line drawn and the position of the other important-looking structures plotted, we came right and slowly proceeded around

Fais until the lookout tower bore 308 degrees true. The sun had set when we stuck the SJ out for an accurate range. It was 7,300 yards, a respectable distance but one at which we knew the 4-inch gun could hit. Of more importance, Fais Island's guns would not bear on us.

The Bells of St. Mary's were sounded in earnest, accompanied by "Stand by for battle surface!" It was a beautiful maneuver to watch. The gun crew and ammunition train were lined up to the gun access hatch. Everything was in readiness in the conning tower.

"All ahead standard. Blow safety and hold her down with the planes, Bill." Bill gave her a 5-degree down-angle, and we were swimming down with safety dry.

"All ahead full. Blow main ballast." The 3,000-pound air roared, and the planesmen fought *Tang*'s tendency to rise. It was a losing battle. We were at 64 feet, then 63.

"Battle surface!"

Three blasts howled, the planesmen shifted their planes, and *Tang* bounced to the surface like a cork. Frank called the initial range, 6,800 yards. "Set!" came from the gun, and I ordered, "Commence firing!"

The first five rounds had point-detonating fuses and were seen bursting in the trees. Then Frank used a rocking ladder of first 200- and then 100-yard increments to insure crossing the target, and applied deflection spots to include the other plotted structures. Though any damage could not be ascertained, the detonations of most projectiles showed as flashes, or momentary looms of light for those landing across the island. With 33 rounds expended, I ordered, "Cease fire!" The remaining 160 rounds we would save for Truk. The empty shell cases were kicked over the side, and we came to the navigator's recommended course for the atoll.

At my request Fraz dropped below and extended my congratulations to all hands, since more was involved in the shoot than could be seen topside. The ammunition train had worked to perfection, for not once was the firing delayed. With the simplest of gun fire control now well tried and proven, I could not hesitate to use the gun if it could further our mission.

It had been a good shoot, primarily a project of *Tang*'s troops with an assist from Frank. Quietly and without any fanfare, his capabilities were becoming evident. It was easy to see why he had been commissioned number one in the prewar emergency officer procurement program.

The subject of conversation in the wardroom that night was the shoot, and from remarks we overheard, it was no different in the crew's mess. It was good to hear something other than gripes about the dearth of Japanese shipping, and this seemed to see us through the following two days of straightaway cruising. We were far enough from enemy bases to permit a daylight grease job on the gun and late afternoon pointer drill. The troops showed such enthusiasm about the gun that I became a little apprehensive of their letdown should we not have occasion to use it. On April 27 *Tang* would again be within range of enemy patrols. They came with an abrupt "Clear the bridge! Clear the bridge!" all jumbled in with two quick blasts. It was Hank's "other" voice, which seemed to blow the lookouts down the hatch and in effect said, "This is no drill."

Ed leveled off at the ordered 100 feet, the first time he'd been called on to take her right on down, and with the added difficulty of right full rudder. Our new course was 225, the bearing of a distant patch of smoke, but closing at six miles as we went under was an enemy plane. Fraz had plotted the probable position of the ship, near Hitchfield Bank. We could waste no time, and *Tang* had climbed to periscope depth just eight minutes after diving.

"Up scope." Jones brought it up smartly; there was not time for the usual caution.

"Bearing—mark!" Jones read 230.

"That's the smoke. The plane is to the right, going away."

From 50-foot keel depth we had two blobs of smoke, now tracked on a tentative course of west and at 10 knots. Three blasts and we were on the surface working up to full power for an end-around, far and away the most thrilling maneuver in submarines. Only in this way could we hope to catch the enemy before he reached Gray Feather Bank and the security of a vast area of shoal water. *Tang* was rolling, but so was the plane, sighted coming in high. Again we made it below, though this time the enemy, a Zeke, got in a little closer. It was probably from Ulul, and those planes were fast enough to give us trouble. Our next two surface dashes gained bearing, but then the Zeke sat on top of us, apparently until it had to return for fuel. Another surface dash got us back in the running before the relief Zeke arrived. Again the sky was clear and again we surfaced. The diesels fired and then came the SD report, "Two miles . . . one mile . . . he's coming in!"

There was a swish below, perhaps of a dud bomb, and the

rattle of machine gun bullets above, but we were buttoned up and on our way down.

It was noon; we'd been at this since 0859, but now the enemy was on Gray Feather Bank and immune from attack. He need not enter deep water again for a hundred miles, and then where? Without other orders we would have tried anyway, but our mission was at Truk, not to the west. Our submarine, especially the lookouts, had performed tremendously. The best time to tell them so was right now. I called the lookouts to the conning tower.

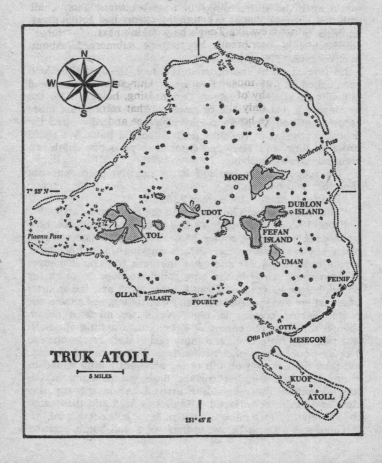

TRUK ATOLL

5 MILES

Quickly the quartermaster took over the wheel and glanced aft with a look of some disbelief. The lookouts came up immediately but with a "Has he gone nuts?" expression plainly discernible. Then it dawned on me. I had not said, "Prepare to surface," but since "Lookouts to the conning tower" is a part of the order, another surfacing was just assumed. I squared them away and have never seen such relief. The four of them seemed to breathe out in unison and drop their shoulders about six inches. The quartermaster, who I now presumed had taken the wheel so as not to be in line to go topside, resumed his duties. After the lookouts, all hands received my thanks. Though the enemy had gotten away this time, with a crew like *Tang*'s he wouldn't next.

Tang caught her breath by running submerged. About midafternoon, the Zekes seemed to have given up their search, apparently satisfied that they had accomplished their major objective, as indeed they had. Our submerged speed was only 3 knots shy of one engine cruising, however, so our siesta had cost us only six miles. Somewhat refreshed, and a little less jumpy, we bounced to the surface and rolled on our way. The seas were friendly, and the night passed without interference.

Blaat! Blaat! and down we went. It was 0719, and the dawn patrol from Truk, a Betty, was on the horizon. It practically confirmed the navigator's morning star fix; we were on the border of our area. Another two hours' surface run would have put us astride the probable shipping lanes from the northwest to Truk. Were any ships moving, that would be the likeliest area, for no sane ship would come from the west off Gray Feather. I decided to leave well enough alone; we now had a full can and could reach the area submerged an hour late. We commenced our all-day submerged patrol, slowing to a quiet 3 knots at midmorning.

A distant plane at 1500 and two floatplanes at 1700 seemed to confirm the intelligence report of Truk's steady buildup since the first air strike, in February. That meant ships, too, and we were eager. Well into evening twilight, we surfaced with the usual cautions but waited a few minutes before starting the noisy turbo blowers. They didn't get started, for the SD that had shown all clear suddenly had a pip at six miles, closing steadily. Fraz, with his sextant, was practically mowed down by the lookouts, who knew of the contact and were on their starting blocks for the dash to the hatch. With decks already awash on "Clear the bridge!" I could not blame them, and made a soft landing myself on the last lookout's shoulders. After going to 60 feet for ten minutes, we returned to radar depth. The enemy was still there. No plane could fly that slowly; for such a constant range it must be circling. We eased on down to 200 feet to have the evening meal in comfort while sound did our searching. The plane finally became discouraged, or low on fuel, because at 2000 all was clear, and this time we stayed on the surface for the night.

This patrol area, across the northern reefs and islands of Truk Atoll, had been one of our submarines' favorites earlier in the war. The North Pass still offered the best possibility of finding a target, for it could handle any draft ship. We had time to give it a few more daylight hours and dived ten miles off the pass before the start of morning twilight. Sound had to be our ears and eyes until it was light enough to see through the search scope, so we rigged for silent running to give the operator every break possible. Shortly after we could distinguish the islands on the reef, a floatplane came by fairly close. It must have been just by chance, for *Tang* had made no electrical emissions that the enemy might detect, and we doubted that his radar on Dublon could reach us or separate us from the northern islands. *Tang* stayed as long as her orders would permit, but here we needed days, even weeks, not hours. At 1100, the last possible moment, we set course for our lifeguard station, 30 miles bearing 110 from Dublon, and commenced the long submerged run to the position east of Truk.

7

It was nearly 1900 when we surfaced. Fraz and Jones hurried with their stars on a fading horizon and confirmed our position. At 1928, SD had our attacking Liberators, coming from the Marshalls, and shortly their blops appeared on the SJ. They provided a good fast exercise for our tracking party. The formation advancing across the scope on each sweep of the cursor was a heartening sight. On schedule, they passed seven miles to the north of *Tang*, and ten minutes later the explosions commenced. They were probably hitting Dublon, which was 30 miles distant, and Ballinger began sending a few hands at a time up to see the fireworks. The Liberators would probably return to Eniwetok or other Marshall bases by a devious route unless one or more were in trouble, when they would ditch at our known position.

Ballinger had taken his own turn topside with us when the first plane closed, ten minutes after the first bombs. It seemed a little early for one of the Liberators unless it was badly hit and was trying to reach us, but how could we identify it? Just in case, the extra hands went below. Suddenly the single pip separated into three. Mel's "Clear the bridge!" left no doubt, but not until after the two blasts and the noises of diving had ceased did we learn that the enemy was dropping flares, obviously trying to pinpoint us. We needed to be back on the surface for two reasons: A Liberator might still be in trouble, and after our long submerged run a battery charge was urgent. The enemy planes cooperated, departing as suddenly as they had appeared, and we surfaced under the quarter moon. A couple of electrical grounds due to the humidity of our all-day dive delayed starting the battery charge, and then the Japanese took over. Their searches were determined, and they dropped increasing numbers of flares as they approached, now using up to four planes. The closest flares were about four miles away, but the planes continued in, disappearing from the radar, probably as they skimmed the seas hoping to catch our silhouette. Dead in the water, *Tang* was undoubtedly invisible from above. There is a time to be chicken; at this stage the battery charge was secured and we dived. After three more dives and short runs to seaward, we were on the 40-mile circle from Dublon, 20 miles from the reef. Perhaps this was beyond the range at which Japanese direction finders could detect our SD radar, maybe moonset was a factor, but I suspect the enemy was tired, just like our whole ship's company, and both sides secured the drill for the night.

Here we were on a mission of mercy, and the Japanese seemed more determined to get our scalps than when we'd sunk their ships, with the one exception of our all-day tussle with the destroyer west of Saipan. At best we had served as a decoy for the Liberators, but when your dives and surfaces come out even, no day is a total loss. Finally the anticipated report came in on the Fox; all planes had made it back. *Tang* was off at three-engine speed, with barely enough time to reach her assigned position for the carrier air strike on Truk.

"Radar interference bearing two four zero, Captain. The executive officer is in the conning tower." There was an air of excitement in the messenger's voice, which I shared equally as I became fully awake. With Fraz on the ball there was no rush. We had both planned on three or four hours of shut-eye, but it didn't look like he'd even turned in. It was 0400, and we'd been on station 40 miles due south of Moen Island for one hour. Thirty-five minutes later the action started with a plane or a flight of planes at 4,600 yards on the SJ. Our section tracking party paid off with an almost instant course determination, toward our task force. There was no time for a coded contact report, so we told the task force commander by voice on 4475, our assigned frequency for this strike. There was no acknowledgment, so we tried twice again blind. After that it would be too late anyway.

It was another 40 minutes before planes showed up on the SD. As usual, when planes were high enough for the SD to catch them, the SJ wouldn't. We had no bearings, only ranges, and no way to determine their course. They could be ours or the enemy's. The next flight in the spotty overcast closed rapidly to two miles. We dived. Thirteen minutes later all doubt was gone, as *Tang* surfaced under flights of up to 50 planes shuttling between Truk and the southwest. With the possible exception of a sinking *maru*, this was the grandest sight any one of us had witnessed.

The tops and then the superstructures of our task force came over the horizon. It was 0815, and here we sat 23 miles from the reef, when in our opinion we belonged up front, as close as we could get. Common sense told us that our planes could not all be lucky, but perhaps none had yet made it beyond the reef. All communications had been checked out; we were guarding the VHF tactical frequency and our specially assigned 4475, and all units and planes of the task force were guarding them, too. Patience is certainly a requisite for a submarine commander, but at this moment I believe I first understood Captain J. W. Wilcox, Jr. I had signals in the cruiser *Chester*. We were receiving an important tactical message sent by 36-inch searchlight from beyond the horizon. My skipper was screaming, "Get it faster!"

Finally the call came, and *Tang* lit out, her screws digging holes with full battery power while the diesels fired. Our destination was a raft two miles off Fourup Island, on the southern reef. There was no emergency speed ahead on the maneuvering room telegraph, probably a holdover from peacetime, when the only conceived emergency was in backing down to avoid a collision. Our telegraphs had just one-third, two-thirds, standard, and full. Ring up full twice and you got flank, also considered before the war to be as fast as a ship could go. When the wartime job to be done became more important than one of the engines, we arrived at a new speed, and why not call it emergency? Instead of ringing up full three times, most of us got this speed by telephone and left it up to the electricians and motormacs (motor machinist's mates) to give the rockcrushers the works. At this moment, Culp and MacDonald were again in charge aft, and *Tang* was rolling. We were out of that static trap, spelled T-R-A-P, of our operational dispatch and meant to stay loose and flexible from here on.

The sight ahead as we closed the atoll would have brought a lump of pride to anyone's throat. Our bombers were peeling off through a hole in the clouds above Tol Island, a hole filled with flak, and diving straight through. For the moment it seemed that the fourth plane of each wing was hit. If they had that courage, we could at least get this survivor, two miles off the beach. *Tang* was not alone as we skimmed Ollan and Falasit islands, for two of our retiring bombers came over to strafe the islands on the reef and fighters arrived to guide us.

"Thar she blows!" It was Jones's Down East twang from our crow's nest. I didn't even know he'd gone aloft. The raft was about four miles west of the reported position, but from an aviator's viewpoint that was close enough. At something over 22 knots, *Tang* was there in ten minutes, conducting an old-fashioned man-overboard drill: a wide turn to place the raft upwind and a needle-threading, slow, straight final approach. The years of conducting this maneuver as a drill paid off in this one moment, as Hank and his rescue party snaked Lieutenant (jg) S. Scammell, Second Class Aviation Machinist's Mate J. D. Gendron, and Second Class Aviation Radioman H. B. Gemmell aboard in three shakes.

While the planes kept any opposition from the beach at bay, we skedaddled six miles to the south. Scammell and his crew were shaken up a little, but nothing that a shot of depth-charge medicine, Lejon Brandy, wouldn't take care of in a hurry. It had to, for we needed the three of them in our new AIC—our aviation information center—set up for this operation. Although we hadn't known it at the time, this project had started at Mare Island, with the customary donations by General Electric and Fairbanks Morse of communication receivers to the two messes. These happened to be the best Hallicrafters, and that suited everyone, as their audio performance was excellent; with them we would get broadcasts from the States and even worldwide. To make them work properly, we needed coaxial cables run from radio fore and aft through the watertight bulkheads. To justify this, another microphone cable was necessary, thus making either mess a potential combat information center. What luck prompted this, we'll never know, but now with a pilot and a radioman aboard who knew all the calls, and lots of the pilots by name, our wardroom AIC, with a large chart of Truk Atoll, was ready to go to work in earnest.

It was 1559 when the next raft outside the reef was reported through our AIC. Again at emergency speed, we set out to round Kuop Atoll, which sticks down south from Truk. A quarter of an hour into the run came another call, a raft close to the area where we'd picked up Scammell and crew. This one we could reach during daylight, a sure rescue, so back we went to a position two miles west of Ollan and one mile off the continuing reef. Again the position was approximate, for our lookouts, the raised scope, and our crow's nest could spot nothing. The bomber and two fighters close by seemed perplexed that we wouldn't follow one of them over the reef to the actual position, which was five miles distant. At least that was the distance on the SD to one of the planes. Fraz plotted the actual position of the raft; it was in the clear and should be able to paddle outside the reef during the night. Right now there was a raft we could reach, even though it would be dark. We set off to round Kuop Atoll and start a night search, feeling confident that Tang's unique ability to monitor distress calls and thus take immediate action augured well for the morning.

All planes had now been recalled, leaving us on our own, as a submarine is supposed to be. We could either dive before the Japanese crawled out of their holes or shoot first and see if we could keep them down. I chose the latter since we could then be proceeding at full power toward the downed aviator east of Truk. White had his gun crew standing by, and my "Commence firing!" was followed almost instantly with the first salvo. The point of aim was the nearest gun emplacement on the southwest end of Ollan Island. Our ballistics of the previous week again proved correct. Frank's curve had plotted so close to a straight line that he settled on a sight bar range of 300 yards less than the radar range. The very first projectile, with its point-detonating fuse, burst nicely low in the trees. The gun crew worked smoothly and unhurriedly as corrected ranges were called every salvo or so to the sightsetter. Frank injected his spots to see an occasional short. The real effectiveness was in the bursts, which must have been showering the area with fragments and preventing the enemy from manning his guns. With Ollan now 8,500 yards back on our quarter and *Tang* pulling away, I gave "Cease fire!" The gun crew dived below through the gun access trunk, and we put the island dead astern. The order was a bit premature, however, for one enemy gun crew crawled out and let fly at us, sending a huge smoke ring rolling out from the beach. The first splash was a big one, 1,000 yards astern on our SJ. The second one we did not spot, but we heard it whump somewhere overhead. It could have been close, for the enemy excelled in his gunnery. Though this added a touch of excitement, there was something to be said for the protection that combat air patrol had provided till its recall.

A 40-minute high-speed run got us clear and into darkness. With only the reefs to worry us, we rolled around Kuop Atoll, then to a spot six miles east of Feinif Island, located on the eastern reef. From there we commenced a zigzag search to the southwest, running a half hour on each leg and firing a green Very star every 15 minutes, one at each turn and one in the middle of each leg. These were not prearranged signals but ones we hoped an aviator would recognize and answer with any one of the pyrotechnics in his raft. It was a rough night for the navigator and not an entirely calm one for me, especially because we closed the reef hourly and my responsibilities brought me to the bridge. The only reply, sighted on some occasions, was a series of red or white flashing lights that changed bearing rapidly, as if flashed along a runway. We were not bothered by the enemy, probably because we used only the SJ, and that sparingly. Neither did we accomplish anything other than assuring ourselves that we had covered the area of the reported raft thoroughly and had given this night our best.

It was now 0330. *Tang* had worked well around the reef,

so we headed out to a proper position for the second day of the strike, hoping to have another chance to find the lonely pilot and crew we must be leaving behind.

8

Radar interference from Task Force 58 waved across our SJ tube minutes after we left the reef. Perhaps it had been there for some time, but our concentration had been elsewhere. If we could note this radar from our low height, surely the Japanese installations atop Tol or Dublon islands had it, too, probably for some hours. The attack had seemed to achieve little surprise the day before; today the enemy would be thoroughly ready if he still had the wherewithal to strike back. With this in mind, we proceeded cautiously to the position we had selected and were stopped, lying to, at the crack of dawn. We were at a focal point of possible rescues, 13 miles closer to the reef than assigned on the first day but still nearly ten miles out. Here we were hull down from the highest points of the outlying islands, beyond their gunfire, but we would be able to watch them with raised periscopes as soon as it got light. We were searching with a half dozen pairs of 7 × 50s, the scopes, and sound as the gray in the east turned to pink. If this array failed to spot the enemy first, nothing would.

"Submarine conning tower bearing zero three five." It was Ogden, Jones's understudy, on the search scope. Both periscopes went down simultaneously. She had to be enemy; *Tang* was the only U.S. submarine assigned to this area. Another single look showed a narrow conning tower and a true bearing change of 4 degrees to the right. *Tang* could reach her submerged. The dive was quiet, as if the enemy might hear us, and *Tang* went to battle stations against a bona fide target for the first time in 48 days of patrol.

Our course was 080, nearly east, to close the enemy's track, and we were moving at standard speed, for he would not be able to hear us above his own surface screw noises. At the end of ten minutes, we stopped our screws momentarily so that our soundmen could obtain a bearing. The enemy had drawn only 5 more degrees to the right; *Tang* would make it handily. Another short run and we should be close enough to call the angle on the bow.

"All ahead one-third." The quartermaster called out our speed as we slowed, fully aware that in such an approach a periscope feather from too much speed could turn the hunter into the hunted. Our speed reached 3 knots, still dropping.

"Up scope." Jones brought the handles to my hands and then followed me up from my squatting position.

"Bearing—mark! Down scope." The angle on the bow was still sharp, difficult to call on a nearly circular conning tower. I said 15 starboard. Frank was doing a good job of analyzing on the TDC. The submarine was coming due south from Otta Pass and making 12 knots; the range generated on the data computer was 4,500 yards. In four minutes the range would be 3,000 and the angle on the bow 30. Our torpedo run would be 1,500 yards if we remained nearly stationary, but we would be closing. "All ahead two-thirds." If we maintained this 6 knots for three minutes, the torpedo run at firing would be under 900 yards, just what we wanted.

"All ahead one-third." Again the only one speaking was the quartermaster, calling our speed by the half knot as *Tang* slowed.

"Up scope." Jones was bringing the handles to the level I indicated. The outer doors were open, ready to fire.

"Lost his screws, Captain!" It was the dreaded report from Caverly on sound. Jones brought the scope up smartly, right on the generated bearing that Frank called. The enemy had dived! We could not fire on the fly without first engaging the depth-setting spindles on each torpedo, and then what was the enemy submarine's depth? A quick sweep and I had the probable reason for our misfortune: Coming in were flights of our own bombers and fighters, maybe a hundred of them. That was the probable reason, but not necessarily the only one. We had quickly passed into that doubtful area of who is attacking whom, aptly compared to a duel in a pitch-black cellar.

We quickly rigged for silent running, for defense as well as to give our soundmen every possible break in regaining contact. Simultaneously, *Tang* was slithering down to 150 feet; we could fire just as well from there, and at least should the enemy make an educated guess that we were at periscope depth, he would be wrong. Sound could hear nothing, though we stopped our screws frequently while proceeding along the enemy's last course. Periscope depth again did no better, and now as in our tussle with the destroyer, we had to disclose our presence first. Our lifeguard job could not be delayed. We turned away, made a short standard-speed run, and hit the surface at full power on the battery. The diesels fired, and we rolled toward the reported position of the previous night's life raft for another try.

The submarine, identified as an RO class, had been heading for Task Force 58. Mel hurried with our contact report, which gave the time and position of diving, her course, and probable submerged speed. On the advice of Lieutenant Scammell, our largest colors were lashed flat on the deck, one forward and one aft of the conning tower. If an aviator thought his fellow airmen would be prone to attack any submarine as a result of our contact report, who were we to argue! The job was barely completed when our AIC made its first report. The time was 0828, and they had been guarding both the VHF tactical frequency, piped in from radio, and 4475 on the Hallicrafter, and had *Tang* on the way 15

Kingfisher (OS2U-2)

minutes before the official report of a raft was received from the flagship.

The downed airmen were two and a half miles off our favorite Ollan Island. Though it was a short run, we rolled in at emergency speed to find what at first looked like a mess but turned out to be a blessing. A floatplane had half capsized in the crosschop while attempting a rescue, but another Kingfisher floatplane had made a precarious landing and on our arrival was towing both his fellow pilot and the raft clear of the island. This action and that of the nearby fighters who were strafing the island greatly speeded up the rescue attempt. Much to its disgust, our gun crew didn't get to shoot as on the night before, instead pulling aboard Lieutenant (jg) R. Kanze and his crewman, Second Class Aviation Radioman R. E. Hill. This was the crew whose raft we hadn't been able to reach on the previous afternoon. Their night of paddling toward the Southern Cross had carried them beyond the reef and made the rescue possible. Back aft, Lieutenant J. J. Dowdle, his Kingfisher wrecked, scrambled aboard. The other Kingfisher had somehow gotten into the air, so our forward 20-millimeter gun crew proceeded with the business of sinking Dowdle's plane.

A cry from aloft brought our attention to one of our torpedo bombers, smoking in a long glide across the lagoon toward our reef. We rang up flank and pleaded for more speed. Then our hearts sank; the plane would surely plunge into shallow water far short of an area we could reach. Our gun crew got its chance as we passed Ollan. The Japanese had cut down the trees during the night, apparently to keep our point-detonating shells from bursting overhead, but in so doing they further exposed their gun emplacements, especially to Frank, who went aloft to spot from our crow's nest. When the plane seemed about to hit, it suddenly climbed sharply with a dying burst of power and glided over the reef into the sea, tail down, in what I supposed was a perfect ditching. In another 20 minutes, Scotty and his men were snaking Commander A. R. Matter plus his crewmen, Second Class Aviation Radioman J. J. Lenahan and Second Class Aviation Ordnanceman H. A. Thompson, onto *Tang*'s forward deck. It appeared that the life raft was only a bridge from the bomber to our boat, and they were wet only up to their knees. I was too busy to do more than simply welcome them and offer my cabin to the commander.

Tang could not dally, for she had another job off the

eastern reef. Our AIC now had talent that would be the envy of any carrier or staff. They knew all the pilots by name—and most of them just by the sound of their voices—and were intercepting the reports and replying by voice over 4475, which was clear of the cluttered tactical VHF communications. They had essentially taken over from the big staff, running way ahead of any directives, and so was *Tang* as she raced for three more rafts. Our AIC was as good for us as for our attacking planes. At the moment we were entering the area of our dawn submarine contact and would have to cross it to round Kuop by the most direct route. Our mission, especially with airmen awaiting, certainly did not allow for the delay of zigzagging or following a circuitous route. Our AIC fixed everything by calling in planes that were returning after their bombing runs. In minutes they had an air cover for us, and never was a submarine better escorted.

Tang was high in the water, with negative, safety, and of course the converted fuel group dry, and with the Fairbanks Morse laying down a mild smoke screen with their overload. There was one more trick, good for an extra knot and a half; maybe we could squeeze it to 2. We had proved it in *Wahoo*, running both ways over a five-mile course in Moreton Bay, near the mouth of the Brisbane River. It required only that one of the turbo blowers be kept running continuously. The low-pressure air kept the ballast tanks dry down to the flood openings and sent a constant stream of bubbles up around the hull. This shield of bubbles apparently reduced the skin resistance of the submarine as she slid through the water. Never had a submarine gone faster, and should the turbo burn up, we still had another, like the duplicate machinery throughout the boat. In short order we had passed through the danger area, and if the enemy submarine was still there, she had but a fleeting look.

Now for the first time this day we had a chance to really observe the continuing attack. This was no 10,000-foot stuff; our dive-bombers were peeling off at about 3,500 feet and carrying their bombs home. With clear skies, the attacks were coming in from different sectors. The flak was more spread out than it had been on the first day, giving the impression that antiarcraft fire might have been greatly reduced. Time and again, it seemed that the dive-dombers would not be able to pull out, but they did, almost all that had not been hit, and some of those that had and were trailing smoke. The obvious devotion of these men, pushing danger aside in carrying out their task, made all of us proud to be a small part of the same navy.

Our AIC now reported that Lieutenant (jg) J. A. Burns had again landed his floatplane from the battleship *North Carolina*, this time off the eastern reef in the vicinity of the three rafts we were heading for, so we requested that he attempt to tow the rafts clear. He was a big jump ahead of us, however, having taken some of the men onto his float and towing the rest to seaward. Since they were now in no immediate danger, we followed our escorting planes to a raft off Mesegon Island, in the bight between Truk Atoll and Kuop. We thoroughly expected to be driven down, so Boatswain's Mate Leibold slipped the towing bridle over the SD mast and secured a life ring and long line to it. We could now tow a raft, plane, or swimmer clear while submerged. Our escorts did such a fine job of strafing that again the Japanese could not man their guns, somewhat to the dismay of our own gun crew, which was standing by below. After another routine man-overboard maneuver, Hank's men pulled Lieutenant H. E. Hill aboard, and *Tang* was off instantly for a swimmer just off the eastern reef of Kuop, about five miles to the south of us. Hill had seen our Very stars but dared not answer.

It was 1330 when we got there, and fortunately a plane had dropped a rubber boat to the pilot, who was already too weak to do more than get half his body over the side. But the rest of him in the water was acting as a sea anchor, preventing the wind from driving him ashore. Fortunately, submarines have a tendency to back upwind. We rigged in our sound heads so as not to break them off on the coral and stuck *Tang*'s bow very nearly ashore. The proper approach upwind was impossible, so a swimmer with line was standing by should the raft drift clear of our bow. But the human sea anchor did the job, and this pilot was pulled aboard as limp as he was wet.

It was 1410, and *Tang* was backing emergency, not because of the beach now drawing away from our bow, but to get on to the loaded Kingfisher floatplane and raft. We were barely up to speed when Chief Pharmacist's Mate Rowell reported that our newest guest, Lieutenant (jg) J. G. Cole, was coming around but might do better with some depth-charge medicine. The brandy was locked up, and we were all busy, so I suggested some diluted grain alcohol, a small quantity of which Rowell kept and accounted for outside of the locked supply. This was what he probably had in mind anyway, and I'm not sure that Cole was the sole recipient.

The Kingfisher was down by the stern with a bashed tail from the seas, so *Tang* came alongside not worrying about crunching a wing. The pilots and crewmen, all nine of them, came over like a pack of hounds let out of a kennel. *Tang*'s new aviators were Lieutenant R. S. Nelson, Lieutenant (jg) R. Barbor, Lieutenant (jg) J. A. Burns, Ensign C. L. Farrell, First Class Aviation Radioman J. Livingston, Second Class Aviation Machinist's Mate R. W. Gruebel, Second Class Aviation Radioman J. Hranek, Second Class Aviation Machinist's Mate O. F. Tabrun, and Second Class Aviation Radioman A. J. Gill—and a happier bunch you've never seen.

Burns's Kingfisher could not have been gotten into the air, so to prevent the Japanese from salvaging it, our after 20-millimeter gun crew took over. Somehow they managed to expend four pans of ammunition before sinking it, perhaps so that each of the crew would have a chance at firing, but I chose to attribute the performance to our moving out of range while working up to full power. It was 1515, and we had to round Kuop, go along the south reef of Truk Atoll, and on to the southwest of Ollan Island. There was the last reported raft. Fraz stepped off our half-hourly positions along this track. It was not encouraging, especially when all planes were recalled, for we could not reach the raft's position till dark, and that would be exactly when we'd need assistance in the inevitable search. The chances would be even worse in the morning after the raft had drifted throughout the night and with the enemy back on top of us.

I dropped below to see what our aviators had to say about it, for they knew what it was like to be adrift in a rubber raft.

"Of course there are the new night fighters," advised Lieutenant Barbor.

"Only the task force commander could authorize that," injected Commander Matter. I didn't even know that night fighters were on the books, much less that such were on the line. That was the complete answer. Our AIC had Admiral Marc A. Mitscher on voice in seconds.

"We'll need two night fighters to locate the last raft, Admiral."

"You'll have three," was his reply. I believe that Com-

mander Matter was a little taken aback that we hadn't
followed the chain of command, perhaps he considered himself in it, but the admiral seemed to like the way *Tang* did
things.

No one liked crossing the area of our morning submarine
contact even though common sense told us we could just as
easily encounter her or another most anywhere. The three
black-winged night fighters that joined us at sunset were
doubly welcome. With one searching ahead and one on each
bow, we approached the reported position. Our periscope
shears bristled with lookouts to replace the scopes that we
could no longer use in the fading light. *Tang* slowed and we
commenced a combing search downwind, the fighters now
looking like black albatross as they flew their search patterns
ahead and on our beams. Our chances of locating the raft
seemed slim, especially when we thought of our recent
experience with aircraft reporting a downed plane miles out
of position. Suddenly, one of our fighters dived, firing red
stars or possibly tracers. The result was a shower of red Very
stars coming up from the sea, well ahead on our starboard
bow. The fighters guided us in and were dismissed with
thanks and Godspeed. Aboard came Lieutenant D. Kirk-
patrick and his crewman, Second Class Aviation Ordnanceman R. L. Bently, who had already set sail for the Solomons,
1,200 miles away, so as to be clear of the Japanese by dawn.
With this kind of determination, they probably would have
made it. It was 1900, and *Tang* commenced a slow-speed
search west of the atoll.

9

Frank had the deck with Mel as the assistant; a better
combination would be hard to find. Fraz and I went below,
rather expecting to see airmen standing around in the passageways, or at least I did. We found only four, three in the
wardroom and one in my bunk. Then I recalled my suggestion to just put 'em on the watch list. Fraz had passed it on to

Frank, our senior watch officer. He and Ballinger had assigned the junior aviators who, except for the three in the wardroom and probably a few in the crew's mess, were now either in their bunks or standing watches as understudies. This did not solve my predicament, for though I had offered my cabin to Commander Matter, I had not intended that it be permanent.

With 22 extra men aboard, making a total of 102, some hot bunking was obviously necessary; as soon as a man assumed the watch, his bunk was available. This would not quite do for the commander, but it led to a diplomatic solution. I do believe Fraz and Ballinger let me stew in my cabin for a while before the chief of the boat knocked. There was not room for three of us in the cabin, so he just stuck his head and shoulders in and addressed the commander: "Your bunk is ready, sir." There are some situations the chief of the boat can handle politely and diplomatically that the skipper and exec can't. He has rare authority. The commander's was the top bunk in CPO quarters and, in fact, a privileged one, for men climbing in and out of the other bunks would not be stepping in his face. Actually, the arrangement was quite proper and even covered in navy regulations, which state that the captain of a ship shall not vacate his cabin for an embarked senior. There is good reason, for if the captain is pushed around, his status, prestige, and authority suffer in the eyes of his crew.

Though Task Force 58 was well over 200 miles away, we continued to guard 4475, partly because there were so many radiomen aboard and this kept them busy, like pounding the anchor chain. One message was both heartening and distressing. Admiral Mitscher congratulated all units on their splendid performance. Sixty enemy planes had been shot down, another 30 destroyed on the ground, small shipping sunk, and Truk's remaining above-ground facilities devastated. We had suffered nine operational losses, and 26 more planes went down in combat. The message closed with a conciliatory statement: Eight airmen had been rescued and "some others" were in *Tang*.

We had assumed that the task force staff was monitoring 4475 with a setup something like ours and keeping a running account of the airmen in *Tang*. We had forgotten the tremendous control problems of the strike and that doubtless everyone was therein involved. They were probably more than happy to have our AIC carry the ball, and our lifeguard results certainly spoke well for this innovation. Should we now open up and tell them? I decided not. It could be hot enough out here in the morning without giving enemy direction finders a chance to locate us. Rarely would a submarine use her transmitter when on patrol in her operating area. There had to be an emergency or urgent contact report, and the voices and laughter coming from the forward torpedo room would tell anyone that all was well this night.

Tang was a happy ship. After the evening meal, the crew's mess and the wardroom became club lounges, enlivened by the stories of those awaiting bunks or coming watches. One thing at once became apparent: Hollywood notwithstanding, airmen could talk without using their hands. What we all learned should have been recorded, condensed to a pamphlet, and promulgated to dispel myths and give facts. We would include some of this in our patrol report, especially their doubts concerning emergency identification signals.

While this was going on, *Tang* was establishing a reputation of her own. The new members of her ship's company were not accustomed to drop-in movies or hot, home-baked bread at midnight served with Taylor-made ice cream, and could hardly believe there would be no reveille for them. Should these men be grounded, we had candidates. Before morning twilight, we took a long suction through each end of the boat and doused the smoking lamp. Our new lookouts had each practiced clearing the bridge in the dark with only the red glow of the conning tower lights to guide them. Their earnestness was so evident that Fraz and I were sure they had been filled with stories of the seas rolling up through the superstructure, but a foot from the hatch as the last man dived below. Of course sometimes, but rarely, this had happened. Besides, maybe this was something akin to bailing out of a cockpit. In any event, with the benefit of dawn's first light and Frank's calm "Clear the bridge," the airmen dived below like pros.

Admiral Mitscher's summation of the devastation on Truk was confirmed on May 2, for during the whole morning watch Scotty reported only one flying boat over the lagoon and a single land plane near Tol Island. That nothing was missed we were sure, for the novelty of manning the scopes intrigued every pilot assistant OOD. *Tang* was in the best position to intercept shipping from the Gray Feather-Mogami Bank area, and our hopes were raised at lunch by a patrol plane searching on a northerly and then an easterly course. A convoy or a single ship might have been ordered back onto the banks during the strike and now be about to make a run for it. On this chance, we moved to the general area of the patrol's search, but one more unidentified plane to the northwest, sighted by Lieutenant Barbor, was our only reward.

It was after 1600, and those men just getting acquainted with submarines might be changing their minds about the luxury of submerged cruising. As a practical demonstration the smoking lamp was lighted at 1830, a half hour before our intended surfacing. Our regular ship's company watched, for the word that was just passed was an invitation to smoke whether one really wanted to or not. Twenty-two men tried in vain, for there was not enough oxygen to keep a match burning or even get a cigarette smoldering.

Three blasts, and a few minutes later a suction, brought all hands back to the beauties of earth with its air well scrubbed by the seas, celebrated shortly by distant fireworks over Truk. It could be anti-aircraft fire and bombs from Liberators, or perhaps the Japanese were just understandably jumpy and one shot had led to the rest. This ended the activity around Truk for the next three days as the Japanese were probably licking their wounds. One floatplane in 72 hours was a good indication of the damage they had received. We continued our search, however, with the SD secured and the SJ never trained anywhere near the atoll. Since one place seemed as poor as another, we worked slowly around to Otta Pass. The only item of note was a serious error by one of our new assistant OODs, who were all qualified OODs in surface ships. Instead of heads that discharged with compressed air, *Tang*'s forward drain lines went to sanitary tanks. A nightly ritual was to blow their content overboard. With 22 extra men and warm tropical waters, the tanks had time to become particularly ripe. This would not have mattered had the assistant OOD headed the ship into the wind before giving the order to blow the largest tank aft. The following breeze carried the stench forward, where our hull ventilation efficiently sucked it in and piped it throughout the boat, setting off cries of anguish. Four diesels on the line and a suction fore and aft put things back in order, though in some nooks and crannies it seemed to linger on, and I wondered if *Tang*'s OODs had connived at all of this.

During the evening of May 5, *Tang* moved out to the designated 40-mile spot to lifeguard for a midnight Liberator strike. The planes were 56 minutes late as their pips closed on the SD and then showed up on the SJ 12 miles to the north of us. Of equal interest to the ship company was radar interference also to the north. It would be *Permit*, entering the area as our relief. The bombs were away at 0110, down onto poor Dublon Island. Good explosions were visible, though most were over the horizon and showed up only as momentary looms of light. The last of our own plane contacts disappeared by 0200, and then enemy planes took over to give us a proper send-off. Their search was persistent, for the Japanese were tenacious fighters. Again, it was that damned SD that we had to use this night. There were no flares; they didn't need them in the moonlight. A passing squall helped us avoid one plane that closed to three miles; for another, we headed up the moon streak so as to present a minimal silhouette. *Tang* moved away slowly, as her luminous wake at higher speeds would aid the enemy. Finally at 0300, with all planes departed and our relief on station, we cranked on a second engine and came to the navigator's recommended course for Pearl.

We were not quite in the clear, for a floatplane, probably from Hall Island, had us down again less than an hour after our dawn trim dive. It obligingly continued on its way. Two SD contacts remained outside of 30 miles but served to keep us on our toes. This was probably well, for the relaxation that unavoidably crept in on the way home could make that passage the most dangerous.

During the day Fraz and I toyed with the message that would be sent to ComSubPac after dark. In an attempt to keep it brief, we punched the big dictionary and a thesaurus, but then we settled on the plainest of English. It read, FOLLOWING AIR MEN ABOARD ALL HEALTHY, and then it listed them alphabetically.

We were not alone in cooking up a message. Somewhat dumbfounded, I read one prepared by Commander Matter, properly handed to me for release. Likewise concise, this one read:

REQUEST RENDEZVOUS EARLIEST FOR TRANSFER AIRMEN
AND EFFECT THEIR RETURN TO PARENT AIR GROUPS

We know that Task Force 58, after a couple of bombardments, would go to Majuro for some rest and repairs. They had been under way nearly as long as we had, having retired to the Marshalls for replenishment after the strike at Palau. We also knew without asking that these 22 men, with the possible exception of one, neither wanted nor deserved rest on the sandspit of a flat atoll. They wanted to go to our rest camp, the Royal Hawaiian Hotel at Waikiki, and I meant to get them there. I silently questioned the authority behind the dispatch, and thought it over quickly; it wasn't the best approach. If this dispatch went out, however, there might well be some damned fool at Pearl or on Task Force 58's staff who would carry the commander's request into effect. Fortunately, among the duties filled by the aviators were those in radio and on the coding board. I sent for the coding officer with the duty; it was Lieutenant Dowdle. He had seemed sort of a rounder, and since he'd had the guts to set his plane down in that crosschop right in front of the enemy, this should be small potatoes to him.

"Will you take care of these," I said, handing him both dispatches. Then I added, "Will you read them now."

He read the long one, at least as far as the listing of names, sort of nodded, then read the other, originated by the group commander. He raised his eyes and looked at me with hard lines of fury drawn on his face. His lips were moving, and I didn't have to be a lipreader to catch most of the "Why that son of a bitch!" Then he understood my nod. Dowdle was my man, and this was right back in the hands of the aviators. After supper both dispatches were keyed through the transmitter, but I strongly suspect that the lead to *Tang*'s antenna trunk had inadvertently fallen out for the second transmission.

It was May 7, and we were entering the area where planes could be friendly or enemy. The simple little SD could not yet be picked up by airborne direction finders, and out here it did add some security as well as some possibly unnecessary dives. The first pip was tracked on by at breakfast time, but an hour later we pulled the plug to avoid a large, low-flying plane. At noon Mel reported a PBM (U.S. Martin patrol bomber) and received the unnecessary instruction to watch it. He'd know what to do.

Blaat! Blaat! Down *Tang* went, with those at lunch tilting their soup bowls to compensate for the rather steep angle. Our PBM might just be coming in to say hello, but with a zero angle at five miles, any plane was menacing.

"Level off at four hundred." We hadn't been deep for a while, and now was a good time to see that all was tight. Besides, our new hands might like to talk sometime about

Martin PBM-5 Mariner

lunch in the deep. All was well, so we dipped down to 500 feet and started the long climb to the surface. It took longer than expected, a good reminder to us for an attack in the future.

It was midafternoon when our SJ kicked the bucket for the last time. The oil had leaked from the modulator unit and it had shorted, but this unit from *Trigger* had seen us through. This delayed a bit a demonstration we had planned, to show the airmen our repertoire of identification flares, but they showed up better after sunset anyway. It turned out that none of the airmen had ever seen them before, so we felt that at least we had accomplished something. But then it was the consensus that they would not be able to see any one of them from the air except the Mark I comet from our Buck Rogers gun, and not even that if they were already attacking. With this kind of assurance, we tucked away the pyrotechnics and decided to rely on our good old two blasts of the diving alarm.

The evening Fox brought congratulations from across and up the line. We were not publicity minded, and our delay in transmitting the list of rescued airmen was just submarine common sense. During this period, doubt, anxiety, and suspense had obviously been building up, and the timing probably brought a maximum impact. There had been sub-air rescues before, but never one like this.

At breakfast Commander Matter thumbed through the

dispatches on the board. "I can't understand why they haven't set up the rendezvous," he commented, "or at least answered my message."

"Well, it looks like they want you all back at Pearl for a little publicity, Commander. It isn't every group commander that gets out and carries the mail!" My comment seemed to smooth his feathers, though I had made it to fill a sudden gap in the wardroom conversation. Perhaps because it was true, the conversation returned to normal as nicely as can be. May 9 came and *Tang* was grinding away the degrees. Wake Island lay 120 miles to the northwest, and seven miles away was an SD contact closing rapidly. We did not question its intent, for a friendly plane would hardly be here at dawn. The dive was twofold, our usual trim and again frustrating the enemy. Another plane near noon closed to 12 miles, apparently just in passing, but now we had another problem, our fuel. At 1300 we slowed to one engine. If the weather held and *Tang* encountered no head seas, we'd make it. Of course there was one ace in the hole, cutting our speed in half and cruising on the auxiliary.

Affecting the new crew members who had joined us at Midway was our failure to put an enemy on the bottom. Rightly or wrongly, the sinking of an enemy ship was the determining factor in classifying a patrol successful. Some-

Submarine Combat Pin

times on the most trying and difficult patrols, no torpedoes were fired. I had experienced this and was sorry for the six new hands, for they would not be eligible for the submarine combat pin. They found an unencumbered champion in Lieutenant Burns, however. As a theological student, he had a way with young men, but I could offer him no solution.

That evening, two of the aviators were speaking of their roles at Palau. We perked up our ears when they commented about the mining. Toagel Mlungui and the other shallow western passes had received about 80 mines, most of them planted on the first day of Operation Desecrate. Frank looked at me and understood the slight shake of my head. This was something within the submarine force; our useless weeks spent there were our business. It would not be spread around in the patrol report, but I would most certainly talk with Admiral Lockwood in private. There were no stone walls in front of his door.

The seas continued calm, and *Tang* crossed the 1,000-mile circle on the 11th. Our luck continued; with 2,000 gallons of diesel remaining of our original 110,000 and with 11,200 miles behind us, *Tang* entered the safety lane. We passed between the buoys, then by the *Arizona* and around ten-ten dock, and moored starboard side to pier 1 at the submarine base.

The reception was not the ordinary one. Fleet Admiral Chester W. Nimitz, Admiral Lockwood, and others were there. As they were greeting each of the aviators, Lieutenant Burns unexpectedly stepped forward.

"Admiral Lockwood," he addressed our force commander, "there are some new members of *Tang*'s crew who joined her at Midway. Is this patrol going to be designated as successful for combat insignia?"

The admiral was a little taken aback, and then he answered, "Why, uh— Why, yes, indeed." Burns thanked him and stepped back, and I'm told that our six new crew members were grinning from ear to ear.

We had in no way expected that *Tang* and the aviators would make headlines and the front pages, with a full page in *Life,* but after all it's the unusual that makes the news. The same crew that had struggled somewhere below 600 feet and spent a day crippled and hounded by a destroyer received no notice other than to have the estimated tonnage of that great tanker arbitrarily cut nearly in half by the staff, but that's the way the ball bounces.

Again working on priorities, payday for the ship's company and buses to the Royal Hawaiian took precedence. The troops' spit and polish had served double this May 15, first for the admirals and next for the officer in charge of the relief crew. *Tang*'s watch officers were gone before noon, and by midafternoon Fraz had wangled wheels. Before leaving the ship, I signed a recommendation that Lieutenant Burns be awarded the Navy Cross for deliberately placing himself in grave jeopardy to save others. Then I joined Fraz.

We glanced back at our ship's washed-out paint job,

running rust by the exhausts. Grudgingly, I admitted that she needed sprucing up. When we would next see her, she would be a camouflage haze gray with white beneath, the color of a gull.

PART IV

Third Patrol
TO THE
YELLOW SEA

1

Not one but two divided highways now led from Pearl Harbor to Honolulu. They were filled with fast late-afternoon traffic, and I thought with some nostalgia of the simple, black, two-lane road that had served so nicely in the late 1930s. The change was necessary, of course, for Oahu was the hub of our expanding Pacific war effort. Unchanged, however, were the Royal Hawaiian Hotel and its magnificent grounds, but a few minutes farther on. The sentry waved us through with a salute, and Fraz completed his first solo in four months.

In minutes we were moved into our suite on the second deck, by chance a deluxe one. A rotunda with powder room had bedroom suites to right and left, each facing the ocean. Straight ahead was the living room, which opened to a spacious lanai. On the back of the rotunda's closet door was a white card stating among other things that the charges were $100 a day. Of course that would have included all of the luxurious furnishings, but some of those had been replaced with items more sailor-proof. It was really better that way, for we'd not have to be over concerned about a dropped butt or a spilled drink. I am not sure who engineered the lease of the Royal Hawaiian as a submarine rest camp, but it was certainly advantageous to both the owners and the navy. The real winners were the submariners.

The division engineer, who handled diverse tasks for the commander, had our mail waiting on the large lanai table. It was all in chronological order, except that the latest postmarked letter had been placed on top before the bundle was secured. Obviously, he had patrolled, too. One letter, one beer from the cooler under the table, and we set out to find Frank, Mel, and the others. As expected, they were at the first reef, where the water was deep enough for swimming without hitting bottom but still suitable for lolling around. The sun was about an hour from setting, and this was the time to start regaining our tans along with limbering up our arms and legs.

There was no rush about this, or for dinner, since it would be served continuously, something that even the hotel's prewar guests could not enjoy. Suddenly, the trials and frustrations of our second patrol, and even the satisfaction of *Tang*'s final task, were all a thousand miles away.

Responsibility for a ship, even in unkeep, could never be completely delegated. The officer in charge of the relief crew could not possibly know a captain's desires as would one of the regular department heads. At Midway this had been of no particular consequence, for none of us was ever more than a half mile away. Here, the 15 miles between the base and the hotel, with no travel after curfew, could have posed a problem except for one thing; Scotty and Bill, together with four leading petty officers, were holding down the fort. Scotty had orders to the submarine base and would take his time at the Royal after we had departed on patrol. Bill had orders to postgraduate school for engineering studies and, like the four petty officers, who were going to new boats, would take his recuperation time in the States. In the meantime, they were available to look out for *Tang*'s interest as the backlog of small alterations was completed. They would call Fraz or me as appropriate.

The first call came at midmorning of the fourth day, relayed by Walker, who found me at the second reef. Fraz had some personnel matters to discuss with the staff, so he joined me in the car that Scotty had sent. *Tang* was still a washed-out, rusty black, but an alteration scheduled but unknown to us, was much blacker. In an attempt to insure good short-range VHF and UHF communications with the surface forces, two new antennas were being installed. Each would stick above the shears to afford all-around performance without blank sectors. Sticking anything unretractable at such a height was bad enough, but the alteration called for their installation plate and angle-iron brackets to be welded to port and starboard of the shears. This structure and the pipe carrying the coaxial cable would make access to our crow's nest practically impossible. Further, the complete array could cause an unacceptable turbulence when we were at periscope depth and making anything above one-third speed, which would be just one more telltale for an alert enemy plane. It certainly appeared that our primary mission had been forgotten, so the next task was to find the base repair officer.

It was not difficult; Commander W. D. Irvin was looking for me. Someone had apparently already told him that I had stopped the antenna work. We met about halfway between *Tang* and the base repair office. He was bristling.

"What's this about your stopping the VHF-UHF installation?" he demanded.

"Not stopping, Commander, just delaying until we arrive at the installation best suited for *Tang*," I replied, maintaining a level tone. It was not too difficult; he was senior to me and I'd had years of practice.

"Well, what's so damned special about you and the *Tang* that the antennas can't be installed exactly as on the other boats?"

Now, that remark didn't seem exactly called for, but since he had asked, I described our crow's nest, its all-around visibility and our means of access to it. Then I expressed my particular intent to maintain our streamlined silhouette, the best in the force, and to avoid the extra submerged turbulence that would be caused by structures hung out to port and starboard. Commander Irvin calmed down a bit, for like most others he obviously had never heard of a submarine with a crow's nest. But he remained unbending.

"Only the force commander can authorize any change!" was his closing remark.

Where had I heard those words before, and would Admiral Lockwood be as cooperative as Admiral Mitscher? I had no choice but to find out, for the alternative would entail redoing the job at sea while en route to our next patrol station. Still, Admiral Lockwood had commanded submarines and might well understand the importance of this to *Tang*. He should not be bothered with this, but big men delegate tasks to subordinates and have more time for what seem to be small things than one might expect. The first part of my brief conversation with him concerned an appointment to discuss future task force-submarine operations, but as I was taking my leave I brought up the immediate problem.

"Admiral, there is one thing you can do for *Tang*. We're about to lose access to our crow's nest unless the new VHF-UHF antennas are installed fore and aft of the shears. Will you authorize it?"

The admiral was quite intrigued with *Tang*'s crow's nest, though he did not delve into the details of how she happened to have one. The conversation revolved around limitations on radar usage, and lookouts, but not the antennas. Then he said simply, "Oh, yes, the antennas. It's your boat, have them installed anywhere you want."

Surprisingly, Commander Irvin was quite agreeable.

"Let's go down and take a look," he said. We were friends again, and that was somewhat important during a base overhaul.

Having Bill and Scotty available during working hours, and this sometimes included most of the night, was not enough. Logically, their real interests were swinging to their coming assignments. There was a solution at hand, however. Our regular watch officers were spending more hours aboard following repair work than if they'd had a day's duty. It would be no imposition to formalize this. Starting in the morning, we'd have an officer aboard who would be responsible for all repairs in our ship, one who would be going on patrol with work done by the submarine base.

Fraz had worked out an excellent arrangement with force personnel. We could choose our replacements from the relief crew and could carry extra hands. For the most part, these officers and men were waiting on submarine billets. We would do what we could to select the best. I would reserve judgment about the antennas, but with everything now apparently under control, we headed back to the Royal, or more specifically, to the beach beyond the banyan trees.

Several boats had returned from patrol, and that always made for an interesting evening. The conversations were broad but always returned to patrol experiences. Just as at Midway, there was much to be learned, especially if one could listen and not talk. It was difficult. Slade Cutter and his *Seahorse* had been down at Satawan, to the south, during the Truk strike, and had piped all of our 4475 voice communications into their 1MC, so they heard it throughout the boat.

"More exciting than any football broadcast ever thought of being," he said, and that was from the man who had once kicked the field goal that was the only score in beating Army.

"That's the beauty of medium frequencies," I commented. "They're not temperamental and seem to get through; of course the enemy hears it, too, but that doesn't always hurt anything." Then I tipped them off concerning the new antenna installations that were in store. Commander Irvin might not remain a friend, but we would be long gone. Of more importance was the experience of one of the boats, which had been fired on while returning from patrol. When another boat said they would have fired torpedoes right down the wakes, it became clear that not everyone was aware of the prohibition against firing on another submarine, except in single-sub Empire areas, unless the submarine was positively identified as enemy. Perhaps a few Japanese submarines had gone free for a time because of this restriction, but that was better than sinking one of our own. So besides the pleasure of seeing old friends and participating in the bull sessions, we all learned a little more about fighting our submarines and of our common enemy as well.

In the submarine force's wartime organization, the division was generally an administrative unit, and though *Tang* like other boats had a permanent division assignment, in practice we reported to a commander present. The squadron commands were usually training officers; some had patrol experience and all had had enough years in submarines to command our wholehearted respect. In patrol operations, however, our orders came directly from the force commander. Admiral Lockwood had an experienced staff to advise him and carry out his directives, but the staff was not in the chain of command. It was proper then, and frankly expected that I would see my boss in private if I had something on my mind, and that I did!

I first discussed with the admiral our earlier operations at Truk, then at Palau and off Davao Gulf, giving our thoughts from on the scene of the inefficiency of the circular submarine disposition. Then I used my express-train example of what an individual submarine might expect.

"That may be what happened to *Tullibee*," Admiral Lockwood injected.

That was my first knowledge of her failure to return. After a pause, I described our simplified operations with *Trigger*, in which both boats retained freedom of movement, and noted that in a similar situation, unknown to either submarine at the time, *Tang* and *Sunfish* might well have chased enemy ships to one another west of Saipan.

"I'm glad to hear that, for it supports my intention for your next patrol, in the East China and Yellow seas. It will be with *Sealion* and *Tinosa*, all operating independently."

I expressed my complete satisfaction—who wouldn't—and then paused again, for the final item I wished to bring up was a bit touchy. It took but a few sentences, however, to point out that if a senior submariner had been ordered to Admiral Mitscher's staff, and if operational control of the submarines had passed to the task force commander for the strike on

Palau, *Tang* and *Trigger* would not have been left guarding mined channels.

This may have been the admiral's first word of the mining; if so, it served to punctuate this recommendation. In any case, he thanked me for my frankness, and I left with the feeling that he was indeed an admiral for every one of us in the force.

It was past time to resume our recreation, but one small task remained. I found Fraz at the officers' club, and we took a quick turn through the boat for just one purpose, to find out how many extra bunks could be swung for extra hands. For the most part, these could be temporary, movable to the forward and after rooms when some torpedoes had been fired. A cursory look showed space for six; we might find more. That job was passed on to the duty officer, and we headed back to the Royal and the second reef, though already discussing the prospects for our coming patrol.

Our troops seemed to have been pretty well swallowed up by Honolulu or the sea off Waikiki during daylight hours. Curfew in town came at dark, and if some strayed the MPs apparently delivered them quietly to the gate. There were more recreational facilities and more organized functions than at Midway. We had all been organized enough, however, and missed the spontaneous sport of our first upkeep. Still, there had been no troubles that we knew of, no mast cases were pending, and already our time ashore was drawing to a close. Fraz, Frank, and I were congratulating the crew and each other over a couple of beers when a messenger brought a sealed letter from the force medical officer, my friend Commander Walt Welham. The doctor had just been informed that the master at arms force at the Royal had confiscated the remains of a tin of alcohol from *Tang*'s wing, and he pointed out that undiluted it could be deadly. This alcohol was supposedly strictly controlled and issued in small quantities for cleaning and drying electrical machinery and optics.

Leave it to a bluejacket, or their combined ingenuity, and they'll figure a way. Getting a five-gallon tin out from under lock and key and then off the base seemed impossible, and then I thought of Walker; his winnings might have been of assistance in finding a way. Frank left to find Ballinger, not to locate any alcohol that remained—that would be impossible —but to insure that it was cut twice. Even then it would be 50 proof. The troops had certainly done better at getting the hard stuff than had the officers and chiefs, who had divided the leftover depth-charge medicine.

Two weeks and a day had passed quickly, but that was all the time it had taken the base to complete the work requests and alterations. We could stay at the Royal another week, but to do so would mean following *Sealion* and *Tinosa* into the East China and Yellow seas. We would then be entering a stirred-up area, when we would like to at least have a chance to hit the enemy first. Ballinger concurred for the troops, though he would not yet tell them why lest word leak to the other two boats. To pacify some, including myself, we would retain our wing at the Royal during the training and readiness period. There was one other reason for returning to our ship early. On board were two new ship's officers and 12 enlisted men. They would have to become accustomed to *Tang*'s way of operating, and we all had to get back into the groove of making real exercise torpedoes pass under real targets.

We started, as usual, with simulated attacks, the tracking parties using problems that had been generated in the TDC and recorded against time. This offered one variation not available with a real target at sea, for when there was confusion, both time and the TDC could be stopped until the doubts were clarified. While this was going on, Hank, Mel, and their torpedomen were loading the exercise fish that we would fire during the next three days. Aft of the conning tower, men not otherwise busy were passing the commissary stores across the deck and down the messroom hatch like a bucket brigade. Almost unnoticed were the engineers, topping off 4A and 4B ballast tanks, now converted to reserve fuel oil tanks. There were no idle hands, and at dusk the executive officer reported the ship ready for sea and our training period.

Our new officers and crew members were not entirely unfamiliar with *Tang,* for as arranged, they had been selected from the relief crew. Only one was thrown into a position of immediate responsibility, Lieutenant Lawrence Savadkin, from Easton, Pennsylvania, our new engineering officer. A dark-haired, wiry, knowledgeable gentleman, he gave every indication of measuring up to his task as he took *Tang* down on the first dive. It was a careful dive, on soundings of less than our test depth, for the alterations to the main ballast tanks warranted a post-shipyard procedure. An extra half hour was involved, but it was certainly not wasted, for it gave Larry an opportunity to get the feel of the boat.

During three days and two nights, *Tang* again went through her paces, with all of the normal emergency drills conducted between practice approaches. Exercise torpedoes were fired on the first afternoon and during the following two mornings. The routine was rigorous, but no more so than during comparable periods when we had been in pursuit of the enemy. In preparation for a long patrol, our OOD and assistant, with section tracking parties, carried the ball, while Fraz shared my responsibilities in overall direction up to the attack position. This would spare us many hours of waiting at battle stations. Our training officer, Captain C. B. Momsen, known for the escape lung and called Swede by his contemporaries, found no escape in his task. He tried to take in everything and as a result was hanging on the ropes. This was a switch, for not entirely in jest, most boats sighed in relief when they got out from under the training officer and on to the relative peace and quiet of patrol against the real enemy.

I called a temporary halt to our operations at noon of the third day. For the benefit of our new hands, I had scheduled an exercise known to no one aboard except Captain Momsen, Fraz, and me. As we went below for lunch, I routinely ordered the OOD to stop and then maneuver on the battery should we pick up any particular roll. Dessert was being served when two blasts took us down, and word came quickly that we had screws on sound bearing 195 degrees true. The OOD was putting them astern and had ordered 200 feet as we paused in the control room. Fraz proceeded to the conning tower and brought us back to periscope depth. The propellers were those of a friendly submarine that had been operating in the area south of us and was trying to close for a simulated attack. As prearranged, we both surfaced. The radar range was 4,800 yards, within reach of steam torpedoes but hardly a distance at which a hit, even on an unalerted enemy, could be expected. Our belief in the advantage of a stationary patrol when a submarine had no particular place to go was bolstered again, though Captain Momsen did not seem to share our confidence completely. As far as Fraz and I knew, *Tang* was the only boat to stop and lie to on patrol, and even we admitted it took some getting used to.

The torpedoes that *Tang* fired had passed under the PC target or sufficiently close to have hit any modest-sized freighter, which would be at least three times the target's length. The final round of drills had gone well, and we were sure that our ship was ready. *Tang* headed for port, and those not in the duty section who wished took the waiting bus back to the Royal.

Hank and Mel, with their torpedomen, now had three days to complete the adjustments on our torpedoes and to strike them below. By midmorning of the first day, a Mark 23 was being eased down the permanent skid, through the slanted loading hatch, and onto its portable skid, supported by chain hoists. The torpedo and skid would be lowered away and moved on crossbeams to their stowage position. Of later manufacture, the Mark 23 steam torpedoes had characteristics similar to the Mark 14s and should perform identically.

Unexpectedly the work stopped, and a hush was noticeable below, followed by the hum of the 1MC. Then in quiet words came an announcement: "Allied forces have landed on the Normandy coast."

I had anticipated that the Allies' return to the Continent would be a moment of great elation, but like others, found that I could not cheer and pray at the same time. If Godspeeds can carry halfway around the earth, then *Tang* was helping 80 fellow fighting men ashore.

By nightfall of June 6, the last of our 16 Mark 23s was below forward. Aft, Mel and his men had finished with the eight Mark 18-1 electric fish, the first ever loaded in *Tang*. Other departments kept pace, and now for the most part two watch sections during daylight hours could complete the loading and final preparations, except for one all-hands function.

Down through the ages, whether it be a share in the plunder or a more formal war prize, the responsible commander received the larger share, for it was through him that this incentive brought results in the field of battle. In more recent times, the substitution of decorations for shares did not alter this. Our submarine force had initially adopted an awards policy that was conservative both in the number of awards bestowed and the time it took for awards to be approved. But wartime losses were resulting in increasing posthumous decorations, nullifying much of the incentive such awards were supposed to impart. So in early 1943 a directive to hasten awards in submarines was approved by Commander-in-Chief, Pacific Fleet (CinCPac). Now the division commander would review the patrol report, question witnesses, and if warranted could recommend that a skipper sinking one ship receive the Secretary of the Navy's Letter of Commendation. For two ships, his recommendation could be for a Silver Star Medal, and for three or more ships, the Navy Cross. Depending on his own award, the skipper could then recommend a specified number of subordinate awards for members of his ship's company, though all had to be approved by CinCPac's Board of Awards. At first, I thought this procedure was too mechanical, but after listening to junior officers at the Gooneyville tell the complete stories of incidents that, of necessity, had been covered by only a sentence or two in the patrol reports, it seemed that this was in fact the best way possible. Regardless, this morning I would attend my first awards ceremony as a skipper.

Tang's officers and crew, in whites, were in formation on the pier. As Fraz, Ballinger, and I looked the divisions over, we were of the same mind: Never had a finer-looking ship's company assembled, nor one as proud. Behind them, moored port side to, was *Tang* in her gull trimmings, haze gray blending into black decks and tank tops. The inside of the bridge cowl, the limber holes, and other voids now showed white. Taken all together, it was a picture I could never forget.

Fleet Admiral Nimitz, Vice Admiral Lockwood, and others arrived precisely on time. The words to the crew were sincere and to the point, and then came the presentation of the Navy Cross to me for *Tang*'s first patrol. Though this was a personal award, I like to believe that the ship's company shared in my pride. In a practical sense, others were affected, for this permitted me to submit recommendations for the award of two Silver Star and two Bronze Star medals, and these nominations would be honored.

The day was still young, and we would not leave until a gentlemanly hour on the morrow. A holiday at the Royal seemed a fitting celebration, though I could not join the others until after lunch with the admirals.

2

The screws were churning, the port one pumping water between *Tang* and the dock, setting her bodily to starboard as she gathered sternway. The prolonged warning blast had stopped, and the line handlers on the pier paused in their task and stood at attention. No one had ordered this; the moment was charged with some emotion, and it was the natural thing for fighting men to do. Port ahead standard killed the sternway rapidly and started our twist to starboard. *Tang* gathered headway and then proceeded briskly along the channel at two-thirds speed. We were right on schedule at 1330 this June 8.

How many times had I gone through this same maneuver? It would seem proper for Fraz or one of the junior officers to take her out, and in peacetime that would be the case. They had their opportunities in shifting berth during our refit, however, and for Fraz, during the training period as well. At that time any possible minor damage could be repaired without delaying our mission. Today if any mistakes were made they would be mine.

The rusting hulk of the battleship *Arizona* was on our starboard hand; I could never give it more than a glance and still keep the clear eye my job demanded, but then came the channel entrance buoys. We were at sea, but in the safety lane, where all submarines were immune from attack, at least by our own forces. Mel took the con and a half hour later, with my nod, brought *Tang* right to the navigator's recommended course, 290. We were on the first leg of our voyage to the East China Sea, 4,150 miles to the west. From there, our patrol could take us another thousand miles to the farthest reaches of the Yellow Sea, and even into the great, shallow Gulf of Pohai.

The seas were kindly, from the southwest. *Tang*'s bow sliced through them effortlessly; the log showed 14 knots.

"Ship rigged for dive" came over the bridge speaker from control. Mel acknowledged and ordered the regular sea detail set, second section. *Tang* could now carry out any submarine evolution; we were on patrol.

Also patrolling, about three miles ahead, was our escort, a bomber making lazy figure eights. We would delay our trim dive until after its release and thus take full advantage of this bit of protection. I liked its constant turning; it would give an enemy submarine fits. There was a second reason for delaying the dive, for *Sealion* was now in sight astern. This afternoon we would test our new UHF-VHF antennas and the low frequencies we might use between submarines, too. Fraz had laid down our track a little to the north. *Sealion* could now pass well to the south of us and still not go much out of her way. Ed and the watch were conducting the tests. With the sharp outline of Kauai already abeam to starboard, I went below to the stack of waiting patrol reports. It was no chore, for at this moment more exciting reading did not exist.

Two words would characterize the control room, quiet business, as if we had been at sea for weeks. This was the result, at least in part, of shortened stays at the Gooneyville and now at the Royal. There had been insufficient time for any of us to fall too far from submarine wartime routine. Now the watch was consciously setting the pace for our new hands, urged by Fraz and Ballinger. Perhaps no urging was necessary, for we were all in the same boat and would share in the results of any mistakes.

In the wardroom passageway, two football legs were slithering down from the overhead. Ensign Richard Kroth, a large, likeable young man from Hamtramck, Michigan, was now getting ready to go on watch. His bunk, one of the new ones, had been hung where the ventilation piping took a convenient jog to starboard. His toes searched blindly for a moment before finding the ladder rung, and then Dick hit the deck solidly. A little more practice and this descent from nearly seven feet might become routine for him, but something for the rest of us to watch out for when going through wardroom country.

A few minutes later, Dick joined us in the wardroom, extolling the virtues of his bunk. Slides providing extra openings in the air supply and exhaust lines were within easy reach; the light, with its long gooseneck, permitted reading in any position; and it would be impossible to fall out of the bunk in any sea. Also considering the privacy, we began to wonder if this bunk should have been assigned to the junior officer aboard.

We dismissed our escort a half hour before sunset with a well done, and the pilot in turn wished us good hunting. The long June days, even at this lower latitude, would permit the bomber to reach Pearl before dark. We were now cruising singly, with our new hands already on watch, and only a trim dive remained on the Plan of the Day. With deference to the cooks, stewards, and messcooks, we changed the time for diving to 2015, when all mess gear would be secured and the new watch set.

The dive would be well observed, for we had a third lieutenant commander aboard, Morton H. Lytle, from Tulsa, Oklahoma. Mort would patrol with us as a PCO, or prospective commanding officer, and would thus take command of a submarine fresh from patrol and as up-to-date as we could make him. The five-year spread in seniority between Fraz and me, with Mort right in the middle, was as it should be. He would not just be standing around but would have a place on the watch list and at times would have other responsibilities that would be to our mutual benefit.

The weighted sacks of trash and garbage had been dumped, the messroom hatch secured again, and two blasts on cue took us down. Larry had compensated quite accurately for the torpedoes and stores of our final loading. To see that all was well, *Tang* swam on down to 550 feet and then back up again. This was a new experience for our new officers and men, but with hands around them taking it all in stride, none of them seemed over concerned. It was an opportunity for Larry to find out now how much pumping was required on the way down and flooding on the way back up again. Things were coming his way one after another, but he continued as if everything was routine.

Back on the surface, the night remained quiet, and having *Sealion* maneuvering to the south gave our section tracking parties a real target to work on with SJ ranges and bearings. We would return this service on the 9th and so alternate en route to Midway. The orders for the night were brief. Other than the course, speed, and engines on the line, they called attention to the standing night orders, items that the watch officers should review frequently and to which I could refer on occasion. They were now typed and pasted inside the hard covers of the 5-by-8-inch Night Order Book, where they would always be conveniently at hand.

Tang was all in the clear except for *Sealion,* and her position was accurately plotted by the section tracking party, so this evening offered an uninterrupted period to consider our patrol. Only 16 months earlier I had been in *Wahoo* when she left Pearl for the same area; she had turned in the top score for the war, eight ships on the bottom. On the table, becoming well thumbed, was her report of that patrol, and though the shipping conditions she had found might well have changed, this report would certainly set the tone for any submarine patrol in these waters. Questions raised by this patrol report I could answer, and surely no submarine was more thoroughly and accurately briefed for her mission.

Nihoa lay to the north at dawn. Fraz and Jones had finished working out their stars, and the plotted position showed *Tang* to be right on schedule. It was our day to maneuver while *Sealion* tracked, so the navigator remained busy drawing in our various courses on ahead. They included straight legs, zigzag plans, and then periods of very gradual worm turns, in which the rudder was held constant at a specified angle and then shifted when the ship's head had swung the directed number of degrees from the base course. The great arcs occurring alternately to port and starboard gave the impression that a ship was wandering all over the ocean, but a good tracking party could usually determine what was going on before it became evident through the periscope.

The tracking exercise continued until late afternoon, when *Sealion* had apparently solved our varied routes and zigzags or had just had enough for this short passage. In any case, Jones had made a tracing that we'd pass to her at Midway so her party could verify its solutions, and she'd be doing the same for us. An afternoon sun line showed that our longitude was not far off in spite of the constant maneuvers, and this we expected, for Larry's engineers had been grinding out 2 extra knots to make up for the loss due to the zigging and wormturning. It would take a round of evening stars, or at a minimum a sight on Polaris, the North Star, to verify our latitude.

All had turned out well with Fraz's evening and the next morning's star fixes, and *Tang* was now cruising singly, the way a submarine was meant to travel. Without the distraction of an accompanying boat, the entire watch was intent on this June 11. Below, items in the press news, which had been copied from the nightly Fox, indicated that the Normandy landings were progressing well except for the Omaha beachhead, where our troops had been stymied. I wondered if we could be as brave and slug it out with the enemy without that diving alarm as a backup. But ours was a different battle in another ocean; we were trained in fighting our submarine, and our thoughts and concentration belonged here.

French Frigate Shoals had been left behind, unseen except for the light green sky on our starboard hand, and we would make our landfall on Midway at daylight. Prompted by an experience when green water had unexpectedly loomed up dead ahead, I changed our course 10 degrees to the south and then wrote in the night orders: *Proceeding on course 300° true at 14 knots, 80/90 on engines 1 and 2. You will note that our track lies 10 miles to the south of Midway. Accurate navigation notwithstanding, keep a sharp lookout ahead, for approaching an atoll during darkness always imposes an extra hazard. Keep me completely informed, and again do not hesitate to call me and the navigator to the bridge.*

I left a call in the usual place for 0500. The call came early.

"Radar signals on the APR-one, Captain." It was the duty chief's messenger, making a report that I had never heard before. I shook my head before the significance sank in. Our new radar detector, installed during our refit, was responsible. Though nondirectional, like our SD, it would keep us posted on the presence of enemy radar. Best of all, it emitted no signal of its own to betray our presence. As expected, this signal soon showed as wavy interference on our SJ and was from a similar radar on Midway. Our visual landfall, on our starboard bow, was made on schedule. An hour later, *Tang* was passing through the corridor cut in the reef. One simple left turn brought us to the fuel dock, next to the old submarine pier.

There was no fanfare connected with a submarine's stopping to top off. Those whose duties permitted usually showed up, however, like train watchers in a small town. This beautiful morning there were two of us, for *Sealion* was just coming through the passage in the reef. It was always a somewhat intriguing sight, and coupled with the convenient hour, the turnout today was sizable. It was good to see friends and well-wishers, too, and the coffee makers were kept busy fore and aft.

We had two pieces of business other than taking on fuel. One of these had been essentially completed en route. Now only the final reading, signing, and mailing remained for my four recommendations for combat awards. I wished that there could be more, but these were all that I was allowed to pass down the line. The choice for the first Silver Star was easy, especially after I had learned of Fraz's actions throughout the night in putting *Tang* in position for the dawn attack west of Saipan. The next choice for a Silver Star was more difficult. Should it be Hank, whose calm direction of the caulking of the torpedo tube may even have saved our ship, or Bill, whose 15 hours of dive without flaw had outlasted the hounding destroyer? I chose Bill, influenced a little by the fact that his new assignment ashore would make this his last chance for such recommendation. The other two, for Bronze Star medals, were shoo-ins, Ballinger, for his participation with Bill, and Jones, who had been indispensable to me on the bridge. More time-consuming had been complying with the detailed instructions and the preparation of citations, but most of the work had fallen on Fraz and his yeoman.

The second piece of business had also been under way, frankly from the day I had learned of our probable patrol area. The manner in which *Sealion* and *Tinosa* would conduct their patrol could have a great bearing on our strategy. We had been quietly listening without fear of disclosing our plans, for up to this time I'd made no decision. Fraz, Frank, and Jones had been our sleuths, and today we'd have the assistance of Walker. He had steward friends on *Sealion,* and there was nothing unusual about his helping serve there this noontime. My own decision was starting to firm up; it looked as if *Sealion* would treat the East China and Yellow seas as another vast sea area and conduct a surface patrol accordingly. *Tinosa*'s previous patrols would indicate the same. This would increase the possibility of their being sighted, so if we remained undetected ships might well be routed our way.

Submarines occasionally have one or two "reluctant dragons" aboard, and in this respect are no different from other ships; and *Tang* was not unique among submarines in never harboring one. A day before we reached Midway, an electrical ground had developed in No. 2 main motor. In peacetime this might require a day or more to isolate and correct. One stubborn case in *Argonaut* was going to require removing the motor until a Fuller Brush man saved the navy $10,000 with $5 worth of special brushes to clean carbon deposits. Strangely, a main motor ground had developed under almost identical circumstances when I was in *Wahoo.* I now tried the remedy my skipper had used then, an announcement through our new chief engineer that we would leave on schedule and make the patrol on the remaining three main motors if necessary. By early afternoon, the ground had been located and corrected. We gladly held a dock trial as a final test. There were no troubles, though now neither Fraz nor I knew whether the ground had been real or pseudo; frankly, we did not care.

Tang was under way on schedule at 1600. *Tinosa* was way out ahead, with close to a half day's run. Now *Sealion*'s course was taking her to the south of us, already hull down. We would next see her at our agreed-upon rendezvous, 15 miles south of Kusakaki Shima, in the East China Sea. Before dark the seas were all our own. Below, I thought momentarily of these three submarines, traversing another 3,000 miles of hostile seas before sneaking along the Empire to its very back door. Then I checked myself; such thoughts were timid. Here I had command of the best fighting ship ever built, capable of going anywhere and sinking any enemy ship. With complete confidence, I reached for the Night Order Book.

The 13th broke bright and clear. Well back on our quarter, to the north, lay Kure Reef, the last navigational hazard for a week. Neither was there any real danger from the skies, and for the present our regular lookouts would concentrate on the seas to the horizon. From our crow's nest and from raised periscopes, we would search ahead, from port bow to starboard bow, for a possible enemy periscope shear. Our posture remained defensive as we passed Marcus Island on the fourth day. It lay far to the south, but *Tang* was not beyond range of its search planes. To make up for our SD, which would remain secured unless absolutely needed, two extra lookouts manned our front porch. As before, they would clear through the 20-millimeter gun access hatch into the sealed-off trunk should we dive. Nothing but seabirds and occasional flotsam came in view.

Tang was now approaching the Nampo Shoto, the string of volcanic islands stretching south from Tokyo to the Bonins. In the center, on our track, lay Sofu Gan, which on some charts is called Lot's Wife. It sticks high out of the sea like a giant thumb and might be considered useless, as it would be impossible to habitate. It was valuable to our submarines, however, for it made a perfect radar target for final tests before entering the Empire areas. Fraz and Jones had enjoyed good morning and evening stars, augmented by sun lines during the day. Their navigation was exact, verified by the SJ radar when it obtained the first contact and range at 38,000 yards, 19 nautical miles. As we approached the pinnacle, our battle stations tracking party put the TDC through its paces, with Sofu Gan representing a stopped ship. The inputs to the TDC of our own course and speed were automatic. Now with the radar range and bearing set in by Frank, the TDC should generate the correct range and bearing of Sofu Gan as we passed by. Additional bearings and radar ranges were checked with the TDC, all close to the computer's solution. Certainly no one could complain about the performance of either piece of equipment. In hope of maintaining the SJ in this present peak condition, we used it sparingly. A sweep or two every ten minutes or so, and then the high voltage was turned off, but the cathode heaters were left on throughout the night. This should keep down the overall heat and perhaps cut down on tube failures, for their cathodes seemed to burn out when turned on, like household bulbs.

Every move, every drill, every test increased our confidence in *Tang* and in our ability to fight her. It was well, for another hurdle lay only two nights away. Our track paralleled the south coast of Honshu, beyond normal search by Empire-based patrol planes. Though we were sure that we could dive before such planes could reach an attack position, our goal was to avoid being sighted at all. There was little reason for the enemy to route shipping across this path when a few extra miles could take it along the safer coastal lanes, through the Inland Sea, and then south along Kyushu, the westernmost of the main Japanese islands. No nation at war would leave her sea areas completely unpatrolled, and it was certainly just a matter of time until our surface passage was challenged. Almost unbelievably, the seas and sky remained clear. We had experienced more patrol activity in areas of the Central Pacific, where the enemy had little reason to search. Could the Japanese be concentrating on *Tinosa* and *Sealion*, called in by the emissions from their SDs? We had a more likely answer when Bergman brought in the press news, copied on the evening Fox. United States forces had invaded Saipan on the 15th. Only four months earlier we had unloaded most of our torpedoes just off Saipan, and the island had taken only a token carrier strike. Now it was invaded and our beachheads were secure. Perhaps loss of the supplies in ships we'd sunk had helped to ease the tremendous task of storming that formidable steep island.

If enemy air forces had been deployed to counter the invasion, they'd be back, and we did not relax. Our position, 200 miles south of Nagoya, the large industrial city west of Tokyo, was plotted on the crew's messroom chart. Along the track to the west were our dead reckoning positions, showing the times we would pass the Kii Suido and then the Bungo Suido, the passages into the Inland Sea. These names brought a tingle to the spine of anyone who had ever patrolled there or even read the reports of boats that had, for at these passes our submarines had received some of their worst drubbings. It was not necessary to exhort our watches to do their level best, but certainly helping in setting the pace was Mort, our PCO. If he were a rank junior and not coming up for command, we'd most certainly try to steal him.

Without incident the Kii Suido and Bungo Suido were left behind, but now coming up was the Nansei Shoto, the island chain leading down from Kyushu and forming a loose barrier to the East China Sea. The name carried none of the thunder of many passes, and in truth the islands would not pose a true barrier to a submarine. But passing them undetected could be something else!

During the intervening hours, the few remaining patrol reports must be digested and then all given the deep six. My laugh when I saw the last report brought Fraz to my cabin. Now, every ship had an artist of sorts. In *Wahoo*, his product had been a comic strip to accompany the press news. *Tang*'s Kassube confined his talents to shipboard characters and events, or occasionally to our operations. The wardroom seldom shared in the former, from which one might conclude that, for the most part, we were the characters. But his drawing of the actual scene during the strike and rescues at Truk had been a masterpiece.

Not to be outdone, *Trigger*, whose report I held in hand, had produced a sketch that expressed her exasperation with the situation *Tang* had shared at Palau. It showed an enormous Bugs Bunny, complete with carrot and crossed knee, sitting atop Babelthuap Mountain. Under his gaze to the west lay *Tang* and *Trigger*, practically side by side and with hungry shark mouths. Back over his shoulder, a stream of small rabbits scampered through the unguarded Malakal Pass. In the usual enclosed cartoon caption, Bugs Bunny asked simply, "Watcha lookin' fer, bub?"

Fritz Harlfinger, rather boldly, had used the full-page sketch as a cover for his patrol report. It seemed to cover most of the points of my private conversation with Admiral Lockwood but insured a rather wider dissemination than might be appreciated. Quite obviously, the staff had failed to understand its full connotation, and Fraz and I laughed at the thought of their trying to retrieve the page from reports already in the mail.

3

It was late afternoon on June 22. Yaku Shima, one of the large islands of the chain, was still 30 miles distant on the navigator's chart. At 1706, still undetected on the voyage, *Tang* dived to close the Nansei Shoto submerged; we would make our surface passage after dark. Our regular submerged routine continued, watches changed, and the evening meal was served. Now in total darkness, but in an area we had thoroughly searched in the fading twilight, *Tang* surfaced for the transit. The submerged run had taken approximately three hours, for the time was 2000, and at this instant 142 megacycle radar buzzed our new APR-1. We would have to learn to treat its buzzes for what they really were, warnings of radar only, for the signal was intermittent, indicating a random training. It most likely came from Yaku Shima, which rises cone-shaped to 6,000 feet, and should *Tang* show on the enemy's screen we could expect a steady buzzing as the operator trained on us.

Remaining undetected, or at least not recognized as a submarine, was still on top priority. To this end, *Tang* was moving along inconspicuously at 8 knots, the speed of a trawler. Our security lay in the dark night, our new camouflage, and periodic searches with the SJ, which was never trained close to the bearing of Yaku Shima. Surely an island outfitted with a search radar would also have the relatively simple receivers to detect the radar of an enemy. Our cautions may have been excessive, but our quick SJ searches were covering the critical areas. Ahead lay Colonet Strait, chosen in part because it is relatively wide, but also because I had navigated *Wahoo* through this same passage 16 months earlier. Somewhat unfriendly, the dark, tall shapes of Yaku and Kuchino Shima loomed on our starboard and port bows. Fraz marked TBT bearings on their apparent high points, then went back to the conning tower to plot them.

"We're right on the line, Captain," came the report, not over the speakers, but from Fraz at my elbow. "Would you like the forward torpedo room to go ahead with the movies?"

It was a normal courtesy request in case the captain should care to attend, though I seldom did. This night I had no idea that they had been delayed.

"Well, they weren't held up, Captain, that is, by anyone's order. The troops just preferred waiting and listening to what's been going on."

That would mean with battle phones manned. The simple transit did not require that, but it could have. Our passage undetected might mean an early contact, and having brought *Tang* this far, I could understand the crew's desire to participate, frankly like my own here on the bridge.

The passage had followed an arc around Yaku Shima and now led between Kuchino Shima and shoal ground to starboard. The continued hours of darkness were welcome as *Tang* slid quietly on through the strait and out into the East China Sea. It was 2300, an hour before midnight, when the navigator recommended our course for Kusakaki Shima and the rendezvous with *Sealion*. The course was set, and below a Western was starting in the torpedo room.

"Radar contact bearing zero four zero degrees true!"

This was not going to be a night for sleep. During the hours from midnight to nearly 0200, we chased an elusive pip that finally faded into nothingness. Possibly it was a submarine, but more likely the radar echo from mountain peaks on the southwest coast of Kyushu. It delayed our meeting with *Sealion* until 0330, but she was waiting on the spot. Dawn was too close to do other than communicate by blinker gun to arrange for our patrolling in mutual support and for another meeting the following night.

Fraz needed no morning stars on this June 23. Barely into morning twilight, Dick cleared the bridge, sounded two blasts, and after the hatch was secured, dropped on down and took the dive. We would relax here southwest of Kusakaki Shima and let the enemy come to us. To the northeast of the island was *Sealion,* patrolling as she saw fit, but we had each agreed to call the other in should a contact be made. Patrolling submerged in what one would call an open-sea area was a new twist for *Tang,* for it approached the patrol procedures of 1941. Submarine tactics had broadened steadily in 1942 and 1943, however, and now with surface search, endarounds, and night surface attacks, our boats frequently took on the character of surface raiders with the ability to dive. Many times endorsements to patrol reports took such tactics for granted, overlooking from the quiet security of an office

desk that each tried and proven development still had its place, though often in conjunction with later innovations. The major factors dictating the tactics remained the nature of the enemy and of the area of operations.

The East China and Yellow seas held everything to be found in the open-ocean areas and the close-in Empire areas combined except one thing, deep water. Only in the region directly to the west of the Nansei Shoto and lower Kyushu was it possible to dive deep and evade below a temperature gradient. Elsewhere, our submarine would be fortunate to have 100-foot depth of water for attack and could not expect over 200 feet in which to hide. By the nature of the coastlines and the shipping routes, contacts might come at sea, with firing close inshore. Sometimes the reverse might be true, and over it all, air patrols, though infrequent, must be expected at any time.

These considerations did not mean that this was a particularly dangerous area or an undesirable one. They did call for hit-and-run tactics, speed in horizontal evasion, and above all, announcing our presence only with our torpedo explosions. Should the enemy so much as suspect *Tang*'s presence, he would route his shipping clear, for a hundred different tracks were available. There would be ships. Our boats had not patrolled here for nearly a year, possibly longer, for *Scorpion*, who had failed to return, may have been lost en route. Finding the enemy and sinking him was solely up to us.

The crew was enjoying a ropeyarn Sunday, taking care of the personal things that had been put aside during our voyage. They deserved some relaxation after the taut transit. Though we had sighted nothing, neither had *Tang* been detected. Continuing the vigilance hour after hour and on into days could be more wearing than when occasional tops came in view. Today, men who had been topside were getting the feel of the planes with others in their duty section. More of the crates of oranges stashed throughout the compartments were broken open, and a general feeling of well-being was evident. It even prevailed into the school of the boat, which was in progress in the forward engine room, and I listened to a short lecture on our Kleinschmidt stills. They were electric, with the salt water heated by an enormous coil area, shaped like inverted peach baskets one above the other. The whole chamber was kept under partial vacuum by electric pumps so the salt water boiled at a low temperature. The vapor, which was pumped out, condensed to fresh water. Each still was about twice the size of a 100-gallon drum, and the two of them satisfied the batteries and our ship's company, who enjoyed a shower a day. It was a far cry from the stringent restrictions on the use of fresh water that prevailed even into the war on submarines equipped with these same stills.

The rumble of distant explosions coming through the hull interrupted the school. The crack of the detonations was not audible on our sound gear or through the hull, so their source could be 50 or more miles away. Independently, our JK supersonic and JP sonic receiver operators placed the explosions to the east. Perhaps they knew *Sealion* was patrolling there. We crossed our fingers and went up to take a look. All was clear at 50 feet, and *Tang* planed up to the surface, ready to roll to a down-angle and disappear, like a whale taking a breath. The horizon and skies remained clear. With lookouts ready and a short shot of high-pressure air to main ballast for positive buoyancy, we scrambled to the bridge. One main engine took a suction down the conning tower hatch. In five minutes, with a fresh supply of air below and the horizon clear above, two blasts took us down.

There was some disagreement, but the average number of explosions counted was 12. They could be torpedoes and depth charges, or just the latter. Perhaps a salvo of *Sealion*'s torpedoes had hit and an enemy ship was on the bottom. We continued periodic high periscope searches, bringing the VHF antenna out for possible messages, but nothing stirred. Air searches out here at dusk seemed unlikely, so we surfaced early into evening twilight while the navigator still had a sharp horizon for his stars, and then the bridge speaker blared: "Hot Ultra from ComSubPac, Captain!"

I recognized Ballinger's concise wording as well as his voice. It called me below.

Dick and Mel had the tape from the coding machine waiting in the control room. Ballinger flipped on a white light over the chart table; all others were red. We ran the tape across the desk:

DAMAGED BATTLESHIP PROCEEDING FROM RYUKYUS
THROUGH NANSEI SHOTO THENCE TO KOBE OR SASEBO
NEXT THIRTY HOURS WEISS IN TINOSA POSITION
SUBMARINE TO INTERCEPT SASEBO PASSAGE

Four thousand miles and we still were not out from under the thumb, but this time no one would object. The Ultra gave the complete situation and designated a commander present, who had been told what was wanted *and not how to do it.* Twenty minutes later a coded message arrived from *Tinosa,* designating a rendezvous at Danjo Gunto. Three engines went on propulsion, the fourth with the auxiliary would struggle with the battery charge, and *Tang* headed northwest until Fraz and Jones could give us a more accurate course. It took but a minute, and we came to 320, a 5-degree change to the right. Hank had the deck; Mort and Fraz joined me in the wardroom, where Jones was waiting with the large-scale chart of the East China Sea. We had a 90-mile run to reach the rendezvous. That gave us plenty of time for our best judgment, but unfortunately, every mile was taking us away from the probable scene of action. Walker served hot coffee to sharpen our wheels, and doubtless also to get a good look at the chart, which we were marking up lightly with possible enemy tracks.

The Koshiki Islands quickly became a focal point. First shoals and then three nearly touching islands extend just over 30 miles to the southwest off the western coast of Kyushu. They thus form a triangular bay, with an entrance a little over 20 miles wide. The pass on to the north, six miles wide and 20 fathoms deep, was marked as dangerous to navigation, but surely the seafaring enemy would consider this passage a lesser hazard than the submarines that might be lurking in the deep waters to the west of the islands. To us, the answer seemed clear: One sub off Bono Misaki, on the coast, to send the contact report and then attack if the enemy was proceeding into the bay; the second boat ten miles west of the southern tip of the islands, to report if the enemy was going outside and then to attack; the third sub to move in north of the pass, also to send out a contact report before attacking.

By this disposition, as we viewed it with *Tang*'s method of operating, at least two, and very probably all three of us could get into attack. Jones copied down the coordinates for each submarine, and Fraz reached for them, already surmising that he was elected to attend the conference in *Tinosa.* As a bit of final argument, should that be necessary, I reached up to the bookcase behind me and brought down a volume of *Sailing Directions.* Specifics of navigational hazards for most any pass in the world are contained in this series, and the Koshiki Strait was no exception. It didn't read as if it were overhazardous to me.

"What are your instructions if Captain Weiss doesn't agree,

sir?" The possibility was certainly remote, but I was glad that Fraz had brought it up. Now was the time to be sure we were thinking alike.

"Just tell him that *Tang* will take any one of the three positions." Now that should mollify anybody. Fraz did not seem completely satisfied, but this was his ball to carry for *Tang*.

Danjo Gunto was still an hour away when the report of radar interference was relayed from the control room. It served as a beacon, and at 0115 on this dark night, Fraz and Gunner's Mate Rector paddled toward the indistinct shape of *Tinosa*. With them were ten movie programs, but more pertinent to the problem at hand were the infrared signaling apparatus and the code for coordinated attack that we had brought along for her.

Time always seemed to pass slowly whenever our rubber boat was out of sight at night. This night it was dragging; over an hour had passed and the conference was still going on. Surely someone would glance at the wardroom clock and realize that morning twilight would come in a couple of hours; reaching the Koshiki Islands undetected and in time to do any good would soon be impossible. What about the problem at hand was so complicated as to require this amount of time? My heart sank at the thought, and I found myself gritting my teeth only to see our yellow boat coming out of the darkness. Fraz, Rector, ten movie programs, and the boat were all pulled aboard in what seemed to be a single effort.

"Where to, Fraz?"

"The Koshiki Islands!" came out of the jumble on the forecastle, and *Tang* was off with a bone in her teeth, the maneuvering room telegraphs calling for flank speed. Not until Fraz had changed to dry clothes and joined us in the wardroom did I ask him about the details. It was enough that we were rolling in the right direction. Looking a little weary, he sat down to a cup of coffee, obviously waiting for my question.

"OK, Fraz, what's our spot?"

"Any one we want, Captain; we've got the islands and the straits all to ourselves," Fraz replied with the usual twinkle in his eye. "*Tinosa* and *Sealion* will be patrolling two lanes, thirty miles wide, to the west. Captain Weiss got pretty mad at my insistence, but finally told us to go to our 'goddamned islands.' "

I wondered if Fraz was just being kind and if Don Weiss's wrath had not really been directed at me. This had been a bit rough on him, but he had come back with what we wanted. It was just too bad the others weren't coming along, but they obviously had different ideas.

Morning twilight came early, and we continued east along the 32d parallel. Our course soon looked like a sine wave as we maneuvered to avoid sampans, which went about their business unaffected by the war. They were not really troublesome, but a small patrol coming south was. We pulled the plug to avoid detection. The hour was 0808, and now we would have difficulty in reaching the strait on time with any battery for a subsequent approach. The choice was not difficult; we could run all day at our present 6 knots and then take our chances on having an opportunity to charge.

Fraz had finished putting our dead reckoning positions on the chart up until evening twilight, when we could surface, and then had carried us on at 16 knots. That would put us off the northern end of the strait at 2200, too late to carry out our plan to catch the enemy still in the strait. However, by heading farther north, and with the SJ to search ahead, we could reach a position to attack any ship leaving the strait at dusk. We came left 20 degrees to 070. All hands tried to catch up on course books or qualification notebooks, and I pulled out a folder of officers' fitness reports. It was no use; our minds were on one thing, and that was as it should be. The informal plan of the day was changed to include a drill for our torpedo fire control party before lunch and then battle stations during the afternoon watch. This fitted in well with our submerged run, for the periodic slowing for periscope sweeps and then charging on again all added realism. There was one other innovation: Behind each of certain key men stood an understudy.

The run toward the coast was uninterrupted. Only a few variations from our course, to give sampans a little more berth, kept our track from being as straight as an arrow. Beam and quarter bearings on distant Fukue Shima to the north had confirmed our earlier position, and now we surfaced in evening twilight for a star fix and the race toward our selected position, 12 miles north of the strait. Two mains went on charge; the other two and auxiliary boosted *Tang* up to 17 knots. She was rolling with a purpose. Soon our track looked like a sidewinder's as we dodged lighted sampans clustered inshore of the 200-fathom curve. The lighted ones

were easy; the hazard lay in those few that had not hung out
lanterns. None appeared to notice us. A third main went on
propulsion as we passed the 100-fathom curve, verified by an
echo-sounding. The 50-fathom curve would come next, but
we could still dive in ten. *Tang* slowed to 5 knots. The time
was 2145 on June 24; the three-day-old moon had set, and we
eased ahead into the black night, waiting.

4

"Radar contact, bearing one five zero, range twenty thousand
yards!" It was Dick's excited voice coming over the bridge
speaker, but probably no more excited than would be anyone
else's. I had never been more certain of joining the enemy
than during these last 24 hours. The Japanese had to run
ships up this coast to Nagasaki or call it quits, and they had
given no indication of doing that. I was not counting on a
first contact within minutes of reaching station. With crossed
fingers, we waited for the range on the next quick SJ sweep.
The enemy would either be emerging from the strait, heading
our way, or entering it, heading south. The former seemed
likely, for even with *Sailing Directions*, entering the strait
could be tricky at night. Still, an enemy convoy could anchor
in the strait and make the safer daytime passage to the south.
If necessary, we could race around the outside of the islands
and greet the enemy at the wide southern mouth.

Considering these possibilities had taken but a minute or
two as we looked over the chart in the conning tower. Then
came Bergman's direct report: "A mess of ships, range still
twenty thousand!"

We pushed him aside momentarily for a firsthand look.
Bergman's description was as good as any for that jumble of
blops. No single pip stood out as would that of a battleship,
but never mind, there were ships and we'd take them as they
came. We were now stopped and had killed any headway so
that *Tang*'s motion would not enter into the tracking problem. Still the pips seemed to mill around aimlessly.

A contact report is supposed to tell what, how many, where, and what doing. Our coded report included only the five-letter group for the word "convoy" and groups giving the position. At least *Sealion* and *Tinosa* could head in at full speed while the situation developed. *Sealion* acknowledged at 2158, just 13 minutes after our SJ contact, but not a dot or dash came from *Tinosa*.

Tracking was now having some success, with courses varying from 270 to 315 and speeds between 10 and 16 knots. A part of the variation was probably due to enemy zigs, confused as the major ships and escorts gained station. It now seemed clear that our first contact had been on the ships as they emerged from the strait and were forming up. Had we kept the pips on the screen, the solution would hve been simplified, for then Bergman would have been able to give ranges on the same ship. Then, however, our SJ might have given us away. Using the SJ only intermittently was a compromise we had gladly made. The tentative course and speed were better than none, so radio fired them off to both boats, answering a query from *Tinosa* at the same time. The hour was 2220.

The convoy now seemed to be settling down on course 280 at 12 knots. Though perhaps this was just a long leg of its zigzag plan, we relayed the information again. The time was 2227, and *Tang* had done what she could to bring the other boats in. The task at hand now required our every thought and effort. The Bells of St. Mary's chimed in earnest for the first time since our aborted attack on the RO class submarine at Truk. This was pure business, and our business was sinking ships; we meant to do just that.

The composition of the convoy, which had remained confused by the smaller pips of numerous escorts and sides lobes of the radar, clarified with the decreasing range and a change of its base course to 340. This placed us in a fortunate position on its port bow as the fuzzy blurps took shape. "Christ!" exclaimed Jones to my left as the individual ships became distinct in our 7 × 50s. He spoke for both of us and probably the whole bridge watch, too. In front of us were six large ships in two columns; the leading ships were possibly large escorts. Between *Tang* and this main body were six escorts, forming a part of two circular screens, 12 escorts in all, extending completely around the large ships. It was a formidable array.

In the dark night, we moved in slowly, intent on sneaking

across the stern of the leading port escort. Jones and Leibold, as on our first patrol, were my second and third pairs of eyes, keeping track of the next nearest patrols to port and starboard. *Tang*'s bow was steady on the leading escort's stern, presenting our smallest silhouette. The escort's wake, still showing a phosphorescence, was close aboard. We would make it across a thousand yards astern, but in so doing *Tang* must cross the bow of the staggered inner screen patrol. Ships and people look ahead, where they are going; we eased out to try again where the inner screen might be out of position.

We paused a minute or two, a half mile from the second outer escort and a little abaft her beam, our course paralleling the enemy's. Fraz came to the bridge to see the situation firsthand, and perhaps by way of encouragement, for he reported everyone quiet and on their toes below. His hushed voice betrayed *Tang*'s mood. Fraz dropped below, and again we headed in, the converging course moving us laterally with respect to the convoy. It was the exact maneuver I had used so many times as an OOD in destroyers. The wake of the escort ahead boiled just off our bow; *Tang* was slicing through it, and again an inner patrol was blocking our path. Only in blind disdain would a captain think he could cross that bow undetected. I hated the enemy's guts, one has to if he's going to fight effectively, but I felt no contempt. We diverged again to the convoy's port flank, close to the quarter.

The opportunities for penetrating the screen and securing a near broadside track, one that would permit a split salvo against two ships, had gone by. But large tracks had worked for others, and we could make them work here. We maneuvered to pass astern of the last outer screen escort and to avoid the trailing inner patrol. If we were successful, our torpedoes could hit on a 150 track, still giving us a target of half the ship's length. For the third time we eased across an escort's wake. It wouldn't work; the inner screen patrol was exactly in position. Or would it! We should be able to see the trailing escort on the starboard flank.

"I've got her, Captain," said Boats. "She's well out there." Leibold ducked, and I looked out over his head, my 7 × 50s paralleling his. Thank God for young eyes; there was her low, sleek shape, but more distant than she should have been.

"All stop. Take the con, Mort."

I heard his "Aye, aye, sir," as I dropped down the hatch. A glance at the SJ confirmed my observation.

"Fraz, get me the difference in ranges to these two trailing escorts and call it up to the bridge." Caverly had the ranges as I was going up the hatch, and Fraz relayed the difference to me in person on the bridge, 2,300 yards. There was our slot!

Tang went ahead standard, changing course 30 degrees to the right, and slid across the stern of the convoy. With the trailing escorts on either bow, we resumed the convoy's course. A third engine went on the line.

I thought for a moment of an incident on patrol in the Solomons. The night had been similar, and a large freighter with a single escort had just gotten by. We surfaced to see her stern still looming up, and I urged my captain to go after her. The thought of his reply still made me boil: "Don't be stupid; a submarine can't attack from here!" My further remonstration would have resulted in an invitation to go to my stateroom. Now here I was in command with a much greater opportunity and a duty to put all that I had learned to test.

Tang was closing quietly but rapidly, the patrols now falling back on our port and starboard bows, as if they were backing down. Reluctantly, we slowed to 16 knots, just 4 knots above the convoy's speed. It meant that we would be in jeopardy for a longer period, for now we would pass between them at only the pace of a fast walk. Motion of an object, however, catches the eye when it might otherwise see only the black night. It was a fine point, one of judgment.

Jones was concentrating on the port patrol and would say nothing unless he saw her turn toward us. If the patrol continued on, she did not see us; that was axiomatic. Leibold was doing the same to starboard, while Caverly below was taking short keyed ranges, and those only when the navigator directed. Our patrols, now close and approaching broadside, had grown into destroyer escort size, with gun mounts fore and aft. At first alarming, their very height was encouraging, for if their lookouts were at bridge level, they could not possibly see *Tang* as a silhouette against the dark horizon; our background was the black sea. The ranges had closed to 1,500 and 1,700 yards; we were not quite in the middle, but we continued straight on our course, still overtaking by 4 knots.

"Our bow's inside their sterns." Fraz's voice coming over the speaker, was hushed but confident. It was well that one of us was shielded from the sight to port and starboard. It would not take much to spook us here on the bridge. We waited tensely.

"Bow's amidships."

We had an overlap. I wondered what quirk brought that sailing rule to mind at a time like this.

"Range abeam, eleven hundred port, thirteen hundred starboard!"

I knew Fraz's reports were, in part, meant to be reassuring, but they did little to ease the situation we saw topside. The next report, with ranges increasing, was almost jubilant, and very probably helped throughout the boat; but *Tang* was now working up to the escorts' bows, where for a short time, the likelihood of being sighted would be the greatest.

We had been in more taut situations, where the immediate danger was greater, but never before in one where all words had been in whispers for nearly two hours. Now the only sounds were the quiet rumblings of our diesels as we drew slowly ahead. Again the speaker, this time barking into the night: "Range two thousand!"

"Come up here, Fraz. This you've got to see!"

My invitation must have been unnecessary, for he was at my shoulder as I stopped speaking. I would like to have seen the expression on his face, but I knew what it was. Fraz, Mort, and I surveyed the situation, and I felt my shoulders relax, naturally.

Astern were sharp, tall silhouettes, menacing, but *Tang* was drawing away. On either flank the long, low outlines of escorts lay in encompassing arcs; those forward were barely visible, blending into the night. Dead ahead, in the center of it all, lay the great, fat sterns of the main body.

The task ahead would be less trying, but it would be more exacting. Mort took the con, and I dropped below for a glance at the chart with Fraz. Ogden's plotting was up to the minute, with our position and that of the main body marked with the time. The convoy had just passed Oniki Saki and would undoubtedly continue on another 25 miles, at least as far as Nagasaki. A finger of the 50-fathom curve lay ahead, but there was no immediate shoal water. We could attack from either flank and, should it become necessary, evade submerged. Our targets would be the two large ships in the port column, three torpedoes each, fired from forward, but all tubes would be ready.

Deciding on our plan of attack had taken but two or three minutes, and the first change was in order immediately. Jones had spotted a small patrol well out on our port bow, just about where we had intended to go. We eased off to starboard to attack the right-hand column from shoreward instead. The increasing swish and phosphorescence along our waterline accompanied *Tang*'s acceleration to 17 knots. Conveniently, the convoy steadied on course north and slowed to 10 knots, helping us gain position. The features of the two ships now in the near column were becoming distinct, and I called them down to control. The after ship was an engine-aft tanker or freighter with plumb cruiser stern; her two-deck after super-structure was topped by a modern, squat stack, and she had a conventional bridge structure forward. The leading ship was a large, modern, four-mast or goalpost freighter with high composite super-structure. Both appeared heavily laden and were most probably diesel-driven, as there was nary a wisp of smoke. I made no attempt to identify the partially obscured ships in the far column, for they were not our immediate targets. Control acknowledged the information, and the identification party would be searching ONI-208J for the probable ships.

"Make all tubes ready for firing." I took over the TBT from Mort and, just to be sure, marked a bearing on *Tang*'s bullnose. A pause and then came the call from the conning tower, "Zero zero zero. Right on."

"All tubes ready. We're ten degrees forward of their beam," advised Fraz. That was the word I wanted.

"Come left to two seven zero. Open outer doors forward. Slow to one-third when steady."

This time I would mark no bearings during the turn. The movement of the bridge rudder angle indicator caught my eye as the steersman met our swing. A glance at the dimly lighted gyro repeater, installed flush in the bridge cowl, showed us steady on, and I commenced marking bearings on the stern of the leading ship. There would be no undetected speed change this night, and Frank's course solution would be better than my estimate through an angle on the bow. I called none.

"Enemy course still zero zero zero, speed ten knots, Captain." Fraz's report made unnecessary my pending question. We had not forgotten our mistakes on the two-stack *Horai Maru* and were double-checking.

"Outer doors are open. Five degrees to go."

I could not speak for the ship's company, but with the moment we had worked months for only seconds away, I could hear my heart in my ears above the idling diesels. I marked another bearing to keep in the swing, as one might follow through on a bird, though not firing.

"Any time, Captain."

"Constant bearing—mark!" My wire was on the leading ship's after mast, the 7×50s now resting steady in their holder.

"Set!" came over the speaker. The counter stern was in the field, its after edge coming on the reticle.

"Fire!" The comforting shudder and zing came instantly. The next torpedo went to her stack amidships, the third to the tip of her bow, and we shifted targets.

"Constant bearing—mark!" The reticle was on the after superstructure.

"Set!" The squat stack crossed the field, about to touch the wire.

"Fire!" Again the heartening feel and sound of a torpedo on its way. The fifth and sixth torpedoes were sent to the forward edge of her after superstructure and to the tip of her bow, zinging on their way.

The tracks had worked out well, giving a longer torpedo run to the leading ship. Thus all torpedoes were under way well ahead of the first possible hit.

"Torpedo run one minute forty-eight seconds, Captain." The conning tower would keep us posted. At the moment we were turning to north again, now with four engines rumbling, ready to roll us into the clear. Evasion would have to wait on the hits and some minutes into the counterattack. In the inevitable confusion, we would find a route out of the area.

"Thirty seconds to go." Fraz joined us on the bridge, and now the times came over the speaker regularly. A whack, a flash, and a tremendous rumble came from the freighter's stern. Then from amidships, and her whole side seemed ripped out. The countdown was resumed only to be smothered in two more explosions. The second ship's stern was a mass of flames, and her superstructure aft crumbled with the second hit. More tremendous explosions and accompanying flashes followed, not timed as our torpedoes, and within minutes escorts were racing through the holocaust, dropping depth charges singly and in patterns. *Tang* was racing, too, for the nearest deep water. The closest escort at 1,400 yards did not see us and passed madly across our stern. We pulled up 5,000 yards from the attack and 7,000 from the projected position of the convoy. Only a great, low cloud of smoke marked the spot where the ships had joined Davy Jones's locker, their pips fading off the SJ's screen.

It was 0000, midnight, only seven minutes after firing our last torpedo, almost unbelievable! The torpedo reload had been ordered; Mort had the deck; Fraz was taking care of another contact report; and I was on my way to the forward torpedo room for a much delayed but necessary visit. Hank's reload crews were already at work, easing a new torpedo home. I could not help comparing their deliberate, unhurried performance to the frantic speed often required by peacetime exercises.

Walker had a cup of coffee waiting as I started aft. "How many'd we get, Captain?" he asked, perhaps having been commandeered by shipmates.

"Why, both of them, Walker. We saw them go," I answered between sips.

"I think there was more, sir," he replied respectfully. I pointed out that there were certainly a lot more explosions but that it would be pretty difficult for him to tell what was taking place from below.

"Oh, I wasn't down here. You were topside so long, I brought your coffee to the bridge. It was so exciting, I dropped your cup down into the superstructure," he added apologetically.

Leave it to Walker; he'd find a way to get in the act whether it involved a tussle with the enemy or getting a hold on a pair of bones.

Fraz had released the desired message to *Sealion* and *Tinosa*, telling them the convoy's position, estimated setup, and that we were trailing. Ensign Kroth had sent it on out without bothering me, and he was right.

It was 0020. There was radar interference to the southwest from one of the boats, probably *Sealion*, but it was so weak that we were sure she could not overtake any ships before they reached the haven of Nagasaki. *Tang* could, and with the torpedo gang completing their reloads, we started off after the one remaining decent-sized pip. Our approach was spurred by an escort, which closed rapidly, but our engine cylinders, which had loaded up with extra lube as we were idling along, now laid down a blue haze that obscured her completely. We presumed the reverse was also true, for she thought we had dived and commenced a depth-charge attack that must have been devastating to the fish. We felt a bit smug about it, but the loom of Nagasaki's lights, probably her shipyards, brought us back to reality. The depth-charge explosions or the escort's radio, perhaps both, had alerted the enemy.

The ship, which we had been closing steadily, suddenly showed zero speed on both plot and the TDC. The range of 7,000 yards became 5,000 and then suddenly 3,800. In minutes our combined range rate was over 40 knots, closing. We had barely time to complete a 90-degree turn when she passed 1,600 yards astern, a modern-looking destroyer escort. She spotted us and closed for a minute, but our team of overload experts forgot everything they had ever learned about mean effective pressures and kept pouring on the coal. The blotch of smoke we laid down would surely mark us as a smoky *maru*. But the enemy was still coming, big and tall, and *Tang* was much closer to the beach than we liked.

"Can we dive, Fraz?" I shouldn't have used that word; it's a wonder someone didn't sound two blasts.

"Not yet, unless we have to."

The DE was giving us a little port angle. She was heading for our blotch of smoke, not us. We eased off to port so we would get further on her bow. An inadvertent patch of smoke brought the DE on and through a repeat performance, but our log showed 22 knots, and each time she gave us an angle the range increased. *Tang* was out to 3,400 yards when her searchlights came on, illuminating the diving alarm for Mort. The sound heads were pulled in, but there was no crunch on diving. Our camouflage apparently worked in artificial light, too, for the enemy still had not spotted us and raced by madly echo-ranging. It had been a rough way to test a paint job, but its effectiveness would never be in doubt again. A quick sounding showed a couple of fathoms under our keel. The sound heads went down, and we moved toward deeper seas.

It was 0200 of another night to remember. Now with time to consider, it seemed that the shallow Nagasaki area would be very unhealthy at dawn, but a little over two hours away. The opinion was quite apparently shared by the whole ship's company, for lookouts were standing by in control, perhaps a subtle way for Ballinger to suggest that it was time to "get the hell out of here."

A search by sound, a single sweep by SJ, each showed our vicinity clear. Three blasts and high-pressure air such as we had never used before, and *Tang* hit the surface running. The turbos had us high and dry in minutes; four mains were delivering full power, and we headed southwest to round the Koshiki Islands. Off the wide southern entrance to the strait, the seas would be deep if not friendly.

5

Sleep was impossible. After reasonably fixing our position with quick SJ ranges on Kami Koshiki, and Shimo Koshiki to the south, the navigator joined Mort and me in the wardroom. This time we did not immediately reach for a cribbage board, for we were already played out by the action of the night.

"Well, they sure fell in our lap tonight," commented Fraz, quite effectively concealing the customary twinkle in his eye and directing his remark to our PCO. Mort sat back and contemplated a moment before saying a word. His usual broad smile came on slowly.

"If the object is to sink ships and avoid depth charges, then I guess this is all right, but I'd hate to think it was going to be my steady diet. I'll take a few depth charges out in deep water any old day."

Mort voiced my sentiment, especially at this moment, but a look at the chart of the Yellow Sea, where *Tang* would be patrolling within a few days, would tell anyone that shallow seas would be our lot. There were advantages to be had in any area, however, and for the time being we would capitalize on the opportunities offered here. Fraz called for the large-scale chart, so here at 0330 we figured on the best plan for patrolling the southern end of the strait. This immediate area held everything. Deep water right up to the promontories on the islands and the mainland would assure us of shots at any coastal shipping, while a submarine lying off the middle of the strait should be able to detect any shipping at night. In the main, we could revert to being a vessel of opportunity here, still do our job, and see if the ship's company, all of us, could get our heartbeats back to a normal 73.

Fraz and Jones were able to get a good round of morning

stars, so further playing of the SJ on the islands to fix our position became unnecessary. At 0500 this June 25, with light gray all around, *Tang* dived for the day. The passage close in to the southern tip of Shimo Koshiki was interesting, as were all close-up views of enemy land. We took pictures through the scope, more for the benefit of our camera buffs than for any reconnaissance consideration, and then moved out into the mouth of the strait. Occasional high periscope searches found clear seas, and the rumblings of distant depth charges indicated that enemy shipping might also be enjoying a day of contemplation. At 1900, however, while *Tang* was withdrawing prior to surfacing, Mel spotted a surface patrol. We avoided carefully, for if she reported the area clear after an all-night search, perhaps the enemy would try to run his merchant shipping tomorrow, during daylight. It could be some time, however, before he would run night shipping again. If this proved to be true, *Tang* would have accomplished a part of her mission, for that would reduce the movement of cargo essential to the war effort by half in this area.

This had been a day of comparative relaxation, but lest we let down our guard, I reached for the Night Order Book and penned special cautions. Then for the record I copied the data on the sinkings observed just before midnight on June 24:

Aobasan Maru class freighter	*7,500 tons*	Lat.	32° 30′ N.
		Long.	129° 35′ E.
Genyo Maru class tanker	*10,000 tons*	Lat.	32° 30′ N.
		Long.	129° 35′ E.

Identification with but oral details of the silhouettes could not be certain, of course, but these were the selections of our identification party. In the quiet of this day, I had compared them with other ships in ONI-208J and could find no fault with our men's choices.

Dick and Frank were in the wardroom. Before they donned their red masks prior to going on watch, I handed them the Night Order Book. Dick took it, as he would be going topside first, and I watched him study each sentence, then place his initials in the lined space before again reaching for his coffee cup. He was jolly, seemingly carefree, but when it came to his watch, Dick was all business. This night we would search well clear of the strait, probably sharing the area with the patrol boat of an hour earlier. There was room for both of us, just as long as we knew where she was and she did not detect us. Our periodic SJ searches would locate her handily. Frank and Dick would be followed by Hank and Mel, watch officers that would give any captain eight hours of calm assurance, but reports of increasing squalls, then the patrol, coupled with an alerted enemy just to the north prevented any solid sleep.

"Radar contact, bearing zero two zero true, range eight thousand."

The report was no louder than any of the others, but every word carried forward from the control room. It was apparently a matter of having my mind tuned as well as my ears. The clock above the doorway read 0424, minutes after the crack of dawn. Fraz would be on the bridge or in the conning tower. Answering bells from maneuvering followed by the slight list of turning to port told me that appropriate action had been taken; there was no reason to rush to the bridge. Over a cup of hot coffee, I realized that *Tang* could undoubtedly develop this contact, and sink it should it turn out to be a ship, without my participation. Fraz was, after all, designated as qualified for command, and I would certainly be losing him after another patrol or so. The thought was sobering and would require continued consideration.

Topside, off in the fog and rain, was a good ship, tracked as having just rounded Noma Misaki, a sharp point jutting out from Kyushu about seven miles into the strait. A glimpse confirmed that *Tang* was already on the enemy's starboard beam, and Ed had rightfully come to a diverging course to reduce the chance of our being sighted between squalls and in the increasing light. My only change in the action that Ed and Fraz had taken was to order, "All ahead full." We would start our end-around to the south immediately.

The light rain and fog hung in irregular scallops, for the most part obscuring the coast but giving us an occasional quick sighting of our enemy. She was a medium-sized mast-funnel-mast freighter with a split superstructure. Surprisingly, she was traveling alone, though hugging the coast for the protection of the shallow water. Already she had passed one danger point, Noma Misaki, but another, Bono Misaki, lay ten miles ahead. What urgency would call upon the Japanese to send this ship out thus, when our submarines were known to be in the vicinity? Did they think that we had been destroyed in the melee following our attack, or had *Sealion* and *Tinosa* been sighted elsewhere, leading the enemy to believe that this area was clear? In either case, we had no complaints, for with more than twice the freighter's speed, *Tang* had gained a position 7,000 yards ahead and but 1,000 off her present track. Less than 2,000 yards from the track on the other side lay Bono Misaki, so a good firing range was insured. Only by reversing course could the freighter avoid the attack.

"When we're all clear, take her down."

Ed acknowledged the order and gave Fraz and me a few extra seconds. Then came his "Clear the bridge! Clear the bridge!" and the two blasts, sounding topside and throughout the ship. I wondered if others were as calm at this moment as they looked. To me it was always a thrill to take a 1,500-ton ship charging below the seas. The lookouts were hitting the deck on below. Ogden whirled the wheel on the hatch by its swing-down handle, setting the dogs, as Ed kept the lanyard taut. The whole procedure was as fast as ever, but gone was a little of the slam-bang of earlier patrols. Perhaps *Tang* had come of age, and I approved.

The general alarm and "Battle stations!" substituted for reveille this June 26. The time was now 0521, just shy of an hour since the original contact. Fraz proceeded with ordering the torpedo tubes readied, four forward and all four aft, as I searched on the bearing where the freighter should break out of the mist and rain. The moments were anxious ones until Caverly reported the sound of heavy screws and then a propeller count of 110 turns. Jones guided the scope a few degrees to the left. There she was, still an indistinct shape, a little farther inshore than anticipated, and with a larger starboard angle.

"Down scope. All ahead standard." Frank adjusted the target dial on the TDC to the estimated new course. A five-minute run would close the enemy's new track. All hands were quiet; only the rush of the sea about our hull broke the silence. The minutes passed on Fraz's stopwatch, four, and now five.

"All stop." Ogden, on the wheel, called out speed from the Bendix log as we lost way, "Five knots . . . four knots." Another minute passed before *Tang* was down to 3, but sound bearings showed the freighter coming on as expected.

"Up scope. Bearing—mark!"

I flipped the handles up, and the scope went down. Jones read the bearing, and I called the angle, 35 starboard. Jones read the stadimeter range from the dial, now just above the periscope well, 3,200 yards.

"Right full rudder; all ahead two-thirds." It was proving to be a typical approach. We were turning in the direction of the freighter's advance until our stern tubes would bear, and would then fire four Mark 18-1 electric torpedoes. They were slower, 27 knots instead of the 46 knots of our steam torpedoes, but only the twist of a knob on the TDC was required to throw in the proper cam so they would take the correct lead angle. Of more importance, these torpedoes were wakeless, leaving no line of bubbles and smoke to alert the enemy or to mark the submarine's firing position.

"All ahead one-third. Open the outer doors aft." I could imagine the excitement in the after torpedo room. This was their first chance on this patrol. Two more setups for Frank followed, and then came Fraz's warning, "Ten degrees to go." That would be the firing bearing for the ideal track. I glanced at the depth gauge, then indicated the desired handle height. Jones brought the scope up smartly; I rode it up another foot.

"Constant bearing—mark!" Jones called it.

"Set!" from Frank. The freighter's stern was coming on the wire.

"Fire!" The shudder, the slight pressure rise, coinciding with a high-pitched whine, for the series type electric motors were up to speed instantly. The other three torpedoes followed, spread along the freighter's length from aft forward. She was a dead duck!

"Christ!" Two of the torpedoes had broached, porpoised twice, and then settled down on surface runs, throwing continuous plumes of water in the air, like the rooster tails of hydroplanes. The time of the 2,100-yard torpedo run was just over two minutes, ample for the enemy, who avoided all of the torpedoes by turning towards well inside their track. All of the exploders operated, detonating the warheads as they hit the beach, if that is any consolation to anyone.

After some random gunfire, the enemy took refuge in a cove just north of Bono Misaki. We commenced an investigation but found ourselves being set toward the beach, so we surfaced and made a full-power dash to the west, unobserved by our late-arriving patrol boat. A day checking the depth mechanisms of our remaining Mark 18-1s was in order, and the place to do this was in the peace and quiet below the surface of the seas. An hour's run seemed ample, especially since nothing had arrived in the skies. Here we had plenty of depth and were not completely withdrawn from possible activity. At 0740, still refraining from any profanity, at least within my earshot, *Tang* dived for the day.

"Sometimes it happens this way," said Mort as he finished his breakfast coffee. It was his turn, and his remarks were pointed at Fraz. We were all thinking, as the conversation soon disclosed, of the rash of torpedo troubles our boats had experienced earlier in the war. Then the failures lay mostly in the exploders, which sometimes had the startling habit of detonating as soon as they armed, 400 yards from the firing submarine. On other occasions, the magnetic feature would set off the exploder just as the torpedo entered the enemy ship's magnetic field, about 50 feet away from impact. It wasn't funny at the time, for not only did the enemy usually escape, but counterattack by any escorts was immediate; I knew, for *Wahoo* had experienced four prematures in this same area. Now as we looked back, we chuckled at the dismay the nearby explosions must have caused on the enemy's bridge. The conversation eased a bit our disappointment and frustration, directing our attention to the next real and serious task. The four remaining electric torpedoes must be made to work properly.

Tackling one torpedo at a time, all parts of the depth-keeping mechanism—the pendulum, hydrostatic diaphragm, the depth engine, the differential valve, and the small air flasks—were checked. When this was completed, each torpedo was suspended by a loading strap with chain fall, then swung and tilted, with gyros running, to check the operation of both horizontal and vertical rudders. With the exception of some stickiness, which was remedied by solvent and light oil, no faults were found, and for most of us, some faith in these torpedoes was restored. The task had taken all day, and we surfaced into another overcast night.

The hours of darkness were undisturbed, as were those of early morning. With improving visibility and then with lifting overcast, we dived at 0958 on June 27 for another day of submerged patrolling. The weather was now to the enemy's liking, for Larry reported a Betty searching just ten minutes after we submerged. At first it appeared that the plane might presage ship movements; but then the general nature of its search, not along any projected track, dispelled this hope. Probably several days would pass before ships ventured this way. Another Betty wandered about in the later afternoon, and then a "Pete" reconnaissance float plane just before sunset completed the enemy's activity for the day. Close to the end of evening twilight, we surfaced into a quiet night to conduct a surface search of our own. Trash and garbage went down in weighted sacks and sanitaries were blown with *Tang* heading upwind. In the middle of these operations, Hudson, the duty chief, called over the bridge speaker: "Ultra for action *Sealion, Tang,* and *Tinosa!*"

Mitsubishi F1M2 "Pete"

6

The message was not a true Ultra as we had come to know them, in that specific enemy ship movements were not mentioned. Instead, the dispatch contained the coordinates of an enemy shipping route. The ports—Shanghai to the west and

Shimonoseki, leading from the Tsushima Strait into the Inland Sea, to the east—were important, however. Ogden brought the chart, with dividers, pencils, and parallel rulers to the wardroom. Fraz went to work with the table as a chart desk.

Navigating unquestionably provides the best way of learning an area. The seriousness and responsibility connected with the work and the constant plotting imprint an almost permanent memory. The first set of coordinates that Fraz plotted rang a bell for me; the second pair confirmed my suspicion. This was turning out to be essentially the same route I had plotted when navigating *Wahoo* here some 15 months before, but that time my skipper had brought the coordinates aboard on a slip of paper just before our departure.

Tang was a long way from Pearl, so we could not be sure of the source of this information. But Japanese ship movement reports, and consequently Ultras, were nonexistent in these waters. Our guess was that the coordinates had been part of a fake message sent in the enemy's ship movement code. The ruse would lure our submarines to the area while enemy shipping avoided it. The period during which the three submarines were to work together was being prolonged, for the dispatch further directed Don Weiss to position us to intercept the enemy. As we saw it, the time for the three boats to fan out and find the enemy's ships was past due. There were probably 60 vessels or more, mostly unescorted, now at sea and ripe for torpedoes. Every wasted day gave the enemy an opportunity to shift more patrols to these seas and to bring ships home safely. To me, this was a perfect example of telling a commander how to do his job instead of properly spelling out what was wanted—and this from across the seas.

Another rendezvous was scheduled for Danjo Gunto which, translated, must mean "meeting place." Again Fraz paddled out into the night, but this time without instructions. He would play it by ear, for we had not yet been hurt by this dispatch. The meeting was relatively short, and Fraz was soon back aboard. With *Tang* heading northward, Fraz joined us in the wardroom. He was obviously waiting for my question, so I obliged.

"We've been banished," he said, but with a twinkle in his eye. Then he explained. Don Weiss had placed his *Tinosa* to the south of the reported shipping lane and *Sealion* to the north of it; he had assigned *Tang* the area commencing 40 miles north of the line.

"And the other boundaries?" I asked.

"Well, Captain Weiss didn't get around to that, and I didn't think we would want to bring it up."

Fraz was enjoying every minute of it, and well he might. As at San Diego, where the southern limits of our training area had been omitted, here the northern boundary had not been specified, nor the eastern and western for that matter. That should guarantee the contacts, and once the enemy was sighted hot pursuit had no limit. We had the whole Yellow Sea.

Our movement northward was slow and deliberate; we crossed the specified route submerged on the 28th and then proceeded northwest at one-engine speed after dark. Again we had one objective: To make our presence known only by our torpedo detonations. To this end, the small APR-1 radar detector was in constant use whenever *Tang* was surfaced. Hour after hour, one member of the radio watch cranked the dial up through its range of frequencies and then back down again. It was a monotonous task, rechecking static and spurious signals that our electrical machinery generated. When opportunity permitted, these were identified and logged, but every now and then the patience paid off. At 2000, Bergman detected a momentary noise that repeated and then developed into the short buzzes characteristic of a revolving radar. It was probably from Saishu To, sometimes called Quelpart, a great island with a 6,000-foot peak that lies 45 miles off the southern tip of Korea. Possibly the signal was coming from Mara To, a small island five miles closer to *Tang* at the moment. Fraz laid down a new track that left both islands farther on our starboard beam to insure that we would remain undetected or at least unrecognized.

The rituals that always followed cleaning up after the evening meal had been completed. Larry had reported us back on course after the short run to windward, and now the noises of a Western movie were drifting back from the forward torpedo room. For two-thirds of the ship's company, this could just as well have been a training cruise, remarkable when you consider that the chart in the crew's mess showed *Tang* about to enter the Yellow Sea, 4,600 miles from Pearl Harbor. It was a compliment to the duty section and a measure of our self-confidence and of our faith in our boat. Lest we forget for even a moment that the enemy was just as determined as we in *Tang* were, I again penned special cautions following the usual entries in the Night Order Book.

The course of 315 degrees true would take us between Kakyo To and Hen Sho, just off the southwest coast of Korea. The evening was interrupted only by the report of sampans and by our occasional maneuvers to avoid them. In the early morning hours, however, weak 95 megacycle radar on our APR-1 and an SJ contact near Kakyo To brought Fraz and me to the conning tower. It need not have, for the section tracking party determined that the contact was actually another one of the side lobes that plagued us from time to time. I did not object to having my sleep disturbed, for there had been doubt, and then especially I was to be called. For the real enemy, it was simpler: Head for him, head away, or dive. Happily, our APR-1 signal did not increase in intensity as we drew near the island, thus eliminating Kakyo To as the source of the radiation and assuring us that we remained undetected.

It was too late to turn in again, so Fraz and I brought *Tang* up close to Hen Sho, a small island in the middle of the pass. Here we dived at 0441, when a just semblance of gray was noticeable in the drizzle and overcast.

The 34th parallel of latitude divides the East China Sea and the Yellow Sea. Our position was ten miles north of this parallel and west of the myriad of islands that make up the true southern tip of Korea. From here we could intercept enemy shipping that followed either the general path of the parallel or the safer route winding through the islands. There could be an additional advantage, for if *Sealion* and *Tinosa,* patrolling to the south, were sighted, traffic might well be routed our way.

Daylight brought low, fast-moving fog patches, not bad in themselves, but the cold water, which was responsible for the fog, chilled our periscopes. Within a second or two after the lens broke surface into the moist summer air, it fogged over hopelessly. The watch was soon using both scopes alternately, one searching while the other dunked. This proved inefficient, almost impossible, so sound and periscopes were backed up with periodic SJ sweeps, with a generous amount of shears exposed momentarily.

The morning wore on, especially for the navigator, as our set and drift varied with each attempted fix. An occasional single ping sounding assured us that *Tang* was remaining outside the 30-fathom curve, however, and should be unhampered in any maneuvers. At 1140 the 1MC hummed in all compartments, presumably to announce, "Chow down!" but the words instead were, "Freighter to the north! Course west!"

The duty chief had preempted the 1MC to locate me aft. The announcement was really not a bad idea, for certainly the whole crew shared an equal interest in any bona fide ship contact. Not until Ogden raised the scope did I become aware that the drumstick I had snitched from the galley was still in my hand. Not too dignified, but I forgot about it when the enemy came into the field.

The scope was vibrating as *Tang* picked up speed, for Mort had already ordered a normal approach course and had gone ahead standard. The major details of the ship were discernible, however, a fine mast-funnel-mast freighter, but with approximately a 60-degree angle on the bow. The generated setup on the TDC checked closely with the observation, and Mort's initial action was the best we could do until tracking showed the freighter's course and speed.

Waiting between periscope exposures while closing the enemy could frequently be more trying than standing by for torpedoes to hit. Then only torpedo failures or an incorrect firing solution could save the enemy. But this freighter was still free and could escape to the islands with the aid of the rain and squalls. We needed to close her track, but most of all we had to maintain contact. A good ten-minute full-speed run was in order, but halfway through we stopped our screws to permit sound to take a bearing. Bergman flipped on the speaker, and the loud *wump-wump-wump* of the target's propeller filled the conning tower. We were closing, but the enemy was drawing left. I let *Tang* coast on down to 4 knots for a periscope observation. The standard procedure for an observation served only as good training, for though the freighter was nicely broad on our bow at 4,000 yards, we were on her port quarter. Overtaking torpedoes would barely reach, and hits would be most unlikely.

"Left twenty degrees rudder. All ahead standard."

A glance at the TDC while we were turning, then running a finger across the target dial and off on the inscribed ship's port bow gave our course. We called it the normal evasion course, one that would maintain the best bearing possible while *Tang* opened the range preparatory to a surface end-around. We settled on 235 and would slow only as necessary for a quick glance at the enemy.

Not long before, such courses were determined quickly, avoiding the delay of plotting, by using a multidialed calculator, resembling a circular slide rule and called an Is-Was. I had reluctantly put it aside as a standby, for even with electrical failure, Frank could crank in the correct picture on the TDC.

Increasing seas as we left the lee of the islands slowed the enemy but did not affect us submerged. *Tang* maintained the bearing on the freighter's quarter, actually gaining at times as the range increased.

"Lookouts to the conning tower. Stand by to surface, four engines." The order, which Fraz announced over the 1MC at my nod, still sent a tingle through my spine and probably that of every man aboard. Ahead lay a race and maneuver impossible to duplicate in other than submarine warfare, and one in which a fair portion of the ship's company could visually participate. Not since our first patrol had we been so involved, but this should be a relatively quick, concise action. Larry took the dive, and I called him up to the lower conning tower hatch for a word of catuion.

"We'll be surfacing into a heavy chop. Don't economize on the high-pressure air. Give her at least twice the normal blow." Machinist's Mate De Lapp, from the air manifold, had moved over below Larry. They were a good combination. How good I was to learn after the three blasts. The time was 1330, an hour and a half into the attack.

De Lapp didn't crack the high-pressure valves, he opened them, probably fulfilling a long-standing desire. This was the time, for we were rolling, working on up to full power on all mains without a moment lost. Only a short blow by the turbos had been required, for the high-pressure air had done a part of their work. Now the bridge was quiet except for the wind and the slap of heavy spray blown against the conning tower fairwater. We were not buffeted by the seas as was the freighter, but in working through them *Tang* took on a rather uncomfortable twist. It was soon forgotten in the excitement of keeping the enemy in sight and not at the same time disclosing ourselves to the freighter or to an ever possible air patrol. Fortunately, the remoteness of this area and the weather almost precluded air opposition.

We had anticipated passing the freighter on an arc at

maximum raised periscope range, but reducing visibility permitted a nearly straight course, and we relied on our crow's nest and the SJ to maintain contact. Occasionally an angle on the bow from a raised periscope would supplement the information for Frank.

We were not at battle stations, but one after another those men and officers with key billets took over. It soon seemed that every one felt that his was a key job, and viewing the problem at hand in its entirety, each was correct. An hour and a half had gone by since surfacing, and the freighter was now 15,000 yards abeam. We were on a parallel track and would now follow the courses recommended by the navigator to maintain the range at about seven and a half miles and put us dead ahead of the enemy.

On each glimpse of the freighter, a bit of information was supplied to our identification party. They had become less hesitant about asking for a specific detail when it was required to solve their puzzle. They had tentatively settled on the *Tazan Maru* and brought ONI-208J to the conning tower, open to the page. It was one of the extra things that could be done on an approach such as this and helped to make it exact. The length and masthead height would be used on the stadimeter.

At 1600 on the button, two blasts took us down dead ahead of the enemy. Frank had the freighter on base course 255 at 7 knots. The range was fine, 16,000 yards. Proceeding with the enemy would delay the attack, but there would be two advantages: She would be farther from any help, and our maneuvers for the desired bow shot would be simplified. With these considerations, we let her overtake us.

A stern chase was always long, and when waiting for an attack time seemed to drag. Another hour passed, but now the freighter was in constant view. It was tantalizing but not easy on the nerves, and I considered turning towards to get it over with. The enemy ship did her part, however, and at 1730 the Bells of St. Mary's chimed again. Compartments reported from forward to aft, and Fraz gave the order: "Make ready tubes three, four, five, six, and seven, eight, nine, and ten. Set all torpedoes to run on ten feet."

That should be enough torpedoes, four forward or four aft, to sink this freighter two times over, but we need not necessarily fire a full salvo. We had discussed the depth setting at some length, but with our experience of the surface runners in mind, and now with choppy seas that tended to make torpedoes broach, a ten-foot running depth seemed the minimum.

Our first maneuver was a dipsy doodle, a gradual turn off the track and then a sharp turn back, like a question mark laid out a little to the right ahead. It brought the bow tubes perpendicular to the enemy's track, insuring a bow shot. This was of some importance, for we would retain our ability to fire from forward or aft on later attacks if we did not use our electric torpedoes now. The enemy did not completely cooperate and zigged towards, requiring a repeat maneuver by *Tang*, but that was par.

Now with the angles I called and the ranges Jones read all checking closely with TDC, Fraz announced, "Five degrees to go."

"Stand by for constant bearings. Up scope." Jones brought it up smartly, all the way. The freighter had no chance of spotting our two feet of scope in this chop.

"Constant bearing—mark!"

"Set!"

"Fire!" Her mainmast had touched the wire, and our first torpedo zinged on its way. The second went to her foremast.

The range on firing was 1,250, the track 90; Fraz called the time of run, 47 seconds. I watched the smoky wake of each torpedo right to its point of aim. There were no explosions; they had passed under the enemy ship. The freighter turned menacingly towards, down the still visible wakes.

7

"All ahead standard. Left full rudder. Flood negative. Take her deep. Grab a sounding." I felt a little silly acting like we had a destroyer after us, but we would not be reattacking this alerted ship now, and besides, if you're not on the offensive, be on the defensive. *Tang* was now passing 200 feet, still 50 feet off the bottom, when quite unbelievably the freighter gave us two very close depth charges. The shoe was on the other foot; they weren't supposed to do that!

Caverly had shaken the depth charges out of his ears and donned his phones again; he reported the enemy's screws drawing away. We started back up, as a quarter of an hour had gone by. Larry approached periscope depth, and the scope was coming up to deck level, to my hands as I squatted for that first look. A shaking whack and rumble sent us back down to think this one over. There had been no planes, and we came to the conclusion that the detonation of a third charge had been delayed, perhaps intentionally with a time device, to keep us occupied while the freighter escaped. We returned to periscope depth, this time into the fading twilight. A sweep with the SJ, and *Tang* surfaced onto the Yellow Sea, all her own.

It shouldn't have happened. To bring torpedoes pushing on toward 5,000 miles, and to have six in a row, six out of our first 12 fail us. That wasn't quite fair; only four had been faulty, but the surface runners had spoiled two others. The thoughts took but a minute, a minute wasted. Our task was ahead.

"What was the last sound bearing, Caverly?"

Ogden read from the Quartermaster's Notebook, "Three five zero true, Captain."

That required notebook, with its thousands of entries, had saved ships from grounding, exonerated or convicted skippers when they had, and served as evidence in collisions, all of this beyond its everyday service to navigators. Now this single bearing could well be a million-dollar entry, spelling the death of an enemy ship.

"All ahead full. Come right to three five zero."

We would work on up to full power once we were rolling and the engine temperatures were normal. Fraz secured the crew from battle stations, and a belated chow was piped down for all hands. It was 2030 in a long, exciting, frustrating day, but this June 29 was not over, for we were heading down the last true bearing of the enemy, just as we had done time and again west of Saipan.

The odor of frying steaks was permeating the boat. Wixon had done it again, changing the menu without authority, or did Fraz have something to do with it? In either case, I would not complain, and one or both of them knew it. The steaks were the best, but the usual comaraderie was lacking. After the meal I found my molars still grinding and with Fraz, Dick, and Frank proceeded to take it out on a cribbage board.

Deep-running torpedoes were not new. At the start of hostilities, it had been assumed that our torpedoes, with warheads of about the same weight as our exercise heads, would keep the depth set. They ran too deep, and the magnetic field of many ships did not set off the exploders. While the bureaus fiddled, some submarine captains, including Mush Morton, commenced setting the torpedoes shallow, to explode on impact; then came the late prematures, drenching the enemy. By comparison, who were we to complain? Wasn't blaming the torpedoes now just the easy thing to do?

Hank and Mel joined us, having withdrawn two torpedoes to check the actual depth set on them. Hank was shaking his head slowly, contemplating his steak it would seem, but this was a habit of his when searching for the right words. In a moment he said it as it was.

"The depth set on both torpedoes is ten feet, Captain, and the depth mechanisms check out, too."

I thanked them for the report, and then Dick posed a question: "Could it have been a Q-ship, sir?"

The thought had certainly been entertained, especially after she counterattacked, but had been dismissed due to her length and clumsiness. Still, we should give her another look. Dick chased aft and returned with 208J, opened to page 215. Those of us who had observed her examined the four photographs and the draftsman's broadside drawing. The Q-ships, a class of five ships, had been built in America during 1918 and 1919 and had a loaded draft of 24 feet. But how much cargo would the Japanese be sending to China? Probably she carried only enough to give her good stability at sea. The unladen draft of these ships was only eight feet. There was our answer, for though not appearing particularly high out of the water, she might quite conceivably be drawing only ten or 12 feet. Our two torpedoes had probably scared the barnacles growing along her keel, for if they had run much deeper, the wakes would not have been visible right up to her side.

Knowing instead of fretting is half the battle. Hank and Mel went after their steaks, and we resumed our four-handed cribbage game. Dick cut a four, a poor card for all of us, and then the phone buzzed to my left. Hank picked it up and repeated the message: "Radar contact bearing zero zero zero."

The change of mood in the wardroom was immediate and most likely reflected that throughout the ship. There was no rush; we finished the game and then Frank accompanied me topside. The dark shape of the enemy was just visible out of the fuzzy horizon, made the more indistinct in the spume of the riled-up sea. Another half hour would pass before we would be able to make a positive identification, but there was little doubt that this was the same ship. Section tracking first had her on course north, then 040, and finally on 070, heading for Ko-To and the ten-fathom curve off the Korean coast. Cutting inside this arc shortened our chase, and *Tang*, now 7,000 yards on the enemy's beam, slowed to plan the attack.

A glance at the chart, and the ideal approach was obvious. In the lee of Daikokusan Gunto, we could set our torpedoes to run shallow without too much fear of their broaching, and an attack after moonset would let us move in to a range at which the enemy could not avoid them if they did. That was some hours away, and again someone had to be cool, calm, and collected.

"Fraz, stay with her here, about seven thousand yards abeam. At moonset, move to five thousand, thirty degrees on her starboard bow, and call me. Take Mort off the watch list for any help you may need, but remember, you're second in command on this boat."

Again Fraz accepted the responsibility with a ready "Aye, aye, sir."

There were really two other reasons for turning this intermediate task over to my executive officer, each based on my own experience. The first but not the more important involved a former skipper of mine who had a special bunk built in the conning tower. Every fish that gnashed its teeth, every spurious bit of static that showed as a possible pip on radar, brought him upright in his bunk. He was soon frazzled and getting the rest of us in about the same condition. Fraz and the tracking party could handle this phase just as well without me, probably better. The second reason was obvious: It had worked before, west of Saipan. I went to my cabin and kicked off my shoes. The only sounds were the seas beyond the ballast tanks.

"The moon has set, Captain." It was Walker with another

heavy coffee mug, which he had confiscated somewhere. It took a moment for the meaning of the report to sink in. All white lights had been turned off, so I needed no red mask. A quick turn forward, and I stopped at the wardroom for another cup before going topside.

"We going to get her this time, Captain?"

"That's right, Walker, one pickle right in her middle." For a moment I wondered what made me say that, then I recalled my thoughts before I had dozed off: a feeler torpedo and then a spread of four if that single shot didn't do the job. With this cup of coffee down, it made a lot of sense. An accurate shot into her middle, especially if she had great, drum-type Scotch boilers, would give an extra explosion, too.

The seas were still kicking up topside, and the enemy's navigation was a little off, the track passing 15 miles north of the islands. As firing from a lee would now be impossible, we would close to a range that would insure hits even with broaching torpedoes. Now, in a pitch-black night, Fraz had to point her out to me, for even with deep ruby-red lights below, a brief period topside was still required for maximum vision. She was there, exactly where we wanted her.

"Let's go to battle stations. I want five tubes ready forward and all four aft. Set all torpedoes to run at six feet. I'll take the con."

Fraz ducked below, and the melodious *bong, bong, bong* of the general alarm carried up to the bridge. In a minute all was quiet.

"Left twenty degrees rudder. Steady on course three four zero."

Tang was 2,500 yards from the track as we turned. The freighter's angle on the bow had opened to 40 starboard when we steadied and stopped 1,500 yards from her track. The seas and wind from aft carried us closer, and we backed two-thirds to kill some of our headway. It would be nearly impossible for her lookouts to spot us looking into this spume. TBT bearings went down on Frank's request; there was no reason for extra ones.

"Outer doors open. Ten degrees to go. Range seven fifty, speed nine, TDC angle seventy-three." Fraz was making doubly sure; it checked with what I observed.

"Constant bearing—mark!" She was coming on fast.

"Set!" Her stack was already in the field, coming on the luminous wire.

"Fire!" A slight jolt, and the torpedo's phosphorescent track was visible, as if skipping through the whitecaps.

"Torpedo run thirty seconds" came over the speaker.

The wake was heading for the freighter's bow but falling aft as she came on, now at her superstructure.

"Five seconds to go."

The wake led to her middle, right to her stack. The 500 pounds of torpex detonated with singular fury, instantly breaking the freighter's back. Her bow and stern sections tilted sharply toward one another under an incandescent cloud of fire, smoke, and steam.

Her gun crew had guts, however, for from her canting bow came a half dozen well-aimed rounds. How they pointed and trained their gun on that tilting platform will long remain a wonder, and their dedication in keeping up the fire until they went under would be a matter of pride to any nation.

Before going on below, I wrote the briefest of night orders and recorded the data on the enemy ship:

Tazan Maru class   *5,464 tons*   Lat.   35° 03' N.
                                          Long.   125° 08' E.

The time was 0130 of July 1, and we headed west for a submerged patrol after daylight and a day of rest.

8

Our dawn position, 40 miles west of Ko-To, lay halfway between the 40-fathom curves to the east and west. This was as good a depth for security as would be found and was also far enough from our attack to be immune from probable enemy countermeasures. *Tang* lolled on the surface with lookouts alert while Larry and his engineers completed the battery charge, then pulled the plug. It was 0540, an hour and a half after the crack of dawn, and the whole ship's company looked forward to a day of relative rest.

Rest we did until 0900, when Hank reported a sailing junk closing from the west. They are stately craft, at least in the eyes of those who have sailed, and perfectly suited, through evolution I suppose, for their tasks. Our leisurely attempts to avoid were unavailing, and rather than use up our battery, I succumbed to Mel's wishes. We would use the junk for pointer drill. It would be a sailor's holiday. *Tang* would not shoot her up, just bring her to and determine, if possible, whether she had passed any sizeable ships to the west. The compartments buzzed even though the troops knew this would be nothing like their shoot at Fais Island. Preparations for a battle surface were never completed more quickly.

Fraz explained our hold-down procedure to Larry, as this method was a holdover from peacetime and not taught in submarine school. To us, it was half the fun. Larry reviewed the steps with the planesmen and auxiliarymen who would be carrying out his orders and reported all in readiness. A somewhat belated "Battle stations—gun!" went out over the 1MC, followed by the general alarm lest someone might still be asleep. Then from a safe distance, well outside any possible small arms fire, we went through the procedure.

Larry kept *Tang* down admirably, first with safety tank dry and then at full speed, with a healthy blow to main ballast.

"Battle surface! Battle surface!" What Chinese word would describe the dismay of that junk's crew to see this monster rear up out of the deep?

Mel and the gun crew held pointer drill until the junk regained her courage, tautened the sheets, and commenced moving off quickly in spite of the calm following the previous day's blow. As prearranged, a half dozen well-placed shots close across her bow brought her to. When we closed, with the 4-inch gun trained on her middle, she doused her great battened sails, probably expecting the worst.

Our attempts to communicate were not proving too successful, though the junk's crew was trying to tell us something. But our crow's nest made further "talk-talk" unnecessary, with a salty "Smoke ho!"

A shower of canned goods that had become wet and lost their labels sailed over to the junk as a parting gift, and *Tang* continued her day of rest by closing the real enemy. It was 1015. The single puff of smoke soon developed into two columns of it, and as we worked up to full power the masts of two ships came over the raised periscope's more distant horizon. *Tang* was on the quarter of this two-ship convoy, now tracked by Ed and the watch section as steaming on course 260. We must have been living right, for had we not surfaced to query the junk, these ships would never have been sighted.

No end-around was routine, but this I believe would be singular in submarines. *Tang* was not called to battle stations; rather, the duty sections were conducting the maneuver, which otherwise would have been trying on all hands. Of course, direction came from Fraz, Mort, or me, another advantage of having a PCO along. It brought to mind some of my patrols in other boats, when battle stations were manned for hours, one time for 12 hours straight, quite unnecessarily. We had come a long way, and perhaps so had this war toward its inevitable conclusion.

High periscope observations could not identify the ships, for just their tops remained in view. The maneuvers of the leader marked her as an escort, however. The second ship, plotted a thousand yards astern, zigged at intervals of from three to 12 minutes, quite orderly, like an unalerted freighter. Only an air patrol could prevent our gaining the desired position, and even then the planes would have to spot us first. To guard against this possibility, two lookouts manned our front porch. We could take as much time as necessary, for the whole Yellow Sea was our battleground. Still, it would be to our advantage to attack before antisubmarine forces could sweep this way.

Though we were following the circumference of a moving circle, making our path a great arc, our 14-knot speed differential was easing *Tang* around the enemy. Three hours had now passed, and the convoy's tops were back on our starboard quarter, nearly in line. The extra lookouts went below, and then on cue came Mel's "Clear the bridge!" and the *blaat, blaat* of the diving alarm. Aft in the conning tower, I heard the reassuring thud of the engine-air and main induction valves as they closed. It called attention to the many unseen men and functions connected with the dive. Now, with negative blown to the mark, Mel was leveling us off at 60 feet. Our trim would not have changed, so one-third speed was ordered immediately. The time was 1322, and we were on the convoy's base course.

There would be personnel changes in several key battle stations this day. The night before, *Tang* had completed the firing of one half of her torpedoes, actually one more, 13 out of the 24. Certain key men had already been designated to schools, staff or new construction, choices of their own. Starting now, they would change places with their understudies, who had stood behind them on this patrol, and would enter into their former tasks only to avoid mistakes. The object was simple; *Tang* would start her next patrol with these key billets staffed by men who had manned them through half a patrol, through the firing, we hoped, of 11 warshots into the enemy.

I believed that the ordered transfer of too many officers and key rates from *Argonaut* and *Wahoo* upon their return to Mare Island had been a contributing factor to their subsequent loss. Like other boats, they had held on to their most important men for as long as possible and then lost them all at once, close to a quarter of their complement. Training our own replacements on the job would permit an orderly turnover and prevent any such raid on *Tang*. Making this possible, of course, were the extra hands we now carried, for otherwise the exchanges could result in musical chairs, affecting billet after billet. This next hour, and possibly the hours to come, might tell if *Tang* had reached a top fighting level that she could maintain on successive patrols.

The enemy came on, zigging mildly and still tracked at a steady 8 knots. Fraz pressed down the short handle on the conning tower's remote control of the 1MC. His "Battle stations! Battle stations!" went throughout the ship. At a nod, the steersman swung the handle of the general alarm, and once again the bonging commenced. This would be the third time we had manned battle stations in two days, fourth if we counted the junk. The actions that followed the first two had nothing in common. Now again, a different set of circumstances might require a whole new bag of tricks.

"Up scope. Bearing—mark!" Jones read 358 as he lowered the scope.

"That's on the large freighter; all setups will be on her unless I change targets. Her angle is not more than five degrees port.

"Fraz, the smaller ship is about fifteen hundred yards closer, on the freighter's port bow. I'll keep you informed separately, and will you keep her on your plot. I'd like two tubes ready forward and aft."

That was one of the beauties of the navigational plot; it was not limited to a single target ship as was the TDC. For the present, we would do nothing but let the enemy come on until the decks came over the horizon. Five minutes passed. With our combined speed as we headed for one another, the enemy would be 3,000 yards closer.

"Up scope. Bearing—mark!" Again Jones read the bearing, this time 350, and I called the angle, 8 port, then stepped over to the chart desk, where Ogden was plotting under Fraz's general supervision. With a finger, I showed the new path of the small freighter, which had zigged and was crossing to the large freighter's other bow. No words were necessary as Ogden drew in the track.

Observations every four to six minutes followed. The convoy was continuing to zig mildly, and ploy showed that its base course would carry it nearly through our position. The range closed, bringing their decks in full view. The small freighter mounted a good-sized gun on a raised bow platform. The bridge, stack, and superstructure were all aft, but of greater interest was a fairly long, sloping, loaded depth-charge rack. We could presume that there was another one aft to starboard.

The attack we would like was perfectly clear, a salvo into each of them, but that required the cooperation of the enemy. Our plans must remain flexible and encompass several considerations: Electric, wakeless torpedoes would not be sighted and, being slower, would allow us an extra minute or so for maneuvering to attack the second ship. Should the salvo at the first ship miss, the second attack could still proceed. If the first ship was hit and the attack on the second failed, we would still have the rest of the day and part of the night to do the second job over again, assuming that any hit would take care of the escort.

The ships' respective tracks were not sufficiently separated to permit firing from between them. To withdraw to one flank would mean abandoning an assured position for at least one attack, because both ships could zig away. We would stay underfoot, maneuvering for a stern, electric torpedo attack on the escort, and then play catch as catch can with the big fellow.

The convoy came on with a small change in base course. Moderate maneuvers put us ahead again, but the escort's patrolling increased. Seldom did she appear on the freighter's same bow on consecutive periscope observations. With broader angles, disclosing more details, the identification party pegged our ships. The escort was of the *Amakasu Maru* class, though probably of the 1940 series, as the pictures showed the bridge forward. The important things for the moment were her length, 270 feet, and the minimum draft of seven feet. The larger freighter looked similar to the *Samarang*

Maru, 357 feet long and drawing a minimum of nine feet. Fraz stepped off the masthead heights from the drawings; we would use the figures of length and height on the periscope stadimeter.

The group was getting close, and there was a great temptation to switch targets, to feed information on the escort to the TDC. It could lead only to confusion, I knew, for her irregular patrolling was superimposed on the large freighter's zigs. Our fire control party would then be trying to solve ahead for unknowns, isntead of detecting a change in the base course or speed. The true plot would suffice for the moment, but the moments were becoming few. I took another setup on the freighter.

"Up scope. Bearing—mark! Range—mark!"

Jones read the bearing, 348, and then the stadimeter as I had left it, with superimposed images. I then gave the angle, it was easy, zero!

"Right full rudder. All ahead two-thirds. We'll be going ahead full, Larry. Take her down to eighty feet."

Zero angles are not always bad, and this one on the freighter practically guaranteed an attack on her escort, now proceeding to the freighter's starboard bow. We had ample time to bring our stern tubes to bear, less time for solving accurately the escort's course and speed.

"All ahead full."

The Yellow Sea swished outside the conning tower, but no turbulence would reach the surface. Fraz announced the recommended course.

"Rudder amidships. Steady on one five zero. One-third speed. Sixty-five feet." *Tang* slowed quickly, not having gained full headway during the turn. The steersman reported steady on our new course and then our speed at 3 knots.

"This setup will be on the escort." Fraz provided the bearing, relayed from sound, and Jones guided the scope, now just breaking the surface.

"Bearing—mark! Range—mark! Angle—mark!"

Routinely, Jones read the bearing and range, but waited until I had given my estimate, 40 port, before reading the angle on the stadimeter. It was our way to insure that I was not influenced by the mechanical stadimeter reading.

"Caverly, grab an echo range."

He trained ahead of the screws so the ping would fall amidships on the escort. "Eighteen fifty," he reported, and then joined in three more setups, with just the accurate echo ranges and the periscope bearings.

"Checks good with escort speed ten knots," Frank reported.

That would be about right, allowing for the extra speed required for patrolling. A quick sweep showed our big freighter right back there, still with a fairly sharp angle.

"Ten degrees to go, Captain. The outer doors are open aft."

"Keep the sound bearings coming."

"Two one five . . . two one three . . . two one zero. . . ." The escort seemed to be creeping across our stern.

"Up scope."

"Constant bearing—mark!" Jones read 206.

"Set!" from Frank. Her stack aft came on.

"Fire!" Fraz hit the plunger, sending that torpedo on its way with a whine. The second torpedo went to the foremast, whining away from us.

"Down scope. All ahead standard." We had to open the distance from the big freighter's track. Fraz called out the time of the torpedo run for the 1,250 yards—90 seconds— and Jones commenced calling them off. Time crept as these slow, 27-knot torpedoes churned on their way. We slowed to one-third speed. Five seconds to go, four, three, two, one and then zero. Time had run out. With an oath on my lips, I managed to change the words to "Up scope." We would attack the big freighter. *WHACK!* The still pending profanity was jammed down my throat. I swung the scope to see the escort's whole stern in the air, then back to find our big freighter already turning away. A shot on the fly would have little chance. Dear God, another night of it!

9

Ballinger had four men standing by, and they manned the scope for a moment each. It was the best way for the troops to get the picture of the final results. No embellishments would be needed. The escort's severed stern had gone down immediately, and now two minutes and 20 seconds after the torpedo's detonation, the tip of her bow disappeared in the frothy boil of the sea. We searched carefully through the area, but there were no survivors, probably because of the detonated explosives aboard her.

A glance at the chart showed that the larger freighter was very probably caught between third base and home, for she was approximately 100 miles from the Korean coast. Should her track veer at all to the south, it would lead to *Sealion* and *Tinosa,* perhaps between them. As agreed, we were obligated to send a contact report, but we would have done that anyway. Dick prepared the message, but it would have to wait, for the enemy was still close and we did not wish to tip our hand.

Tang's batteries still showed nearly a full charge, for our submerged running and speed had been minimal during the approach and attack. Now we were trailing the freighter at 6 knots, which we could maintain handily until dark and still have enough juice left for a possible submerged attack.

The freighter pulled away steadily, with an estimated speed differential of 5 knots. At least the book said her top speed was 11, and under the circumstances she would hardly make less. The time for the next hourly contact schedule with *Tinosa* and *Sealion* was coming up, and with the freighter still in view on the horizon, I was hesitant about surfacing to send a contact report. The freighter had certainly stationed lookouts, just as had the naval tanker, and they would be searching westward, where *Tang* would be a silhouette. As a compromise, Hank brought us up to SJ depth and then eased *Tang* skyward till the lead to our flat antenna would drain free of salt water. Radio was ready, and Bergman keyed the message through twice, blind. There was no receipt, and Hank eased *Tang* down again, surely unsighted by the freighter's lookouts now peering through her smoke.

Dick had the con and with volunteers waiting in control manned the scopes continuously. Vibrations at our speed made searching difficult, but they were looking for only two things, a change of course by the enemy and the air patrol that would surely search down the freighter's wake. No planes arrived, and the enemy continued on a straight course for the coast. We wondered about this ship, for she seemed to be a Japanese version of our Hog Island freighters, which had been designed to carry Allied supplies during World War I. They had eventually been sold for scrap, mainly to the Japanese, who ran or towed them to the Far East. It seemed that out of each four they had put together three operating ships. Since the start of the war, they had been absorbing our torpedoes, though most of those in this China trade had gone free.

The submerged chase would last another three hours. Leaving explicit instructions to call me if sight of both freighter and smoke was lost, I went below for a turn through the boat. My thoughts on the coming night reflected, in part, my concern for some of our men, principally the new hands. They had not been thrown into this sort of thing before, especially two day and night attacks back to back. It was different with Fraz, Ballinger, Hank, and others, for we had done this before and were somewhat calloused. We had learned to take these dangers in stride and would probably be more hesitant if suddenly faced with boarding the shuttle at Times Square. The turn did me good, not just in stretching my legs, but in exchanging a few words here and there with the crew about our attacks and late successes. The men's determination bolstered my own, and their confidence was brought home sharply in the crew's mess. On their chart, the track of the enemy had been carried almost to the coast, where it ended in a large black X. I had the message.

At sunset, the enemy was marked by a great, low funnel of smoke, hanging above the horizon due to the mild following wind. It brought to mind a distant tornado and well might be a prophecy for this night. We were unhurried and waited for dusk, when the last chance of air cover would have vanished. Lookouts were standing by, and De Lapp gave us a healthy blow, bringing the decks clear. The turbos started and so did all mains, three working up to their full power rating while the other with auxiliary went on charge.

I marked a bearing on the middle of the black cloud ahead. "Zero seven eight, Captain," came over the speaker. "Make it so." *Tang* was rolling on the enemy's tail.

The tail was a long one, for the freighter had conjured over 11 knots from her coal-burning power plant. Our 18 knots was steadily closing the gap, but too slowly when I glanced at the chart and considered the arc *Tang* must follow to avoid detection. In the 30 minutes since we had surfaced, that one main had jammed her full output into the can. Now the future would have to take care of itself; we needed that other diesel on propulsion. She pulled her weight like a Belgian, removing any overload on the others.

The moon that had set at 0020 the night before would be up another 50 minutes, until after 0100. That meant our night would remain fairly bright even up to midnight. I looked at the chart again and then raised the scope to be sure. To the south, the horizon was quite distinct; so also would be the silhouette of a ship, especially a close one. I would not prolong this until moonset but would dive in the first good lee for a submerged attack.

We were now using the SJ freely. The accurate tracking and navigation showed that *Tang* would have to pass the enemy ship up moon and to the south of Ko-To to insure against losing her in the islands to the east. Full power and extra turns just shy of smoking had *Tang* waiting with about three minutes to spare as the enemy approached the southern tip of the island.

It was 2224 when we dived a mile and a half off Ko-To and 1,200 yards north of the enemy's track. As soon as Dick leveled *Tang* off, the Bells of St. Mary's were sounded for the third time this day, still July 1. Manning stations and preparations were more rushed than previously, for the enemy was only 6,000 yards away and closing at nearly 400 yards per minute. Stations reported and tubes were readied, four forward and two aft, as the freighter passed the southern tip of the island. Suddenly my periscope bearings failed to keep pace with the TDC. Three echo ranges by Caverly, coinciding with three periscope bearings, put the TDC back on; the enemy had slowed to 9 knots, probably taking a deep breath at reaching the apparent protection of the island.

Tang was already closing the track for a straight bow shot. "Fifteen degrees to go. Outer doors are open." Fraz had allowed an extra 5 degrees for a rapid bearing change.

"Ten degrees."

I was following the freighter's stack continuously, Jones calling the bearings.

"Five degrees."

"Constant bearing—mark!"

"Set!" from Frank. Her after well deck came on the wire.

"Fire!" Torpedo sounds were in the background, but there was no time to contemplate. The next torpedo went to her well deck forward.

"Both hot, straight, and normal," reported Caverly.

"What's the time of the run?"

Frank called the firing range, 500 yards; Fraz was interpolating out loud for the torpedo run of 460 when a frightening whack and explosion shook us. It shook the enemy far worse, apparently setting off a cargo of munitions. A short section of the bow was all that remained as Fraz bowled me off the scope and watched it go, timed by Ogden in another 20 seconds. Our second torpedo was in there somewhere adding to the destruction or had been robbed.

Four minutes after the torpedoes were fired, *Tang* was on the surface poking around in the debris. Again there could have been no survivors; we would have seen them in the moonlight. Somewhat awed by the finality of the attack, we rounded Ko-To and proceeded northwest, toward a position 60 miles out into the Yellow Sea for our usual patrol.

10

It had been a classic approach and attack, ending with a firing range to our liking. There were submariners who frowned at getting so close underfoot, where an enemy zig in the closing minutes could drive a submarine down. By and large, they were not the ones who sank many ships, though in certain places there could be advantages in staying on the flank. Here in the Yellow Sea, if a submarine was driven down before firing, there was a good chance of being able to make the approach all over again. If not, she still had her torpedoes and could find another target.

These things, of course, made up the general conversation in the wardroom and probably aft in the crew's mess, too. Fraz had laid down our track, a straight line, and joined us. His quick apology for grabbing the scope was unnecessary. I really should have handed it to him when the last torpedo was on its way; he rated the gesture, though there had been quite a bit going on at the moment. Fraz was in the middle of the conversation in a minute. I listened and approved, even of a jibe or two directed at Mort. *Tang* was clicking and Mort knew it, for he had participated in everything that had taken place. How could anybody aboard feel other than satisfaction at the way this patrol was now developing? Five ships down and we still had five steam torpedoes plus two electrics waiting for targets.

To an observer, our operations this day might have looked routine, even simple. Finding and sinking a freighter and a converted escort with the odds stacked against them was no great feat. But he would be forgetting that *Tang* had secretly rolled 5,000 miles to get here, and that every one of a thousand mechanical devices had operated properly. To our ship's company, today's success meant that every man had performed his task without error. To Fraz and me it meant one thing more. We had changed horses in the middle of the stream; the recent understudies had performed admirably, and we would stay on top of the enemy regardless of personnel transfers.

Dawn was coming earlier as we worked north. After Fraz and Jones had taken a round of stars, more to keep their hand in than for any immediately required exact navigation, *Tang* dived for the day, and we made it another ropeyarn Sunday. Masts of two trawlers poked over the horizon at midmorning, but no one suggested surfacing to look them over. Perhaps we were not ready for what might be beyond. Before lunch, Mel reported that they had gone below the horizon of our raised periscope. They had gone their way, and we had gone ours, but sighting fishermen rang a bell. The Fourth of July was but two days away, and I checked the menu, which I had signed too casually. Fraz and Wixon had not let me down. There in New England tradition was salmon and peas for the 4th. Of course, it was actually salmon loaf, but one can't have everything.

At my desk I penned careful night orders, for it was at a time like this, following prolonged action, that we could unconsciously let down our guard. Then on the preceding page I recorded the ships we had just sunk, together with their positions:

Amakasu Maru class	2,000 *tons*	*Lat.*	34° 37′ N.
		Long.	123° 46′ E.
Samarang Maru class	4,000 *tons*	*Lat.*	34° 38′ N.
		Long.	125° 12′ E.

That would not only be a matter of record but would also give the oncoming OODs and duty chiefs something to think about.

July 3 passed quietly. Men broke out their course books and worked on their qualification, making up for the days their studies had been set aside. Such effort was another of the reasons for carrying replacements. A new rate and qualification were keys to a new billet, which would not necessarily be open in *Tang*. Some men would stay, and others might be looking for milder assignments. With men ashore waiting for the chance to come aboard, Fraz could comply with most requests for transfers, but *Tang*'s requirements came first. Once we had begun patrolling such requests had leveled off, however.

Upon surfacing at dusk, *Tang* headed northeast for a rendezvous with *Sealion*. Her radar signal appeared on our SJ at 2200, and just 50 minutes later Fraz and his bow hook were paddling out into the Yellow Sea toward our friend. She was barely visible at 500 yards, even under a bright moon, but our yellow life raft stood out plainly. The fact that I kept my 7 × 50s glued on the raft may have been in part responsible for its apparent visibility.

Fraz was to deliver an oral invitation for Eli Reich and his *Sealion* to accompany us counterclockwise around the Yellow Sea. We would operate independently but in mutual support, and I would guarantee targets for *Sealion*. The rubber boat also carried ten movie programs, a second reason for the meeting. An hour passed before the lifeboat returned, and willing hands snaked Fraz aboard and out of the way so the flat film tins could be struck below. Fortunately, *Sealion* had not exchanged movies with *Tinosa*, so we did not get our original films back, but the troops felt that even those would be better than the ones they had just seen. Now with this consideration all squared away, I ducked below to speak with Fraz.

Mort and I were having a cup of coffee when Fraz, in clean, dry clothes, joined us. I shivered as I remembered what the temperatures had been when I was here in *Wahoo* in March, 1943; exchanging visits between submarines would have been virtually impossible. But *Wahoo* had had the area all to herself back then. Eli Reich had decided not to bring *Sealion* north with us but to head directly for the Shanghai area instead. I could not blame him. Having operated closely with Don Weiss's *Tinosa* while we were more or less banished, he had been somewhat restricted and obviously would now want to go it alone. Eli was familiar with that area, having served on the China Station before the war and, as I remember, after hostilities commenced. Fraz had further discerned that both *Sealion* and *Tinosa* had indeed patrolled on the surface with SDs on and had been driven down frequently. *Sealion* had sunk her first ship of the patrol while en route to this rendezvous. Fraz withheld nothing about our method of operation, so they could try it for whatever it was worth. There would be one thing lacking, of course, for we would not be patrolling in a manner that would cause the enemy to reroute his shipping past someone else, as had the other two boats. Our normal patrol would continue to be submerged with high periscope looks during daylight.

By blinker gun, we sent *Sealion* a Godspeed and good hunting, then set course for a position we had previously selected. It lay on the direct route between Daikokusan Gunto and Osei To, close to the Korean coast. The time was 0005 of July 4, and three engines were pushing us up to 18 knots for the race to the passes, a race against dawn.

The assurance I had sent to Eli was not an idle invitation. When the East China and Yellow seas had been stirred up in March of 1943, the shipping seemed to vanish. *Wahoo* found it skirting the coast from the Shantung Promontory, north past Port Arthur–Dairen, on east though Gaichosan Retto, down the Korean coast, around Choppeki Point, and south through the inshore areas *Tang* had just patrolled. *Tang* was working counterclockwise along this track for a reason. The Japanese might hold up shipping scheduled for China until adequate escorts were assembled, but the ships already at sea or those returning from China would have to make it on their own. That meant traveling the long way around, and *Tang* intended to meet them, not follow them.

Opportunities to copy or even read the press news had been limited. But while *Tang*, one ship in one of our smallest forces, was busily occupied, grand operations had been under way. Piecing together the sketchy one- or two-line press reports gave us a fair knowledge of the progress. Normandy's beachheads were secure, with Allied forces now cutting off the Cherbourg Peninsula, and Cherbourg itself, bombarded from the sea, was perhaps about to be liberated. Closer to us, Saipan had been taken except for stubborn resistance at the very northern end. And closer still, the Battle of the Philip-

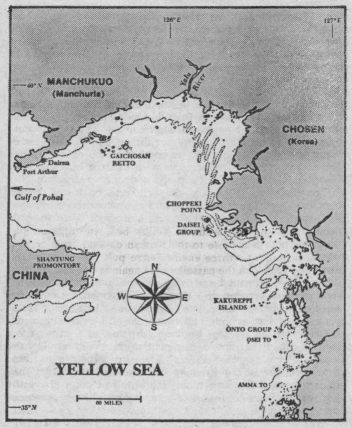

pine Sea had been successfully waged. We would have to wait for *Time* and *Life* to find out what had really transpired, but in the meantime excitement was not lacking.

Hank reported increasing clouds at 0230 and a sounding of 30 fathoms. The clouds could be a characteristic when approaching this coast, but our landfall would not be made until after daylight, while moving in submerged. Minor changes in weather would not be of great importance, therefore. A further report of complete overcast at dawn was significant; with sharp lookouts, we could now continue on the surface, at least for a time. Fraz came below, without stars, and apprised me of the latest situation, fair to good visibility but with a very low ceiling. I joined him for coffee, as we still had some plans to discuss for the day. Our planning was interrupted by answering bells from maneuvering .We listened.

"Ship bearing zero four five!"

The three digits signified a true bearing; she would be to the northeast of us and, we hoped, coming south. The rudder was full right as we passed through control. The OOD would be putting the contact astern, not diving, so without fear of being trampled by lookouts, we climbed to the conning tower and then on to the bridge. Astern, above the horizon, were heavy, black masts and the top of a wide bridge structure.

The time was 0408, and the action to be taken seemed obvious: Open the range for secure raised periscope observation, move onto the enemy's track, and shoot when the ship came by. In the middle of the Yellow Sea, we might try just that, but here islands restricted our movement, and as luck would have it, a small fleet of fishing vessels was sprawled out along the path *Tang* must follow. There was but one thing to do, and we threaded our way at full power through 13 sampans and between two trawlers. Fishermen are supposed to be about before dawn, like farmers, or so I had been led to believe, but just as they had been east of Danjo Gunto, the vessels were on random headings, drifting, and with nary a sign of life. From above, our maneuvers would surely have looked like a seagoing slalom. The very presence of these fishermen during our drive to get ahead of the target may have been a boon. The enemy's bridge had crept above the horizon, and this confusion of sampans could have prevented our detection.

We did not press our luck; now 5 degrees on the enemy's bow, we slid below the sea. All dives were supposed to be the same, but one from full power with the enemy in full view had a bit added, like the kickoff of a football game. We added a little more by not slowing—the controllermen would just shift the load to the battery—for a final trim would have to wait for another time and place. This short burst would not take much out of the battery and could put us in perfect position. Frank had gone to the TDC and Larry to the dive, so our first team was already manning the key positions. We watched the TDC's target and submarine dials turn slowly, the inscribed ship now pointing at us. *Tang* slowed to two-thirds speed for a quick look.

The scope vibrated in the rush of the sea, but not so much as to seriously blur the image. Jones lowered the scope, and we went ahead standard. I liked a part of what I saw, the massive bow, broad superstructure and bridge, the great, heavy masts. Perhaps we had forgotten what a big ship looked like, but everything suggested an auxiliary warship. It would take a broader angle, uncovering more details, before we could further identify her, but the angle she now presented was the part I did not like. It should have been zero or slightly port; it was 10 starboard. The ship had zigged away, but we were hot after her!

We didn't know what might be in store, so the Bells of St. Mary's chimed again. The time was 0516, ten minutes after we had dived, and if a submarine was going to have early reveille, this way would raise no objections. There would be another ten-minute run. After battle stations were manned, I dropped down to control to have a word with Larry, for shallow water could make this a taut one. Boatswain's Mate Aquisti was on the bow planes, working nicely with Motor Machinist's Mate Robertson, at the stern planes. They both had the feel of the boat, like good steersmen, but what was more, their mutual cooperation left nothing to be desired. The glance told me all that was necessary, and I returned to the conning tower.

Fraz had readied five tubes forward and the two with fish aft. Halfway through the ten-minute run, we stopped our screws momentarily so that Caverly could check the bearing of the enemy's propellers. It checked with TDC's. *Tang* had coasted down to 5 knots and a further midpoint check was in order. Jones brought the attack scope up to my hands.

"Bearing—mark!" Jones read 315; it also checked, but it would not have for long, as the angle on the bow was 50 starboard. The ship had zigged away again or was changing her base course toward the coast. Jones read the stadimeter range on his knees, opposite an assumed masthead height of 100 feet—4,500 yards, not a suitable shot. We could only stay with her as our speed and endurance would permit while steering whatever courses would maintain the best possible true bearing. To converge and close the range would only result in ending up astern, in a hopeless position. *Tang* was rolling again at standard speed, and we let five anxious minutes pass as we paralleled the enemy. The next observation confirmed our suspicion; we were abaft the shp's beam, and she was heading directly for the shore. For the moment we did likewise, while Fraz and I took another look at the chart. A great bulge of the ten-fathom curve, extending about 15 miles from the coast, seemed her obvious destination. Everything hinged on what she did when she got there. Of one thing we were reasonably sure; she would not turn left, back toward where she had come from. The other possibilities we meant to see firsthand, and *Tang* was rolling at full speed.

First sharp and then broadside views had permitted identification details to flow to our party. With the moderately raked bow, mast, heavy bridge structure, more masts and king posts, large superstructure and heavy stack aft, and finally a cruiser type stern, they had settled on the *Kurosio Maru*. I could not disagree at the moment, but the much heavier masts, king posts, booms, and platform astern indicated a conversion, possibly to a seaplane tender or aircraft transport.

Spurred further by this probable identification, we went to the one-hour rate. This did not mean that our battery would be completely exhausted at the end of an hour, but we would then have to cut our speed radically, down in steps to a crawl in any later evasion. The really important details were the masthead height and the overall length. These figures for the stadimeter could be doubly important if we were forced into a long-range shot.

A half hour had gone by. We made few observations, and many of these were discouraging, as her zigs at times showed us within 30 degrees of her stern. Fraz motioned for me to come to the chart. "It looks pretty hopeless, Captain," he said quietly and privately. Fraz was right, not just because of our position, but also because the bottom was shelving rapidly at our plotted location. I wished I had not seen the true presentation; my argument was with the enemy, and I succeeded in pushing all else aside, except acceding to quick soundings and rigging in of the sound heads.

Fortunately, perhaps, my attention was now absorbed in dodging sampans. They were everywhere, and any one of them could ruin a periscope. It was a case of taking a look through a shaking scope, then easing off a bit toward the next clear area and trusting we were in it for the next squint. Amidst it all came Caverly's sounding, four fathoms under our keel, not critical yet. The navigator seemed relieved, or perhaps resigned, and we continued barging ahead.

To our surprise, at high speed on her almost straight course, *Tang* was maintaining the bearing on the zigzagging enemy, now about 6,000 yards on our port bow. Fraz reported her now crossing the ten-fathom curve almost simultaneously with Caverly's "Three fathoms." We killed our way momentarily for a proper look.

"Up scope." A look and I flipped the handles.

"All ahead full. She's turning right!"

A glance at Fraz's chart showed her just north and west of Amma To. We were back up to speed when Ballinger stuck his head up the lower conning tower hatch: "Plenty of battery, Captain." It was the report I wanted to hear. We would make a last dash to close this ship and shoot on whatever track she presented. Our dash was curtailed by soundings of two fathoms, one fathom, and then the echo merged with the outgoing signal. This was it.

"All stop. Up scope. Bearing—mark! Range—mark! Angle —mark!"

Jones read 340 and 2,800, then waited for my angle estimate. I called 75 starboard; Jones read 80. Frank called the setup on the TDC, 2,500 firing range, 105 track, but asked for quick bearings since the enemy had slowed. We obliged, and the scope went down.

"Ten degrees to go, outer doors are open forward."

I glanced at the depth gauge, 58 feet. "Hold her down, Larry!"

"I can't, we're aground!"

"All back full. Up scope." Jones brought the handles to my hands. I must have looked like a reptile, squirming on the conning tower deck, but there she was. "Constant bearing—mark!"

"Set!"

"Fire!" and the first torpedo went for her big stack aft. The next fish went for her middle, and the third forward.

"Left full rudder." We picked up a swing to the right with our sternway.

"Shift the rudder, all ahead full, steady on two zero zero."

"Hot, straight, and normal." The call came from JP by battle telephone. We had practically forgotten our topside-mounted sonic receiver. I wondered what shape the torpedoes were in, for now I could consider what had barely crossed my mind before firing. Torpedoes were supposed to duck about ten feet on leaving the tubes before gaining their set depth. That habit, this time putting them into the mud, might account for a somewhat muffled zing, but JP showed they were otherwise all right. The warheads were something else. Would mud jammed into the impeller recess on the bottom—the impeller that armed the firing mechanism—wash clear during the run? The answer came in two tremendous explosions, and I thanked God that I had been too busy to consider all of these things beforehand.

We slowed for a look; only the bow, stern, and masts were sticking out of the sea. A sweep around and we surfaced, surrounded by 34 fishermen, understandably awe-stricken. They were quick to recover, for in some sampans men were shaking their fists at us while from others came the overhead clasped hands of a boxer's salute. We assumed that they were Japanese and Koreans respectively.

The time was 0601, five minutes after firing. Astern, for Fraz had brought us to 270 now that our business with this ship was over, were about 50 survivors in the water but with several large lifeboats. We could not have dived there had we wanted to close, and the thought of welcome deep water overcame any curiosity. The stern had sunk before we surfaced, and now the bow went under in a bubbling, foaming sea.

Three engines were driving us west, the others charging. On our port bow was smoke, black smoke, and then the hull of a ferryboat, about the size of those that plied between San Diego and Coronado. Water was boiling from her stern as we passed; we were both running, and I wished we could tell her to close the dampers lest she explode a boiler.

With all trawlers or other craft with antennas now hull down and unable to report our course, we headed north to continue our counterclockwise search. At 0900, with the location of our attack 40 miles away, Mel took us down for the submerged run to our previously selected position toward Osei To, up the Korean coast.

11

The enemy would have to search a semicircle with a 40-mile radius, about 2,400 square miles, to have any hope of finding us. By that time, *Tang* could well be another 40 miles away. Frankly, the one chance of locating us passed when patrol planes did not show up during our dash to sea. That possibility had caused us to dive earlier than we liked. Without any design on our part, *Tang* was very close to her original track and could pick up the plan at the point where she had turned south. There would be some modifications, for we were five hours behind and with far less battery gravity. We could move along at 3 knots for the rest of the day and have enough extra for a reasonable approach, but that would not get us to the passes. It did not matter; they would still be there tomorrow, and this morning's attack had been a grand way to celebrate Independence Day. Just possibly the ship's company would take the Old Man's salmon and peas in stride if that helped sink ships. Actually, there was a trick to cooking good canned peas that I had learned from Romero, the chief commissary steward when I was a junior officer. You just drain off the juice and boil it down, seasoning it with salt, pepper, and plenty of butter. Then just before serving, you dump in the peas and bring them to a quick heat. Well, we'd see how they turned out today.

In the wardroom, the conversation did not stray far from the last attack. This was Fraz's tenth patrol, and he'd neither seen nor heard of anything quite like it. Mort just shook his head slowly. But actually, without escorts to oppose us, it was a straightaway approach with only a few twists. After all, a submarine was not truly aground till she was high and dry. Like Fraz, I was aware of no other case in which a boat had run aground and was backing full while firing. But I had known one submarine that would have gone after this ship exactly as *Tang* had. I did not voice this, nor did I mention the image of Mush Morton across the table saying, "Tenacity, Dick. Stay with the bastard till he's on the bottom."

A late breakfast for all hands had done much to prolong the festive mood, even for the messcooks, as shipmates were lending a hand. The watch, of course, was all business. In the conning tower, one scope was manned continuously and both for high searches every 15 to 20 minutes. We would remain a bit on the defensive until we had an opportunity to jam some more energy in our batteries, but *Tang* was still on the prowl.

The morning went quickly, and everybody seemed to enjoy lunch, for the cooks had let their imaginations run and had turned out beautiful salmon loaves. Quite likely this was in part due to some encouragement by Fraz and carried out by Dick. The afternoon was quiet until 1500, when the distant rumblings of depth charges commenced, 58 miles distant to be more exact. It was always nice to know where the antisubmarine forces were working, especially when they were miles away. The rumblings remained faint and finally ceased as we moved slowly north, approaching the Korean coast where it juts out to the northwest. Fraz had been up to the conning tower a half dozen times to identify landfalls and finally Osei To, the one we were looking for. Frank reported it abeam at suppertime. We were doing well and relaxing when the wardroom phone buzzed. Mort picked it up and said calmly, "Here we go again, Captain. Dick's got smoke beyond the Onyo Group."

I couldn't place the islands but knew they must be just inshore; there weren't any to seaward except Osei To. Fraz left to start the tracking; Mort and I followed a few minutes later, giving tracking time to get organized.

The situation was not impossible but far from good. The enemy was heading south between the islands and the coast a treacherous area for a ship not familiar with the shoals. We examined our chart for any place where we might attack outside the ten-fathom curve, for the moon would be coming up full, and a submerged attack would be required. There appeared to be one chance, a high-speed end-around right back to the vicinity of the morning's attack. That area was undoubtedly still infested by enemy antisubmarine units, but maybe they would have retired by the time we arrived. It was something we would have to find out, for there was no alternative.

The lookouts were in the conning tower, and preparations

for surfacing had been completed. I commenced the customary careful high-power sweep around, over the moonlit island and land silhouettes, across the darker horizon to the south, and then along the sharp edge of the Yellow Sea, scalloped by clouds still colorfully illuminated by the sun now below the sea. I found myself retracing an arc for no particular reason —or was there one? I swung back again; a slight discoloration clashed with the sunset, the faintest wisp of light brown haze.

"Bearing—mark!"

It had become doctrine in *Wahoo*, and now *Tang*, not to switch ships. Stay with the one you have in hand until it's on the bottom, then go after the next one. But for most every rule there's an exception. Besides, these were not ships yet, just smoke and light brown haze.

"Bearing—mark!"

It was still there, faint but changed in shape. Ogden had read the bearing, 185, which Fraz converted to 265 true, no change in bearing; *Tang* was close to her track.

"Right full rudder. All ahead standard."

This ship was coming from the west or we would have seen her earlier. She was upsetting my traffic flow predictions, which bothered me not one bit, especially since she would get us out of another inshore scrape and into deep water, where a submarine belonged. Never could a shift of targets have been completed more quickly.

Fraz recommended course 290. It would take us clear of Osei To more rapidly, and then *Tang* could get on the surface, charge batteries, and look over the enemy. The island was soon on our quarter, and three blasts sent us up onto a flat sea, under the light of a full moon. Three engines fired, two to go on charge and the other for maneuvering. The time was 1953, still early in the evening, and there was no hurry. We could wait right here for the enemy to come over the horizon, but to insure an attack seaward of the 20-fathom curve, we would move slowly west. Though all practical considerations told us that contact with the enemy would soon be regained, the passing minutes were anxious ones. Caverly searched with the A-scope, which was becoming standard practice when examining a particular bearing or sector. There was nothing random about his search as he moved the reflector, examining every degree about the suspected bearing. Knowing what he was looking for, and assisted by local radar conditions, Caverly had a single dancing pip on the screen that quickly rose to half the viewing height. Tracking commenced immediately with this accurate range of 18,500 yards and the enemy bearing just slightly on our port bow. No immediate maneuvers were required as we quietly closed our target.

Some excitement was building up, noticeable in the voices making routine reports below and in one report delivered in person to me on the bridge. It did not seem logical, for up to now this approach offered no real troubles such as we had faced this morning. That was probably the answer. Then we had been too busy to look beyond the immediate problems, while now we had time to think ahead, each about his particular coming tasks. Mine was to sink this ship with but two of our four remaining torpedoes.

The report made to me on the bridge concerned the specific gravity of our pilot cells in each battery; we had enough for any submerged maneuvers. I was tempted to shift the two engines from charge to propulsion and close the enemy but restrained a natural urge to move in to the attack. It might work, but to take full advantage of the circumstances, exact solutions by tracking came first in putting the ship down. Our single pip danced, and now an inversion layer, or other phenomenon that helped radar and vision alike, brought the target into full view, in a mirage. The range was 15,000 yards; she sat there on an artificial horizon, smaller but otherwise as she would normally appear at half the range. Even the freak atmospheric conditions were on our side.

Within a few minutes, Fraz came to the bridge to report that he was satisfied with the solution of the enemy's course and speed. The range had closed to 9,000 yards, and we discussed briefly the possibility that the enemy might also soon see us on a false horizon. It did not seem likely, but I secured the battery charge in anticipation of diving. The range continued to close, and I considered how clearly silhouettes stood out in a moon streak; tonight we were that silhouette.

The range was 7,500. I cleared the bridge, counted the lookouts as they went by in the moonlight, sounded two blasts, and stepped down the hatch. Ogden set the dogs as I held the hatch closed with the lanyard. The dive took two seconds longer than usual. The time was 2041.

As ordered before he went below, Larry leveled us off at 47

feet for radar tracking. The Bells of St. Mary's chimed again, and *Tang* was into her ninth attack of this patrol. Bergman now took over radar, and Caverly went to sound. With accurate periscope bearings, Frank changed the enemy's speed to 9½ knots. The solution continued to check, and we eased on down for a moonlight periscope attack.

Never, at this stage, could a submarine captain have had more accurate information nor have had his boat in a more favorable position; but then there were few, if any, other crews with this total experience. The silhouette soon developed into the one we had seen in mirage but now with more details discernible. Her bow had a very pronounced rake. Between the bow and bridge stood an extremely heavy tripod mast. Her bridge appeared mushroom-topped. Another heavy tripod mast lay between the bridge and large after superstructure, which was topped by a large, short stack. As yet her angle had never been wide enough to expose her stern. Ballinger came up head and shoulders through the lower hatch, waited for a proper moment, then announced that the identification party could find no such ship in the books. The reason became evident on the next zig, a wide one. At 4,000 yards, her side glistened in the moonlight; she was a new ship.

Fraz had ordered the tubes readied when we went down to periscope depth, the last two containing torpedoes forward and aft. At range 3,500 he ordered the outer doors opened, for maneuvers by the enemy, not those that I would order, would determine which torpedo room fired the last of its torpedoes first. That was well, for a part of payday was probably riding on it. The tactics we would use were fairly simple and revolved around nice timing and a good call of the angle on the bow after her next zig. If it put her track too close, we would pull away and fire from aft. If her zig was broad, we'd turn towards and fire from forward.

Caverly was now matching my periscope bearings with sound. The range was 3,000 yards as generated from the TDC, and a zig was due at any moment. The scope had been up continuously but now was down to water-lapping height. The enemy was closing at 300 yards per minute, and our 3 knots added another 100 yards to that.

"She's zigging, Captain!" Caverly had caught the change in sound due to her rudder before the ship's swing was perceptible. It was the mark of a real soundman, not just a listener.

"She's zigging left!" I called. "Right full rudder. All ahead standard. We'll fire on this leg. Stand by for a quick setup before we pick up our swing.

"Bearing—mark!" Jones called 358. "Range—mark!" He read 2,400. "Angle twenty-five starboard." Jones lowered the scope.

"Steady us normal to her track, Fraz."

Tang was picking up her swing, which at first had seemed much too slow. So slow that I had glanced at the TDC's presentation to see that our bow was indeed drawing ahead of the enemy as it should. With 15 degree to go, Quartermaster Welch put the rudder amidships and then met her swing. *Tang* settled on 355, almost north, and continued to close the track. Another glance at the TDC showed the enemy broad on our port bow.

"All ahead one-third."

Caverly commenced calling sound bearings as the noise of our own screws subsided. Frank nodded, indicating that the bearings checked with those generated by the TDC. Welch called our own speed, 6 knots, 5 knots.

"Up scope." Jones brought it up to my hands and then guided me to the correct bearing. The enemy ship was in the low-power field. I shifted to high; the angle was opening as it should. Caverly supplied three echo ranges to go with my next three bearings and angles on the bow.

"It's all checking," said Frank.

"Ten degrees to go." She was big and broad, a massive, loaded ship, a beautiful ship.

"Constant bearing—mark!"

"Set!" The scope was steady as her decks raced across the reticle. The after superstructure came on.

"Fire!"

The torpedo left with a good zing. The second torpedo went to her bridge. Fraz announced the time of run, 30 seconds. Jones was already counting, "Twenty-five . . . thirty, thirty-one, th—" Explosions, shaking explosions rocked us, but the great tripod masts were tilting toward each other; the enemy ship's back was broken. Jones took a look and a few seconds later said, "She's gone, Christ, all of her!" The twisting, grinding, breaking-up noises came over sound and through the hull in increasing intensity. It was a frightening, sobering noise and should serve to keep any lookout on his toes for weeks to come.

Flotsam was but 500 yards dead ahead, and we surfaced to

pick up possible survivors. The time was 2131, just three minutes after firing. The lookouts spotted one man, who ducked under the overturned lifeboat. It took Leibold's grapnels to hold the boat alongside and bursts from White's tommy gun to scare him out into the open. Our ship's company was better at shooting torpedoes than in rescuing this one reluctant survivor. Finally, enmeshed in heaving lines, he was dragged aboard to a kinder fate than awaited him in the Yellow Sea. Rescuing this young man had taken more time than the submerged approach and attack, but it had provided activity for the troops and filled a sense of obligation for all of us.

Japanese antisubmarine forces were 50 miles behind us, or so we believed. Having no desire to verify this, I ordered three engines on the line, and *Tang* headed north with two celebrations to mark our Independence Day:

Kurosio Maru	10,000 tons	Lat.	35° 22' N.
		Long.	125° 56' E.
New Maru	10,000 tons	Lat.	36° 05' N.
		Long.	125° 48' E.

12

Our prisoner was dubbed Firecracker before he was brought over the bridge on the way below. He seemed to be in reasonable shape, at least as viewed by moonlight. That is, until he saw the conning tower hatch and the glow of red lights below. To him, it must have looked like the fire pit or some American inferno. Firecracker stiffened and went into convulsions, and only with the aid of Chief Pharmacist's Mate Rowell was the poor lad ushered below.

The course north should keep *Tang* in the clear for the remainder of the night and give all hands an opportunity to return to normal fighting trim, eager but rested and sharp. The brief night orders were written accordingly, but the night did not cooperate. Within an hour we were tracking another target, which was zigzagging leisurely, as if it owned the

Yellow Sea. Not until well into the approach could we make it out, a sailing junk beating to windward. We should have known what we had by her movements and the direction of the wind long before the sighting, but we probably would have closed to look her over anyway.

The tracking and partial approach had taken us south of

Sailing Junk

the Kakureppi Islands, so the navigator laid down a new track to leave the islands well clear and then awaited my decision for the coming day's patrol. The original plans for moving up the coast had been so interrupted by contacts and approaches that our track looked as if we had been playing leapfrog. *Tang* would normally have arrived off Choppeki Point in due course and with plenty of torpedoes. We were not objecting to a single one of our side excursions, but it would be a shame to come all this way and not spend a little time off that advantageous promontory. With but two torpedoes left, which meant none for defense after an attack, our approach to the point required good timing and preferably a reconnaissance before moving in to attack. Just to the south of Choppeki Point lies the Daisei Group, with good water all around and a natural channel between the islands and the promontory. Off these islands we would be able to see what was going on and even move in to the south of them for attack in the channel. Fraz moved the arm of the drafting machine till the rule passed through our position; its other end passed over the center of the three islands. It was good to have an exec and navigator thinking along the same general lines with you, especially when he would not hesitate to point out an object if he saw one. The bearing on the protractor was 340, and *Tang* came to it. With our present speed on this track, we would be approaching the Daisei Group before dawn, and I changed the night orders accordingly.

The days were getting a little shorter by the calendar, but this could not begin to match the extra daylight as we approached Manchuria. Jones called the navigator for morning stars, and a glance at the luminous dial on the clock showed 0245. A half hour later, two welcome blasts took us down into the shallow though still protective seas.

Rumbling distant explosions commenced at breakfast time, reassuring in that they gave the general location of the enemy effort, way to the south. They also served to reignite the conversation that had been running since our previous dawn attack, a rehash of the whole episode as various individuals had seen it, which helped all of us relax. We did not get too far unwound, however, for Hank sighted distant smoke. The time was 0917, and section tracking went to work with only true bearings of the puffs of smoke, beyond the Daisei Group. They drew slowly to the right, showing that the ship below the smoke was traveling south, inaccessible in six fathoms of water. The sighting and tracking practically guaranteed an early attack off Choppeki Point, for the coastal shipping was still running and had to round this promontory.

Fraz and Jones needed no stars this night since our OODS had been able to keep our position plotted with bearing lines on the three islands. The time was 1952, the period late in evening twilight just before the near full moon would rise. *Tang* surfaced and commenced the three-hour run to seaward around the islands and then to Choppeki Point. There we could fire in 17 fathoms and have our torpedoes hit any ship trying to round the point. Fraz brought the chart to the wardroom as was customary when there was more to consider than could conveniently take place in the conning tower. The sailing would be clear, but our approach should be cautious, with the APR-1 searching the frequencies for enemy radar. Certainly if the enemy had an installation to spare, this would be a natural location. Lying submerged off this point, unsuspected, would be like hunting with your rifle laid across a stump and pointing down the trail. I circled a 30-fathom mark that lay about ten miles northwest of the tip of Choppeki Point.

"Is that where *Wahoo* sank one of her ships?" Fraz inquired.

"No. That's where Mush Morton dealt me a twenty-eight cribbage hand."

"I can't think of any better criterion," said Mort. Fraz extended *Tang*'s track to the circled mark, Mort reached for the cribbage board, and our grand strategy session was over.

Tang's mood was obviously one of cautious optimism, cautious because the old hands knew we could not stay ahead of the opposition indefinitely. If the enemy resorted to escorting his ships past dangerous spots, as he did around the main islands, then this was the place to start. We did not have long to wait, for the radar presentation became confusing just before 2200, with a side lobe and several multipulse echoes, such as we had experienced on our first night in the East China Sea. These could be reflections from distant mountains falling almost in phase with later outgoing signals, but they could also be a ship at 15 miles. Perhaps it would be fair to say that we shared in the confusion, for differentiating one from the other was time-consuming and would remain so until Ed had a chance to operate on our SJ, giving us an additional knob that would vary the pulse rate. This, he assured us, would solve our present problem, but it would have to wait for another patrol.

We had coasted two miles beyond our selected spot, essentially stopped to see if one mountain to the north would move. It remained stationary, but a new pip showed up to the northwest. It too could be a secondary return, but if so the echo was coming back from a mountain range in Manchuria. We killed our way completely, and the pip moved steadily away from Choppeki Point. *Tang* did likewise, hot on its tail.

Again my theory of a southward traffic flow was somewhat incorrect, though understandably no one mentioned it. We were too busy anyway, for the original contact was at 29,000 yards, and we had now tracked it out to 34,000. Under an almost full moon, we commenced a long, long end-around. Fraz broke out an old-fashioned mooring board, a pad of sheets with a compass rose in the center, bearing lines coming out radially, and with evenly spaced concentric circles. The sheets were designed specifically for plotting relative movement situations. This was such a problem indeed, for *Tang* must pass from 17 miles dead astern to nearly ten miles ahead, all beyond the enemy's sighting range. Further, this must be completed before the enemy reached the sanctuary of Gaichosan Retto. Fraz plotted our course legs and recorded the times. We would make it with a few miles to spare, but just to be sure we worked on up to full power.

Tang rolled under a still-rising moon and on a rippleless sea. The run to our diving position would take three and a half hours, the submerged approach and attack at least an hour more. This would be another one of those nights, or more exactly, nights and mornings, for firing would come near dawn. There was a great temptation to stay on the bridge or in the conning tower and to share in all of the excitement of this maneuver. Then I thought of a former skipper, the one with his bunk in the conning tower, and wished to avoid similar mistakes. Fraz, Mort, and Frank could conduct this end-around; after all, two of them were qualified for command. I could relax and then conduct the approach and attack. There was a difference this night, however, for we had all enjoyed a good measure of rest on our all-day dive, and this would be the last maneuver against the enemy on this patrol. Staying clear of the mechanics of the plot and TDC but generally at hand seemed a good compromise.

Ballinger had temporarily moved Firecracker from the after torpedo room to forward. It was a logical move, for even handcuffed to a bunk, he could disturb the firing aft. The young man was recovering remarkably from his ordeal, perhaps helped by being the center of attention and by Rowell's ministrations. Topside again, the enemy ship was abeam, her silhouette now identifying her as a freighter of conventional size for the China trade. The end-around was going well, following almost exactly the tracks that the navigator had moved to the true plot. Another 90 minutes and we would dive. I went below for a turn aft and found men up and about as space would permit. Two ahead of me, proceeding through the engine rooms, gave each main a reassuring pat, and I was tempted to follow suit. The shaft tachometers in maneuvering showed an even 345, about ten turns high. Culp was in charge, and we were both satisfied. The after torpedo room was all business. Their true test would come with the firing plunger.

"Captain, you put us in position, and we'll blow her out of the sea!" Chief Torpedoman's Mate Weekley had put his finger directly on our mutual responsibilities. I went forward to carry out mine, pausing in the messroom to look at our second plot; *Tang* was moving in ahead.

When I reached the bridge, the enemy was astern, with a sharp angle and on a parallel course. We had time for a final accurate check.

"All back two-thirds." I watched over the moonlit side. "All stop." *Tang* was dead in the water.

Radar ranges and TBT bearings went to plot and TDC; there were no other inputs. The enemy was closing at 9 knots, exactly as tracking had previously found, but the double check increased our confidence.

"All ahead two-thirds. Dive when I'm clear, Ed." Two blasts took *Tang* down, and battle stations sounded as our ship leveled off. The time was 0227 on July 6.

The freighter came on, overtaking us, becoming more distinct every minute till a predawn mist set in and her shape disappeared completely.

"Bring her up to forty-five feet, Larry." *Tang* took a modest but steady up-angle and leveled off. Bergman, standing by on SJ, called, "Range five thousand. Bearing one seven zero." That would be a relative bearing; she was just off our stern to starboard and coming on nicely, her present track just 500 yards to starboard. We went back down to wet the scope, now hopelessly fogged, and Caverly called the bearings of the freighter's propellers as she closed.

Both the surface mist and the fogging of the periscopes had resulted from the very cold water and the moist summer air here in the northern Yellow Sea. The patch of mist was now behind us, but the fogging periscope lens persisted. The enemy could be viewed for only a second or two on any one exposure, but frankly this was all I dared to use in a close-in day approach. The angle was now opening but hard to call. Caverly backed up the observation with a single pulse echo range, 1,100 yards.

"Left full rudder. All ahead full," I ordered.

Fraz ordered the course for a 90 track with zero gyros, and I watched the TDC presentation as we pulled off the track. Our stern was now ahead of her bow. Welch was meeting our swing.

"All ahead one-third."

"Ten degrees to go," called Fraz.

This would be a new one for me. I could get the "Constant bearing—mark" off handily, but the "Fire" on a separate exposure might be too early or late. I considered firing on generated bearings, most submarines did, but with only two torpedoes, I'd stick with our bow-and-arrow method.

"Constant bearing." Jones raised the scope on the generated bearing. I swung it ahead to amidships and called, "Mark!" Jones dunked the scope and raised it immediately.

"Fire!" The mainmast had passed the wire, but the after well deck was still on. The torpedo went out with a whine.

The second double dip was more accurate, and our last torpedo was on its way for her foremast, its whine fading out in a few seconds. The range was 900 yards, the gyros near 180, the same as near zero for a bow shot. Both torpedoes were running at six-foot depth. Ogden called off the seconds; they should hit on the 60th and 68th. I gave the scope to Fraz and Jones; my job was over, and they could work out a hurried dunking sequence. The scope broke the surface ahead of a shaking detonation. The time was 0320.

"Her whole side's blown out!" Another whack and explosion followed on time. "She's capsizing!"

"Take the con, Frank, and take her up. The lookouts can follow later. Move us in to any flotsam."

Immediately, three blasts took Tang to the surface, and Frank conned her in a quick turn to close the small amount of wreckage that was visible in the pale gray dawn. The largest piece was a portion of a lifeboat; there were no survivors. We could not dally, for radar had two contacts at 16,000 yards, closing.

13

Every effort, every maneuver would now be pointed toward the accomplishment of one task, cruising home safely. Perhaps the two pips were belated escorts; we did not wait to find out. Now, just five minutes after the contacts, *Tang* was nearly up to full power and the range was opening. The course of 190 would take us past the Shantung Promontory, the great peninsula of China that juts about 200 miles into the Yellow Sea and forms the southern boundary of the Gulf of Pohai. This would be the first leg of a large arc, curving to the east, which would pass well clear of the scenes of our recent attacks. Should someone viewing our track chart characterize us as running scared, he would be absolutely right. When the torpedoes were expended, it was the only way to run.

By 0600 we had put 50 miles of Yellow Sea between us and the position of our last attack. Hank pulled the plug on schedule, and *Tang* slid under the sea, on down to 100 feet for a leisurely cruise at 4 knots. All hands would have preferred 6, but then we would have to charge batteries on surfacing, and there would be insufficient gravity for possible submerged evasion should we be driven down. Our speed was a compromise weighted toward safety, as was our depth.

Tang continued along her track, and hands not on watch did just what they pleased. For the majority, that meant sleep. Like our storage batteries, which could receive enormous amounts of energy when flat, so these young men stored away their sleep. By midmorning men were stirring about, some caught up on sleep and others perhaps still too keyed up to stay turned in. I fell in that latter group and examined two weekly menus awaiting my signature. I signed them but drew question marks on each evening meal. Fraz gave the word to

Wixon, who had no trouble in rounding up volunteers. Two at a time they sorted the cold room, a few degrees below zero, bringing all steaks, roasts, and fresh-frozen strawberries to the front for daily consumption. All hands fully understood that none of this was to be turned in to the base, and no one objected.

As we were sitting down for lunch, the rumblings of distant explosions came through the hull. Sound was able to obtain a reasonably broad bearing on the source, approximately the reverse of our course. It was reassuring, but we needed more than an educated guess about what was going on above the surface. Fraz left to take us up for low and then high periscope searches. All was clear, but we remained at periscope depth. Fraz returned with the chart that I had requested and watched, while having his lunch, as I sought out a 36-fathom spot north of the promontory. I'm sure that Fraz could visualize more exploring, or at a minimum a new track to plot.

"Now this is where Mush Morton dealt me my twenty-nine cribbage hand, one chance in fifteen million. I have it framed, with each card signed by a different officer." Fraz seemed relieved that I had nothing serious in mind; the others in the mess commenced figuring the odds and in a concerted effort finally agreed.

"Do you still feel lucky?" asked Fraz.

"Well, that is one of the reasons I asked for the chart." We got out the cribbage board and Fraz proceeded to pin my ears back, which simply verified that my luck was now concentrated in torpedoes and enemy ships. It then occurred to me that in all of the excitement of the attack and getting on our way, I had still not looked over the findings of our identification party for the last ship. They had worked fast and diligently, and it was quite possible that we would have had more misses without their determinations. They had settled on a ship similar to the *Osaka Maru*, on page 132 of ONI-208J. The silhouette pictured certainly looked like the broadside I had seen on firing, and I thanked them for their assistance.

Everything had gone well this day. Sunset was coming in anther half hour, and any enemy patrol planes would already be en route to their bases. There was nothing holding us back, so I went to the conning tower, advising Chief Hudson and Mel to make preparations for surfacing as I passed through control. Frank was on the search rope. I took the attack scope, and we searched carefully in low and high power. All was clear, and three blasts sent us up to continue the 700-mile run to the Nansei Shoto and the boundary of our area.

This evening I penned a well done in the night orders and then proceeded to list the cautions I would demand as we headed home. On rereading, the two messages did not seem to belong on the same page, but that was the way they came to mind. As before, on the previous page I listed the data on our last enemy ship:

Osaka Maru class   *4,000 tons*   *Lat.*   38° 40' N.
                                                 Long. 123° 40' E.

Any further considerations were interrupted by a quiet knock, and with my answer, Walker stuck his head past the curtain.

"I think we're in the news, Captain," he reported. I stepped across the passageway to hear Tokyo Rose, who frankly presented the most entertaining program available. No specific submarines were mentioned as sometimes was the case, but dire fates were predicted for submarines that foolishly entered the East China and Yellow seas. Excellent music was followed by the usual funeral march. If the Japanese were bothered now, wait until a few more ships failed to make port. Actually, the program served to emphasize my night orders, and I should have thanked Tokyo Rose for the cooperation.

Tang rolled throughout the night and continued at full power into morning twilight, the change barely perceptible under the bright moon. Sunrise came, and we now expected a patrol plane within an hour. The lookouts were cautioned accordingly, and before the sun had barely cleared the horizon, two blasts took *Tang* down. Probably a seabird, I thought, but Dick had followed a caution in the night orders and had answered the lookout's report with two blasts. It was a plane, a Betty off on the southern horizon. We watched it through the scope, continuing on its way. *Tang* did likewise, submerged.

Only true seabirds and an occasional sampan came into our periscopes' view throughout the rest of the morning. The dawn patrol would now have returned by another route, so after careful high periscope searches, we got up for another full-power run. After nearly seven hours, with 150 miles behind her, *Tang* looked forward to running on the surface on into the night. Tokyo Rose and friends obviously thought differently, and a distant patrol plane sent us down. It was 1914, shortly after sunset, and all planes should have returned to base. We watched it continue on its way, apparently unaware of us. Or was it? We had seen this same thing en route to Saipan. We waited another 30 minutes, then resumed our race through the evening twilight.

Our course was now 125, heading into the loom of a full moon. Our APR-1 picked up 250 megacycle radar with random train, perhaps a brand-new installation on Danjo Gunto, our old meeting place. The time was 2055. An hour later, when we were between the islands and the southern minefield described in the JICPOA (Joint Intelligence Center Pacific Ocean Area) supplement to our Operation Order, SJ reported five pips at range 16,000 yards, dead ahead! The range was suddenly 12,000, and right full rudder put them astern. Well, we couldn't say we'd had no warning, and I wondered if Tokyo Rose really was a turncoat. Certainly her antics were too corny to fool a bluejacket.

I had discounted the effectiveness of this reported minefield on both my voyages to the East China and Yellow seas. This was based in part on personal experience in trying to maintain a minefield off the Golden Gate. It was a peacetime test, and the cases were loaded with concrete. Every blow would break some of the mooring cables, and the mine cases would end up on the beach. In one instance, they had further found their way to a ranch, where they served as unique gate markers. One good typhoon would likely do an excellent job in sweeping this field if it really existed, and then the floating mines would be a hazard to the Japanese. As I viewed it, a minefield here would serve no real purpose, though planting a pseudo field by including the coordinates in a code that was suspected of being broken could be useful to our enemy. These were my theories, but we would not put them to a test this night.

Tang commenced a reverse end-around to get on the enemy's quarter, a much more prudent position for any further investigation and clear of the minefield, pseudo or not. Our section tracking party was doing well, but this was developing into a task for the first team. The group had been on course 310, nearly the reverse of our original course, then on 340, and finally 060. Apparently they were shifting their front to intercept us. It was too late; the combined speeds accelerated our maneuver, and *Tang* was already on their quarter. The night had become lightly overcast, with the moon breaking through occasionally, but still with excellent visibility. We closed the group cautiously to obtain information that could go in a contact report to *Sealion* and *Tinosa*. At a range of 10,000 yards we could observe blinker signaling but still could not make them out with 7 × 50s. Any good-sized ship would have shown up clearly, so based on their maneuvers, signaling, and size—or lack of it—we classified this as a killer group, probably directed by the early evening plane. We would report their presence after clearing the area, but now we slunk away and then bent on the turns.

I had elected to pass through the Nansei Shoto a little farther to the south this time, using the Nakano Strait. There was no particular reason for this selection other than avoiding the more common passages. Our track through the remainder of the night was thus more southerly and, we hoped, deceiving. Still rolling at full power, we dived at 0500, well outside of possible contact by enemy radar. A diving position 30 miles closer to the islands would have been more desirable, but the hunter-killer group and our ensuing investigation had put us behind schedule. Continuing further on the surface would likely tip our hand, disclosing our intended route to the Japanese. They would then have all day to muster antisubmarine forces. Thus, diving here was a compromise, as was our submerged speed of 4 knots, for all mains would be required for another full-power run, when we next surfaced. Should enemy patrols outfox us, or just get lucky, *Tang* might need a near full battery to shake them.

More planning and figuring were taking place for this transit than for any one of our approaches and attacks. This was in part due to the time involved, for we could plan ahead, knowing exactly where we would go. It would be foolish to consider that the enemy was not doing likewise. Our close brush with him pointed the finger to his probable efforts. In all of this was one more factor, one that had been so beneficial during parts of this patrol: the bright moon. Still bright, and rising at 2130, it would benefit the enemy, especially should *Tang* still be in transit.

The day was uneventful, but a tautness and extra note of seriousness were discernible on surfacing. It was early, 1600, for we had to make up the lost time, and a five-hour run lay ahead. All engines went on propulsion or the battery charge.

When the first enemy radar registered on the APR-1 at 1940, *Tang* was already rolling with four engines on propulsion. The next hour was quiet, but one minute after we sighted Gaja Shima light, a searchlight commenced sweeping the horizon to the right of the islands. The time was 2106, and we went to full power. Seventeen minutes later, the APR-1 had 153 megacycle radar, strong but with random train. At 2145 the signal steadied at highest strength. The enemy was tracking *Tang;* that was a twist. The maneuvering room answered the signal for emergency speed.

We were already between Gaja Shima and Taira Shima, racing through the strait into a rising moon. As we passed Nakano Shima, the steady 153 megacycle signal reached a maximum; that was its location. But radar is not a weapon, as some would want to classify it. The signal doesn't bite or shoot projectiles and should be considered assisting equipment. I found it a little difficult to go along with my own thesis, however, especially when five small surface patrols moved in ahead from port and starboard. There were no prescribed procedures for such a situation. I chose to run the gauntlet and not let them bluff me into diving.

Fraz came to the bridge from a quick turn below and reported all men at their battle stations. Each word, each order was being relayed by the telephone talkers, and you'd hear a pin if it dropped. Quite admittedly, we were all in the middle of a small drama.

"I'll take them one at a time, Fraz, and give way just enough to get its true bearing drawing aft. We may close another in doing so, but then we'll do the same with it. I'll call the bearings as usual, and you keep me posted on the true bearings."

Fraz caught the plan and ducked below with his usual cheerful "Aye, aye, Captain."

Though the patrols would probably not have our speed, they could give us trouble from their advantageous position ahead. Unless their movements were coordinated, however, our tactics should work. If not, we had that small button to starboard on the cowl to take us down. The range rate had picked up as the patrols headed towards. We gave way to the nearest one on our starboard bow. She held the bearing for a minute or two and then drew aft. The next was also to starboard because of our turn. We were being driven diagonally across the channel, but we now had two in back of us.

The next maneuver to starboard was closer, but it took care of two more patrols. The last one had no chance as *Tang* outran her to the open sea, our hearts pounding.

The time was 2300; the whole maneuver with the patrols had lasted but 15 minutes. We had had our seagoing slalom off Amma To, now this was like a punt return. True, there were fewer tacklers, but these were playing for keeps. Again, I believe the whole ship's company breathed out in unison, and to ease the adrenaline, the electricians proceeded with a shoot-'em-up Western in the forward torpedo room.

Fraz, Mort, and Frank joined me for coffee. We concluded that the enemy had done well with what he had. *Chidoris*, or faster patrols, could have forced us down for a 20-hour dive due to the moonlight, but here in 200 fathoms we were assured of good temperature gradients, and successful evasion would have been just a matter of time. We were 20 miles south of the 30th parallel, almost 600 miles due west of Sofu Gan. That pinnacle lay far from inhabited islands, so our present course of 090 needed no change. Neither did our speed, for having been just 30 days on patrol, we had fuel to burn, and *Tang* rolled on through the night.

A flying boat after breakfast and a flare fired by a friendly submarine, which surfaced about 4,000 yards on our quarter, provided the only excitement for July 9. The smoke bomb was a bit sobering; and enemy submarine could have been in that position. It impressed on all hands that *Tang* was not yet out of the woods. For the benefit of the other submarine's fire control party, we would include the target data in our patrol report. To make enemy tracking difficult, *Tang* had been using a course clock, which moved a false lubber's line. The steersman kept the line on the compass card course and, depending on the cam selection, our ship wandered about her base course. Neither this nor a conventional zigzag plan would thwart an attack by one of our boats, and I would give the enemy the same capability. Well, we had used the clock in taking the advice of a senior, and now I secured it. The ten percent increase in speed along our base course would cut a day from our voyage and, for my money, reduce our chances of being torpedoed by at least one-eighth, assuming that we would be ordered again to Pearl.

The required message reporting our departure from patrol and the results went out to ComSubPac after dark. We also included the information on the small killer group and the previous night's passage, for possible use to *Sealion* and

Tinosa. Our eight sinkings ought to set the staff buzzing in the morning. At dawn *Tang* was nearly buzzed, too, by a transport plane heading south through the Nampo Shoto. Its mission was obviously not antisubmarine, and 15 minutes submerged cleared the skies. Our track left Sofu Gan over the horizon to the north as four mains moved us back up to a safe speed, our fastest. Any submarine that spotted our shears would hardly have time to maneuver before we had passed by. Again *Tang* was "rolling down to Rio."

No one had complained about our daily rich diet, but why we were not all breaking out with strawberry rash or suffering from protein poisoning would doubtless mystify the doctors. On a turn aft toward midnight, I found the duty cook still busy over the galley range. At a glance, he seemed to be trying the texture of his handiwork between thumb and finger, as if judging pastry dough. Curiosity got me; I had to inquire.

"Oh, I'm just trying to get the texture of Firecracker's rice the way he's used to it, Captain. We've been cooking it too hard," our new ship's cook, Roberts, replied. He was so sincere that I just could not remind him that Firecracker was, after all, a prisoner, not a guest.

I had not paid any particular attention to our prisoner other than to have received daily reports; there hadn't been time. This apparently was not the case with our crew, who had quite quickly developed a combination of sign and oral language that worked satisfactorily. The information obtained about the young man and his understanding of the status of the war would have made up a small dossier. The important facts, as far as we were concerned, were the name of the ship, the *Yamaoka* or *Amaoaka Maru,* her cargo of 7,000 tons of iron ore, and ports of call, Tientsin and Kobe. Of course Firecracker's real name, Mishuitunni Ka, and his hometown of Kyoto were of interest, as was his belief that Japan had captured the Hawaiian Islands and half of Australia. The truth would come down hard some one of these days.

Nightly now, as we were trying to use up the movies along with the steaks and strawberries, Firecracker would be brought forward, handcuffs and all, for the evening show. There was no longer any doubt that he had become much more of a crew's mascot than a prisoner of war.

A congratulatory message came from ComSubPac on the evening Fox of July 10. Not received too well by a part of the ship's company was the second half of the same dispatch, assigning *Tang* to Midway for refit. Fraz and Jones laid down the new track, a bit to the north of our present one. Field days and compartment-by-compartment inspections went ahead, while Yeoman Williams typed the stencils of the patrol report. All the while, four main diesels drove us on through crisp Pacific seas. Our report on crossing the 1,000-mile circle went out on the 12th, giving our arrival time. *Tang* enjoyed two 13th's and at high noon of the 14th passed through the reef.

All of the dignitaries that Eastern and Sand islands could muster were on the dock, along with the band, which was smartly drawn up in formation. We had anticipated some of this and had half of one section at quarters in clean, scrubbed dungarees and white hats. Except for the line handlers scurrying to take the mooring lines aboard, everyone on deck was at attention. From my position on the bridge, *Tang* looked smart indeed. The bandmaster gave a nod, but before he raised his baton, Aquisti, our accordianist, stepped quickly from behind the conning tower, playing the Midway Hymn. I was as much taken by surprise as the bandmaster. Somehow the lines were secured and doubled up, while those at quarters chanted, a few horribly off key:

> Beautiful, beautiful Midway,
> Land where the gooneybirds grow,
> Beautiful, beautiful Midway,
> The goddamnedest place that I know!

the new track, a bit to the north of our present one. Fish

PART V

Fourth Patrol

OFF THE COAST
OF HONSHU

1

The usual formalities of an arrival were not restored; it would have been impossible, but on this day *Tang* could do no wrong. The troops had undoubtedly anticipated this and had taken advantage of the opportunity to blow off steam. Only one incident marred our otherwise happy landing, the arrival of four Marines. Six-footers, they had come complete with handcuffs and blindfold for Firecracker. It came close to being too much for the crew, who were already lining up to draw their monies. Ballinger interceded and went one step further, securing a signed receipt on a supply chit for one prisoner of war in good health. This seemed to mollify some, but others looked like boys who had just lost a pet.

Captain Edmunds left the ship, perhaps to affix a padlock to his freezer and liquor cabinet, but Commander John M. Will stayed aboard. We had been assigned to his division for our upkeep, and as Commander Submarine Division 62 (ComSubDiv 62) he would lend such support as was required to insure the best of repairs. His resourcefulness in meeting the materiel needs of our Southwest Pacific submarines in the lean months of 1942 was well known, and now *Tang* would benefit.

Most of the crew had vanished, each member with a ten-spot, and Walker was explaining our pantry's baking oven to his temporary relief, probably itching to be on his way, too. I invited the commander to walk through the boat with me. It was not necessary for me to comment, for *Tang*'s department heads and their counterparts on the relief crew were discussing the work requests on the spot, though I took the opportunity for introductions. The spit and polish spoke for itself. Commander Will had gathered more information about our ship in these few minutes than would have been possible in an hour's discussion. In fact, this was our pre-repair conference, and I saw him ashore.

Fraz had finished all business except the final checking of

the stencils of our patrol report, and Yeoman Williams was standing by to make any corrections on the spot. Fraz had made one change by lumping our attacks 4 and 5 together as 4A and 4B. It was a small point, but now the reader would know immediately that these concerned one ship, finally sunk on the later attack. I turned on to the final blue sheet preceding the tabulations, to paragraph (Q) Personnel:

(a) Number of men on board during patrol	76
(b) Number of men qualified at start of patrol	55
(c) Number of men qualified at end of patrol	59
(d) Number of unqualified men making their first patrol	18
(e) Number of men advanced in rating during patrol	17

What an introduction those 18 new men had had, 9,700 miles in 36 days, ten attacks, eight verified sinkings, and only three depth charges—and those from a freighter. Jones and Williams headed for ComSubDiv 62's office with the report and the track chart tracings. Fraz and I were close on their heels, but we turned left for the Gooneyville. A few minutes later, we joined Frank and Mort in the corner room. With feet propped up and a beer in hand, we rehashed the patrol. It was here that the small trials came to light; the depth-setting spindle that would not re-engage until a minute before firing; the failure of a ready light in the firing panel, indicating that No. 2 torpedo tube was not ready, but corrected by battle phone. None of these problems had affected the safety of our ship, and I was proud that the individuals on the spot had solved each one, and in time. I shuddered to think what might have happened if one more item had been added when we were aground, backing full, and firing.

Submarines were never officially scored or rated, for there were so many variables affecting a patrol. By the very nature of antishipping patrols, however, a keen competition between boats did exist. Already, *Tang* was moving up the ladder, and Frank was discussing the results of our latest foray.

"I read all of the patrol reports at sub school and all I could lay my hands on since; there's been no patrol like this," he commented.

"You missed one, Frank."

"The *Wahoo*'s fourth," joined Fraz.

He was right, and I pointed out some interesting similarities. Each sub had suffered a like number of torpedo failures, though after one surface runner, *Wahoo*'s had been prematures. Both had put eight ships down, but *Wahoo* had accounted for two of her smaller ones by gunfire. For sentimental reasons, and love of that fine ship, I was quite satisfied that the results had turned out this way.

Our dinner on the second evening with Captain Edmunds and Commander Will was delicious. The salads and mashed potatoes, decorated by the Filipino stewards, were beautiful. I caught Fraz's look as he sawed through a slice of tough beef, however, and we lowered our eyes lest we'd explode in thinking of our past actions and the nice steaks we'd been enjoying. It was a relaxing evening, though we were surprised that our hosts were already familiar with our patrol report. The commander's yeoman had obviously run the stencils through immediately, and we were not averse to filling in some of the details. For certain, we did not have to embellish the facts, but the place to swap stories and to learn what was going on was still the Gooneyville.

Or was it? We excused ourselves early and dropped by the corner room to see who was around. None of our contemporaries was in sight, so we inquired.

"Oh, they're probably over at the senior officers' bar," was the courteous reply. We found it, but why we needed a bar and a steward to serve bottled beer was beyond us. Then we found we were expected to pay for each bottle instead of picking up the tab upon our departure for patrol. The small building and bar had been built, we were informed, so that the junior officers could supposedly kick up their heels elsewhere than right under their skipper's or exec's nose. What they were supposed to do on this gooney-infested island that needed shielding was beyond us. Those who had seen to this construction had unwittingly undercut the finest war patrol school in existence, for at that corner room ranks were never considered, and there the junior officer, coming exec, PCO, and skipper learned from seniors and juniors alike. We would not snub our friends from other boats, but *Tang*'s senior officers agreed to spend an appropriate amount of time at the Gooneyville hangout and keep that corner room buzzing at least while *Tang* was in port.

Included in the submarine talk was an update on Cherbourg, which had fallen to the Allies on July 1. The port and facilities had been demolished by the Germans and the harbor mined, so it would not be usable for a couple of months. Closer to us, *Albacore*, *Finback*, *Bang*, and *Stingray* had been positioned as scouts prior to the Battle of the Philippine Sea. They were further backed up by *Flying Fish* off San Bernardino Strait and *Seahorse* off Surigao Strait in the Philippines. These two had made contact with the Japanese carrier forces and formidable battleship force and got off their contact reports as required. Commander J. W. Blanchard and his *Albacore* got one or more hits in the new carrier *Taiho* on June 19, while my classmate Herm Kossler with his *Cavalla,* en route to relieve *Flying Fish,* torpedoed the carrier *Shokaku* on the same day. Both carriers sank. The main battle between the carrier planes of the Japanese and Task Force 58 had taken place on the 19th and 20th, and was described as The Marianas Turkey Shoot. About four times the forces were involved as in any previous encounter, and Japanese losses in planes probably precluded their being able to engage our combined forces again. No one had to mention that the loss of two carriers, one probably the Japanese flagship, had had a significant effect on the outcome.

I might just have to reconsider submarine actions in support of fleet operations, but in this case the submarines had been able to act independently, and their great value, other than the sinkings, was in contact reports from exact positions. Still, only two out of seven fired torpedoes, and for the others it had been a long patrol, as *Tang* well knew.

Completion of the work requests was staying right on schedule, but on this turn through *Tang* I was surprised to see my surf and deep-sea rods still secured in the overhead. They had been brought along for just such places as Midway, and last time were in nearly constant use. Ballinger provided the answer. There was now a recreation department on the island, complete with outfitted sportfishing boats, and even manned by specialists. Well, tomorrow the fish fry and ball game would take everyone's mind off their own and Midway's problems.

As before, the day started off with softball and beer. The game between the deck force and the engineers was the only one recreation had scheduled, however, and things hardly got warmed up before chow was down. The beer was good and cold, though short on quantity, but the fish fry was something to behold. Packages of fresh-frozen fillets from Boston had been allowed to thaw. They were then opened, and the fish were dipped in batter and dropped directly into hot cooking oil. The entrapped moisture practically exploded, and those who escaped a burn or two were just plain lucky. After recreation had secured, Frank took a volunteer working party to the Gooneyville and returned with all of the available cold beer. It saved the day. Before long, men were lolling along the beach, some taking a swim, and others sailing gooneybirds into the air with a gentle assist from the windward wing. With very little breeze, the albatross seemed to like the help in becoming airborne.

The gooneys would not change, but Midway had. The island was no longer a frontier, and it was time for *Tang* to be on her way. A private letter from our chief of staff, Captain Joe Grenfell, preceded our Operation Order and contained the necessary information for Fraz and Jones, who would need to draw detailed charts from the base. The last part of the letter would go on the bulletin board in the crew's mess:

Incidentally, Mishuitunni Ka insisted his name was Firecracker. CinCPac's intelligence questioned him for a week before they got him to say anything other than "Ten thousand tons," and say he was the toughest nut they've had to crack.

The *Yamaoka Maru* was not 10,000 tons but 7,500, and was carrying that amount of iron ore. If it is any consolation to *Tang*'s crew, she was on her maiden voyage to Tientsin and was returning to Kobe fully loaded.

The letter had Fraz laughing. "I guess I might as well tell you," he said. "Whenever you saw Firecracker coming to the movies, it was a reward for saying the tonnage of his ship was ten thousand. Sometimes the troops would feed him ice cream, but in the end they had him so well indoctrinated that if you'd just point to the middle of any good-sized ship in 208J, he'd say, 'Ten thousand tons,' without fail."

We had more serious things to discuss, for a short training period would start in two days, and I would now follow through on a decision I had made when having Frank surface *Tang* and close the last flotsam. A part of this period would be his, to make approaches and fire torpedoes, so that without reservation I could designate him as qualified for command. In the other part of the training period we would schedule a few indoctrinal depth charges. These would be primarily for our new hands but for the rest of us as well, for not since the tooth-shakers of our first patrol had *Tang* really been depth-charged.

Preliminary loading was routine, and there was no evidence of tampering with any of the frozen meat cartons. Frank made practice approaches on the first underway day, sandwiched between emergency drills for our two new officers and eight enlisted men. On the second day, his exercise torpedoes were hot, straight, and normal. A message from the target ship remained puzzling indeed, for the PC reported that one of the torpedoes still had its propeller key in place. Perhaps they were referring to the propeller lock, a rugged bronze device that slipped over one blade and between others of the counterturning propellers to prevent accidental firing. A check showed the propeller locks from our torpedoes still aboard.

Perhaps we would find out more about the locks ashore, but now came our depth-charge indoctrination, apparently the first conducted at Midway for some time. It had been necessary, of course, to notify all commands, and so the word spread, resulting in a fair number of spectators. *Tang* dived, keeping both scopes well above the surface, and the PC rolled by at maximum speed. The charge at 200 yards was approximately as expected, the whack followed by the rumbling swish through the superstructure. The next charge was scheduled for 100 yards but fell somewhat closer and did a fine job of indoctinating all hands. It should have been milder, but apparently the shock wave and detonation reflected from the hard coral bottom reinforced one another. Coinciding with the whack came the sound of a ton of bolts being dropped into our superstructure, or so it seemed. It was a reminder not to judge the proximity of a depth charge by the intensity of the sounds alone, and at least those ashore and on the PC had enjoyed a grand show.

The best part of the day had been Frank's performance, and now I faced the same dilemma as had my skipper before the war. If I sent in Frank's qualification now, he would probably have transfer orders waiting when we returned from our upcoming patrol. I could then lose both Frank and Fraz and this would approach the situation that obtained in both *Argonaut* and *Wahoo* preceding their losses. For selfish reasons, but also in the best interests of our ship, I would ask Commander Will to hold up forwarding the correspondence and his endorsement until *Tang* was heading back.

It had always been the privilege of a captain to be last in visiting the dentist; there was no one to prod him. This morning, the dentist proceeded directly with putting four small fillings in one tooth that was giving me no trouble, and to my query about cleaning my teeth said, "Oh, we take care of that during the afternoons." I was no expert in dentistry, but in the past cleaning and examination had always preceded any drilling. I assumed that I should have dropped in on the previous afternoon, but did so this day instead. The dentists were not in evidence, but I received a thorough scaling by a competent technician. When I returned aboard, Chief Ballinger posed a somewhat blunt and unexpected question, but that was his privilege.

"Did they charge you for cleaning your teeth, Captain?" Then without really receiving my answer, he exploded. "Well, I just found out that those bastards have been charging our troops five bucks apiece, and no one could get a dental appointment in the afternoon because the dentists were always out sportfishing!"

I thanked him for the report, turned on my heel, and headed for ComSubDiv 62's office where, in slightly more formal language, I repeated what Ballinger had told me.

The morning of July 30 broke on a nicer note. As a result of the recommendations hustled into the mail right here a month and a half before awards for Fraz, Ballinger, Jones, White, and Leibold had arrived, and for me the Legion of Merit for my conduct of the rescues at Truk, as well as a third Silver Star from my beloved *Wahoo*. Happily, a belated award, under more recent directives, had also come for Hank from *Tambor*. Commander Will made the presentations, and we could not have been more proud of these shipmates.

While we were still at quarters, Commander Will called Hank front and center again, and proceeded to read from a card attached to a large manila envelope: "Presented to Lieutenant (junior grade) Henry J. Flanagan, United States Navy, in recognition of his fifteen years of service in the furtherance of torpedo performance and capability." The commander then withdrew a beautifully finished mahogany plaque bearing the same inscription and mounted with a highly polished and horribly mangled propeller lock. Hank received the plaque in good grace, helped by a cheer from his torpedomen and a good laugh by all.

In the wardroom for coffee, Hank was reading his real citation when he blurted out, "I finally made it, after fifteen years I finally made it!" Then Hank, who had fleeted up from seaman in Uncle Sam's regular navy, read from the citation:

"Lieutenant (junior grade) Henry J. Flanagan, United States Naval *Reserve*."

"Well, move over, Hank, we might as well join your club," Fraz commented. "The captain, Mel, Dick, and I are the only regulars left."

Tang's final loading proceeded in the afternoon in an unhurried manner, with steam fish forward and electrics aft, and then continued on the 31st. By 1500 she was topped off with fuel and chow, and the lines were singled up. After a sincere Godspeed, Commander Will had left for an appointment, considering, no doubt, that we were taking the action required by a dispatch delivered by the base while he was aboard. In part he was correct. The message, from ComSub-Pac, directed that we leave witnesses to the dental shenanigans. Well, the force commander had sent the message he felt necessary, and we were making the only reply possible:

WITNESSES HAVE IMPORTANT BATTLE STATIONS
AND ARE NEEDED IN TANG ON THIS WAR PATROL

Only Fraz's formal report of ship ready for getting under way remained before casting off the lines, but now *Tang* had one man missing, Walker. Shipmates had him aboard in short order, though with his fists full of bills. His trip to buy money orders involved a repeat performance, and another detail was sent to round him up. We had a compulsive gambler!

It was 1555, almost an hour after our scheduled departure, when the base took in the lines. *Tang* backed quietly from the dock and twisted toward the basin's entrance leading to the dredged channel. Ahead lay the slice through the reef. The coral heads disappeared, and at my nod Hank ordered, "Rig ship for dive," then brought us to the navigator's recommended course, 270 degrees true. *Tang* was on her fourth war patrol.

2

Numbers 3 and 4 main engines were driving us through the moderate summer seas on a duplicate of the route we had followed on our last foray. Lieutenant (jg) Charles O. Pucket was standing his first watch as OOD on patrol. He was teamed with Hank, so little could go wrong, and nothing that couldn't be taken care of by the diving alarm. Small and light-complected, Charles was from Chattanooga, Tennessee, and had come to *Tang* from the relief crew. The recommendation of our senior petty officers who had now been detached was in the main responsible for his orders. It might not be the Navy Department's method of making assignments, but so far the selections were working out well for us.

I was about to go below when Fraz joined me on the cigarette deck, the out-of-the-way area aft of the shears. It was his way of giving me a chance to speak in private of anything that was on my mind. He was probably thinking of our rather unconventional departure, but we spoke instead of Midway, now below the horizon but with its position still marked by an area of aquamarine sky. How tremendously its location had affected Japanese strategy. The Empire's South and Central Pacific outposts had all become secure in operations following Pearl Harbor. Japanese conquest of Midway and the southern Aleutians would have completed a perimeter of bases from which their patrol planes could keep track of our naval operations. With the U.S. Pacific Fleet a shambles, a move against Midway was considered imminent, and *Argonaut* had patrolled there for two months awaiting the action. A submarine with two 6-inch, 53-caliber guns and 78 mines to defend an atoll, but she was the best our navy could do. Japan had the capability back then but delayed too long. When the battle did come, in early June, 1942, the enemy split his forces and lost four carriers to our one. Our victory in the Battle of Midway was won dearly, for nearly all of our torpedo bombers were lost. But their low-altitude attacks had diverted the attention of the Zekes and permitted our dive-bombers to carry out their task against the fleet so successfully. Now it was evident that this battle had been the real turning point of the war in the Pacific.

Douglas SBD Dauntless

We had just received our finest refit, so even though no longer near the van, Midway continued to make it possible for *Tang* and other submarines to be there. The charts Fraz and Jones had brought aboard told of our general destination, but I wished that those men in the relief crew and others who had worked on our equipment might have seen our Operation Order. Ballinger would now have posted the pertinent part in the crew's mess, and to all hands the directive would more than formalize the rumors; it would provide a thrill and a serious challenge as well. The first lines read: "When in all respects ready for sea and patrol proceed by route south of

Kure Reef to the Nampo Shoto and areas 4 and 5. Conduct offensive patrol against all shipping. There will be no friendly submarines in the adjacent areas. . . ."

To any seasoned submariner these two areas had long held the greatest possibilities—and the thunder, for they covered the whole south and a part of the east coast of Honshu, the main central island of the Japanese Empire. We had rounded up a goodly number of pertinent patrol reports, some dating back to the first months of the war. The tactics might have changed since some of these earlier patrols, but the areas had not, and there was just a chance that some of the tactics had come full circle. We would have only a week to study the reports, for they would all go to Davy Jones's locker before we entered the areas, or at least before moving onto soundings.

We would make our trim dive in the evening after all the mess gear was secured, trash dumped in weighted sacks, and the ritual of sanitaries completed. It had proved to be a good time on our last patrol, and on surfacing would be followed by the movies. Here was our ship on the same course, at the same speed, following the same routine, and now another pair of football legs was blocking the passageway forward. They belonged to Ensign Basil C. Pearce, Jr., from Palatka, Florida, who had come to *Tang* on the same recommendation as had Charles. In a moment his feet were solidly on the deck, and after an apology, which was unnecessary but did no harm, Basil followed me into the wardroom.

It was good to see and hear the wardroom buzzing again, and never had a cup of coffee at just the right temperature, hot, been served more quickly. Fraz had already told Walker that I chose to consider his antics in holding up *Tang*'s sailing a part of our leave and recreation. How could it be otherwise when, in truth, all hands had enjoyed this episode; and besides, pending mast cases were not compatible with the requirements of patrol.

The watch schedule worked in well, giving Basil the first dive. Larry stood in the background, no doubt gritting his teeth a bit, but I had seen worse dives by experienced officers. Our seasoned planesmen and chief would help any dive, of course, but if we concentrated on our new officers, they should be ready by the time we reached the Nampo Shoto. Such demands on young officers, especially ones who had not had an opportunity to attend submarine school, would have been deemed preposterous as late as two years before. We were not asking for a total performance, however, just one that would get our ship safely below, to where shipmates could assist if necessary.

This evening Fraz brought down the chart, with the position of his star fix plotted and then run ahead to 2000. We were doing well and would pass Kure Reef during the night. A change in course would be in order but could better wait until after the morning star fix, when we would not be turning toward a shoal during darkness. The only time that the cautions demanded by good seamanship might take second place was when in pursuit of the enemy. This night I penned normal night orders, but with additional information stressing some points for our new officers.

Proceeding on course 270° true at 80/90 on two main engines. The SD radar is secured and will be turned on only with my permission. The SJ heaters are on. Require sweeps and reports by the operator every 10 minutes, and search continuously commencing a half hour before morning twilight till daylight.

When in the conning tower, and as time permits, reread the standing night orders. Make all required reports and demand the reports you are to receive.

Do not be lulled by the 2,500 miles between us and the enemy's front door. He can be here just as surely as we will be there.

Do not hesitate to call me to the bridge, or to dive.

Our new course was 282 degrees true. We had come right the 12 degrees at 1230, after Frank's noon sun line had verified our latitude. He was still our senior watch officer but at times would take himself from the list during this transit to navigate. The opportunity to work with both Fraz and Jones could be invaluable. Others were learning, too, for our short training period had been only an introduction for Charles, Basil, and our eight new unqualified men. Some dives were scheduled, but others were not so that this training would approximate the expected operations off the Empire. In order not to slow the transit, fire control drills were held while we cruised on the surface, using sound bearings and propeller noises generated by *Tang*'s shaving brush-microphone method.

These propeller sounds were serving a dual pupose, for *Tang* had a new gadget. I had long thought it archaic for a sound operator to count a ship's propeller beat with stopwatch in hand, keeping in phase with the rhythm by either a hand motion or a bouncing knee, like a bandleader. Then came the quadrupling or doubling of the count if its duration was for 15 or 30 seconds instead of a minute. Detecting a speed change, except for an experienced soundman, was likewise time-consuming, sometimes coming too late to correct a firing solution speed error. There were instant-reading tachometers for engine revolutions, even strobe disks for home phonographs; why wasn't there something to give us an instantaneous reading for propeller sounds? A pulsing sound or note that the soundman could match with the propeller rhythm seemed a workable solution.

Back in December, I had been walking past Sherman Clay & Co. in San Francisco when a metronome in their window caught my eye. I went inside to find that they had an electric one, the works contained in a small, gray metal box. A husky knob swung a pointer along a curved scale, which was already graduated in beats per minute, and the range covered that of the propeller beats of merchantmen and heavy ships. For fast screws, like a destroyer's, the metronome's beats might be matched with every other propeller swish. Time would not permit official purchase by the U.S. Navy—and such a device for a submarine would certainly raise some eyebrows—so, still feeling flush with recently acquired submarine pay, I bought my ship a present.

We had figured various ways of feeding the metronome's beat into the audio end of the JK sound receiver so that the operator would hear it in his earphones, but the task had low priority, and we were seeking perfection. Our coming operations, where information from sound could be of special importance, had changed all of that, and Midway mounted the little gray box on a bracket adjacent to the receiver, where the soundman, with his headset pushed off his ears a bit, could hear it direct. There was no coercion, but our soundmen found it worked fine on the propeller sounds we generated in the forward torpedo room. Some would reserve judgment till we had a real enemy ship, but as the captain's gadget, the metronome was undoubtedly assured of a fair shake.

At general quarters, when they were on watch, but especially in the wardroom, we were getting to know our new officers. My first impression of Charles as a quiet Southern gentleman needed some modification. Charles fitted in with the rest of us, and when it came to throwing an acey-deucey or pegging out, he could be as noisy as anyone else. With Hank, Frank, Dick, and now Basil aboard, the wardroom needed but one to round out a basketball team. Basil, like Dick, was a real all-American boy, pushed into growing up by the serious threat to our nation; he would fit in anywhere.

Before *Tang* crossed the arcs of possible enemy air patrols, I made my customary inspection of our boat. It was for one purpose, to assure myself that all was secured for sea. Someone else's word in this was not enough, for unless he had slugged it through a hurricane or typhoon on the surface, he could not appreciate its importance. One piece of heavy gear adrift almost surely meant injuries and damage as well. The walk-through took little time, for loose gear had been well lashed. Having observed the effort, I would not have to give the matter another thought on this patrol.

Fraz dropped by my cabin after dinner to advise me that we would be within range of patrol planes from Marcus at dawn, and this threat would carry through until patrols from the Nampo Shoto area might be expected. It was just a double check, for we had changed to the east longitude date, which was always confusing, and he knew I would want to include extra precautions in the night orders. We would meet the small additional hazard with extra lookouts, as we had before. At my invitation, he occupied the preferred chair, my bunk, and we studied the ship contacts he had tabulated from reports of previous patrols in our areas. They were not yet plotted but listed by date with corresponding latitudes and longitudes. Over the past several months the contacts had dropped off steadily, and a glance at their latitudes showed practically all of them to the north, close to Honshu, on coastal shipping. We had no patrol reports from the last quarter, but a private message written by Admiral Lockwood covered that. I handed the penned note to Fraz.

Dear Dick,

I want to tell you why I am sending you and your *Tang* right back to the Empire, with hardly a breather. We have had two poor, and now a dry patrol in these areas, the boats reporting a dearth of shipping.

Intelligence reports indicate that the merchant traffic must be there, and I am certain that *Tang* can rediscover it.

Sincerely, and Godspeed,
C.A. Lockwood

Fraz read the note and didn't bat an eye. "It requires nothing that we wouldn't do anyway," he commented, and in every respect he was absolutely right.

"Well, we don't need intelligence to tell us that the ships are there and running. The war is still going on, so they have to be either loading or at sea, but I don't expect that we'll find them off soundings, or off the ten-fathom curve for that matter. Of course the admiral's note underlines my responsibilities."

Fraz's answer was a nod. We both knew that this note was a compliment to our ship and offered a challenge to each of us.

Tang continued to enjoy yachting weather, with flying fish skimming away from her bow. Our camouflage seemed to be serving a dual purpose, for nightly a few fish would land on deck. Walker undoubtedly had something to do with the supply brought below, for Frank reported meeting him topside before the crack of dawn, waiting to scurry about the deck as soon as their white shapes were visible in the first gray light. Fish for breakfast remained the captain's prerogative, though now others shared, especially Frank on Friday for, he pointed out, he was a good Catholic and thus a bona fide "fisheater."

Unlike the Nansei Shoto, whose spacing makes it troublesome for nearly 150 miles below Kyushu, the Nampo Shoto has a convenient passage. Forty miles wide, it lies between Mikura Jima and Hachijo Jima. The track that the navigator had laid down on our chart passed ten miles south of Mikura Jima. Only about eight miles in diameter and rising to nearly 3,000 feet, this volcanic island would make an excellent radar target and serve as our landfall as well. This was *Tang*'s destination on August 8, as clear dawn promised another fine day.

The yachting ended abruptly with Basil's booming "Clear the bridge! Clear the bridge!" He had hooked them up in series, which was fine as long as the lookouts didn't freeze in their tracks. *Tang* slid under the sea for 30 minutes, until a Betty bomber at about eight miles disappeared on to the south. The time of the sighting was 0950, and if there were still some who didn't believe we were in enemy waters, another bomber at 1410 was the convincer. The range on this sighting was too great for identification, and this was as it should be. We were reasonably certain that neither plane had sighted us, but Bettys had played tricks on us before. With a full can, and plenty of time on our side, we cruised submerged for an extra half hour, content that no Zekes or other fast bombers arrived.

Tang was on the last leg of the transit, on course 273 degrees true, and according to our navigators, Mikura Jima should loom up at midnight. A cheer carried forward from the crew's mess; someone just going on watch or perhaps just relieved had won their pool. The time was 2359, and on a hunch, based in part on reports of possible nearby radar installations, *Tang* moved quietly 20 miles into her area, southwest to Inamba Jima. It is a small pinnacle, uninhabitable, and was thus even more suitable for checking our SJ. This would serve as a reference point for our submerged patrol at dawn.

3

Jones had plotted all of the available ship contacts in this immediate portion of the Nampo Shoto and had drawn in a median. It turned out to be a convenient north-south line about halfway between Inamba and Mikura Jima, and *Tang* would patrol along that track on this August 9 as she worked her way toward Honshu. The final checks of the SJ and TDC were completed, and two unhurried blasts sent our ship beneath the calm though slightly rolling seas.

Our chances of a good ship contact had, of course, been reduced by the Japanese loss of the Marianas in June. This very loss, however, increased the importance of the Bonins. Lying halfway between Japan and the Marianas, these islands were ideally situated as a base for interceptors that might then thwart any planned bombing raids coming to the Empire from Saipan or Guam. Building up the necessary facilities would require shipping, two-way shipping, and the previous day's patrols might well indicate that some of this traffic was under way. In any case, this was a better spot to patrol than in the open sea between here and the central coast.

The day wore on but with willing hands standing by for

turns on one of the scopes. Though on frequent searches the lenses were 26 feet above the surface, nothing but the two islands came in sight, not even a sampan. Still, it was turning out to be a good day for our men and officers, for this was their first opportunity for full watches on the planes and with the dive. For each section, *Tang*'s plank-owners gave demonstrations in the art of slow-speed control on down to stopped and then balancing.

We had worked northward slowly, across a submerged mountain 300 fathoms down, good for a Fathometer test, when Basil sighted possible smoke to the west, beyond a small pinnacle and reef called Zeni Su. Fraz had searched with the same high scope by the time I reached the conning tower, and I followed. Neither of us could identify anything, but as we had long ago learned from reports from lookouts, no tentative sighting could be discounted. Three blasts sent us up into the fading light to investigate. Radar and 7 × 50s searching out into the night found only Zeni Su, a nice-sounding name but a treacherous shoal and pinnacle. The search had not taken us far off our track to the coast; we were unhurried, and nothing was lost.

As it turned out, the short jaunt to westward showed the desirability of continuing on the same heading so that we might then approach Honshu normal to the beachline, directly to an open bight west of Omae Saki. This position lay close to the middle of our two assigned patrol areas and seemed a good place for a starter. More important, shipping between Nagoya and Tokyo and from other ports would be visible for miles as it proceded along this straight coastline, thus practically guaranteeing a successful submarine torpedo attack. Another feature, and perhaps of greater significance to the submariner, was the 100-fathom curve. In this vicinity only, it curves to within one mile of the ten-fathom curve and three miles from the beach. After an attack in this position, *Tang* should be able to reach deep submergence in 15 minutes, maybe less.

Of course the enemy knew all of these things, too, but there was only one way to find out what he had done about them. Even with our dogleg, there were only 70 miles to go. The battery charge was completed before midnight, and we moved in slowly, now heading due north. Not knowing what may lie ahead and having time to think about it is not a good combination, but we resisted our natural urge to close the bight during the dark night. An unsuspected patrol boat

might then thwart the reconnaissance that was a part of our
mission and a subsequent attack, too. Better that we continue
closing slowly and dive for a daylight examination of the
beach as well as patrols and shipping.

A quick SJ sweep and a single ping sounding checked
Fraz's position; *Tang* had passed the 300-fathom curve 15
miles west of Omae Saki and was now six miles from the
shore. Just a semblance of gray showed in the east, and the
coast of Honshu appeared only as a fuzzy line to northward. I
followed Fraz below, and then came Charles's "Clear the
bridge," the diving alarm and the roar through the vents. We
were on our way for a close-up of Hirohito's main island and
perhaps his shipping, too.

The time was 0441, and now we would go through a period
of blindness until there was sufficient light for the scopes.
With two scopes, one of them could certainly have been designed for better light transmission. The British had long had
such a scope, but our construction had followed the ideas of
submarine warfare as visualized in the Geneva Convention, of
a submergible raider that would bring an enemy ship to and
then sink it only after all hands were safe in the boats. Of
course, this could only be done in daylight. It was a nice
thought, put forth after the "war to end all wars," and none
of us would have objected if it was in any way practical. That
was the basis for our temporary blindness, but the solution
was now at hand due to the development of a radar scope. It
had more generous optics and was consequently an excellent
lightcatcher. We'd make another try for one at Pearl.

"Bearing—mark! Range—mark!" came from Frank on the
search scope, trying out his new qualification. Fraz called
the bearing, 55 degrees, and Ogden, ducking under him, read
the stadimeter range of 12,000 yards as the scope went down.

"It's a PC type, Captain, nearly hull down. The angle is
forty port."

I liked Frank's positive report; he did not hem and haw
but made his one estimate. As in answering a true-false quiz,
the first estimate of an angle was generally the best. There
was no action to be taken, for the patrol was crossing from
starboard to port, except to see if a ship might be following.
This was asking too much in such a short time since our dive,
but now both scopes were busy, one searching to the east and
the other following the PC type escort off to the west and
checking relative bearings with sound. The range had actually
been closer, for Ogden had read the stadimeter opposite a

100-foot masthead height, which was our practice until a ship was at least partially identified. This patrol probably had a height of 70, and that would have to be reduced to the height above the horizon.

Walker brought coffee to the conning tower, but Fraz and I decided to have an early breakfast to go with it. Now with Frank at the con, this might be our only chance in what could be a busy day.

"I think we should have moved in closer, Fraz. It's the same old thing, two of us on the bridge and we get too cautious," I commented halfway through a plate of bacon and eggs.

"Speaking as the navigator, I like just what we're doing. We could have been right underfoot, and that PC could have spoiled our whole day. We're not rushed."

We were cooperative but frank, almost a must in joining the enemy. Already, even before breakfast, we knew there would be shipping. That PC was not out here pleasure cruising, and we had the time to wait for the big ones. The hours might be a little wearing, and some shifting of the watch would be necessary, especially as we closed the ten-fathom curve, where we could afford no mistakes. Fraz, Frank, and Ballinger would take care of this, with my stipulation that our two new officers would take the dive with one of our experienced officers and, not known to them, would have the backing of our most experienced petty officers when in the conning tower.

The morning watch had been relieved a full hour when the 1MC hummed in wardroom country, followed instantly by "Captain to the conning tower!" This use of the 1MC indicated a contact or an emergency, and I was on my way up the ladder. The contact was there, but the emergency had passed; *Tang* was on the beam of a large engine-aft ship, which was passing unbelievably close to the beach. Her escorts were three patrolling bombers, but they made little difference, for at 6,000 yards we were hopelessly out of position.

Battle stations had been sounded automatically, and now we tracked the ship on down the coast, not losing sight of her until the TDC's generated range had passed 13,000. She was making 12 knots, and had we first spotted her at that range, *Tang* could handily have reached an attack position. The responsibility was still mine, and in all fairness, tracking a ship until it disappeared was quite a different thing from making a first sighting, especially under these circumstances.

SOUTH COAST HONSHU
Kii Suido to Inubo Saki

30 MILES

135° E 136° E 137° E

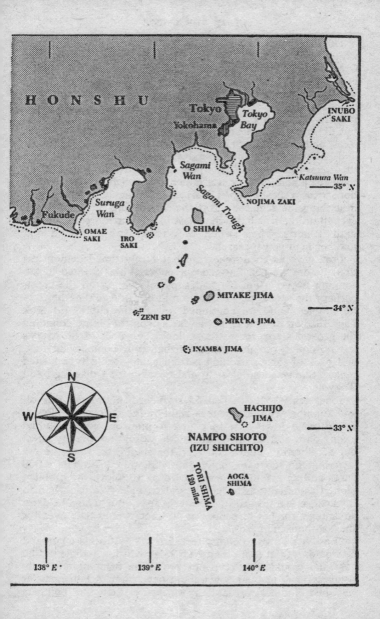

This forenoon drill led to a discussion in the wardroom, while Fraz took the con and Ballinger assumed the dive. Obviously, Ed felt guilty, but that was squared away in a hurry. None of us could say that we would have sighted this ship earlier, but we could go over carefully all of the things to look for in spotting a distant enemy ship that was close inshore. The puff of smoke or light brown haze, of course, but the mast, canted or straight, that did not match with the trees, and the relative movement, or lack of it, between trees and poles as the submarine moved parallel to the beach were the items to discern. An inconsistency might disclose the masts of a ship, and even a hunch was worthy of reexamination, witness the *Yamaoka Maru*. I still knew no better way of describing the required effort than by saying, "Just put your eyeball on the beach, up the coast to the horizon, and squeeze until it hurts. Then switch eyes for a sweep around and another high-power search."

Fraz gave us an unrehearsed but nicely timed demonstration. Before we had finished our coffee, I was wanted in the conning tower again. He had a patrol coming up the coast, perhaps the same one we had seen at dawn. Avoiding her was no problem, and we continued toward the shore. Ed took back the con and let us get as far as control before sounding the general alarm for battle stations. The Bells of St. Mary's left no doubt; our man of action had four bombers in sight, and back of their patrolling pattern came an old type loaded tanker. She was also close in and heading for Omae Saki and Tokyo.

Jones read 352, I called 55 starboard, and *Tang* was off and running with 15 degrees right rudder. Fraz and Frank would come down with the course to intercept before we had swung past, and the moderate rudder would not greatly affect our acceleration. Jones had read the stadimeter range before lowering the scope on down into the well. With this 8,000 yards and an assumed enemy speed of 10 knots, the problem plotted essentially as an equilateral triangle. We each had to traverse a leg toward the eastern apex, but *Tang* held an advantage, for her torpedoes at 46 knots would take over for the last thousand yards.

"Ease her down to eighty feet, Larry." With this command he would not put more than 2 or 3 degrees down-angle on the boat and would thus keep our propellers from momentarily rising as *Tang* pivoted down about her center of buoyancy. It was just another precaution to insure that the bombers overhead would not sight a slick or swirl about our props in the flat, calm sea.

We were settled on course 050, on what might be our only leg of this approach. This was a new situation for most of the crew, since the enemy could not zig away and an attack was virtually a certainty. There were disadvantages, too, for time would not permit the frequent observations that made for precise tracking. The hour was now 1020, ten minutes into the approach, and we slowed for a sound bearing and possible look. Caverly called 345 true; we had gained a little but could not afford the delay of an observation. Better that we save a few moments for quick checks before firing. Standard speed rolled us on.

It was 1030, another ten minutes into the run, and as we slowed Larry brought us up to periscope depth. Caverly called the bearing, no change. Welch called our speed, 4 knots. Jones awaited my nod and brought the scope up smartly; I rode it on up till the lens was clear of the surface. The enemy was coming on big and fat, completely black, and with an ungainly tall stack aft.

"Bearing—mark!" Jones read 315 relative.

"Range—mark!" He read the stadimeter on the way down, 1,300 yards; Caverly's echo range corrected it to 1,200. There were three minutes to go. The outer doors were open forward. Another periscope bearing and echo range checked with the TDC's presentation. *Tang* was steady on course. The clock read 1034.

"Five degrees to go," Fraz warned. Jones had the scope's handles at deck level. I glanced at the depth gauge, right on at 64 feet, and held my hands at waist height; the handles rode up into them.

"Constant bearing—mark!" She was racing across the steady wire.

"Set!" Frank called. Her stern came on.

"Fire!" Fraz hit the plunger—he considered this his prerogative—and our first torpedo was on its way with a healthy zing. The second and third fish went to the tanker's middle and at her bow. A quick sweep showed three bombers still out ahead, the fourth was not in sight. I did not search.

"Right full rudder. All ahead standard. Get a sounding, Caverly." We would be turning toward deep water during the torpedo run. Fraz checked the prepared card opposite 1,200 yards for the time and read 58.8 seconds. We would not worry about the tenths, just the whole 35 seconds to go—and the sea bottom, for Caverly had just reported two fathoms under our keel. With but 12 feet for vertical maneuvering in any evasion, we might as well stay at periscope depth, at least until the torpedoes had time to do their work. The 58 seconds for the first torpedo had passed, and now an additional 15 seconds for the next two. There were no explosions.

We slowed, steadied on due south, and sneaked a look. The tanker was still proceeding, but a few seconds later, two minutes after our firing, she reversed course to the left. We pulled in our neck, rigged in our sound heads, grabbed another sounding, and started deep, now thoroughly expecting a bomb or aerial depthcharge attack. Our surprise came when we rolled on the bottom, but our submarine was tough and could take things like this. At least all hands now knew that we were getting them into the safety of the deep as fast as possible.

There would be no more hunting in this vicinity today, at least not of the kind we wanted, so after reaching 400 feet we came right to course 250. This would keep *Tang* outside the 100-fathom curve for a time while we caught our breath and still parallel the coast for possible later contact. Nothing stirred.

"Would you like to go over the firing data now, Captain?" Fraz inquired after we had reached the wardroom. It was certainly a good time, here in the quiet with nothing likely to disturb us, but it was too soon after the attack. The excitement and frustrations of the morning would need an hour to subside, and then we would be able to examine our failure more logically. The morning was not a total loss, however, for we now knew of one place to intercept ships that were plying between Tokyo and the many ports to the west. That the enemy would continue sending ships along this flat stretch of coastline without the proper surface escorts seemed doubtful indeed. Still, this was a part of the game, and while the Japanese worried about the Omae Saki area, we would attack elsewhere.

An hour after the firing, with no screws, pings, or other sounds on the JK or JP, we started the climb to periscope depth. Our ascent was cautious, leveling off at 80 feet while Larry adjusted the trim. The quick low-power periscope sweep and the careful highpower search disclosed nothing except the shoreline to the north, not even a plane. A sounding showed us across the 100-fathom curve, a little farther to the north than expected but on the line for an afternoon patrol off the Irago Suido, the strait leading to Ise Wan, the large, shallow bay below Nagoya.

After lunch, Frank and the battle stations tracking party reran the complete approach through the TDC. Again the Quartermaster's Notebook was invaluable. Between the information from it and the true, or navigational, plot the whole situation was recreated and run through to its conclusion. Frank, Mel, and Dick brought the results down to the wardroom. In addition, they had made a largescale plot of the firing, which showed the torpedo tracks and that of the enemy. We should have had hits, at least two of them; with an average torpedo track of 110 degrees—torpedoes coming in on the target from 20 degrees abaft the beam—large variations in the enemy's course would result in practically the same lead angle. We could have had some speed error since firing just 24 minutes after first sighting was something akin to shooting from the hip. Still, the final setups included accurate echo ranges to go with exact periscope bearings, and these positively fixed the tanker's position and checked the speed determination.

It would be easier if we could find a simple error, something that we could correct before the next firing, but now we were considering the torpedoes themselves. We had heard zings as they left the tubes, but our own screw noise had blanked them out as we turned toward deep water. The planes had not sighted their wakes, which would have led right to our firing position, or surely we would have been attacked. Still, something alerted the enemy about one minute after the torpedoes should have hit. We were in part guessing, but there seemed only one conclusion: The hard bottom off Honshu had not been as kind to our torpedoes and their warheads as had the mud at Amma To, and this could also account for their not exploding on the beach 2,000 yards beyond the tanker.

I do not believe that any one of us was sure that we had arrived at the correct answer, but we were most certainly not trying to blame the torpedoes. A miss was a miss regardless of the cause, but on subsequent attacks we would try to fire from deeper water if possible. Distant depth charges brought the discussion to a close. Sound located the detonations in a broad band across our stern, and we were quite satisfied not to be able to see the enemy during a single search with 20 feet of scope. It was 1500, and we changed course to the southwest to keep well clear of Daio Saki. The four hours to dark passed routinely, giving most hands an opportunity to rest up. The time was 1920, and three blasts sent us toward the surface to continue our search for the enemy.

4

All had appeared dark through the scopes, but now with 7 × 50s and the faint light from the upper limb of the moon, our lookouts would spot any ship or patrol that crossed our horizon. It gave us a secure feeling, as did the two diesels jamming energy back into *Tang*'s batteries. When the gravity was sufficient for another day submerged, we would move on to the southwest coast of Honshu, an easy hour's run ahead. For the moment, our position below the shoals extending down from Daio Saki seemed ideal. Any sizable shipping would have to pass at least five miles south of the point, and contact would be almost guaranteed. The topside watch was quiet and intent.

There was a mixture of business and pleasure below. Willing hands were beating down a mound of dough on the forward starboard table in the crew's mess. It had obviously risen more than usual in our long, hot dive and was attracting more attention than the acey-deucey. To port, at the far end of the crew's washroom, two hands from the duty section were taking their turn at running the sacks of accumulated laundry through the machine. They would then hang it on lines in one engine room, and since it was well marked each man could easily retrieve his own. This nightly detail insured clean skivvies daily and provided a change of pace for those involved. Aft, electricians and motormacs were at their stations in the engine rooms and maneuvering, meticulously following the curves that guided the charge. In the battery wells, below the living spaces, others were checking the specific gravity of the pilot cells and then recording the ventilation flow meters in the living spaces above. It was all business, serious business except in the forward torpedo room, where the usual movie was in progress before a full house.

The whole scene would surely have given anyone a feeling of satisfaction and confidence.

A pause in the movie to announce that the smoking lamp was out indicated that the battery charge was on the finishing rate. The extra hydrogen now being generated would be carried away by the blowers at their maximum speed; still, every precaution would be taken to insure that there could be no explosion. The announcement also meant that we could move in to the coast and carry out any operation, night or day, even both if need be. We were not unhappy at leaving this spot, for Daio Saki, according to the intelligence supplement accompanying our Operation Order, had 252 megacycle radar. It did not show our APR-1, which was coupled to the raised SD antenna, before surfacing nor after our decks were high and dry. Still, an enemy radio technician could just be completing the last connection on a new modulation network, and one pip would eliminate surprise. At least these considerations provided a good enough reason to get on with our exploration, which anyone would prefer.

The coast loomed up black, a bit foreboding and eerie as we followed the 100-fathom curve due west to within five miles of the shore. The curve turned southward, down the coast, and its line served as a ready-made track for Fraz and Jones, one from which *Tang* departed to investigate various locations but which remained as a safe guide. Except for a 15-mile straight portion, the coast was marked by large and small bays with intervening sharp headlands, some with deep water nearly to the cliffs. The best of these promontories was Miki Saki, about halfway down the coast, and we doubled back at midnight to insure reaching it before the crack of dawn.

Frank temporarily filled in for Fraz as had Mort in the Yellow Sea. Perhaps having two execs was the answer for successfully patrolling the Empire, for now Fraz and I had nearly four hours to get in shape for another inshore day. We relaxed with Mel and Charles, who had just come off watch, and reviewed what we had seen while waiting for Adams's apricot turnovers to come out of the oven. We were unanimous in the opinion that no ship had sneaked by so far this night, but I was alone in believing that the enemy had to run some night shipping. Surely the enormous losses he had suffered made getting the available bottoms through without delay all the more imperative. But night or day, we meant to find and sink his ships.

An hour or so passed before the heat from the battery charge was dissipated and the cool predawn air returned the living spaces to normal. It was still not a night for sleeping, as Frank and the OOD kept me informed of *Tang*'s progress up the coast. Then came the anticipated report from Frank: Nigishima Saki was abeam and we had slowed as directed. The next point, only five miles farther on, would be Miki Saki. The duty chief, Hudson, had the morning watch relieve a few minutes early so as not to confuse the pending dive. Fraz gave the course to the point, 280 true, and *Tang* came to it. When we steadied, Miki Saki's black shape showed up dead ahead. The time was 0400. Eighteen minutes later, three miles from the point, Dick's firm "Clear the bridge" and well-spaced blasts sent our ship below the sea.

Tang continued on course, blind for the next half hour. Then details gradually became discernible, first the shore and then almost simultaneously the bow wake of a patrol and smoke. Before we could reach an approach course, this escort and a large engine-aft ship had ducked around Miki Saki into Kada Wan and then down the coast. Whipping around that point at full speed, exposing themselves for only minutes, had been a smart move. Even if in position, a submarine would have had no time for tracking, and for the moment we all knew how Casey at the bat must have felt.

The enemy's patrol activity increased steadily. At least one echo-ranging patrol was in sight almost continuously, and another cruised back and forth about 1,000 yards off Miki Saki. The action of this latter patrol dictated our own tactics; *Tang* would simply do the same 2,000 yards farther out and move in to attack the next ship. By presenting a minimum angle for her ping, we would probably not give her an echo, and there was plenty of water for evasion if we did. Fraz joined me for a late breakfast. Dick and Larry had already finished but stayed for more coffee and perhaps to hear if we had anything to say. We did, but not about the first ship; that was already in the past. I could tell what Fraz was going to say by his smile and the look in his eye.

"This is the spot, Captain." I answered with a nod.

"That makes five of us in agreement," said Larry. "I'm including the Japs, of course." He had hit it on the button; find the patrol activity and you'd find the ships. Larry handed me the phone, which had buzzed to my left. The Japanese had just added something new, simple, and possibly effective to their antisubmarine arsenal; Mel had a small-craft in sight, resembling a landing craft, carrying six lookouts. He also reported the wind dying. Fraz went up to survey the situation, and I followed shortly after.

The sea had become smooth and glassy, and just cutting in our position now required minimum periscope exposure lest it be sighted. This was made more difficult by the speed required to overcome the countercurrent setting us to the south; we had to slow before each look so that our scope would show no feather. The inshore patrol did not help, either, for just as we were regaining our position, so it seemed, we would be forced to steer courses across the current in order to present a minimum angle and thus were set to the south again. It all made for a trying morning, further aggravated by the small-craft, who did a good job of making a nuisance of herself. The situation became more serious at 1244, when a modern-looking gunboat, loaded with depth charges, forced us on down as she passed nearly overhead. On our way back to periscope depth, sound detected loud pinging on a bearing different from the gunboat's. Jones and Fraz quickly had the general course plotted as coming up the coast. This antisubmarine patrol was not as big as her ping, but what she lacked in size she made up in savvy. When abreast of Miki Saki, she turned directly toward our scope and succeeded in bluffing us off the 50-fathom curve as we kept our stern to her. The reason for this tactic became apparent when a tanker nosed out of Kada Wan, to the south, and ducked around Miki Saki with *Tang* again in no position to attack. In fairness to our ship and Hank, who had been on the scope, lucky timing by the escort was a big factor. The patrol was back on our quarter when she turned towards, and to swing toward her would have meant presenting our broadside to her ping before our aspect would again sharpen. With a ship in sight, an aggressive submarine commander would have done this anyway, but the ship had come minutes later and Hank was not in command. It was my responsibility, and next time we would turn towards and go under the SOB.

In midafternoon we were still at it when quite suddenly our periscopes commenced fogging as they had in the Yellow Sea. A check with the bathythermograph gave us the answer; changing tides were bringing cold seas from the deep to the surface near shore. Our chilled lenses now fogged almost instantly on exposure to the humid midsummer air and would not clear for several seconds. The longer exposures led to the sighting of our scope by the pesky small-craft. She was tenacious and extremely difficult to shake, remaining in our immediate vicinity for over an hour and probably calling like mad for assistance from one of the patrols. This tomfoolery came to a screeching halt with the Bells of St. Mary's.

We had smoke, two columns of it, coming up the coast, and *Tang*, now a bit to the north in shaking the small-craft, was off on a high-speed run into Owashi Wan. Welch took the wheel, Jones stepped over as my assistant on the scope, Ogden went to plot, Caverly to sound. In moments the immediate battle stations were manned, and an air of confidence seemed to permeate the conning tower. This would be no fly-by-night approach and attack; we'd be all set for these ships when they came by. The time was 1635, over 12 hours into the dive.

Fraz had plotted the approximate track of the tanker that had slipped by early in the afternoon, and a spot on this track was our destination. At standard speed down here at 80 feet, we would cause no turbulence and should leave our small-craft still searching some four miles behind out in 80 fathoms. *Tang* should still have 40 fathoms, or nearly 180 feet under her keel, when she reached the track, and that was more than we had enjoyed almost anywhere in the Yellow Sea.

The half-hour run passed slowly, seemingly minute by minute. I held up both hands, fingers extended, and Fraz ordered all ten tubes ready for firing, torpedo depth six feet. The order and subsequent reports seemed to make the time pass more quickly. With five minutes to go, we slowed to two-thirds speed, and then one-third.

"Bring us up to sixty-four feet, Larry." The up-angle was modest, but *Tang* leveled at periscope depth quickly and took a slight down-angle that would counter the bow's tendency to rise on firing. Welch called our speed and Caverly the sound bearing. We had guessed right; the enemy was on our port bow, and Jones guided the scope to the correct bearing before the lens broke the surface. Marks for the bearing, range, then angle, and the scope was down. We went ahead standard, and then I described the enemy to the fire control party; the telephone talkers would send the word throughout the ship. The columns of smoke had become two mast-funnel-mast split-superstructure freighters. The leader was medium-sized, about 5,000 tons, the second in column somewhat smaller. On our side of them was the gunboat that had driven us deep, while ahead a smaller escort was apparently patrolling. Best of all, both ships were heavily loaded.

Six minutes at standard held the bearing, but a tapping sound broke the silence in the conning tower.

"No change in speed, Captain, still seven two turns," Caverly reported, and Sherman Clay's metronome had become a part of *Tang*'s sound and torpedo fire control equipment. There was time only to acknowledge the report, for even with the enemy's slow speed, firing was but minutes away. Identification had now classified the larger ship, a *Biyo Maru* freighter. Fire control had her on course 020, steaming at 6 knots. Fraz gave the course for a 100 starboard track, 290, and at my nod Welch brought *Tang* to it.

"Open all outer doors forward."

"Seven degrees to go, Captain." Fraz's was the best report of all; it had been a rough two days, and in minutes we'd be getting the hell out of here.

"Stand by for constant bearings. Up scope."

"Fast screws bearing three four zero, Captain!" Caverly was not excitable, but with this report he came close to it. I swung left and Jones brought me on. It was the gunboat with a zero angle, this side of a thousand yards, and with a tall, white V for a bow wake. At 20 knots it would take her over a minute to reach us; continuing with the attack was automatic.

"Constant bearing—mark! Keep her sound bearings coming, Caverly."

"Set!" came instantly; Frank sensed the urgency.

"Fire!" and the first torpedo was zinging to intercept the leading freighter. Two more fish followed, and then a similar spread of three to the second ship in column. Never could individual torpedoes, each to hit a point, have been fired more urgently. I swung left to the sound bearing of the gunboat. With the scope in low power, she filled the field. I had misjudged her range or speed, but if she had once had our exact position, she had lost it during our water-lapping periscope exposures. Now she was boiling past our stern, apparently having mistaken the direction of *Tang*'s motion, and was out of position for an immediate attack. Ogden was counting the seconds till our first torpedo should hit, "Five four, three . . ." I swung the periscope back to the leading freighter in time for the first explosion, right in her middle. It must have ruptured her Scotch boilers, for the ship broke in two, practically disintegrating. I took a final bearing of the gunboat, then gave Jones the scope; I had more pressing interests in conning *Tang* to put the gunboat astern. Though she had missed our position before, she would now have six converging torpedo wakes leading right to *Tang*'s firing point. Her turn would be far enough away to insure being at full speed for her attack, but she could be back within two minutes. With a conscious effort to sound calm and assured, I ordered, "Flood negative. Take her deep. Rig for depth charge."

5

Fourteen thousand welcome pounds of salt water surged into negative, accentuating the down-angle and pulling *Tang* bodily toward the deep. Watertight doors were being closed and dogged; bulkhead clapper valves in the ventilation lines were being secured; and all machinery not required for maneuvering was shut down. It seemed painfully slow, until Ogden timed two sharp detonations as our fourth and fifth torpedoes; only 66 seconds had passed since firing! The gunboat would have to be our proxy in observing the results. She would be coming in from near astern and was already echo-ranging. It would be comforting to know there was a temperature gradient above us that would deflect her howling pings, but getting a bathythermograph card in these seconds would have been difficult. The knowledge would really make no difference, for on reaching a path just off the ocean floor, we would be below any gradient that existed.

There had been various staff recommendations concerning personal protection during depth-charging, such as lying in one's bunk, relaxed. Since most of these were not very realistic, submariners at sea did what they liked as long as it was compatible with their battle stations. Some preferred standing in the clear, where they'd not be bashed by solid objects and such. Others liked to hang on tightly, for the very same reason. My position when conning by sound was to remain wedged between the large pipe housing the SD mast and the battle stations sound operator, specifically Caverly, who had already turned his left earphone outward.

The gunboat was now closing fast from slightly on our port quarter. The very low bearing rate and the intensity of her screws both spelled *close*. Any maneuver would throw our bow or stern closer still; there was but one order: "Keep her going down, Larry!" If we lost one sound head, we still had another. The bearing rate suddenly picked up. Caverly trained right and had the gunboat going away; she would have dropped. She had, but between ear-splitting, wracking explosions Welch heard me order, "All ahead full, left full rudder!" As arranged, Caverly got a sounding, and Larry was on the way to 180 feet, two fathoms off the bottom. Maneuvering poured in the juice, and by the gunboat's fifth pass all detonations were to shoreward. There had been 22 close ones, and now compartments checked in from forward aft. No damage except light bulbs; we should have more with flexible portions above the threads. Even better than the reports was the unmistakable twisting, scrunching, breaking-up noise, loud in the direction of the enemy, easily audible even above our screws at 100 turns. We rigged for normal submerged cruising.

In 38 minutes we were back at periscope depth watching the gunboat, 4,000 yards back on *Tang*'s quarter. Beyond her was the other escort, at the approximate scene of the attack and apparently picking up survivors. One plane was now circling the area; nothing else was in sight. The time was 1821, only 40 minutes after the attack, but it seemed like a week.

In the wardroom, Larry was slowly shaking his head and looking down at the green poker cloth as if it were spread out for a courtmartial. Before I had a chance to compliment his excellent control of our ship, he spoke up.

"Captain, if I'd known depth charges would be like those, I might just have stayed in surface ships."

"Larry, they seemed close because you're not used to them. When we get some that are really close, these won't seem too bad. Just wait and you'll see."

Larry looked up in disbelief, and Fraz, sitting across from him, was able to keep a sober face. I wasn't and confessed: This was my tenth patrol, and that lousy gunboat had laid them down faster and closer than any I had experienced before. If *Tang* were not blessed with the new deep hull, we'd probably be wrestling with repairs this very minute. The confession perked Larry up, and he reached for the cribbage board to get us back in fighting trim, while Fraz took a turn through the boat.

Fraz returned shortly and reported that he had observed almost identical reactions by the troops fore and aft, a reassuring pat on our ship's pressure hull. It was no wonder, for with the sea about a submarine acting like a solid in transmitting any quick shock, a detonation of sufficient severity to move her violently could crush her as well. Some submarines had returned from patrol with dimpled hulls, bashed inductions, and jimmied hatches. Lesser damages involved the distortion of various fittings or the breaking loose of fixtures, and almost traditional in this latter category was the captain's washbasin. But today our light bulbs had borne the brunt of the enemy's wrath. I nodded when Fraz raised his hand to his mouth and tilted it as though sipping from a glass, and he went aft to disburse the depth-charge medicine. For most of the troops the brandy would celebrate the sinking rather than soothe jangled nerves.

Willing hands were helping with the torpedo reload while the evening meal progressed, probably with the knowledge that the movies could not start until the job was done. Our 5 knots had carried us well to seaward, but the depth charges kept rumbling. On surfacing, we found that the area astern was being swept by searchlights, and we knew that if the good Lord had not been on our side, we might be back there looking for an opportunity to surface and run for it. The time was 2010, and all engines went on charge or propulsion. Fraz gave the new course, 108 degrees true. It would take us back past Inamba Jima for a day or so of quiet patrol in deep seas.

We had broken the ice, but our start was not auspicious. Nine torpedoes expended with one ship down and another damaged was nothing for *Tang* to crow about. We knew that the second, smaller *maru* had sunk, for there had been nothing left after the *Biyo Maru* class freighter had disintegrated to make the sobering breaking-up noises. Thirty-eight minutes later there was nothing in sight. Her best speed could not have taken her clear in that period. Still, the same rules applied to all of us, and visual evidence was required for the credit of a sinking. That was frequently easy enough early in the war, and even now in a few areas like the Yellow Sea. In some boats back in 1943, the camera club would be ready for daytime shots through the scope, and quite often had the opportunity. Now, with the ratio of escorts to ships practically reversed, cameras, even official ones, remained in the lockers during attack. At least this was so in *Tang*, though anyone could hang his camera around his neck if he wished. Actually, we had been fortunate to see the first ship break in two, for only the choice of basing our initial evasion on visual information rather than blind luck had made it possible.

The orders this night contained the course, our speed of 18 knots, and the searching instructions. In the second paragraph I penned heartfelt congratulations to all hands. Staying within a patrol's echo-ranging distance hour after hour had not been easy, and I doubted if any of our boats had ever done so before, but it insured joining the enemy. The troops knew that I had patrolled in fast company, but had they known that this was also my first experience in so slugging it out, some might have had heart failure. Somewhat regretfully, it might not be our last, for Admiral Lockwood's letter left us little choice. At least we had found one way to put ships down in this area.

Frank and Charles were in the wardroom when I laid the Night Order Book on the table. At hand was ONI-208J with slips of paper, one containing latitudes and longitudes, inserted at pages 220 and 230. It was a helpful gesture by the identification party, and we recorded the ships as usual:

Sunk:

Biyo Maru class freighter	5,425 tons	Lat.	34° 12' N.
		Long.	136° 19' E.

Damaged:

Akasi Maru class freighter	3,057 tons	Lat.	34° 12' N.
		Long.	136° 19' E.

It was the first I knew of the identification of the second ship, but quite a bit was going on at the time, and the pictures shown did seem about right.

While we were making the entries, some weird sounds floated aft from the movie in the torpedo room. I had to laugh with Frank, Charles, and Adams, who was serving me coffee. The crew had selected a Dracula film, perhaps to ease them back to normal gradually, but since the volume seemed unusually high, the choice might be for my benefit.

Only the reports of the completion of the battery charge and of Inamba Jima on our bow and then abeam to starboard disturbed the night. Maneuvering bells and the feel of our ship told me that we had slowed on station, and I went topside for a look at the sea before we dived. Even in the first gray of dawn, the calm, almost oily surface was discernible. It would be a day for caution even in this remote spot.

Charles called an unhurried "Clear the bridge." Each lookout dropped to the step at the foot of the ladder, using the hand-grabs as dual firemen's poles, then ducked clear and on below. If one of our new men was among them, he had learned quickly. The two blasts had initiated the dive, and now *Tang* was sliding below the surface in the same spot where she had dived on the first day in the area. Perhaps Basil was hoping for another chance to locate his smoke, but what all hands would like best was the 155 miles that separated us from the scene of our depth-charging.

We had been too busy with our own little battles to think much about the rest of the war, but an item in the press news put us back in our proper place. Our forces' assault landings to retake Guam, which had been a U.S. possession for 40 years before the war, had commenced during the last week of our refit. We had just assumed that with command of the air and sea for bombardment, all had gone well. The Japanese, however, had made every effort to reinforce the island, bringing its troop strength to an estimated 50,000. Guam had finally been secured just two days before, on August 10.

Further consideration of the item and breakfast were interrupted by a call from Charles. We had a patrol boat in sight. The enemy was out early, for the wardroom clock read 0736. Fraz took this one, maneuvering to give the patrol a reasonably wide berth. As the morning progressed, we had our first tussle with the Kuroshio, or Japanese current. It sets about 065 degrees true in this locality, with a drift of anywhere from one to 3 knots. At our position, perhaps also affected by the tides and the islands, the drift appeared to be maximum. We found ourselves being set directly toward Mikura Jima and had to run to the south to stay clear of the island. In mid-afternoon, quite unexpectedly, depth-charging commenced. Planes and patrols were now in sight on every observation, and then came smoke in the direction of our dawn position.

Tang was off on a long submerged run, making the maximum turns she could hold till dusk. Our attempt to maintain contact with the smoke failed, but we gave it a try at full power upon surfacing. Fraz's plot showed the futility of continuing, however, for even a 6-knot enemy ship would reach the sanctuary of Tokyo Bay ahead of us. We had simply guessed wrong, as our evasion of the early-morning patrol could just as well have been to the west. That might have led to timely periscope sighting of the enemy and a successful submerged attack. Perhaps we were not using the talent embarked in *Tang* to its fullest. An arrow on a compass rose for Walker to spin could certainly do no worse.

"Why not let him spit in his palm and hit it with his finger?" suggested Frank, and we might just do exactly that.

As our chase had taken us close to Sagami Trough, south of Tokyo Bay, continuing on for a crack at any shipping along the southeast coast of Honshu seemed only logical. On the seaward side of the peninsula that forms Tokyo Bay, this 70-mile-long section runs from Nojima Zaki in the south to Inubo Saki in the north. Any traffic between Tokyo and ports to the north would be vulnerable when rounding each of these points. Fraz laid down the track and recommended our new course. *Tang* steadied on 046 and we went below for a very late evening meal.

The chips weren't falling our way, but this did not seem to affect the exuberance of our young officers. Mel and Dick came off watch as cheerful and optimistic as ever and seemed to lift the spirits of the rest of us. A report of weak radar signals of 260 and then 150 megacycles when Nojima Zaki was nearly abeam rang a bell for Mel.

"That one-fifty is the same frequency radar that steadied on us in the Nakano Strait," he recalled. "If they have surface-search radar here, they're expecting ships," he continued. Fraz sent for the Quartermaster's Notebook, having remembered another frequency for the Nakano Strait. He thumbed it through and conceded that Mel was almost correct as he read 153. There was a logic in Mel's appraisal that we might prove before the skies again turned gray.

At 2300 we turned left toward Katsuura Wan, an open bay only 20 miles up the coast from Nojima Zaki. Just short of this roadstead, a finger of the 100-fathom curve extends to within two miles of the beach. We would attempt to stay close to this deep area and spend the remainder of the night inshore. Closing the enemy's coast on the surface would never become routine, but a thoroughly competent navigator helped.

The coast is long and low and this night seemed deserted. *Tang* was never more than three miles from the shore, so visual or SJ radar contact was assured, but nothing moved. The only sign that the peninsula was even inhabited came at 0300 when wood smoke commenced rolling from the beach. The aroma was so pronounced that we could almost see it. The inhabitants were probably withdrawing charcoal from retorts and restocking them, but knowing the source of the smoke did not help the visibility, which dropped quickly to zero. Even a radar approach would have been futile, so we withdrew for a submerged patrol at dawn, still wondering if the enemy knew he had a new submarine defense right at hand.

We cleared the smoke by proceeding to the southwest well off the ten-fathom curve, and then Basil took us down in the gray of dawn. The concave shoreline insured a distant sighting of any coastal ship, with ample time to close to an attack position. *Tang* had been submerged over two hours on this August 13 when the anticipated call came from Hank on the periscope. Maneuvering bells brought Fraz and me to the conning tower on the double.

Hank's contact was smoke, not up or down the coast, but off to the southeast. A second true bearing showed that the enemy was drawing right, undoubtedly heading for Tokyo Bay. *Tang* was off to intercept at the best sustainable speed. Four bombers, and later a surface patrol, prevented a surface dash to get on the enemy ship's track, and our 12-mile high-speed submerged approach fell short by three miles of reaching a firing position. Frank and Fraz practiced calling angles on the stern of a fine medium-sized freighter until she disappeared around Nojima Zaki.

This was our drill and contact for the day. After surfacing at 1921, we took one more turn up the 100-fathom curve to Inubo Saki and then headed toward the Tori Shima area of the southern islands. *Tang* would not be able to cover the 300 miles before the next night even at full power, so we rolled south at a comfortable three-engine speed. Comfortable till dawn, when Ed's "Clear the bridge!" and two blasts sent us down. The time was 0429, close to our usual time for diving at dawn, but this time we had submerged for a yacht. The craft was not on a pleasure cruise, however, for a closer look showed heavy machine guns and extra antennas. What she was doing here, 40 miles east of Hachijo Jima, we meant to find out and at the same time keep her in sight as a target for our 4-inch gun crew if nothing worthy of torpedoes showed up.

Though my intentions were not announced, not even whispered, the ship's company sensed the plan and started with such preparations that stopping them would have been difficult indeed. It was entirely possible that the yacht had plans that included *Tang*, for numerous planes kept our scopes dunking, and her maneuvering prevented our surfacing for high periscope searches. The troops experienced some anxiety at midafternoon when we lost their target, but a dash on the surface between planes regained contact and all was forgiven.

After the last plane had apparently retired, we surfaced to check all guns, and then Ballinger passed the word, "Battle stations—gun!" The general alarm pealed with all of the authority that would accompany a full-fledged torpedo attack. At range 7,000, I ordered, "Commence firing!" Dick and Mel took it from there.

The yacht was tenacious and wiry, twisting and turning and closing the range at every opportunity. Her weapons seemed to be the equivalent of 20-millimeter machine guns but maybe larger, for she kept us outside of 4,500 yards and stayed on in deflection. The shoot provided a good example for my argument against having a single gun forward, since at the point while we were opening the range, our 4-inch came against the stops short of the conning tower and would not bear. With the slow rate of fire, about seven seconds per round, it was impossible to stay on the yacht for more than one or two hits after Mel had spotted the splashes on, and only eight sure hits were observed. They were good ones, however, exploding in her side and upper works, and demolishing her deckhouse.

After 88 rounds, I ordered, "Cease fire," so we'd have the remaining 40 rounds for defensive purposes. To me, the enemy still seemed under control, and I thought it best not to mention a somewhat similar incident, though at much shorter range, when the enemy's crew had come up from the sheltered side and thumbed their noses at us as we withdrew.

The activity gave the troops something to talk about as we proceeded down the island chain. This was well, for only daily dives to avoid bombers and one depth charge from a Mavis bomber marked our surface patrol off Tori Shima. Again, however, we caught up with the war by the brief, nightly reports of press news. Allied forces commenced landing on the south coast of France on the 15th and the buildup was continuing. Hitler had another front to face, and this should be the beginning of the end in Europe.

Kawanishi H6K5 "Mavis"

It was 1410 on the afternoon of August 18. *Tang* had been down an hour for another bomber, marking time in this area, and was about to surface.

"Fraz, let's head in and get a ship!" His answer was a broad smile and an OK sign.

6

Any change of mood usually spread quickly through a submarine, probably due to the physical closeness of the whole ship's company. Even experienced hands who might otherwise be conservative were caught up in a chase and often turned out to be the more aggressive men. Their knowledge of what had to be done and how to do it was, of course, a factor, and when the enemy was joined you didn't stand in their way. There was no enemy in sight, nor in all probability would there be for another 300 miles, but the three engines on the line and our new course were all that was needed to spark a feeling of enthusiasm within our ship.

Our few days of open-sea operations were a necessary part of this patrol, and more might follow. I would be remiss in not trying to find the enemy in waters where we could take full advantage of our strong points in attack and evasion. That, for the moment, having proven unproductive, we would attack the enemy on his terms, and our beeline track toward the southwest coast of Honshu told all hands where.

Kantori Saki, our destination, is the next sizable promontory to the south of Miki Saki. A shallow, low coastline extends northward without interruption for some 20 miles. Thus, sufficient tracking of all ships coming down the coast should be possible. Those heading north might get torpedoes shot from the hip. In either case, *Tang* should be able to reach deep water within minutes. Fraz had brought the chart to the wardroom with our estimated positions marked along the track. If *Tang* could stay on the surface undetected until the following noon, a submerged run would put her in position to attack after dark. My night orders emphasized the key points.

Proceeding on course 312° true at 18 knots toward Kantori Saki for inshore patrol against the enemy. Our success can depend on reaching the promontory undetected. Search with the SJ continuously during the night. Man the search scope at dawn, and station two extra lookouts at sunrise.

Inform me when the battery charge is completed, and call me to the conning tower or bridge for any contact this night which is inside 10,000 yards. If in doubt, dive first.

I entered the usual call, this time for 0400, and handed the book to Walker for delivery to the duty chief. A few minutes later I walked aft to the control room on my way topside. De Lapp was standing the duty chief's watch with Hudson. That was the way it would be for the remainder of this patrol, as those about to make chief petty officer worked into the new responsibilities they must assume. The watch was staggered so that the best from our experienced duty chiefs might rub off on those who would fill out that watch list. It was a continuation of the program we had commenced a patrol ago to insure that *Tang*'s key billets were all filled by seasoned hands.

It was well to look ahead, but now Fraz and I had to concentrate on the present to be sure of *Tang*'s arrival at the exact spot to intercept the enemy whenever he chose to move along the coast. On topside, the lower limb of the near new moon had set and a light overcast was blanking out all but the brightest stars. Even the turbulence along the limber holes and our wake were barely visible on this black night. We could not have ordered conditions more to our liking, for they practically guaranteed an uninterrupted night. Still, on such a night there often arose an unconscious tendency to relax, even ever so slightly. On the way below, I mentally pictured myself as the OOD as I reread my night orders; they seemed adequate.

Before dawn, Charles reported a drizzle and low overcast. We would have ordered this, too. Extra lookouts were posted nonetheless, and we rolled on through the morning. Fraz's dead reckoning position at noon showed that *Tang* could now close Kantori Saki submerged. With deference to the Kuroshio and to insure reasonable battery gravity, I put off our dive for an hour but welcomed Basil's two blasts sending *Tang* down still undetected.

The submerged hours could well have been spent on Fraz's educational program, the course books and qualification, but when closing the enemy's coast none of us could concentrate on such things. The watches, library books, and acey-deucey games took precedence on this August 19, that is, until evening chow was piped down a half hour early. The change was just to permit all messes to be squared away before surfacing. With improving visibility, Fraz had obtained high periscope bearings of Kantori Saki and Shiono Misaki to the south. His lines crossed close to our dead reckoning position, and now three blasts sent us up into the darkness of the night. The time was 1904.

The run in to the coast just north of Kantori Saki must have given Fraz and Jones fits, for as they were attempting to fix *Tang*'s position, we were following an irregular worm turn in avoiding sampans. Nothing interfered with our closing to 5,000 yards from the beach, however, and here we were assured of finding any ship that dared to pass. Evenly spaced dim lights, perhaps a mile apart, were now visible along the shore. They were possibly lighted buoys marking the six- or seven-fathom curve and meant to guide shipping in those safe shallow waters. This was the thought that first came to mind, and it led us to believe a ship might this minute be approaching the point where it would become distinguishable on the SJ. As time went by with nothing moving, we thought of typical watercolors or prints showing a Japanese fisherman at the end of his small pier. There could be night fishing going on out there, with lanterns hung out to attract certain fish. Further contemplation was put aside as a patrol boat came down the coast to seaward of us. When she was nearly abreast of our position, she slowed and her silhouette sharpened. So did *Tang*'s as we turned toward the patrol and deeper water. Holding our breath a little, we waited; no one spoke. And then her silhouette broadened as she completed a 180-degree turn to proceed back up the coast.

It was never boring this close to the enemy's shore, but his patrol boats added a little spice and exhorting the lookouts became quite unnecessary. The midwatch took over, and we stayed in the same vicinity with only the addition of 156 and 256 megacycle radar to record. Its signal strength was just medium, three to four on a scale of five, and Ed reported that it was nothing like the signal from Nakano Shima on our last patrol, which had put the needle against the pin. Since it didn't bite, we'd ignore it. Compared to many nights this had been calm indeed, but the continuous waiting and searching had been tiring, and the gray in the east was welcome. Hank took us down in his calm, unhurried manner, which always turned out to be as fast as any other dive. We would wait for the enemy submerged. The time was 0450, August 20.

We had moved in a thousand yards, to two miles from the beach, before diving and confirmed the 50 fathoms shown on the chart by a single ping sounding. During the short time until we could see through the periscope, a morning mist had set in. It could be confined to a shallow layer above the surface but should burn off with the warmth of day. In any case, we were not significantly hampered, and it might even provide some protection against having our scope sighted. An early contact, a ship from the southwest whipping around Kantori Saki, seemed likely, so Fraz and I stood by in the conning tower during the first crucial hours and then joined the others for breakfast as soon as the forenoon watch had relieved.

We might have known, for the phone buzzed before we

had started eating. It was an inshore patrol, and we avoided by presenting our stern until she had passed. Her position gave a probable track for any ships that might follow, however, and we moved in another thousand yards. Fraz stayed in the conning tower for a sounding as soon as the patrol rounded the point and then came down for another try at his bacon and eggs.

"Twenty fathoms, Captain," he reported. "There should be one along any time now, Adams, hurry up with my breakfast!"

It wasn't clear whether the second part of his report was for me, Adams, or just a general warning to stand by. It became academic a half hour later when the hum of the 1MC stopped our conversation.

"Captain to the conning tower. Ship bearing zero two two."

"That puts her inshore," Fraz commented on our way up the ladder; he had the whole picture in his mind already.

Only the tops of two masts and smoke were visible above the mist, but the separation of the sticks confirmed the navigator's estimate. Welch had taken over the wheel, not waiting for general quarters, and rang up standard speed seemingly ahead of my order. Fraz gave the course, 290, straight for the beach. The Bells of St. Mary's chimed, and *Tang* was on the prowl, ducking under sampans en route.

We were no more than up to speed when it was time to slow, now in 15 fathoms if the chart was correct. Larry had us right on at 64 feet; Jones brought the scope to deck level, Caverly called the sound bearing, and I rode the scope up. It was all routine.

"Bearing—mark! Range—mark!" and the scope was down. Fraz corrected the bearing from relative to true, 017. Jones read the stadimeter, 9,000 yards, and I called the angle on the bow 20 port. We had a good setup on a modern, medium-sized, engine-aft freighter. The escorts were two SCs, or sub-chasers, well clear to seaward on her port beam and bow. Unless they changed their patrol stations, we would fire from a position halfway between the escorts and the enemy ship.

On succeeding setups, plot had the freighter well inside the ten-fathom curve, and we closed the track slowly with tubes ready forward, and aft should she veer out to seaward. Plot and TDC had practically identical solutions for the freighter's course, 217 and 219; each had her speed at 8 knots. Caverly's bearings and constant screw beats checked.

"Five degrees to go, Captain," Fraz warned. "The outer doors are open." We would fire on a 123 track, so the torpedoes would come in from about 30 degrees abaft her beam. Jones brought the scope to waist height and then followed me up.

"Constant bearing—mark!"

"Set!"

Her stack came on. "Fire!"

Fraz hit the firing plunger and the torpedo left with a healthy zing. The second torpedo was aimed forward; her foremast came on the wire. "Fire!"

Again Fraz hit the plunger, but the torpedo left the tube with a resounding clonk and did not run. We could fire another, but at 900 yards our first torpedo was halfway there. Ogden was counting for the 36-second torpedo run, 30 . . . 35, 36, 37, 38, and so it went for another half minute, when the first torpedo exploded inshore.

Caverly grabbed a sounding during the rumble following the detonation. It showed but three fathoms under our keel, hardly enough to provide additional protection. We took the first eight depth charges at periscope depth, which was all right since we could see that the enemy was going to miss and was better than burying our head in shallow enemy seas, but we'd take deep water anytime. The detonations were not severe and came as single attacks instead of the salvos that had thundered down at Owashi Wan. This was probably the SCs' tactic due to the limited number of charges carried, but it could have been just as frightening had we not had both of them in sight.

Short bursts of speed with each detonation were carrying us to seaward, away from the patrols. A welcome sounding showed 40 fathoms under our keel, a depth where we could increase speed with small chance of being heard. Larry put us into a slow glide toward the bottom. All was quiet except for continuing depth charges astern. As *Tang* passed 200 feet, we heard Larry's expected order, "Pump from auxiliary to sea." De Lapp would now be cranking up the motor of the drain pump. But instead of the hum of the pump we heard shouts.

Fraz dropped down and came back to report that two of the motor's metal fingers, which held the carbon contacts, had broken off. It was not critical; we could blow ballast from auxiliary to sea, put a bubble in safety, start the noisy trim pump, or even hold *Tang* up with the planes while making repairs. Fraz did not interfere, and Larry requested permission to use the trim pump. The request before starting up the trim pump had become standard procedure if it was to be used in pumping to sea during evasion. We would not forget our experience west of Saipan when the destroyer had stayed with us hour after hour.

De Lapp and the auxiliarymen completed silver-soldering the fingers shortly after we had leveled off. The failure had not been serious this time, but it brought home to all hands that our ship, just like any one of us, was not infallible. On the brighter side, the depth-charging had stopped after a total of 30. Though none were close, it was always a somewhat shaking experience, and all hands could use some relaxing time. There would be no more ships today; the seas were friendly in the deeps, and there we stayed, heading slowly to the southwest.

While Charles and Basil practiced changing depth, the rest of us threw our ideas on the table, trying to come down with a logical reason for the miss and the failure of the second torpedo to even run. Perhaps more to the point, Hank and Mel left for the torpedo rooms to help check the hardware.

7

The first and then the second dog watch had been relieved. All hands had finished the evening meal, and we were a half hour into the evening watch when three blasts sent *Tang* to the surface. Following the pattern of our slowdown, we would charge batteries here at sea and let the boat cool down before moving on to the coast. There was no rush, for we were now confident of finding a ship at nearly any daylight hour. I only wished that the same confidence extended to our torpedoes, for we had not determined any sure cause for their apparent failure—theirs or ours.

On to the west lay Shiono Misaki and Ichiye Saki, where we would attack, this time late in the afternoon, which would be closer to the shelter of darkness. We were not on the defensive, but we were acquiring a better and more sympathetic understanding of the problems that had undoubtedly beset our immediate predecessors in these areas. With similar torpedo performance, getting any ships from outside the 20-fathom curve would have required more luck than any boat might expect. Even inside, we were having our troubles.

Radar on 82, 99, and 261 megacycles, apparently from Shiono Misaki, buzzed the APR-1, but nothing came of it. The night remained quiet on till dawn, when Mel pulled the plug in the deep water off Okinokura Shima. We would move in slowly to give both the training and qualification programs an opportunity to regain some of their lost momentum and then join the enemy.

The Japanese had other ideas, sending a large ship and two escorts around Shiono Misaki heading eastward and out of reach. It was like dancing a fly ahead of a hungry trout; Fraz's Plan of the Day went into the GI can, and we were off to intercept the next ship. The course of 315 was far to the left of Okinokura Shima, but our ship moved like a fiddler crab directly toward the island due to the Kuroshio. The mooring board had proven correct again. *Tang* would be in an ideal position by noon. In the meantime we would search continuously, as a light chop made any sighting of our scope impossible.

Dick's shout brought us to the conning tower. He had a modern, engine-aft ship at a range of 8,000 yards, with her escorts well out ahead. She was heading west and offered a possibility; *Tang* was off and running. The time was 1039, not yet two hours since the first contact, and this time the general alarm involved all hands. For a time all looked good, for the enemy was slowed by the Kuroshio. The 3-knot current would not upset our torpedo attack, but a component of the current was affecting us. A 3,000-yard torpedo run was the best we could do; even full speed would have done little better. There had already been two ships, however, and there would be more; we'd wait for the next one.

Another two hours passed, and now the bottom lay 14 fathoms under our keel. No ship could get by to shoreward. We turned left to parallel the beach, our 2 knots matching the Kuroshio, and waited; waited four minutes for Jones's salty "Smoke ho!"

This was what we were looking for, smoke and then a ship far enough off to track. The Bells of St. Mary's rang out over the 1MC for the second time in two hours, and the compartments reported so quickly that the troops must have been still standing by. The ship was now in sight at 9,000 yards, the bearing placing her practically on the beach. We had a medium-sized, mast-funnel-mast freighter escorted by two SCs, and a whale killer. Tracking soon had her on 290, exactly parallel to the coast, and coming on at 8 knots. The approach consisted primarily of ducking under the two SCs and turning left for a stern shot. Everything was falling in line for a 110 track and a firing range of about 1,600 yards when Fraz gave the customary warning, "Five degrees to go, Captain."

I had but one area of doubt. Had the freighter, in close to the beach, been subjected to the same current as had *Tang?* If not, our speed determination could be in error by as much as 2 knots. I would cover this possibility by spreading the wing torpedoes. Jones had the scope at deck level and brought it up smartly to my hands.

"Constant bearing—mark!"

"Set!" came from Mel. Her stack amidships was coming on.

"Fire!" The first electric torpedo was on its way with a whine. The second Mark 18-1 went to a point one-quarter of a ship's length ahead of the bow, the third to a point the same distance abaft the stern. If all was well, the first torpedo would break her in two. If we had some speed error, the first and second or the first and third torpedoes would hit. If we were way out, even beyond any logical guess, the second or third torpedo would hit. The time was 1317.

We settled down to the long wait while the 27-knot torpedoes cruised on their way. The first hit should come in one minute and 50 seconds. Caverly gave us encouragement, for their whine was now blending in with the freighter's prop noise. Ogden called the seconds to go, "Ten . . . five . . . three, two, one, zero." There was no explosion. I held back an oath during the additional time required for our second and third torpedoes, and managed to swallow it during those 16 seconds. We had another minute's run to seaward before the enemy was alerted by the explosions of all three torpedoes on the beach. We did not stop to admire them, and Larry had us leveled off at 200 feet when the first depth charges let go.

They were not very close, and now with soundings as a guide, *Tang* reached deep submergence. The enemy had dropped 20, but our 100 turns had kept everything aft, including some late-arriving pingers.

Frank, Mel, and Dick made a thorough check of the firing bearings, the actual gyro readings that had been recorded, the depth set, everything. Then in addition to setting the problem into the TDC, they broke out the Mark 8 angle solver. It was a slightly modern version of the prewar Mark 6, popularly called the Banjo. Most of us had wrestled with the latter, and if the correct graduations on the sliding arms were properly positioned over the curve with the correct color, you could read the right combination of gyro and lead angle if no one bumped it. The Mark 8 had clamping arrangements to overcome this difficulty and could come up with a solution as accurate as that of the TDC. My spread had covered any possible speed errors, and the coast of Honshu had taken care of the enemy's course. Depth settings, hydrostat spring calibrations, and rudder throws notwithstanding, one or more of our torpedoes had run deep.

We had no wounds to lick from the enemy's depth-charging, but perhaps more serious, our confidence in our ability to put the enemy on the bottom was a bit shaken, and our pride, at least my own, was a little bent. There is but one thing to do when you fall off a horse, swing back in the saddle immediately. We had to keep slugging it out with the enemy, but I would at least be hesitant to attack on his terms, inside 15 fathoms, with erratic torpedoes. Luck had been on our side, but with our firing position pinpointed for the enemy and no hits to confuse him, the coin could easily flip the other way. There was only one solution, conduct some test firings where we could observe just what our torpedoes were doing.

Fraz was in complete agreement with the decision, which was good since the plan called for disposing of three or four torpedoes. There remained only the selection of an appropriate place, and Fraz went back to the conning tower to check on the possible positions.

The Kuroshio added 3 knots to our speed over the ocean floor, carrying us beyond Shiono Misaki by noon. A half hour later we came left, following the coast well to seaward toward Miki Saki. Frank reported Kantori Saki in sight at midafternoon. It marked the halfway point to Miki Saki, and the

Kuroshio had determined the place and time for the firing; we would enter Owashi Wan, just to the north of Kuki Saki, at midnight.

On the surface midway through evening twilight, our two navigators had a fine, sharp horizon. Their exact position for a departure could be doubly important when making the landfall this night. The engineers and electricians scurried with the battery charge, and both torpedo rooms buzzed. *Tang* seemed to come out of the doldrums, for all of the old hands knew what a night probe such as this might hold.

The dark shape of Miki Saki loomed up at midnight and Kuki Saki minutes later. A single diesel moved us quietly around the points and into Owashi Wan. The bay was as black as the night and seemed to hold no resemblance to the roadstead I had seen through the scope. But those had been fleeting glimpses, and details of the shoreline were not on our minds. I slowed to one-third speed to provide more time for considering the contour of the land. Fraz and Jones were not finding everything to their liking either, for bearings and ranges of known landmarks did not jibe with the chart. Of course, the charts were not completely accurate, and the SJ's side lobes added a bit of confusion. All fell in place when the bridge speaker blared, "Contact one point on port bow!"

Bergman had a pip where no pip ought to be. We stopped and the bells chimed below for the third time since morning. With radar to coach us on, we now had a long, low shape in our 7 × 50s that was otherwise indistinguishable against the dark background of the land.

We remained stopped while tracking worked on the ship's course and speed. It did not take long, for her speed was zero, too. Stopped or anchored, was she viewing us? It took no encouragement to start moving slowly on a great arc to get her silhouette to seaward, away from the black background of the land. We were tracking all the while and clear of the Kuroshio or its countercurrent; the enemy ship still plotted in a fixed position. She definitely had her hook on the bottom, well out in the bay.

Now with the starlit sea as a background, we could make her out, a large patrol, anchored two miles in from Kuki Saki and asking for it! I shifted propulsion to the batteries so there would be no diesel sounds, for they would carry across this bay on such a still night as do noises on a lake. All tubes were made ready, for contrary to the War Instructions of the

1930s, which specified one torpedo for such ships, a patrol or destroyer might require any number of torpedoes; I knew. Our torpedoes aft were set on three feet.

Speaking in whispers, we closed slowly, heading directly for the patrol ship's beam. At 1,500 yards, identification became positive. The fore and waist guns, a structure abaft the bridge, and now the long depth-charge racks; it was surely the gunboat that had harassed us during our first visit, topping it off with those tooth-shakers.

At 1,200 yards I twisted ship to bring our stern tubes to bear, a bit apprehensive while we presented our broadside silhouette. But nary a thing stirred aboard the gunboat as far as we could tell. We were now in position to fire a Mark 18-1 electric torpedo, and its minimal wake, should it miss, would not necessarily alert the enemy. There was an additional advantage; we were already heading away from her should she suddenly come to life.

The outer doors were open aft as I conned *Tang* for a zero gyro angle shot. The binoculars rested untouched in the after TBT receptacle, checked below as on 180 degrees, dead astern.

"Set below." We were steady on her middle.

"Fire!" The torpedo left with the characteristic whine. All of us on the bridge watched as the wake petered out after a run of a hundred yards or so, when the torpedo evidently headed down. A loud rumble occurred when the torpedo should have been halfway to the gunboat. Caverly had tracked the fish until the low-order explosion; there could be no doubt that it had indeed hit bottom where the chart showed 250 feet of water.

The time was 0142, and feeling that the enemy must surely be alerted, I twisted *Tang* quickly to bring her in alignment for a second straight shot, taking all of the care that we had with the first torpedo. *Tang* was steady as a rock, the wire right amidships, when I received Mel's "Set below."

"Fire!" was almost instantaneous. The torpedo left with a reassuring whine, and its phosphorescent wake stretched out into the night, visible almost to the target. But there was no explosion or other noise as it apparently passed underneath the enemy. The time was 0144.

Fraz had joined me on the bridge, expecting an explosion, for Caverly had tracked the fish down the correct bearing. There was no need for consultation; we had one salvo of three left aft and were circling for a bow shot. The question mark turn, steadying, and now closing to 900 yards, seemed slow, but Mel's "Set" came instantly following my "Mark."

"Fire!" and a Mark 23 steam torpedo, set to run on the surface, left with a zing directly for the enemy's middle. Though *Tang* was stopped, absolutely steady, and the torpedo had zero gyro angle, it took a 30-yard jog to the left before settling down toward the target and missed astern.

We were still whispering, though the last two torpedoes must have roared past the gunboat. Her crew was waking up, however, or at least someone was about with a flashlight. They would have to hurry, for a "Set" came from below. The wire was on her gun mount forward, lest this torpedo jog also.

"Fire!" It jogged left but then settled down for her middle, running close to the surface. The run would be 40 seconds.

"Come on topside!" It was going to hit, and my invitation was meant for Fraz, but most of the fire control party and others, too, reached the bridge. The explosion was the most spectacular we had seen, topped by a pillar of fire and tremendous explosions about 500 feet in the air. There was absolutely nothing left of the gunboat, but we had seen enough of this ship on this and previous occasions to provide the designers with everything but the blueprints.

Now knowing that our torpedo difficulties were mainly in sluggish steering and depth engines, we bent on full power to reach the security of the deep seas. There we would temporarily convert *Tang* to a submerged torpedo overhaul shop, staffed by men whose lives might depend on the quality of their work.

8

The course was east and dawn met us after a run of 60 miles. Dick slowed to one-engine speed, as instructed by the single entry in the night orders, and took our ship down for the day. The exacting work on our six remaining torpedoes would start routinely, or so I thought, but Hank had the preliminary findings ready at breakfast. It had been the whole department's idea to start immediately after the attack, but in a compromise work on the torpedoes had replaced standing their normal watches. Hank and Ballinger had arranged the minor juggling of the watch list, and this was just another example of the flexibility that came with having a few extra officers and men in the ship's company.

The findings practically pinpointed our troubles, for three of our remaining six torpedoes had horizontal, or depth-keeping, rudder throws of from three-quarters to a full degree heavy, or deep. It was at least expected after our test firing, and in itself justified expending those torpedoes, at least as far as we were concerned.

How could this happen in torpedoes that had been run through the base torpedo shop, with preliminary and final adjustments made by experts and witnessed by Hank and Mel on the check-off lists? The answer is that it couldn't with handcrafted torpedoes from the Naval Torpedo Station. There the differential valves and control engines were hand-lapped, and other mechanisms were fitted to each torpedo in a way comparable to the production of a Rolls Royce.

The torpedoes under consideration, however, were put together from components that had been manufactured in dozens of different locations. The people making the castings and doing the machining could not visualize the whole torpedo. Even more important, they did not have an active hand in making the whole thing work. So the improper rudder throws existed all the time but were not discovered because the rough valves and engines would stick in their travel and give what seemed to be correct readings. But our task was ahead, and during this day the valves, steering, and depth engines would be operated and operated until they lapped themselves in, or at least were sufficiently worn in to have rubbed off any rough spots. By late afternoon, Hank reported both torpedo rooms ready for the final calibrations and tests.

In anticipation, the air compressors had brought the pressure that had built up in the boat back down to a normal atmosphere, jamming the air back into the banks. Inter-torpedo room rivalry was put aside by Hank's 6-foot 4-inch mandate. Mel, with First Class Torpedoman's Mate Foster and his men from aft, went forward and joined Hank, Chief Weekley, and the forward gang. More than pride and reputation was riding this afternoon. The depth springs were calibrated under the correct atmospheric pressure and then each torpedo in turn was suspended as had been done in the East China Sea. Each was then fired with its high-pressure air only, spinning the gyros and admitting the air to the control valves and engines. Then came the swinging in azimuth to check the actual operation of the vertical, or steering, rudder. Next came the tilting to check the honesty of the horizontal rudder. The same cooperative effort followed aft, and now no holds were barred, the rooms were in competition again. Just prior to loading, the men painted fresh eyes on each warhead to help guide it to the enemy. No real torpedoman would think of loading a fish otherwise, and frankly neither would I.

It was 1900 when we surfaced this August 22 with the troops exuding confidence. I thoroughly believed that they had done their part, and I meant to do mine. Our heading was 012, directly toward the scene of our first attack of the patrol, where we had missed the old-fashioned black tanker west of Omae Saki. We would move north slowly; there was no rush, and our attacks would be cold, calm, and calculated!

Checking the torpedoes had taken precedence over food, and the wardroom was enjoying a late evening meal. The fresh ocean air more than made up for the warmed-over sogginess. On the table to go with the meal was the determination by the identification party. The gunboat, as we had chosen to call her, was new to all appearance and unlisted in our publications. The party had used the notations from the Quartermaster's Notebook, which had been made at various times when the ship was in sight, and the length determination by the stadimeter, which Jones remembered. It all fitted together in a neat paragraph.

GUNBOAT: Flush deck with raised gun platforms forward and amidships mounting estimated 3-inch double-purpose guns. Aft of midship platform was a goalpost structure, probably for sweeping, topped by a lookout or director platform. Her stern has two very long horizontal depth-charge racks, holding 14 counted depth charges a side, and what appeared to be Y-guns on the centerline. The length is between 225 feet and 250 feet measured by stadimeter, and standard displacement estimated to be 1,500 tons.

They had put together more than I remembered, and it would go into the patrol report as they had prepared it. This turned the conversation to the current results of our patrol. One freighter down, another damaged, a patrol yacht damaged, and now a gunboat blown to smithereens. It was a motley array to say the least, but the gunboat did add a bit of respectability. Truthfully, the ship was pure gravy, for we would have fired those four torpedoes whether she had been there or not.

"Suppose we hadn't seen her," Frank ventured, and that led to some lively possibilities arising from torpedoes racing aimlessly across Owashi Wan. But she was in our bag, and we now had a chance to make more of this patrol and perhaps really hurt the enemy.

At 0100 Frank reported *Tang* in position on the 50-fathom curve west of Omae Saki, and I went topside as we moved slowly into the wide bight off Fukude. There, 6,000 yards from the long beach, we were certain that no ship could pass undetected, and the burning navigational lights spurred the hope that the enemy might try.

The remainder of the midwatch passed with Fraz up and available. The morning watch came on, and Basil took us down quietly. It was 0417, and this time our dive was in the best possible position to intercept the enemy. We had not long to wait, for bombers commenced searching at daylight. A half hour later the first surface patrol hove in sight, coming westward from Omae Saki. Our periscope searches would be cautious this day, and I took the scope until she had passed. Fraz would take the next one, but now only planes remained, searching methodically along the coast.

We were at breakfast, as usual, when the phone buzzed. Ed had smoke toward Omae Saki, and since it had just come in view, the ships would be heading our way. The time was 0803 as Fraz and I left the wardroom. As expected, the enemy ships were nearly aground as they hugged the coast, and *Tang* could finish that job! Just as Jones swung the handle on the general alarm, Walker appeared with our two cups of coffee, no mean trick to balance while climbing up a ladder and through a circular hatch. We would have time to drink them, for *Tang* was off on a four-minute dash to close a hulk off Fukude, undoubtedly one of our subs' handiwork. A position 1,000 yards to seaward of the wreck would insure the short-range attack that we wanted. The enemy course had to be about 280, the direction of the coastline; we would concentrate on the speed determination. The periscope bearing before our dash, converted to true, had fixed the enemy ships' position as 10,000 yards up the coast, and now as we slowed, the next true bearing would fix it again. It would be a simple case of time and distance run, a problem for a third-grader.

Welch was calling off our speed, and Caverly with his metronome was beating out the enemy's propeller turns, 130, a good clip. The log was down to 3 knots when Jones brought the scope to my hands. I checked it in low power and Jones raised the scope with me as if it had a built-in follow-up system. A single sweep and the scope was down.

"Left full rudder, all ahead two-thirds. We're inside three SC escorts and have two medium freighters. I'm turning for a stern shot. Angle on the bow twenty port."

"All tubes are ready with outer doors open, Captain." Fraz's report made unnecessary my pending query. Our stern was staying ahead of the enemy on the TDC. We would steady on 190 for a broadside track. Welch acknowledged one-third and would steady us on. There would be one more setup before the constant bearing. The scope came up in time to observe an unexpected zig towards, putting us underfoot. A full-speed dash succeeded only in getting us between the two freighters, which had zigged and were now on a line of bearing. They boiled past, about 200 yards ahead and astern, followed by a third, smaller freighter previously unseen. All three of them were too close; our torpedo warheads would not be armed at that short range.

When you tried for a range inside of 1,000 yards it sometimes happened this way; but we still had our torpedoes, and at least that was an improvement. Perhaps we should be grateful that they had not wiped off the attack periscope and that depth charges weren't raining down.

Tang had been secured from battle stations for a half hour when an old type destroyer closed our position. She resembled our World War I four-pipers but had two stacks and long depth-charge racks that must have cleared out the arsenal. The suspicion that we had been spotted seemed almost certain with the arrival of a floatplane and then four bombers. The planes did not bother us as much as the ear-splitting echo-ranging of the destroyer, the pings blasting through our hull as she closed the range.

"Set all torpedoes on two feet and open the outer doors."

None of us wanted to shoot this ship, feeling that a better

one could be just around Omae Saki, but she could force our hand. When the range was just inside 1,000 yards, the destroyer commenced circling us slowly, very slowly, counterclockwise. We kept our bow pointed at her; we had no choice. She continued her search, sometimes coming very close, and I shifted the scope to low power, not just to keep her in the larger field but so the planes, especially the floatplane, could be observed, too.

I had made water-lapping looks during approaches, perhaps a hundred or more, some very taut, but never before ones that continued on like this, wherein we were forced to keep her in constant view to attack before she could. The tip-off would be a shift to short scale, the increased ping rate showing that she had an echo. It could come at any instant. A half hour passed and she continued, never closer than 500 or 600 yards, but seldom outside of 1,200 or 1,300.

We maneuvered slowly, following a smaller circle inside the destroyer's and keeping a bead on her so there would be no last-minute twisting and attendant swirl to disclose our presence to the floatplane. Caverly had the slow swishes of her screws on the speaker, keeping phase with the metronome. I was calling angles and ranges continuously lest we be forced to attack, and by battle phone the situation went to all compartments. Perhaps I should put our stern to her so that we could sneak away when she gave us a large angle and still shoot if necessary. But turning now would present a broadside to her ping; we had to hang on to our present position and wait her out.

The destroyer gave ground first, leaving her circle and moving slowly to seaward. The time was 1017; we had been under her thumb for nearly an hour. Her new tactic smacked of Miki Saki, where the patrol had searched the point before turning seaward to drive us out of position. Now that I was able to use a little more scope, the reason for the destroyer's search became apparent. To the west, under the bombers, were the masts and broad bridge structure of a big ship coming our way along the coast.

The destroyer had accomplished a part of her mission by dragging us to seaward in her maneuvers, which surely would have plotted like penmanship circles drawn across a page. It was nothing a high-speed run could not rectify. With a single call of "Starboard five, range thirteen thousand," we were off and boiling, still at battle stations. Besides the planes, the big ship had escorts, but we'd worry about them later. For the moment, this approach was such a breeze compared to the last hour that we were relaxing our shoulders while Chief Culp and his controllermen drove us toward the enemy's track. Ten minutes into the run *Tang* slowed, Welch calling out her speed as she lost way.

The periscope observation was routine, but the ship was not. Her angle had now opened, showing her full import. The decks of her long midship superstructure were dotted with white uniforms, as was her upper bridge. We had a big naval transport for our torpedoes instead of that destroyer. The scope was down and we were off on another run to further close the track. I took the moment of quiet to give the escort picture, especially to Caverly on the JK-QC and Bergman on the JP forward. The transport had a large PC or DE ahead, an SC on her bow, and an LST (landing ship, tank) plus a PC astern. I'd do the worrying about the planes overhead.

Again we slowed, Welch calling out our speed from the log each half knot, and Caverly a constant stream of bearings. Mel was checking them against the TDC, giving reassuring nods. I glanced at the computer's presentation; we would fire on this observation, perhaps a double dip of the scope.

"Get echo ranges to go with my setup." Fraz stepped aft for a moment to be sure that Caverly had the word and then moved over to the TDC.

"Fifteen degrees to go for a one hundred track, Captain. The outer doors are open, all torpedoes set on six feet."

Jones had the scope ready, having trained it on the approximate bearing by twisting the tube with his hands, and followed me up.

"Bearing—mark!" Jones read 345.

"Range—mark! Angle ninety starboard." Caverly called 800 yards; Jones read 700.

"It all checks, speed eight and a quarter," called Frank, and the scope was back up.

"Constant bearing—mark!" Jones called 354.

"Set!" came from Mel. Her after deck was coming on. This was it!

"Fire!" Fraz hit the plunger. The first Mark 23 left with a healthy zing, and the reassuring pressure hit our ears.

The second and third fish went to the middle of her long superstructure and under her forward deck. The whole ship's side was manned by sailors in whites, exactly as had been the big naval tanker west of Saipan.

"Right full rudder. All ahead full." We would attack the LST.

"All hot, straight, and normal." Those beautiful words came from Caverly and Bergman almost simultaneously. Jones was helping our torpedoes on their way with his raised fist. Ogden was counting off the seconds—11 more to go. We slowed and Mel called the new relative bearing. The scope came up, a sweep in low power and back to the transport. The smoky wakes were fanning out toward her middle; the torpedoes themselves would be 75 yards farther on. There was nothing that great ship could do; she was a dead duck.

The crack of a detonation and the roar of the explosion jammed Ogden's 30th second back down his throat. The hit was in the after section of the superstructure, the shallow torpedo ripping out a section of waterline the size of a freight car. The next hit was just forward of the long superstructure, under the short forward deck, and gave her a down-angle of about 20 degrees, which she maintained like a diving submarine.

The LST was heading for the beach, and a sweep showed no ship or plane paying attention to our immediate position, so Fraz and Frank each took a squint of the sinking transport, followed by Ballinger. It was not just pure generosity; we wanted extra witnesses to watch her go.

Some ship or plane dropped two depth charges, nicely spaced so Caverly obtained two soundings. Following the bottom, 100 turns on the props cleared us out of the area. For once, counterattack of the submarine seemed to be of second priority, undoubtedly as the survivors were picked up. Ten full minutes passed before the charges rained. *Tang* was then snug at deep submergence, and two hours at high speed followed by gradual slowing kept everything astern, including a multiship echo-ranging search. The enemy was persistent, apparently staying with us, and we came back to periscope depth for the advantage of a visual observation. Masts, four of them, were fanned out across our stern, but the howling pings were not as disturbing now that we could see the ships' tops. It was so easy to think that echo-ranging was getting closer that watching the enemy as soon as it was reasonably safe had a mental as well as a tactical advantage.

Our patrol had been punctuated by disappointments and triumphs, but each had added to our total experience, and especially to that of our new hands. In just over three weeks they had participated in more action than I had seen in

Wahoo's two long early patrols. As I watched Basil going about his duties with confidence, it was evident that he had already acquired the pride I had hoped for.

During the afternoon, volunteers commenced sorting the freezer room; this patrol now promised to be of no longer duration than the last. Darkness was trebly welcome, for the three blasts of the surface alarm would herald a rush of God's fresh air, then frying steaks, and a full-power run away from the enemy, now back on the dark horizon.

9

Jones had spent a part of the afternoon over the chart with his tracing sheet firmly secured in place, apparently oblivious to the sonar search going on behind us. Keeping busy was the best way to keep the enemy from getting on your nerves, but Jones's task had become a necessary and continuing chore. After a week our tracks were crossing on the navigator's chart, and a glance at all of the tracings now showed a confusion of lines. They were visual evidence of our hit-and-run policy, always trying to put at least a hundred miles behind us after an attack, and preferably twice that figure. It was not just a measure affecting our immediate safety but one that we hoped would confuse the enemy. Our torpedoes, whether they hit or exploded on the beach, were announcing the presence of a submarine. The Japanese had those positions plotted, but without the tracks they would certainly attribute them to more than one submarine, maybe three or four. How could they be expected to know of our extra fuel capacity and attendant long legs when our own force engineer and operations hadn't? At least this should disperse the enemy's escorts.

At the moment *Tang* was charging through the night and before dawn would have added another 160 miles to the 3,000 that Jones had added up roughly, 3,160 miles just in these two areas.

"That should provide the DivCom with his endorsement,"

Fraz commented as we relaxed with after-dinner coffee. " 'Excellent area coverage is indicated,' " he intoned, of course needling me a bit about the endorsement I disdained. This time there might just be some periods of running scared. Midway was only 2,500 miles away; we had the fuel, and if it could add to our safety and help promote this patrol, we'd not carry any excess back.

"I'm still wondering about that destroyer we had this morning." Frank had changed the specific area of the conversation a little, but turning entirely away from the morning attack would be like forgetting an Army-Navy game with the last play. It was routine to discuss any attack, sometimes to find out what went wrong, but going over what went right was a lot more fun and sometimes just as important.

"Maybe she never did train her sound gear far enough aft," said Mel. "As I remember, we were almost continuously on her quarter." I was pleased to have the junior officers join in, for they were flexible and could come down with fresh ideas. Without a watch to stand, I had been mulling over the subject for some hours, and Mel was close to my conclusion. I threw it on the table to see what comment it might elicit from others.

"I figure she had a fixed sonar and was searching by maneuvering in lazy circles. We stayed on the inside, keeping our bow to her, and as Mel said, never did get off her quarter for any appreciable length of time nor into a forward sector where she could have obtained an echo."

"Could it have been just a Fathometer we heard?" asked Dick. None of the rest of us had considered this, but it was as plausible an explanation as any other. A Fathometer is just a vertical echo-ranger; its pings would sound the same and could drive a submarine out of position just as effectively as horizontal echo-ranging and might even make a contact. Many an attack had been thwarted by random depth charges, and the combination of an old type destroyer with long depth-charge racks and a powerful Fathometer could have been successful, too. That is, if we had not unwittingly done the right thing, not through any logic other than remaining in an attack attitude. One thing was certain, however; the failure of the destroyer to make contact would remain a pleasant mystery.

We had received no identification of the transport during the attack, partly because of the few observations and little information sent to the party. Had it been a normal attack, the ship could not have been typed anyway, for she was nowhere in the books. The party had done the next best thing, submitting a paragraph for the record:

The Naval Transport would appear similar to *Buenos Aires Maru,* page 45, if she were given a raked bow and her stack cut down level with the highest point of her superstructure. The gross tonnage would be about 10,000 and the standard displacement 15,000 tons.

We checked ONI-208J again and none of us present who had seen her disagreed. I recorded the latitude, 34° 37′ north, and the longitude, 137° 50′ east, and to ward off any questions added one sentence, *This was not a hospital ship,* since the identification book contained a small note saying that the *Buenos Aires Maru* had been designated as such. The night orders were again brief, my congratulations having gone over the 1MC. *Proceeding at three-engine speed on course 247° true to pass Shiono Misaki before dawn and attack shipping on southern coast. When the battery charge is completed at about 2300, put the fourth engine on propulsion and work up to full power. Call me topside for any contact inside of 10,000 yards or dive.*

A turn through the boat, the report of increasing seas from the west slowing us a knot, the completion of the battery charge, and then the expected radar signals from Shiono Misaki, all of these made the night go quickly. It was speeded further by an SJ contact out at 10,000 yards. The time was 0336 on this August 24, and section tracking was sufficient for the moment. With Hank, Charles, and Frank assisting, the tracking went smoothly. It was like old times, gaining position ahead with a surface dash on an enemy ship making only 6 knots, but we had not yet made her out in this darkest part of the night. The run carried us toward the beach from the 100-fathom curve, and now we had a second ship, close inshore and seemingly larger. As the first contact was probably an escort, we shifted targets. The Bells of St. Mary's called an 0428 reveille to go with battle stations, and moments later Larry took our ship below the seas.

Our approach went smoothly on to a generated range of 3,000 yards. Then in the dawn light the ship commenced signaling with yardarm blinkers and maneuvered away, displaying a super load of depth charges and efficient looking guns. We kept a bead on her, but like the destroyer the day before she could foreshadow a real target. None of us regretted that her maneuvers took her shoreward, never giving us a suitable setup. It appeared that she had been relieved by a second patrol, which kept us occupied for the next two hours. The troops, a few at a time, finished breakfast. And then, too late, we saw the second escort lead a medium-sized diesel tanker out of Kazampo, just east of Ichiye Saki, and head for Shiono Misaki hugging the coast.

This promised to be a busy day, and we went down to breakfast before another interruption could turn it into lunch. The time was 0950, and over an hour went by before Dick's call came from con. He had a *Hishun Maru* class patrol with two stripes on her stack coming down the coast. Two stripes should mean something, perhaps designating a command ship, for the escorting along this coast was obviously from point to point, seeing a ship through a danger area, rather than accompanying her all the way between ports. It avoided the slowdown of convoy operations and certainly made for the most efficient use of the available escorts. With this in mind we moved to the 40-fathom curve on sighting smoke beyond Ataki Saki, guessing that the escort commander would be returning. He was there, all right, on the very next observation, coming back west and leading two large freighters close to the beach. Welch swung the handle on the general alarm, and *Tang*'s battle stations were manned again.

The freighters were in ballast or riding high. Still 13,000 yards away, we should have no difficulty in making the necessary run to close the track. An escort similar to the *Hishun Maru* following astern offered no problem; neither did two destroyer types, one just to seaward of each freighter. *Tang* was on a long run in, and we'd take a look from the 30-fathom curve. It was always a long wait, but finally Fraz gave me a nod.

"All ahead one-third." Maneuvering answered, but with the bells came reports of light screws and echo-ranging on our starboard beam and quarter. When Welch called 3 knots and Jones brought up the scope, I trained first to starboard. We had two PCs, not yet threatening, though the one on our quarter was obviously already to seaward of our position. Left to the freighters showed them coming on, and against the background of the beach they were definitely painted white. This was unusual and so were the maneuvers of the destroyers, which were patrolling with a worm turn, a sine wave track, each still abeam of her respective freighter. *Tang* was charging in again, and the next observation

would be from about the 25-fathom curve. The ocean floor
shelved very slowly, and we had time to consider further the
details of our last observation. Were the destroyers searching
with fixed sonar, or were they momentarily expecting torpedoes and wormturning to add to the difficulties facing the
submarine? Further, what were the PCs doing this far to
seaward, considerably outside of a submarine's firing position? We slowed again; the situation was changed only by the
addition of another PC to starboard. The scope was down,
and I looked over the situation on Fraz's chart. Neither of us
liked the pending long torpedo run, but we'd see what
developed at an estimated 20 fathoms. We were now moving
in at a somewhat cautious two-thirds speed.

Again Welch rang up one-third speed. Caverly swept
around and had the jumble of freighters' and destroyers'
screws on our starboard bow as expected. Further to starboard and across our stern, he now reported light swishes of
four patrols, the two on our beam somewhat close. Jones had
the scope ready and brought it up for one of our water-
lapping looks. The sweep was quick and the scope was down.
We'd need to move in another thousand yards for the shot
we'd want, in to 15 fathoms. But what disturbed me as much
were the PCs, now five of them, poised in an arc between us
and deep water.

"Fraz, this situation stinks!" I remarked, straightening up
as Jones lowered the scope.

Fraz's thumb pointing seaward and his pleading expression
fortified my decision. No exchange of words was necessary.
Routine orders sent *Tang* into a great descending curve, the
half turn of a helix, toward the PCs and friendly seas beyond.
In all compartments our troops quietly went about rigging
for depth charge.

10

Our speed was two-thirds, not sufficient to permit the patrolling PCs to hear our screws, but the 5 knots was bringing us

around handsomely. Fraz and Jones had used their Ouija board in arriving at the depth of the sea, and Larry was about to settle us two fathoms off the bottom at 90 feet. Rather than dispute the navigators' figure, I ordered the sound heads rigged in. It need not be for long, and at the moment Bergman, with the topside-mounted JP head, was doing a masterful job in reporting the low-pitched pings of the enemy. Larry went through to a 3-degree up-angle in leveling off, not unusual and advantageous on this occasion. The stern didn't hit, so neither should the sound heads.

We had the choice of heading off to pass between two PCs, giving each of them the opportunity for a broadside echo, or of heading directly beneath the one nearly ahead and presenting a minimal angle. The fine line traced by the stylus of our bathythermograph showed a minute horizontal movement at our present depth. It could signify a temperature gradient ahead. We repeated the sound head procedure while going down another 50 feet and passing directly beneath a PC. The seas were kind, and we cruised to deep water below a 5-degree gradient, which would reflect all but a fraction of each enemy ping.

One depth charge, perhaps dropped in disgust, bade us farewell, and we commenced ringing for normal submerged cruising. *Tang* had ben completely on the defensive since the decision to break off the approach, and the immediate rigging for depth charge had obviously soothed out our withdrawal. This became especially evident when Fraz and I compared it to the simultaneous rigging and evasion following the first successful attack of this patrol, out of Owashi Wan. It would seem that some rigging for depth charge could take place during the approach, thus speeding the transition to the defensive after firing. We each knew of boats that operated that way, but in them the spark that turned a ship's company into a fighting unit seemed to have been snuffed out along the way or never was ignited at all. They had sunk some ships, but not many.

Tang would continue on the offensive just as long as she logically could; we'd worry about evasion when the time came. It had come this day for several reasons: The enemy at least suspected our presence, or had made a good guess, and true surprise was lacking; *Tang* was being forced to attack from a precariously shallow position and would have no torpedoes left for defense; and the enemy's antisubmarine unit was already in place, waiting for us to shoot. Retreat has its place in any battle, even in a submarine's. We could find a better spot, with conditions more to our liking, and we still had our last three torpedoes.

The patrol was young, a week shy of a month, and timewise we could afford a ropeyarn Sunday. But the waxing moon dictated otherwise, for now late in the second quarter, it was shining bright at sunset. An extra day and it would be low above the horizon and a definite hindrance to a submarine wanting to surface and make a run for it. We could avoid the worst of this by attacking tomorrow.

The horizon was clear late into evening twilight, when we surfaced under a three-quarter moon. It was 1930, the evening meal was over, and only routine dumping of weighted sacks held up another high-speed run. Fraz had laid down a track that would take us well clear of any possible radar detection from Shiono Misaki and then northeast past Kantori Saki and back to our old stomping ground near Miki Saki. We would not be moving onto this point nor into Owashi Wan but to a lesser point about five miles to the southwest called Nigishima. It is tipped by a small island lying about 300 yards off the point, and any sizable ships would have to pass to seaward. Further, the motorboat patrols that we had observed before near Miki Saki—and who had observed us, too—did not range this far. With 50 fathoms close to the seaward side of the island, it appeared a natural for our last attack.

The squalls reported to be gathering should make the passage more secure, but with the sudden change in the weather, I went topside to see for myself. Fraz was already there, and though the lookout efficiency and even that of the radar were reduced, this would affect the enemy without radar more adversely. I was on my way below when Hank's firm voice called me to the bridge. There, unbelievably close and parallel to us, was a submarine. Radar called 1,100 yards, and I called, "Left full rudder!" putting her astern. We had moved out to 5,000 yards when tracking showed that she had turned away also. The battery charge was complete. All engines went on propulsion and *Tang* rolled at full power in a midnight end-around. We did not get far before the pip on the SJ's A-scope became smaller and then disappeared altogether; she had dived. We ranged ahead on her original course and then stopped and waited. A long hour went by; she had not surfaced and her submerged speed could now be bringing her within torpedo range of us. It could be a case of who was hunting whom, and without reluctance we bent on the knots and headed for Nigishima Saki.

We were too keyed up for sleeping, and over a cup of coffee Fraz and I talked over the possibilities, joined a few minutes later by Hank and Basil, who had come off watch. Could we have missed a Fox that told of a friendly submarine? It did not seem likely, but we would have wanted to observe this submarine in daylight to be sure. Franz left for a moment and came back with some notes. This was the area where four torpedoes had missed our submarine *Tautog*, and we concluded that the enemy had outfitted at least one submarine with radar and she was looking for us.

Diving was but two hours away. Fraz would be up the rest of the night making our landfall, and then I would con us in while he navigated. There was time, however, to kick off my shoes; and in the quiet, perhaps fortified by the excitement of the last two hours, I decided on our tactics for the coming day. I doubted that they had been tried before; they hadn't in *Wahoo,* and that covered most everything that submarines had ever done. More important, they should be new to the enemy and would avoid the difficulties we had experienced in attacking the *Biyo* and *Akasi Maru.*

The two hours passed quickly and at 0420 we slid under the sheltering sea a mile and a half from Nigishima Saki. As insurance against being caught in left field, we continued in to 1,500 yards off the rocks. As expected, patrol activity commenced within the half hour, but it turned back northeast short of us. In the calm, we now learned that Tokyo Rose had again pointed the finger at us, but encouragingly had used the word "submarines." Our hit-and-run tactics had the enemy confused, but he was doing a pretty good job of getting under our skin. Perhaps by this night we would have evened that score.

Mel called me back to the conning tower at breakfast, for one of the PCs on a return trip south was continuing directly for us. At a periscope range of 2,000 yards, we headed down, rigging for depth charge as she closed. *Tang* was at 275 feet, two fathoms off the bottom, when the PC passed directly overhead, her sound bearing suddenly shifting to the reciprocal. As I expected, she gave no indication of suspecting our presence, and we were close to evasion depth if she had; we rigging for normal submerged cruising on the way up. She was back again within the half hour, heading up the coast, and we went through a repeat performance. Again our vertical evasion worked perfectly, even though we had but a slight gradient, and some of the troops began to share my confidence in the maneuver. Listening to the PC's screws and pings growing in intensity till they were overhead and crossing our fingers that neither speeded up, indicating a contact or depth charges, did pick up the heartbeat a bit and would take some getting used to by all of us.

Fraz, who was supposed to be making up for a night without sleep, could not stand being outside of the activity and joined me for the second double pass. Mel kept the con and handled the PC's southward leg so well that Fraz and I went below for coffee. My smile brought a query from Fraz.

"I was just thinking that with more time in submarines than Mell, I was essentially put under hack for shifting the *Argonaut* from one berth to another. The U.S.S. *Beaver* made port early, before dawn, and we were in her berth. I had the duty so I backed clear, but I was not yet qualified."

Fraz shook his head. He, too, was well aware of the tremendous changes submarine service had undergone since the start of the war. He reached for the cribbage board, which might serve as a sort of therapy this day.

After one more double pass, the PC was relieved by a *Hishun Maru* class patrol. We were not leaving everything up to Mel, for planes in sight continuously indicated coming shipping. Flying low, they also limited our periscope exposures and the opportunity to fix our position. The counter Kuroshio had moved us southwest a mile, off Adashika Wan, when smoke appeared around Miki Saki. Battle stations sounded for the first time this August 25, a slowdown since yesterday, but our targets here looked better. Their tops were now in view, a medium mast-funnel-mast freighter and a smaller one with engines aft. Their track plotted across the narrow entrance to the bay, and we turned left for a stern shot with our last three torpedoes. The enemy came on and then turned unexpectedly into Adashika Wan, giving us a 130 port track with a range of 1,700 yards. It would be a reasonable shot, but not with our last torpedoes. Possibly influenced by their port quarter escort, which was about to wipe off our scope, we broke off the attack and bucked the current back to Nigishima Saki. *Tang's* speed over the bottom was only a knot, but two hours after the sighting, now 1335, she was back in position.

Time had not dragged, but the hours since dawn had been

wearing and we welcomed a period of inactivity. It lasted 54 minutes, ending when Frank sighted smoke to the south. As the tops and then the hull came in view, it proved to be another patrol with a deep-throated pinger, sounding like a pile driver over our supersonic JK. Her hull, however, had the chunky lines of a minesweeper, and as she drew closer a motor sailer or work boat came in sight about 100 yards on the sweep or patrol's starboard beam. The two appeared to be sweeping. Our sonic JP, which amplified sounds just as they would be heard with your ears under water, took this delightful moment to report scraping and clonking noises, as though heavy chains were being dragged along the bottom. This certainly fortified the visual impression that they were sweeping for us.

Fraz went forward and *Tang* went down. The pile driver continued on JK as the range closed. We had 250 feet of sea above us when Fraz returned. The best he could say was, "I don't think so," and then the pile driver shifted to short scale. We were almost glad to exchange the cables and chains that had seemed so logically possible for the enemy's sonar contact. We waited, there was nothing else we could do, and then a low cheer filled the conning tower as the enemy shifted back to long scale, having passed us up for a bump on the bottom. Still, we'll never be sure he wasn't sweeping too!

It was now 1530. We had spent just over an hour with the sweep, and as she continued driving piles to the northeast, two and then three patrols moved in to search the area. They, at least, were not fitted for sweeping, though avoiding the three of them required almost continuous trips close to the bottom. The action and the possible decisions now required more experience. Fraz had the con for the moment. Since something was obviously brewing, I flipped the eavesdropping switch on the Voycall at the head of my bunk. I could now listen in on both control and the conning tower and thus judge when I should go up to take the con. This could, of course, be rather dangerous to my pride, but it had saved countless trips to the conning tower or bridge, and had permitted enough horizontal exercise to keep me going. Word from con of distant high-frequency echo-ranging drifted through, followed by a hushed statement from control that surely expressed the sentiment of the whole ship's company: "Jesus Christ, I wish the Old Man would get rid of these three goddamned torpedoes!"

The duty chief's messenger brought the official word of the

echo-ranging from down the coast, growing louder though no ships were yet in sight. In the conning tower, the JK speaker had been turned on. The high-pitched, squeaky pings, like steam from a radiator valve, were the same as those we had heard the day before. Though its peak was above the range of our receiver, the intensity increased steadily, and on the next observation four escorts were in sight. The Bells of St. Mary's chimed for what all hands certainly prayed would be the last time on this patrol. Happily, the last three PCs had shifted their activity to Miki and Kuki Saki just to the northeast, apparently satisfied that our vicinity was safe. For the moment, Jones and I were able to search at will. This was well, for passing rain squalls were obscuring the coast, and we needed the earliest contact possible on the ship that must be following.

The report "Battle stations manned" was almost immediate, giving the impression that the ship's company had already been standing by, which was very probably the case. Now I heard Fraz's order to make torpedo tubes ready aft. The enemy ship was not yet in sight, but on the next observation her two masts poked out of the squall, followed by her long, low hull.

I called, "Starboard eight," Jones read, "Range eight thousand," and *Tang* was off to move onto her track. From there we could pull off anytime for a stern shot as she came by. The time was 1743, a half hour since hearing her escorts' pings. Fraz called the time for our run, 15 minutes. We slowed for a midpoint squint and a range; all was well and we continued on. Another six minutes passed, and we slowed again. Caverly immediately had her screws beating 90 turns by metronome but abaft our port beam; we had crossed her bow or she had zigged to seaward. The next minute seemed interminable, but with Welch's call Jones and I took a quick sweep and the scope was down. I gave Fraz the OK sign and ordered left full rudder. The angle was 10 port; *Tang* was inshore of the enemy ship, and we were coming to the reverse of her course for low parallax firing. Our torpedoes would leave in the direction of the enemy's motion and their gyros would then take them to the right to intercept.

There was now a moment during the turn to describe our target for the identification party and very probably all hands, too. It was not difficult; she was a heavily loaded, medium-sized diesel tanker, the identical ship that had slipped by us out of Kazampo yesterday morning. The overall speed of under 2 knots must have been nearly intolerable to the enemy; we meant to make it impossible.

We had steadied on course 223. The escort that I had first seen across the tanker's deck, forward of her after superstructure, had now dropped nearly astern. The other three were fanned out on her starboard bow, while a fifth ranged ahead. None of them could interfere with us, and there was still time to turn away for a straight stern shot. The navigator tabooed this; there was not room between us and the island. I would now want echo ranges to substantiate the stadimeter, for the data computer's angle solver must account for the advance and transfer of each torpedo to the point where it settled on its gyro's course. An error in the range set into the TDC would result in a displacement of the torpedo at the target.

Fraz reported the outer doors open; the enemy was coming on. We would get one more setup and then shoot. Jones brought the scope to my hands as usual, and I rode it up. Caverly was standing by.

"Bearing—mark!" Jones read 292.

"Range—mark!" The scope lowered and Jones read 1,100 yards; Caverly called 800 from his echo, 300 yards out!

"Oh, Christ! I got a reciprocal on the rocks," Caverly said and trained the sound head 180 degrees to bring the echo-ranging QC elements on the tanker. We tried again, and both checked at 900. Only seconds had actually been required, and now came Fraz's warning of 10 degrees to go. I glanced at plot; the projected firing range was under 600 yards, no problem since the Mark 18-1s armed before 200. The TDC now read 700, with enemy course 033 and speed 8. It all looked good, but with no escorts on our side of the tanker, we'd take one more range before firing; it would never be heard amidst the array of pings on our port hand and could make this the most accurate salvo we had yet fired. This time Caverly, Jones, and I were all at the ready.

"Any time, Captain," said Fraz, stepping over to the firing panel. Jones raised the scope from deck level to my hands, and I stationed the wire amidships on the tanker.

"Constant bearing—mark!" Caverly called a range of 600. Jones read the bearing. "It all checks," said Frank, backing up Mel.

"Set!" Her after superstructure was already coming on, and now her stack.

"Fire!" Fraz hit the firing plunger, and the first torpedo was on its way. The second fish went amidships. But the third

I aimed a quarter of a ship's length ahead, for the middle of three escorts, nearly on a line of bearing.

Caverly was tracking the torpedoes, all running normally as Ogden called out the seconds. At this range even the slow Mark 18-1s would not take long. The time was 1805.

"Torpedo run forty seconds," called Fraz, both to us and over the 1MC. All 88 in the ship's company were apparently urging these torpedoes on, some men close by quite audibly. They had been babied, checked, and rechecked. If ever torpedoes were to run true, these should. They did; the first with a whack and disintegrating explosion that crumbled the whole after section of the tanker, as if she'd been constructed of poorly reinforced concrete. The second torpedo finished the job. I swung left to the escorts ahead and gave Jones a thumbs up for the search scope. They had not recovered from the shock of the first two explosions, and the leading escort never would; our last torpedo had just blown her to pieces.

What was left of the tanker's bow had now sunk, and the stern escort was making a run for where the tanker's quarter would have been. Expecting some close ones, we put her on our port bow to work toward deeper water, rigging for depth charge on our way.

11

The depth charges rained, but not close, for the enemy obviously had not the faintest idea of our firing position. To close the escorts now solely for the purpose of reaching deep water by the shortest route was certainly not in our best interest. We eased off to starboard and proceeded along an arc, keeping track of the nearest escorts by sound and water-lapping looks. At the end of about ten minutes, the initial barrage stopped, but we had now obtained deepwater soundings with the enemy abaft our beam. Any curiosity concerning the enemy's tactics after the escorts regrouped was put aside. Larry took our ship on down in a long, slow-motion glide and trimmed her off at an even 500 feet.

Our course was 116 to pass Aoga Shima, safe in the central Nampo Shoto. Any course to the east, as long as our 100 turns outflanked the enemy, would have been satisfactory. But knowing that *Tang* was proceeding along the general route for Pearl gave us all a lift. The Japanese were tenacious, however, for bearings of their echo-ranging showed a search extending across our stern from quarter to quarter. It was 1915. Over an hour had passed since the attack, and if we were to observe the enemy it had to be now, before the end of evening twilight.

Standard speed assisted Larry's long climb to 100 feet, where we slowed while he adjusted the trim and then proceeded smartly on up to 60 feet. The enemy was not close, but neither was he as far astern as we would have liked, for the bright moon lay dead ahead. We would be in its streak on surfacing. *Tang* was holding her own, perhaps drawing away slowly at 100 turns; we speeded up to standard. The time was now 2000, and off on our starboard bow, at about the same elevation as the moon, lay a single black cloud. It was not large but big enough. Its bearing was drawing slowly to the left, and I had never expected to hear a conning tower cheer for a cloud. Preparations for surfacing were completed; we stood by, moving up to full speed on the battery. The cloud started across the moon's face; a minute later three blasts sounded, then a cheer rang through the boat as *Tang* hit the surface.

The time was 2039, and one at a time the diesels took over the full-power load lest we leave a telltale blotch of smoke. We could probably outrun the enemy's escorts anyway, but there had been enough excitement for one patrol. Again we had one objective, and for the moment our props at 315 turns were taking care of that. Of lesser importance, though perhaps not in the minds of the ship's company, was a delayed evening meal, announced by the aroma of frying steaks coming from the hull exhaust.

Enemy radar signals on 142, 242, and 306 megacycles weakened rapidly as we withdrew, and searchlights astern were soon lost in gathering rain squalls. Now with even the weather rooting for us, Fraz and I left our ship in Dick's capable hands and went below to see if the steaks were as good as the smell would indicate. The formality of waiting for the captain or executive officer to be seated before serving was normally waived by them when under way if they would be delayed. Watch officers, of course, completed their meal in time to assume the watch by a quarter of the hour. This night, all the officers except Dick and Ed, on watch, chose to wait for us. It was a compliment, but also with this meal would commence the rehash of the day and the patrol. It was natural, and probably no different from the stories swapped back at camp after a day's hunt. In a factual sense, ours was hunting to the nth degree. I do believe that an air of relief greeted my characterization of the day's tactics as being suited to a particular problem and set of circumstances, and so at least indicated that this would not become *Tang's* modus operandi. It seemed best not to point out that when fighting the Japanese in their front yard, the tactics used this day were applicable off every deepwater promontory. I would be the first to admit that a submarine would never feel completely comfortable in staying underfoot. But compared to the minimum-angle tactics we had used earlier in this patrol, it was considerably less dangerous, for the enemy would already be past the drop point for depth charges by the time he detected the sub, and the sub could be halfway to deep water.

Our conversation was accompanied by the score of *Flying Down to Rio* showing in the forward torpedo room. All of our movies were of course repeats, but it happened that this show with Fred Astaire and Ginger Rogers was the only one I had attended on this patrol. There was a remote possibility that it was having a rerun for my benefit, though most probably for the suggestion contained in the title. If so, I had the message.

"What's our fuel status, Larry?" This was normally a daily report but quite understandably had been pushed aside this day. Frank handed Larry his notebook, which he'd apparently left on the sideboard in anticipation.

"On surfacing we still had fifty-five thousand, and we're burning five thousand a day at this speed, that is outside of charging batteries," Larry replied, checking the figures in the notebook.

"That would get us to Pearl with at least seven thousand to spare, Captain," Frank volunteered. The two had obviously been advised by Fraz to be primed for the query.

"Let's let her roll for the present and see what auxiliary can do about pumping up the battery during the next day or so."

It was fun to observe *Tang's* officers remaining maturely serious but unable to totally suppress a boyish glee at the thought of a high-speed run from Honshu all the way to

Pearl. Perhaps they were thinking the same of me. It was a far cry from peacetime steaming at the most economical speed, but other than the added safety such a run afforded us, it was far and away the most economical move in the overall war effort. Since departing on her first patrol, day in and day out including refits, *Tang* was averaging one enemy ship on the bottom every 12 days. In dollars and cents they would be worth several million dollars apiece, and many times that figure to the enemy since they were irreplaceable. So it was very easy to justify to ourselves the three days we could save now, for we would be able to depart on patrol again just that much sooner. And should any staff nitpicker dare to raise an objection, we could throw the figure of at least a million bucks on the table.

My night orders and congratulatory message to the crew seemed familiar on rereading. I thumbed the pages back to July 6, the day of our last attack in the Yellow Sea. Except for listing the cautions and course ahead of the congratulations, the entries were almost identical. The message had worked well before; there was no reason to change except to record the data on this last ship and escort. The identification party had found no picture of the tanker in the publications, undoubtedly because she was too new. The escort, however, appeared to be a *Kushiro* type, and I recorded them as had become customary:

1 *medium diesel tanker*	5,000 *tons*	Lat.	33° 55′ N.
modern, new appearing		Long.	136° 13′ E.
1 *Kushiro Maru class*	600 *tons standard*	Lat.	33° 55′ N.
escort vessel (PCE)	*displacement*	Long.	136° 13′ E.

Walker brought a cup of coffee and took the Night Order Book aft to the duty chief. Only the muted sounds of the racing seas beyond the pressure hull and the reports required by the standing orders disturbed the hours till daylight.

In overcast, scuddy weather, *Tang* rolled past Aoga Shima. It was 0800 of August 26, and 3,325 miles of unobstructed seas lay between us and Pearl. We continued making knots throughout the day, and the required departure message went out to the force commander at midnight. Included in addition to the results was a general statement of where and when and under what circumstances we had found the enemy. The message should delay the next boats for the Empire until we would have a chance to talk to them at Pearl, Midway, or by rendezvous at sea, but that was staff business and ours was to bring *Tang* back safely. With this in mind, our first running dive was scheduled for midmorning. In peacetime this term would describe any dive with way on, but ours would have a variation. Those involved in the mechanics of the diver were cut in on exactly what we would be doing; the rest of the ship's company would soon find out.

Basil's two blasts initiated the dive exactly like any other. Fraz, on the search scope with the prism fully depressed, watched forward. As soon as he called, "Decks awash!" I ordered three blasts. *Tang*'s downward momentum carried her another few feet in a long, shallow dip, and then she was on the surface at cruising speed. The pit log showed that our speed had dropped 3 knots, but the whole evolution had taken only four minutes. Using an average of the speed reduction, we had been set back only 200 yards in our run for the barn, instead of five or six miles by a normal trim dive. The troops liked it, and this dunking dive told me that *Tang* could go on down, which was all I needed to know. Frankly, it was enough different to be fun.

In February of 1943 I had enjoyed two birthdays and felt none the worse for it. There would seem to be a chance in four that someone in the ship's company would have a birthday on the day *Tang* recrossed the international date line. Yeoman Williams had gone through the individual records prior to our departure and had made up a birthday list, and now I took a look at it. Two fell on this August 30. Tomorrow would be August 30, too, and that meant two days of celebrating birthdays. When the cooks and bakers had such an incentive, they could do wonders, especially when in competition. For two days now, the humdrum meals of steak and strawberries would be topped by cakes the equal of Blum's in San Francisco.

Frank was polishing his navigation, department heads were preparing their base work requests, and those not on watch were polishing their compartments. Fraz and Williams were bearing the brunt of turning my longhand into an intelligible patrol report, but on occasion Fraz would accompany me when a particular compartment was ready for inspection. In the pump room, the vertical pipe housing the SD mast had a peculiar bluish-purple stain that caught my eye.

"Oh, you missed that at the end of our last patrol," Fraz volunteered. "I'll tell you about it down at the Royal." I would have passed it off as unmixed bluing in the priming paint now showing through the well-scrubbed finish, but the twinkle in his eye showed Fraz had a story more suitably told over a cold beer. That was not far away, for this night we reported passing the 1,000-mile circle and gave as our arrival 0900 on September 3. Ballinger posted a copy of our dispatch in the crew's mess; it would serve as a target date for all hands.

Our dunking dives continued, but one day out of Pearl, Ballinger reported a problem; our ship's company would never be able to finish the steaks. There was little doubt about his thoughts, that those frozen fry cuts could be the makings of a luau-steak fry that would demonstrate to the new recreational specialists how things ought to be done, and I was confident that the combined ingenuity of the troops would triumph again. Frankly I was glad that our Taylor ice cream machine was securely installed with its compressor in the pump room and not as a single unit, or the crew would take it to the Royal, too.

The dawn came on bright and clear. In fact the visibility was too good, for back on our quarter to the southwest was a searchlight signaling FORM ONE EIGHT, or in plain language, "Fall in astern." Ogden took delight in sending IMI's (repeat), INT's (interrogatory), in fact every operator's signal in the book, ending with a JIG (verify and repeat) as we went over the horizon. Having come this far safely and now in the homestretch, *Tang* would not submit to peacetime protocol.

A full section in their scrubbed dungarees and white hats, this time including Aquisti lest there be another surprise, looked sharp indeed as they faced ships in the harbor. No better men fought any ship. First in, we chose our berth, and bowing to nostalgia I stopped the screws after ten-ten dock and ordered 15 degrees left rudder when the end of the pier lined up with the second palm tree. It used to work; it still did, and *Tang* brought herself alongside for a one-bell landing.

The usual fanfare awaited, a bit more formal than at Midway but just as sincere. There would be three or four more boats arriving, in column if they had been caught by that FORM ONE EIGHT, so the troops were quickly free to go about the business of drawing their monies and boarding the awaiting buses for the Royal. Of the people who greeted us, one of the most welcome and respected was Commander David C. White. He had commanded *Plunger* at the commencement of hostilities and had departed December 11 for

the Kii Suido, just to the west of the areas we had patrolled.
There he sank the second Japanese ship of the war, and one
of the depth charges *Plunger* received in return was so close
that it expanded the port vent riser aft, jamming the stern
plane shafting and temporarily putting the planes out of
commission. As ComSubDiv 43, he would be our division
commander during this refit and accompanied the officer in
charge of the relief crew and me through the boat. In the
crew's mess he paused to look at the troops' tabulations, 18
ships and 150 depth charges, all but a handful of the ash cans
received on this last patrol.

"It's a rough area, isn't it," he commented, and he should
know! We walked on aft, climbed up through the torpedo
room hatch, and the commander politely went ashore. The
troops' spit and polish had not gone unnoticed, and we'd get
our ship back shined up and ready for sea.

In the wardroom, Fraz had all of the paperwork practically
buttoned up. Frank was assisting by calling the totals from
the rough tabulations: 20 ship contacts with 31 escorts, 22
separate patrol craft, and 41 bombers. It didn't appear that
the enemy was about to say uncle, but more important than
these figures were those concerning our men. Fifteen had
made new rates, and another 18 had qualified in submarines.
The work had been going on for months, of course, but
completing the taut requirements on this patrol was worthy of
special credit. Perhaps it was further proof that some men
excel under stress.

Williams and Jones were on their way. The relief steward
served us good coffee and then proceeded to put our gear in
the back of the sedan at the head of the dock. With no alarms
or 1MC to hurry us, we took our time before heading toward
the Royal and the first reef.

PART VI

Fifth Patrol
IN THE
FORMOSA STRAIT

1

We had not kowtowed to Hank Munson and his *Rasher,* who was trying out his two years seniority with that FORM ONE EIGHT, but now we faced a new problem. Our beautiful suite at the Royal was reserved for the Pearl Harbor Commission, admirals with 30-odd years seniority who were still investigating the holocaust. I could not blame them for commandeering the best but wondered what pressures had forced Admiral Lockwood to admit them when even he would not come to the Royal except as a guest. It wes probably a direct order from Admiral Nimitz, or more likely from Commander-in-Chief, U.S. Fleet, Admiral Ernest J. King in Washington. The commission would undoubtedly continue its study indefinitely, and with the added incentive of such accommodations, who could blame the admirals?

Fraz and I were not accustomed to walking away from problems, big or small, and this one loomed big at the moment. A surreptitious inquiry with the assistance of the chief master at arms, a former chief of the boat, disclosed that the commission had not shown up for months, but since the suite had been scrubbed and polished to a T, it was being kept vacant for the day when the commission might return. Chiefs of the boat, present or past, are wonderful men, and armed with this information and fortified by my brand-new commander's insignia, I found regaining our former accommodations to be a simple matter. In fact, they were now even more luxurious, for the original rugs, drapes, and other beautiful furnishings had all been replaced.

With our suite secured, the last letter from stateside read, and two beers under our belts, we headed for the rendezvous at the first reef. The surf was unusually high due to a kona, or wind from the Big Island. Only now, as the adrenaline subsided, was it evident that we were tired, exhausted, worn out. But it was nothing that a few days or possibly weeks would not rectify. At the moment, the physical support of the foaming sea was our therapy, though understandably none of the ship's company ventured on to seaward this evening.

Hank Munson joined us for chow, laughing about his visual signal and claiming that it was just a gag. We were not topside when the other boats entered port, so we couldn't say if they were in column, but we were perfectly willing to give him the benefit of the doubt. After all, we shared a common enemy, and that alone put any differences aside. Further, *Rasher* had just completed a fine patrol with five ships down, and they were not coming easily as the war progressed; we knew. This night, as all first nights in from patrol, was not measured in hours of rest but rather in the exchange of yarns and the camaraderie that holds between men who have shared similar experiences and dangers.

We had enjoyed routine sleep on our return voyage but awakened truly refreshed for the first time on September 4. It was well, for already important business awaited us at the submarine base. During her shakedown and subsequent patrols, our ship had logged sufficient nautical miles to have taken her twice around the world. The initial marine growth on her underwater body would have been killed by the antifouling ingredients of the plastic bottom paint, but on their faint skeletons new plants and animals would have thrived. To maintain *Tang*'s speed and endurance, a docking and bottom job were in order.

I regretted the passing of the all-hands toil of scraping and wire-brushing the bottom as the water receded. Though working from punts snubbed in close to the hull made it an arduous task, this and the subsequent painting were chores of pride that offered each hand an equal chance to work on his ship. The fact that the troops on this one occasion could ignore everything they had ever learned about proper topside painting and just slap paint on the bottom, themselves, shipmates, and even on unwary officers or chiefs who had been unnecessarily taut merely added to the esprit of this field day.

Alas, dock workmen with high-pressure hoses and a few others to brush out the spots would now complete the preparations. The plastic paint would then be sprayed on by professionals and the ship undocked with only a few of our ship's company involved. Among them would be Fraz, Frank, and Mel, plus a few selected hands, and on this morning all but Fraz and Frank had gone on ahead. Frank was driving and dropped me off at squadron headquarters, for this was the time for him to handle our ship. Without my presence, his judgment would not be tempered by thoughts of what I would desire, and thus with his sole direction, *Tang* would dock handsomely. Word would pass through the crew, and Frank's prestige would rise several notches as had mine, with the troops anyway, following the *Beaver* incident.

My business was with Commander Submarine Squadron Four and had been briefly though completely stated on a single sheet. I doubt that one page had ever received more thought and care by a skipper and his executive officer, for it could affect Fraz's whole future. After a cup of coffee, I handed the letter to Captain C. F. Erck and watched his expression as he read. The first paragraph summarized Fraz's experience, now a total of 11 patrols, probably more than any contemporary. In addition, it pointed out that he had been designated qualified for command for more than a year. The second paragraph described his performance and fighting ability and stated that we were doing the enemy a favor by holding Fraz in his present billet when he should be fighting his own ship. The next paragraph recommended that he attend the special PCO school at New London to catch his breath before taking his own command. An equally important reason for sending him to PCO school—that some of his knowledge might rub off on others—was left out. The last paragraph, which should be the clincher, simply stated that *Tang* had trained officers in excess of complement and a suitable relief as executive officer and navigator was aboard.

Captain Erck raised his head and started to nod, but a prolonged blast from the waterfront delayed any immediate discussion.

"I didn't know any boats were getting under way this morning," he commented while walking over to the window to see what was going on.

"That's *Tang*," I volunteered. "The executive officer will be docking her," I added.

Captain Erck blinked a bit, obviously not quite attuned to my reasoning concerning such delegation of responsibility. A few words of explanation were in order but were forestalled by a polite knock on the office door. In walked Fraz.

"Who has the con?" I inquired, trying not to show any surprise.

"Oh, Mel is backing her clear," he replied. Then he added, "Frank will be putting her across the still, of course."

"You certainly have confidence in your executive officers,"

the captain commented and by the use of the plural signified his approval of the basic request.

I had business with Commander White and Fraz with the personnel office, undoubtedly to grease the skids for the preparation of his orders. Knowing Fraz, he'd probably sit down at the typewriter himself and leave nothing to chance. We'd meet after lunch at the dry dock.

Tang was high and dry with an exceptionally clean bottom. Apparently the first semblance of marine growth had washed away in the fresh to brackish waters of Mare Island Strait. Since then, our short periods in port and speed at sea must have prevented the expected accumulation. Our zincs were another matter. These plates, about six inches wide, a foot long, and a half inch thick, were secured with cap screws to the struts, propeller shafting, and the area around the stern tubes. Without them, the electrolytic action between the bronze propellers and steel hull would erode and pit the structures about *Tang*'s stern. Higher on the atomic scale, the zincs went into solution first. Ours were gone, so the docking was necessary if for this reason alone. Since undocking would take place in the morning we wasted no time in heading for the Royal.

Surprisingly, with the surf nearly as high as before, we moved out handily to the second reef for bodysurfing shoreward. This would have been the time and place for my prewar board. More of a paddleboard than a surfboard, it measured 15 feet long by 17 inches wide, and was four inches deep. Hollow and tailing off gradually to a narrow transom, it would catch practically any wave with just a paddle or two, but it was a devil to steer. Kamaainas would shout when they saw it coming and give it a wide berth. Fraz and I spoke of those days and wondered if such would ever return. Perhaps, we concluded, though knowing they could never be quite the same.

The undocking and return to the base the next morning were routine, so we were soon free to take care of other business. Mine concerned another pitch for a radar periscope, called an ST. Its 3-centimeter radar, one-third of the wavelength of our SJ, would undoubtedly remain immune from detection for months, maybe till the end of the war. Radar, at least our own, had not played an important part in our last patrol except as an aid to navigation. None of our patrols held much in common with one another, however, and with the enemy closing the radar gap, we needed this ST scope to prolong *Tang*'s advantage. I didn't think much of the staff comment that our submarine didn't seem to need one anyway. A couple of them should have been on our front porch when we penetrated the convoy in the East China Sea. Thoughts of that night still sent goose pimples up my spine. But true, we had not been shot at while on the surface during this last patrol except by the patrol yacht, and that was of our own making. Still, our last patrol was in an area of daytime operations, and surely in the offing were operations requiring more difficult nighttime penetrations. *Tang* rated the facilities to conduct some of them submerged, but in spite of previous requests, she was not listed for the installation.

I suspected that *Tang*'s lack of success in getting an ST was the result of a missing comma or dash between the words "radar" and "periscope" in a précis of our third patrol report prepared by a reporting senior. Referring to certain approaches and attacks that were in part conducted by radar and then periscope, his brief called them radar periscope attacks, and this at least implied that *Tang* had the installation. As it developed, this would have made no difference, for as of the moment there was no ST available at the base. Still, the confusion pointed to the dangers of trying to further condense an already brief and exact report. Better that interested parties read the words of the submarine commander.

Fraz and Frank had enjoyed better luck and had laid the groundwork for changes in personnel that would follow our established pattern. Not one of those men who had manned key battle stations during the last half of the fourth patrol would be touched, and again we would pick replacements for others from the relief crew, all volunteers for *Tang*. Frankly, this was more important than the ST, and we headed for the Royal again in good spirits.

The first week had passed with seemingly more time spent at the base than at the Royal, at least daytime hours. This had affected few of the troops, however, who organized what turned out to be the luau to top all luaus. In the wartime rationing, meat points were as scarce in the Islands as anywhere else, almost as scarce as young ladies. Apparently the word of steaks had brought the latter out of hiding, and our single junior officers now had second thoughts concerning the advantages of commissions. But that was just one day, and with the available recreation interrupted little by business, we kept pace with our ship in returning to fighting trim.

Already we had begun conjecturing concerning our next patrol, and the logical guess was not to our liking.

For over a year now, small groups of boats had been patrolling together, at first under the command of an embarked division commander, but later under the senior commanding officer. The Pacific was too vast for division into a grid as the Nazis had quite apparently done in the Atlantic. If a contact were reported, the great distances would normally preclude headquarters' vectoring boats to intercept, and the convoys themselves were too small for any large-scale operation. The direction thus fell on the senior skipper, who did not have the secure reliable communications the task demanded. It seemed to be the hope that a hot boat, by direction and example, could impart some of its fire to others in the group or wolf pack. I hadn't changed my opinion that the boats could do better on their own, and areas for operation were not yet at a premium. Our recent areas, 4 and 5, could take four or five submarines and really stupefy the enemy. Neither had I changed my opinion that the spark that ignited a hot boat had to come from within, and to date the total sinkings by only one wolf pack had exceeded those of *Wahoo* or *Tang* in the Yellow Sea. We'd cross our fingers and hope for another independent patrol but of course would carry out whatever our next Operation Order entailed.

The Pacific war was accelerating, and to keep pace our submarine tenders were now deployed to Majuro and Saipan. They were in essence mobile bases and subordinate commands operating just as had Midway. Direction and patrol assignments remained under the one command at Submarine Base Pearl. Thus the same clean directives continued while the boats enjoyed a shortened turnaround time. Since January our boats had sent well over a million tons of enemy shipping to Davy Jones's locker, but the enemy showed no sign of succumbing. Perhaps the acceleration might speed that day, for he had but an estimated 4 million tons left. We were considering these things and working ourselves back into a fighting frame of mind when a driver brought a note from the admiral.

The message merely asked that I drop by to see him at my convenience, which of course meant immediately or he would not have sent a car and driver. A word with Larry, for his engine overhauls would be a determining factor, and Fraz, Frank, and I were off for the base.

"How soon could you be ready to head west?" the admiral asked. "All the way west," he added.

I had not arrived unarmed, having spent some hours during the past week at briefings, and had a pretty good idea of the urgency. The Leyte campaign, in which General Douglas MacArthur expected to return to the Philippines, was shaping up. In preparation, there would be carrier air strikes to the north and south to interdict enemy supply lines and destroy reinforcements. Most important, engagements with the Japanese fleet before this campaign was over were almost guaranteed. Now *Tang* would have a chance to be in the midst of all of this.

"Four days, sir," I answered, "but there is one thing I request in return."

"Yes," he said, not seeming surprised and as if encouraging me to continue. The few words I had to say had been well rehearsed mentally, and I barged ahead.

"Admiral, *Tang* has been banging out patrols at nearly twice the customary rate. Most have been short, but so has every upkeep. My ship needs an ST scope, and I need something to take back to my crew. I'd like our next upkeep scheduled for Mare Island."

"I appreciate what you say, and I'll take care of it," Admiral Lockwood replied and extended his hand to seal the bargain. "By this morning's report, you may have trouble getting a load of torpedoes," he cautioned, and I departed to start the wheels in motion. Fraz and Frank were both waiting, and fortunately for the moment, *Tang* still had two execs. Fraz sent for Hank, Mel, and Ballinger, while Frank reversed the overhaul of two mains, which were half disassembled in the after engine room.

Since all torpedoes were 21 inches in diameter, even most foreign ones, we anticipated little trouble in finding a load, though it might be a motley one. Torpedo shortages had cropped up occasionally throughout the war. Back in late 1942 one boat took a load of Mark 10 torpedoes on patrol when others were having troubles with later torpedoes and their magnetic exploders. We had all chuckled at the endorsement to the patrol report: "Even though attacking with Mark 10 torpedoes and obsolete inertia exploders, three valuable *marus* were sent to the bottom." We would be tickled to find a few of them today, but another's misfortune solved our problem. *Tambor*, Hank's old ship, would be indefinitely delayed in proceeding on patrol due to main propulsion troubles, and the base commenced removing her complete load of Mark 18-1s and delivering them to *Tang*. A composite load with at least some steam torpedoes forward would have been preferable, but the fact that *Tambor* had accepted these told the story of another temporary shortage. *Tang* would sail on schedule, but in the middle of the preparations came another all-hands evolution.

How men can toil at striking stores, fueling, loading torpedoes, and carrying out the dozens of pre-patrol tasks and an hour later appear as if ready for a military inspection will always be a wonder. But our crew at quarters this September 22 would match the best in the fleet. It was well, for punctually as always, Fleet Admiral Nimitz and Admiral Lockwood, with an entourage such as we had not seen since returning with the downed aviators, proceeded with presenting awards for the third patrol. A second Navy Cross to me; a third Silver Star to Fraz; Silver Star medals to Frank and Jones; Bronze Star medals to MacDonald, Weekley, Ogden, and Caverly; and the Secretary of the Navy's Letter of Commendation with ribbon to Montgomery, Robertson, Kivlen, Andriolo, Aquisti, and Wixon. In addition, under the revised instructions, Hank received a Silver Star for the first patrol, so if I had erred in that choice between Bill and Hank, it was all squared away now.

These presentations were not all, however, for more important than any one or all of them combined was the award of the Presidential Unit Citation. Signed for Franklin D. Roosevelt, it cited the actions during *Tang*'s first three patrols, and from this moment every man who served in *Tang* would wear the ribbon with its blue, gold, and red horizontal stripes, and with a star if aboard during the actions cited.

It was not something that one scored, but with the recommendations submitted as a result of our last foray, I believed our ship now led all others in personal and unit awards. In any case, no submarine captain could have been prouder of his fighting ship and men.

We had retained our billets at the Royal, and this evening I finally learned the story behind the purple stains in the pump room. Cases of Welch's grape juice were being struck below when provisioning ship for our third patrol. Our radiomen had volunteered for this working party, so slipping a few cases into the adjacent radio shack became a simple matter. Thus on board was the major ingredient for home brew to liven up Midway upon our return. The brew had worked, in fact during the hot dives it had worked too well and couldn't be capped or stopped. The purple froth oozed from the brewing area in the back of the spare parts lockers, down through openings in the nonwatertight deck, and thence to the bulkheads and SD mast housing in the pump room. Scrub as they would, the radiomen could not completely eliminate the purple stain, and there was no paint aboard with which to cover it. It did not matter, for the auxiliarymen had now invited themselves to the party.

It had all taken place in an unused shack on Eastern Island, with the two gangs rowing over from Sand Island after dark. The brew had some kick but was apparently also a potent uretic. Stumbling in the dark in answering the urge, one of the auxiliarymen had stepped hip-deep into a hole or burrow filled with rats. His shouts and the frightened, squealing rodents running about and over everyone had a sobering effect that brought about a retreat across the harbor, back to the sanctuary of Gooneyville.

I was undoubtedly the last to learn about this escapade, but it need not have been so. There were few my age who had not tried their hand at home-brewed concoctions during Prohibition, though I suppose it would have been impossible to pass on the benefits of experience. One thing for sure, *Tang*'s troops were no sissies.

Fraz's orders had arrived, and I signed the detaching endorsement before our one-day training period, albeit with a bit of a lump in my throat. We had been through much this past year, and with results that neither of us could have accomplished without the other. The skipper-exec was a unique relationship in submarines, but I was confident that with Frank I would be blessed once more.

Our day under way was really a post-repair trial rather than a training period. As before, we did sandwich in a round of emergency drills for our new officers and men, but we moored at a respectable hour so that those who wished could spend another relaxing late afternoon at the Royal. Though not many left the base, we found the swim to the third reef and beyond was now a breeze and returned to our ship physically tired but relaxed and mentally refreshed.

In the solitude of my cabin after dinner and cribbage, I reviewed my ship's readiness for this mission, my thoughts reaching back to the lay of the ways, which had determined the north and south poles of *Tang*'s magnetic field. The Nazis used this characteristic of all ships to trigger their magnetic mines, and the immediate antidote had been the shipboard installation of great degaussing coils to counter the ship's magnetic field. In a later substitution, this field was sufficiently reduced at dockside degaussing stations. So *Tang* was demagnetized, as a jeweler does a watch, but her residual magnetic character would never change.

Along the way our ship had acquired other traits that would remain a part of her. Many of these had intensified on succeeding patrols, for the unusual had become routine in our operations, while the expectations of the ship's company were ever increasing. The constant flow of new hands in no way lessened this, for her reputation had spread and was the very reason they sought billets aboard. The determination to live up to her name and to better her previous performances had become a driving force, defining *Tang*'s unchangeable character as a fighting ship.

So Fraz's departure would not materially effect our ship's performance, and neither, I would have to admit, would my own inevitable detachment after another patrol or so, one with the designated PCO aboard if possible. Presumably, I would then assist in the direction of our sub-air rescue, which would become a major mission. But this was in part conjecture, and my thoughts belonged with the task immediately ahead. Frank's quiet knock speeded my return to the present as he entered to report all hands aboard and *Tang* ready for patrol. The clock over the doorway read 2200.

2

Hundreds of patrols had now originated at our base, some boats returning routinely as had been our lot, but others continuing on to the Southwest commands. With departures almost a daily occurrence, one might expect them to be considered commonplace, routine. This had not been our experience in the past, and if this September 24 was any indication, the sincere formalities would continue till the curtain was rung down on the war.

There had been ample time for the officers and crew to exchange words with friends, for *Tang* would not get under way until 1300. Now, as Frank and I awaited Commander White and Vice Admiral Lockwood, we spoke of our enemy, wondering if his submarines also departed on an air of formality. Probably, we surmised, but guessed that the wardroom coffee would be replaced by a saki toast to the emperor.

Walker's coffee was obviously still considered better than that at headquarters, for the admiral had allowed ample time to enjoy it. We did not speak of the patrol, for not until on station would we find out what might be in store. The conversation instead turned to the Empire areas, their possibilities, and our mutual hopes for the future. The diesels fired on schedule, and we adjourned topside. The Godspeeds were accompanied by firm handshakes, and I saw our visitors ashore.

Base personnel snaked the brow over to the dock in seconds—and then took the lines, but not fast enough, for the admiral, by chance in position, caught the bow line; he was everybody's admiral and stood at attention with others on the dock, but with his fingers in his ears for the five seconds of our prolonged blast.

With "All back two-thirds," the diesels stopped purring and got down to business. *Tang* quickly gathered good sternway and "Left twenty degrees rudder" pulled the stern into a great arc around the finger piers and into the basin beyond the base. "All ahead two-thirds; shift the rudder" killed the sternway, and our ship headed out the channel.

The harbor was quiet and had for the most part assumed its pre-war appearance. Now the capsized *Oklahoma,* which would have been on our port hand, had been righted and moved for refitting. The *Tennessee,* only damaged, had been rapidly repaired and had nearly stolen our ice cream machine back at Mare Island. The *Nevada,* hit repeatedly and holed forward, had been beached on Waipio Point, now on our starboard hand, and then quickly repaired. Together with *Tennessee,* she would be engaged in the very campaign *Tang* would support. How ironic that our fleet, which had been caught in port on that fateful day when seemingly it should have been at sea, had really survived due to this very circumstance. If our ships had been off soundings, such a surprise attack would very probably have sent the majority of them irretrievably to Davy Jones's locker.

When first viewing the holocaust on returning from patrol in late January of 1942, I should have looked beneath the tears streaming unashamedly down the faces of those at quarters with me. I would have seen jaws set as was my own, but all had then become a blur. The same determination was apparently reflected across the land, for otherwise we could not now be closing the clamps on the enemy.

But that was in the past; ahead lay the open antisubmarine net, the red and black channel buoys to port and starboard, and down their corridor, the sea buoy. *Tang* entered the safety lane, and two more diesels went on the line. The maneuvering room would add turns slowly as the engines warmed up until we reached full power. When Captain Swede Momsen had informally characterized our ship as having two speeds, full or stopped, it was not entirely in jest. It all depended on whether or not we had someplace to go and of course the fuel on hand. At this moment, the destination was clear and the fuel no problem.

Dick, now a lieutenant (jg), took the con as we headed west along the line dividing the two operating areas in the submarine sanctuary. They were unoccupied at the time, and the shortcut would save a dozen miles. At my nod, he ordered, "Rig ship for dive." We were reading each other five by five, and no other words were necessary. Circling ahead was the PBM that would escort us till dusk should we wish. Frank was calling a round of bearings and then went below to plot our departure position. A few minutes later, on the heels of "Ship rigged for dive," came the navigator's recommended course, and we came to 284 degrees true, paralleling the Islands. The regular sea detail, first section, assumed the watch, and *Tang* was on her fifth patrol.

The quiet, businesslike manner of our departure, of the transition from the Royal to patrol, augured well for this mission and should lend confidence to the whole ship's company. Our immediate destination was our friendly atoll, Midway. This accounted for the leisurely hour of our departure, for we would thus arrive at dawn of the second morning. At the moment, Dick was still turning over the watch to Lieutenant (jg) Paul T. Wines from Ridgewood, New Jersey. Called Tiny, he would obviously round out *Tang*'s basketball team and by his jolly nature would fit in well. He would share the afternoon watch with Larry, who was now our senior watch officer, so nothing would go wrong.

On watch with Ballinger as duty chief was Leibold, who like others had advanced a rate. A second class boatswain's mate but a year before, he would work in as chief of the boat on this patrol. Frank dropped below, and we scheduled a dive for 1530 so Paul could get his feet wet. In the wardroom, Adams served us the first coffee of the patrol, and it was difficult indeed to tell that our ship had just spent three weeks in port.

Tang was rolling, and at 1525 Kauai already lay well back on our starboard quarter. We released our escort with sincere thanks and received a Godspeed in return. In minutes the PBM was but a spot above the eastern horizon, probably under full throttle heading for the golf course. After brief instructions to Paul, I proceeded below. The dive was intentionally slow, following the peacetime sequences to best demonstrate all the elements involved. We had not done this since our initial dive and training period, and though it might seem a step backward, it was akin to reviewing the precautions for handling explosives and reminded all of us to be alert for any irregularity in a dive. Failure to note a crucial item was not unheard of and in some boats had led to disaster.

With Larry's previous compensation and immediate coaching, the dive was surprisingly smooth. Perhaps this was a good way to commence a training period, and we'd consider it for the next full one. Now Paul was going through the more deliberate and cautious procedure of surfacing, where the submarine, not the enemy, picked the time. With the first surfacing in enemy waters, the reasons for the caution would be evident.

Frank's evening star fix showed us behind by a half dozen miles, so Larry picked up the phone to speak to Chief Culp. A few extra turns would have us back on schedule by morning, when we would be to the north of the island chain. A jog in our track would come up shortly after passing Nihoa, and we welcomed this northerly route as an overdue change. Sooner or later an enemy submarine with endurance and patience would surely get off a shot at the traffic along the virtual highway to the south. Of course our more southerly routes were never the same, and that held true for other boats, too. Still, our present track followed an almost unused corridor as far as we were concerned.

Our speed made the moderate seas race by this night, and though muted by the ballast tanks beyond our pressure hull, the sound was of a plunging waterfall. The quiet movements on changing the watch and the punctual hushed reports in accordance with the night orders told that all was well with our ship, and the night passed quickly.

We had made up the six miles lost during the dive and would add a like amount by afternoon. A second dive would be in order, this one for our other new officer, Lieutenant (jg) John H. Heubeck from Baltimore, Maryland. He and Charles had swapped jobs, which was agreeable to all concerned, though we would miss Charles's quiet Southern humor. John had the forenoon watch with Ed, and after Ballinger checked with Parker, *Tang*'s new chief commissary steward, lest pies and things might be in the oven, two blasts took us down. Our ship had almost dived herself the first day, giving the appearance that except for the reports and blowing negative to the mark, the diving officer could pretty much twiddle his thumbs. Accordingly, I had asked Larry to upset the trim a little. How much is a little? One or the other of us should have told Ed, who was a bit taken aback at our unexpected down-angle and the ensuing gallops. But we all found out in a hurry that in John we had a second Mel, who had that fine feel of diving from the very start. On the surface again, I looked at Frank and we both nodded; *Tang* would not be lacking in competent officers.

Extra activities to help time fly by continued to be unnecessary. Eight hours of watch, meals, school of the boat, studies, a book or an acey-deucey game, perhaps a movie, and the day was gone. This afternoon we threw in battle stations with a complete approach and attack. Periscope and sound inputs were again from our folder of time-versus-bearing plots, which had now become so extensive that it was impossible to recognize a particular problem from the first few zigs. Caverly's bearings were especially realistic, for he had learned to throw himself completely into the problem, even switching on the speaker so the whole party could hear the shaving brush-microphone screw noises. Mel was setting our own ship's ordered course and speed into the TDC so *Tang* could continue along the navigator's track independent of the problem. I could not speak for Paul and John, but I'm sure that for the rest of us real torpedoes could just as well have been on their way. A few more drills would have them in the swing of things; it was impossible not to become involved.

Topside again, Frank shared my feeling of confidence, and then joined Jones, who had brought his sextant and watch to the bridge for an afternoon sun line. It was rather a precautionary position line, unnecessary with a good round of evening stars, but sometimes invaluable should the sky cloud over before dusk. All was going well, but a falling barometer bore out the weather briefing Frank had attended just prior to our departure. Anyone living in the northern hemisphere knows that with September come storms, especially at sea. In the fall, it had not been uncommon for returning submarines to circle Midway for days while waiting for the winds and seas from the south to moderate. Only then could a safe passage through the reef be assured. Should this be our lot, we would proceed on our mission, bypassing the atoll and the opportunity to top off. In anticipation of this possibility, every tank in our ship not reserved for fresh water and trimming had been filled with diesel fuel. We could still carry out our mission but would then have to forgo the advantage of being on station well ahead of other operations.

French Frigate Shoals lay 20 miles to port. *Tang* was doing well, but seas commenced building up during the night. They did not slow our speed of advance since, for the most part, we were riding in the trough. Our hot SJ raised a pip on Eastern Island at 0500, right on schedule, and I knew the satisfaction Frank must feel with his first landfall. We slowed and maneuvered to insure the customary long, straight approach to the channel. After we steadied on north, the seas commenced pushing us on. We could not slow or back down, for that would only accentuate the yaw that had come on with the shelving bottom. It was difficult to leave the steersman alone when one moment the bow was 30 degrees to the left of the slot through the reef, and a few seconds later in the same attitude off to starboard, heading for angry surf breaking over the coral. Seemingly, he could dampen out the yaw about the ordered course and keep the lookouts from climbing the shears. But should he try to overcome the natural forces, too much or improper rudder could indeed broach our ship, when she would otherwise continue in the right direction, though on wild headings. *Tang* would pass nicely through the reef if I just gritted my teeth, which would also insure keeping my mouth closed. They were anxious moments, nonetheless, but with a ship's length to go she settled on course, bisecting the slot into the harbor.

It was 0700 when we came alongside the fuel dock. In spite

of the hour, friends were down to greet us, though we saw no dentists. Frank and I turned down a luncheon invitation from captains Edmunds and Will with some regret, for there had been a great innovation at Midway. Instead of carting the garbage to leeward of the island in the old scow, they had for some time now been spreading it out on the coral sand. After it cured in the sun for a day or so, a bulldozer covered it over with a thin layer of sand. The whole project had taken months, but Midway now had rich soil and raised vegetables unobtainable elsewhere, even in submarines during the early weeks of patrol.

No special instructions had been issued concerning Walker, and he seemed in excellent spirits upon our return from the morning's courtesy calls. Diplomatically, we did not inquire, especially since the captains accompanied us for a cup of our good wardroom coffee. It wasn't long till the diesels fired, and we went topside. The fuel hoses were on the dock, the mooring lines singled, and after the handshakes and Godspeed captains Edmunds and Will stepped ashore. The brow was on the dock, and the last lines let go as I reached the bridge. At the end of the prolonged blast, "All back two-thirds" moved us quickly from alongside. Hands on deck paused at attention in response to those on the dock and then went about the necessary checking and securing topside. "All ahead two-thirds. Right fifteen degrees rudder" brought *Tang* onto the range. Ten minutes later she passed through the dredged slot in the reef, directly into the seas rolling up from the south. The time was exactly 1200, September 27.

3

Again we had fuel in every tank and corner, but the dead reckoning positions along the track, which Frank had diligently plotted, would all have to be stepped off again. The three-engine speed that we had planned would expend too much energy in fighting the seas. If we could believe A. M. Knight's *Modern Seamanship*, the direction of the wind and seas, and our own barometer, two days at the most would move our ship beyond this storm. There, a third engine would really count, and it was just common sense to take advantage of the natural movement of the storm before increasing our speed.

Pertinent parts of our Operation Order were now posted in the crew's mess, and after stepping off the new DR positions, Jones would be tacking up their chart, too. The posted Operation Order read:

> When in all respects ready for sea and patrol on or about 25 September 1944, proceed at best speed by route north of French Frigate Shoals to Midway for topping off as weather permits. Thence follow track north of Marcus, between Volcano and Bonin islands, south of Ryukyus and into Formosa Strait. Adjust speed so as to arrive on station if possible prior to 12 October. Friendly submarines in the Bonin-Volcano area will be informed of *Tang*'s transit. As seems desirable the patrol area may be extended northward into the East China Sea, but your attention is invited to the JICPOA Supplement to this order, and particularly to the Ryukyu and other minefields detailed therein.

The general nature of the order would undoubtedly stir the imagination of the troops, but they would probably deduce that some specifics were included in private communications still in my desk safe, as had been the case in the past. But the only additional information had been given to me orally— Task Force 38 would strike Formosa on October 12. Frank's expected course recommendation came over the bridge speaker, and at my nod Paul ordered, "Come right to two six seven." With small variations as might be indicated by the star fixes and sun lines, this would remain our heading until just before entering our area. Paul and John would continue standing their watches with our most experienced officers, topside as OODs and then exchanging for the conning tower watch, which might best be called operations. We would try to funnel as much of the activity their way as possible during this transit. If their performance during the past three days was any indication, they would be able to take most anything in stride by the time *Tang* reached her area.

The seas continued to be brisk, with eight-foot waves and whitecaps through September 29, but our ship was riding well, very nearly in the trough. Well, that is, for everyone except Caverly and a few others. Since the commencement of our shakedown, whenever the seas kicked up a bit Caverly had been the first to feel it, and a kid's potty hooked to his belt had become a trademark. As time went on, the presence or absence of the ornament proved to be more reliable than our barometer in predicting coming storms or their passing. On more than one occasion, Caverly was encouraged to accept pending jobs on the staff, once actually leading to his detachment. A last-minute reshuffle of the paperwork got him back aboard, for though he dreaded his seasickness, his hate of the enemy won out, though antipathy to the staff may have tipped the balance. Finally, at morning fire control drill on the third day from Midway the pot was missing, and a third engine went on the line. By late afternoon, *Tang* had moved into friendly seas under clearing skies.

Before we encountered a real storm the usual inspection was in order. It was set up for midmorning, and as I had already seen that everything forward was secured for sea, I joined Frank in the forward engine room. I was rather surprised to see our junior officers gathered in a group.

"I suggested that they be here to see what you demand on these inspections," Frank volunteered, and that seemed a good idea to me. They saluted and I returned it, looking them in the eye as is customary. They stepped aside and I stepped forward—directly into the open hatch to the engine room's lower flats, about five feet below. The bottom ladder rung broke my fall, but also my left foot. Hollywood would have one bouncing back from such an accident, but when you're doubled up, nauseated, and with a sweaty brow, you've had it. Some minutes later, snaked up from the lower flats, I hobbled forward and Frank continued the inspection aft.

Submarine pharmacist's mates are the best in the world, and I'd match their knowledge and skill with that of the country doctor. It had been proven in all sorts of doctoring, including lesser amputations and even appendectomies. Chief Larson took one look, straightening my foot and damned near sending me to the overhead, and then announced, "You've got some small broken bones—I could feel 'em, but they're pretty straight now—and one hell of a sprain, but there's nothing they'd do ashore that I haven't done except to take some X rays, and I already know about what they'd look like."

Those were the words I wanted to hear, so I was relieved

of the necessity of pulling rank had they been otherwise. Stretched out in my bunk and with my club of a foot propped up on the bulkhead and the Voycall by my ear, I'd command orally over the squawk box.

Tang was now within patrol plane radius from the Bonins, and Frank stationed extra lookouts forward as had been our custom. The daily dives continued, and then unscheduled ones as Bettys from the Bonins or the Volcano Islands seemed to concentrate along our track. The contacts were most probably just the result of our passing through the enemy's normal search patterns, and by all reports we seemed to get below without being sighted. If there was doubt, we would alter our track during darkness to foil a vectored enemy submarine. But Frank was confident we were still undetected, and I shared his feeling.

Hearing all of the reports, from the lookout's initial call to the diving officer's "Satisfied with the trim," without participating physically was contrary to my previous experience, and I wondered how the realization that *Tang* could get along without me, even through the torpedo fire control drills, would affect the troops. Finally, I chose to consider it a compliment to our ship's training. Judgments, maneuvers, angles on the bow, and torpedoes that hit would salvage any lost prestige.

The Bonin and Volcano islands were behind us, and on the night of October 4 came our first opportunity. An Ultra for action to *Trigger* and *Silversides* included *Tang* as an information addressee. They had departed Pearl a few hours ahead of us, stopping at Saipan for topping off, and would be patrolling as a two-submarine group off the Nansei Shoto. The Ultra alerted the boats to an enemy weather ship east of the Ryukyus. Frank brought the chart, and I hobbled to the wardroom, where we could lay it out. The position plotted only 50 miles south of our track and but a 40-hour run ahead, less if we put a fourth engine on the line and worked on up to full power. We considered the possibilities. There seemed little doubt that *Tang* would reach the position first, and the experience leading to our very first attack dictated that any submarine with a chance should go after every target. A weather ship might not be much of a target, but she could be of inestimable value to the enemy in the brewing engagements. Besides, entering your area with a ship already on the bottom was most any submariner's dream.

Fortunately, weather ships usually occupy a station, so we

expected little trouble in locating this one. A few hours in searching should do the trick, and then there'd be a long submerged run from over the horizon. A ship, any kind of ship, was all that was required to perk up a crew, and with some misgivings I allowed members of the gun crew on deck to grease their gun. If we could polish this one off with the deck gun and enter the Formosa Strait with a full load of torpedoes, *Tang* would be a jump ahead indeed.

In the morning, Caverly went forward again wearing his trademark, though we had only picked up a long, easy swell from the southwest. It had helped in kicking aboard some flying fish, so one's loss was another's gain. The day passed quickly with extra drills, and with satisfaction I listened to Frank going through the periscope procedure with Jones. The weather ship would be Frank's to sink, and I would only advise after contact that he move in to where a single torpedo would be sure to hit. His first ship and only one torpedo to put her down, but that had been my lot. These and similar thoughts kept cropping up during a night made fitful by increasing seas and then at 0300 by the report of a falling barometer. The sound of mounting seas now came through the ballast tanks, great muffled roars, but they were mild compared to the screaming winds and crashing seas I could hear over the Voycall. Remembering a near disaster in *Wahoo*, I ordered the lookouts below; the OOD had the protection of the bridge cowl and should be in no immediate danger. We'd assess the situation at daylight. But soon the thunder of green water on the bridge and a rising stern as *Tang* commenced seasledding dictated a change in plans. Only one order was possible or we'd lose the watch overboard and flood the inductions: "Button up the ship. Shift propulsion to the battery and slow to steerageway."

The immediate pressure on my ears told me that securing had already been in progress. That's my exec, I thought. Not so pleasant was the last barometer reading before the boat was sealed, 27.8 inches; it left no doubt about the severe nature of the storm. Dawn was breaking, however, and having come this close to the reported position of the weather ship, we'd stay on the surface and search with raised scope. An attack would be impossible, but we could perhaps stay with the ship and fire later.

It did not seem credible, but the seas increased, forcing us to run before them in an attempt to hold down the roll. Good seamanship would have dictated diving long ago and running under the storm, but finding the enemy ahead required high periscope searching and one could not dive except in the extreme. The extreme came suddenly, with violent rolls dumping me over the guardrail of my bunk and onto the deck. Frank came quickly; he needed my help in the conning tower and had brought Chief Larson, the two climbing the bull heads along the passageway. A shot in my foot and the support of about a size 14 sand shoe, laced tight, had me standing on one foot and a club in no time. Frank and I headed aft, hanging on as we could, but when we reached the control room *Tang* took a violent roll to starboard. I landed on the after end of the high-pressure air manifold, with my face about a foot from the bubble inclinometer on the forward end of the low-pressure blows. It read 70 degrees, and there she hung, obviously broached by the seas.

"Jesus Christ, is she ever coming back?" I heard myself say.

Frank had his own troubles, having landed spread-eagled on the open knife switches of the IC switchboard. The 110 volt AC juice had him doing a jig as he tried to get clear, but somehow he called out a cheerful answer: "Sometimes they don't, you know!"

In all of his gyrations, Frank must have crossed himself, or the good Lord thought he had, for we eased back to 60 degrees for a couple of rollers and then slowly righted. Frank scrambled up the ladder to the conning tower, and I followed, mostly pulling myself up with my arms. Jones raised the search scope, perhaps saving the attack scope for business after we pulled clear of this mess.

When submerged, looking through the scope gives the viewer the impression that his eye is just above the surface of the sea, at the position of the lens. When the boat is on the surface, it's like looking out and down from a 55-foot tower. I was looking up at a single monstrous wave, so big it had normal waves on its crest, which were blowing out into spume as it rolled in. Reflexes made me duck momentarily just before it hit, and then green water, solid green sea, went over the top of everything, burying *Tang* scope and all. Amazingly, the scope was still there when the wave rolled past. I had expected a mangled tube, if indeed it was not broken off above the roots. Jones lowered away lest the next wave finish it off.

With a bit more speed to help the steersman and—right after waves thundered overhead—quick scope exposures to con our stern exactly at the seas, we got the roll down to cycles ranging from 45 to 20 degrees. We knew exactly where we were, in the dangerous semicircle of a full-fledged typhoon, where the great circular winds are augmented by the speed of the advancing storm. Our present position was untenable, for we were being pushed ahead in addition to our own turns, and our total speed likely equaled the advance of the storm. We could thus remain in this dangerous semicircle for days, even into the Ryukyus to the immediate north.

Having already come to control on the assumption that we would dive, Larry came shoulders-high into the conning tower to report on conditions below. For once, the crew's living spaces were better than either CPO quarters or wardroom country, for the troops who were up and about had simply wedged themselves on deck between the bunk tiers, and others had just hugged their bunk frames with both arms. So, not relying on a silly guardrail, none of them had fallen. Larry would take charge below.

We had long since forgone the option of diving, for our ballast tanks were divided port and starboard and had individual floods and vents. A short-lived loss of stability accompanied any dive, and with rolls such as we were experiencing, the down tanks would flood first and could capsize the boat. True, we might juggle the vents, but that was something we would not try for the first time under these conditions. There was but one option; we had to turn in front of the seas that had just knocked us down.

4

The maneuver would have to be fast; there could be no hesitating, lest we founder while broadside to the seas. Culp and the battle stations controllermen went aft to maneuvering; Welch took the wheel. Our ship had just reached a maximum roll of 45 degrees to port, then starboard, and was now down to 35 degrees, then 30. With fingers mentally crossed, I ordered, "All ahead standard." De Lapp, by the inclinometer in control, sang out, "Twenty-five degrees," and Jones raised the scope. A great wave was rolling in, but not so vicious; it would barely top the lens. The sea shook the periscope, blurring any further vision.

"All ahead full. Right full rudder." Our stern started to port. The next great wave rolled up our starboard quarter, laying us over to port as it passed overhead but accelerating our turn. *Tang* rolled through the trough and took the next monster on the starboard bow. It knocked her nearly over, shook her, and buried her, but could not stop her swing. Frank called the new course, the reverse of that which we had been trying to steer.

"All ahead two-thirds. Ease the rudder to fifteen. Meet her. Steer two one zero."

Though the typhoon would still dictate our course, no longer was it driving our ship into the Ryukyus, nor could it knock us down. *Tang's* motion was, nevertheless, that of a wild, plunging roller coaster, and though it was midmorning, control reported that only a few hands had come to the messroom. For them, fortunately, baking had been completed before midnight, and our toasters were secured and could not get adrift. But the report of hot tea instead of coffee to go with the toast seemed a bit on the sissy side. Of more importance was Larson's report of no injuries; it seemed impossible, but a submarine lies so deep in the sea that it does not have the dangerous whip of a surface ship. Not to be forgotten, however, was Frank's continuing the inspection after I had fallen down the hatch, for a single piece of loose gear could easily have broken some bones.

Our best steersmen, working in pairs with one on the maneuvering room telegraphs, used their skill and our screws to keep *Tang* heading into the seas. For five taut hours, they kept *Tang* on course, coached by Frank, me, and the OODs on the scope, for the seas determined our headings. Quite suddenly the wicked seas changed to mountainous swells under torrential rains. The winds moderated, became confused. Were we at the eye of the typhoon, where we could now head into the safe semicircle? For a quick check we tried cracking the hatch to obtain a new barometer reading. It wouldn't budge, held tight by increased atmospheric pressure. High-pressure air was bled into the boat, a full half inch, to free the hatch; the barometer read 28.4. The increase showed we had missed the center but were pulling out of the typhoon on what would now be the safe trailing side, or more accurately perhaps, the typhoon was leaving us behind.

Now able to choose the course, we came to 267, our original heading, and stationed the regular watch sections. This should be safe until the navigator could fix our position. At 1700, we fired two mains with the engine-air induction open only to the forward engine room. At worst, a slug of seawater would go to its bilges. With all under control, Frank and I went to the wardroom. I propped up my foot; the shoelaces, still as Chief Larson had tied them, were now loose. I had hardly noticed when the shot had worn off; there were more important things going on. Confident that the shoe had something to do with the decrease in the swelling, Walker had arrived with a smaller size, a 12 this time, and laced it up tight, apparently with the idea of squeezing my foot back to shape.

Over coffee, Frank and I spoke of the Ultra that had put us in the predicament. One of two things had obviously taken place. Perhaps intelligence had incorrectly broken the enemy's message, which could have been reporting the position of the typhoon at a specified time along its projected path rather than the position of the weather ship itself. This seemed likely. Another possibility involved the advantage that accrues if you know your enemy has broken certain codes. We had evidence of the Japanese using this in an attempt to save their naval tanker west of Saipan. If this message had been designed to sucker a submarine into a typhoon, those involved were undoubtedly sitting around a bottle of saki, laughing at the predicament they might be causing their enemy. Still, if offered the same opportunity, we would surely coin a comparable dispatch. There would be only one difference: We'd be laughing over a bottle of beer. Nature might have taken care of the enemy ship, but it was difficult to conceive of a weather ship being caught in a typhoon, especially one from such a seagoing nation.

On the more serious side, we talked of our fourth patrol, when our ship had taken the best the enemy could throw at her and had shaken it off, going about her business. Now she had taken the worst that nature, even with the aid of bungling humans, could hand out and had shrugged that off, too. Surely the whole ship's company, including our new shipmates, considered with me that *Tang* was the toughest ship in the world.

Dawn of October 7 broke, still with great swells and occasional confused chop. The normal watch manned the bridge, giving the SJ and the scopes a rest, but the seas held our ship to two-engine speed. Finally the scudding clouds broke away, conveniently in time for the navigator's evening stars. I watched Frank and Jones with a bit of envy, though there was nothing to prevent me from taking a round of stars if I wished. Jones's competence made me wonder if my introduction to navigating might not have been more pleasant had I enjoyed an assistant with his experience.

Frank brought down the chart with his position run up to 2000. The typhoon had carried us 60 miles from the position shown on our DRI, and we thanked our lucky stars that the encounter had taken place well clear of the Ryukyus. I recalled an experience at sea with a hurricane packing 100-knot winds and spoke conservatively when I estimated that the winds of this typhoon had half again the speed. In the height of the seas, there was no comparison. We were not just guessing, for in the Quartermaster's Notebook were recorded various periods during which the scope had been completely buried, the longest being 14 seconds. Sketching the wave crests in their most modest form, and arriving at their speed from the recorded frequency, *Tang*'s junior officers calculated that on occasions a minimum of 40 feet of sea had rolled above the lens of our scope. I would not dispute their figure nor would Frank, we had seen the waves, and 95 feet from crest to trough seemed conservative.

We came left 15 degrees, for the typhoon had pushed us from south of the track to north of it. This course would put *Tang* back on the line by dawn, and I penned the first regular night orders since the Ultra. They were overdue.

Proceeding at 80/90 on engines 3 and 4. Our course is 252 degrees true, and I anticipate no course changes throughout the night. We can now encounter surface patrols, however, and it is your job to spot them first. If the enemy is sighted put him astern or dive and then call me. Air patrols are possible at dawn, and the duty chief will caution all oncoming lookouts accordingly. We have come 4,600 miles, but the next 500 are as important as all of the miles behind us. At 0600, or on advice of the navigator, change course to 267. Keep me completely informed in accordance with the standing night orders.

Adams took the night orders aft, and the sound of movies from forward indicated that all was well with *Tang*. Most remarkably, none of the ship's company had received more than a bump or scrape during the wild gyrations; they were apparently as tough as our ship. The pegs on the cribbage board had not been greased for some time now, and I found a more than willing opponent in Frank. Having observed his predecessor, the executive officer probably assumed that this was one of his informal collateral duties, and if so he was absolutely correct. Frank pegged out on the rubber game, but more important was our formulation of plans for our initial days in the Formosa Strait.

October 8 saw moderating seas, and a third engine went on the line. A torpedo fire control drill speeded the morning, leaving the afternoon for a ropeyarn Sunday, while extra lookouts searched for planes. They were possible at any time now, for Okinawa Jima lay only 200 miles to the northwest, but no patrol challenged our passage. Three diesels drove *Tang* on into another day when a firm "Clear the bridge!" and two blasts sent us down. I searched carefully in the bearing of the patrol plane and could not be sure; it seemed to flap its wings. But I decided to keep that to myself, for the speed of clearing the bridge and the dive were excellent. A last drill in the afternoon showed no rough spots. The next time we heard the general alarm, we would have an enemy ship in sight.

At dawn, Sakishima Gunto was beyond the horizon off our starboard bow. Our landfall would be on Ishigaki Shima, about 150 miles east of northern Formosa, or on Formosa itself, which would come up dead ahead. Chiefs Ballinger and Leibold consulted with Jones, then came to a proper decision: The official landfall would be on Formosa, not Ishigaki. It was well for the troops to settle such things in advance, for I presumed it had something to do with their pool.

The 11,000- to 13,000-foot mountains of Formosa loomed up dead ahead at noon, officially 1158, while Ishigaki never did show. A fourth engine went on the line, and we built up to full power to insure our transit into the strait during darkness. A bearing on Iriomote Jima, just west of Ishigaki and now abaft our beam, cut in well with two peaks ahead. After plotting, Frank recommended the new course, 320.

"Make it so," I said, and the navigator gave the necessary order to Basil with the deck. Our new track would pass between Yonaguni Jima, now in view to starboard, and the northeast coast of Formosa, a handsome 60-mile-wide passage.

Dusk came and there was no challenge from the enemy. But technically *Tang* was still in the Pacific, or as printed on our chart, the Philippine Sea. We came to 340 to give the headlands more room before rounding the northern promontories. There was time for coffee, and I dropped below only to hear the control room speaker: "SJ contact broad on starboard bow. Range eleven thousand yards."

5

By the time I climbed to the conning tower, Frank and the OOD had slowed and put *Tang* on a converging course with that of the enemy ship, which could be heading from the Sakishima Gunto to the strait. It was a likely path for a freighter, but not for an unescorted one. Her speed was further discouraging, for plot's first estimate of 12 knots would be high when compared with the cargomen we had encountered. Still, in this vicinity ships were making the long haul between the Empire and the southwest, and faster vessels would be employed.

The guessing stopped at 7,000 yards when the low hull became more than just a blurp. Masts or goalposts were not yet visible, so we continued closing cautiously, and then the outlines firmed. We had not seen the goalposts because there were none, but the compact superstructure located about a third of a ship's length from the bow confirmed our suspicion. Left 15 degrees rudder put an enemy patrol astern, and a third engine took us on our way.

Looking aft, Frank and I recalled the incident following our first attack in the East China Sea when we were at full speed closing a destroyer escort only to find out that she was taking the same action. It had been a truly frightening experience and could have happened again right here had we not used caution in our approach. Perhaps our ship had matured a bit. We were, of course, disappointed that this had not turned out to be a suitable target, but in the past patrols had meant ships, and this would be an area to investigate

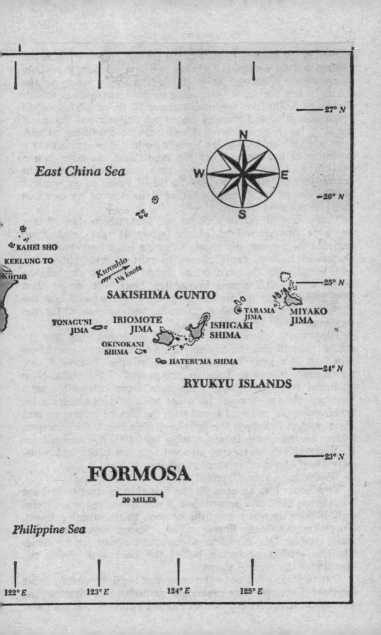

East China Sea

KAHEI SHO
KEELUNG TO
Kiirun

Kuroshio
1½ knots

SAKISHIMA GUNTO

YONAGUNI JIMA

IRIOMOTE JIMA

OKINOKANI SHIMA

ISHIGAKI SHIMA

TARAMA JIMA

MIYAKO JIMA

HATERUMA SHIMA

RYUKYU ISLANDS

FORMOSA

30 MILES

Philippine Sea

27° N

26° N

25° N

24° N

23° N

122° E   123° E   124° E   125° E

further in the coming days. For the present, the best place for finding worthy targets lay ahead, and our interest, especially the navigator's, shifted from the fading shape astern to the points on our port bow. According to the contour lines on our chart, the 5,000-foot mountains about 30 miles inland sloped down abruptly, and starting about ten miles from the coast the land lay near sea level. This could be confusing at sea, even in daylight, for the land might be hull down with only a structure or beacon to show the land's end. At night, when navigating in part by radar, the small single structures might not reflect the impulse. I shared a bit of Frank's concern and readily agreed to soundings rather than slowing as cautious navigation would dictate.

There were 80 fathoms under our keel, which showed that we were not shoreward of the selected track, and *Tang* barreled on through the night. Kiirun, a large, well-protected, deepwater harbor, came abeam to port at midnight. Larry and John, with the midwatch, would take us around the northern tip of Formosa in another hour. We would then slow and head to the southwest down the coast and into the strait. Only a single-line night order was necessary, for the navigator would be about.

The course change left to 245, leaving Kahei Sho to starboard, and slowing to one-engine speed were reported on schedule. An hour later *Tang* was off the Tamsui River, which leads inland to Taihoku, the capital of Formosa. Now sheltered from the Pacific, the seas were calm. It was a welcome change, for in the quiet we could concentrate on seeking out the enemy. I toyed with the idea of getting up and about and switched on the light to double-check the luminous figures on the clock. It was coming up 0400. A moment later the duty chief's messenger stepped into my cabin and whispered as if afraid of awakening others.

"We've got a ship, Captain."

Two hours into an area till the first ship contact must have been some kind of a record, but it would become meaningful only if the ship was put on the bottom. In the conning tower, Torpedoman's Mate Foster called, "Range seventeen thousand, closing," the direction undoubtedly added for my benefit. The section steersman pulled the knob and swung the handle for the general alarm.

Our position relative to the coast was ideal. Now four miles off Puki Kaku, we were practically assured of an attack as the enemy came up the coast from Pakusa Point. Lacking a radar periscope, we had two options: We could continue closing and fire from the surface, or we could run with the enemy and fire submerged after dawn. To keep our options open and to give more time for tracking, we reversed course, prompted a bit by the first speed check on our enemy of 14 knots. Though the considerations had taken only a minute or so, our combined range rate of 24 knots, 800 yards per minute, had already reduced the range to under 15,000 yards and would have brought on the attack within another 15 to 17 minutes.

While Frank and I examined the chart, tracking took advantage of the additional time to verify the enemy's speed, which at least raised the possibility that the ship might indeed be a large patrol. Shallow soundings to shoreward of the enemy's projected track practically dictated an attack from seaward. On the surface, we would not then have the advantage of the dark land background, and for a truly short-range shot, the enemy would have a fair chance of sighting *Tang*. Thus on this ship, the best chances of a sinking would follow a submerged approach, wherein a range well inside of 1,000 yards could be sought.

As a daily part of normal navigating, Jones had already figured the time of morning twilight. Frank plotted the enemy's position for that time; the waters were good, with at least 20 fathoms unless the base course was altered shoreward. Frank then picked up his compass and spun a circle with a half mile radius about the point, and I do believe he expected that *Tang* would lay the ship down in its center.

Without further interference, Ed on plot quickly confirmed TDC's estimate that we had a good-sized ship chasing us. This was based primarily on the timing of the zigs but was backed up by Bergman's view of the pip on the A-scope. We would know for sure shortly; we slowed to drop back on the enemy's port bow. Chief Leibold accompanied me topside to the after TBT, and we commenced searching a narrow sector on the starboard quarter. With the advantage of a known bearing and not having to cover a whole sector, Boats had the blurp ahead of the lookouts but only whispered the sighting so as not to interfere with the pool.

She was low and chunky, as a sharp angle aspect should look, and my visual bearings were being read from the repeater below whenever I sounded the TBT's buzzer. The angle was now opening and I called port 15 then turned the TBT over to Boats while conferring with Frank. We had a cargoman, apparently diesel, for there had not been any smoke. There was no time for extra conversation, as the navigator must con *Tang* onto the enemy's track. I continued to call bearings, then an enemy zig to starboard, but not angles on the bow since either TDC or plot would now be more accurate. The silhouette sharpened to zero, which I did call below.

"Any time, Captain." Frank now had *Tang* in position to dive. Boats went below, and I stopped a moment with John, our battle stations OOD, just to tell him to go ahead with a normal dive when I was clear and to assure myself that he knew all but his four lookouts would then be below. The pause was fortunate, for the expected first inkling of gray that marks the start of morning twilight was not yet noticeable. Jones did not make mistakes, but we had all neglected to consider the mountain range only 35 miles to the east with peaks up to 9,000 feet high. It was acting like a curtain drawn up from a sill and would delay the time when the scope would first be usable. A full ten minutes passed while we ran with the enemy, but fortunately the setup was a relative one and we still enjoyed the situation originally sought, though transposed three miles up the coast. John's "Clear the bridge!" was firm and unexcited, the two blasts methodical, and *Tang* slid under the sea.

As we slowed for Larry's trim, Caverly picked up the enemy's prop and for some seconds switched the noise to the speaker. It was the hefty *thump-thump-thump* of a single-screw ship and batting out 140 turns by metronome. Though the sound bearing checked closely with TDC's, at least showing no major change, remaining blind at such a crucial time tried our nerves. My reply to Larry's "Satisfied with the trim" was an immediate "Bring her up to forty-five feet," to expose our SJ reflector. Bergman's single SJ range of 4,500 yards and bearing 150 showed a zig toward shore. At standard speed we followed suit while easing back down to periscope depth.

Firing would come in less than ten minutes, and the torpedo rooms made ready tubes 1, 2, and 3 forward, and should there be a wide zig to the left, tubes 7, 8, and 9 aft. Four minutes into the run I ordered, "All stop." Jones raised the scope when Welch called, "Five knots," but Caverly beat us with a bearing. His 140 was a good guide, and now the enemy's silhouette was sharp in the scope. I could see a good half ship's length, but that was still just a 30-degree angle on the bow, so I called it to go with Jones's relative bearing of 135. Standard speed closed the track. After *Tang*'s run to the firing point, the torpedo run would not be over 1,500 yards, and much less should the enemy zig towards. Another three minutes passed and we slowed just enough to get a vibrating look. I called, "Port sixty," and then in succession, "Port forty-five, port twenty, port thirty." I would guess that new members of *Tang*'s fire control party figured that the Old Man had one hell of a time making up his mind, but the plank-owners knew we had the enemy in the middle of a zig and probably with a new steersman who had swung past the ordered course. He would never zig again, not horizontally anyway, for this was the firing leg.

"Open the outer doors forward."

"The course for zero gyros and a ninety track is one two five, Captain."

"Make it so."

Frank was forgetting no details in readying the ship and providing his part of the necessary information. I'd see if I could match him on the scope. Two quick setups checked. This big freighter, with raked bow and squat stack, was so heavily loaded she had little more freeboard than a tanker.

"Any time, Captain."

"Range eight hundred."

"Stand by for constant bearings. Up scope." Jones had the handles in my hands with the scope practically on.

"Constant bearing—mark!" The wire was on her well deck aft.

"Set!" came from Mel. Her 14 knots brought her stern on quickly.

"Fire!" Frank hit the plunger and instantly came the slight shudder, the momentary pressure from the poppet valve, and then the whine as our first torpedo went on its way. The next two, aimed amidships and forward, seemed to leave the tubes automatically. Frank read from the prepared card opposite a torpedo run of 670 yards and announced the listed time of 47 seconds. Already 30 seconds had passed since he first hit the plunger. Caverly switched on the speaker again and trained from the freighter's prop to the high-pitched whine of the torpedoes and back again until they all blended together. We forgot the counting, but the exploders didn't, the first two detonating with instantaneous fury. In seconds, when the cloud of smoke had blown clear, only the tilted bow was in sight, seeming to back down into Davy Jones's locker.

Without advance preparations, three blasts took us to the surface. Those closest to the hatch grabbed available binoculars and substituted for the regular lookouts, following me and John to the bridge. We conned *Tang* in among the flotsam, but there were no survivors. Amid the wreckage, however, were several half-swamped, empty landing craft. Could the enemy be moving war materials north? Now with ballast tanks nearly dry and four engines purring, we headed southwest down the coast while working up to full power. The time was 0455, and the normal watch section relieved. They could take *Tang* down just as fast as the battle stations team, and now two-thirds of the ship's company could catch its breath.

In the wardroom I openly congratulated Frank since this was the first sinking in which he had participated as executive officer. Reserve officers hold commission dates that fix their seniority among all officers in the navy and are in all respects equals. Our most senior reserves were still about a year away from command, and Frank was among them. He would make lieutenant commander upon our return from patrol and most assuredly deserved the qualification for command that also would be waiting.

6

We hoped to reach Pakusa Point, where we would have an unobstructed view up and down the coast, but would move beyond to deeper water if the sky and sea remained clear. The mountains that had foiled Frank's plan to have the ship laid down within the circle now gave us a few extra minutes of grace in a delayed sunrise. Pakusa Point was already on our port quarter when the lookout guarding that sector spotted the first plane. It was distant, perhaps over land, but Dick's answer was two blasts. Our ship slid down quietly to patrol submerged throughout the long day.

As was often the case after a night of it, all hands were hungry, and Ballinger's request to go ahead with breakfast was readily granted. The good breakfast seemed to substitute for the lack of sleep, and the wardroom conversation revolved about our fortunes in making this early contact and attack. Of equal importance were the apparently exact fire control solution and the torpedo performance. The first two hits were right under the points of aim, and as had frequently been the case in the past, there was nothing left for the last torpedo. The patrol was young, but *Tang* was clicking; Frank knew it, too, and brought the discussion to the extremely short sinking time.

"She had only a few feet of freeboard," I volunteered, "and our torpedoes exploded at six feet below the waterline. They just plain blew out her side and the tops of her cargo holds and engine spaces, too." Then, for Paul's and John's benefit, we reviewed the previous torpedo troubles we had experienced, primarily in depth keeping, and why we set ours to hit a few feet below the waterline along the ship's side. Having watched sinking times change from hours to minutes, even seconds, as *Wahoo* commenced setting torpedoes shallow, I could speak of the finality of blowing a ship's side out.

The conversation would go on, but Frank and I decided to take a periscope view of our area and the coast of Formosa just to see what it all looked like in broad daylight. Mel's previous reports of planes over land or close inshore had changed my mind concerning a patrol off Pakusa Point. It was no Miki Saki or Nigishima Saki as far as depth of water went; in fact, we would have to move out over ten miles to gain a depth greater than 30 fathoms. Horizontal distance from the scene of our attack seemed best, and we were continuing on course 225 down the coast.

The sight of four planes on one low-power sweep rather surprised me, though closer examination in high power showed them to be landing and taking off from several airfields. I intentionally made no comment and handed the scope to Frank. He took the sight in stride, as if he'd expected it, and proceeded in attempting to identify the somewhat indistinct points along the low, nearly straight shore. Welch recorded the bearings and our ship's heading so as to convert each bearing to true for plotting. While the navigator was going about the task of identifying the points and plotting, I raised the search scope for a careful study of the land, one that I might remember. Mel and one of the watch section lookouts took turns on the attack scope so that my search could be uninterrupted, and I followed the coast slowly. Another sweep with the prism raised a bit covered inland to the mountaintops, and the land I saw looked as fertile as the Sacramento Valley. The view brought home the importance of this great island to the enemy as both a strategic frontier and a rice bowl. It suddenly became all the more evident that every torpedo must count.

No surface patrols were sighted as we proceeded southwest at 3 knots. Could it be that they believed we were still north of Pakusa Point, off Puki Kaku? It did not seem likely, for we knew the enemy's quick response. A considerably greater possibility was the failure of anyone to note or at least to report the attack. It was all over so quickly that now only the discovery of the flotsam would tell the enemy of a disaster. Our faith in this theory was shaken a bit at midmorning when enemy planes commenced passing over our vicinity. Frank was getting some necessary and ordered shut-eye, so I tried out my new sand shoe in checking this out and found that I could walk on my heel with little pain. Land-based bombers were aloft, and we tracked them on to shore, directly into the wind, which had backed around to the east.

I went to the conning tower again just before noon. The watch had relieved and Hank was just lowering the scope after a normal search. "It's all clear, Captain," he reported. "I've just completed a sweep." I had come up primarily to observe the seas for myself, but the fast sweep and careful search were still automatic. Satisfied, I swung back to the coast, for this stretch of shoreline was new and I might distinguish a landmark or two.

"Bearing—mark!"

Hank read 282, not quite smothering a goddammit. It shouldn't have happened to our most conscientious OOD, but the masts of a ship put aside other considerations. The steersman had called our ship's head, and we laid down the true bearing line through the enemy's position.

"Head for him, Hank."

Letting him close the enemy might bolster his prestige, and until we found out which way the enemy was heading no other action was required. Hank steadied our ship on 147, and I went down for lunch. It might be my only chance. White, with the chief's watch, had had an ear to the hatch and knew we had a ship in sight. So, of course, would everyone aft, and I decided to see how long it took the grapevine to reach the wardroom; it might take Hank's call reporting the bearing change to the right or left. But I had forgotten Walker and his trips back to the galley.

"We goin' to get this one, too, Captain?" he asked, obviously enjoying the moment. The phone buzzed, and Hank reported the enemy ship drawing left.

"Come left to zero four five and go ahead two-thirds, Hank," I ordered, having cheated a bit in mentally figuring the reciprocal of our former course ahead of time.

The time was 1220, still October 11, and *Tang* was off on a long chase. We had another option, for using our best sustained submerged speed, we could undoubtedly intercept the enemy by midafternoon. A glance at the chart showed that the enemy ship would continue inside the ten-fathom curve in following the coast. Our attack from seaward of 12 to 15 fathoms should be successful, but *Tang* would then face a shallow-water evasion with a near flat can. It was a combination we could not accept as long as there were other possibilities.

By 1300 the increasing winds had churned the shallow waters till nice depth control at 60 feet was becoming difficult. Section tracking already had a reasonable speed estimate based primarily on true bearings of the enemy ship, which essentially fixed her position along the coast. There was no reason to fight the seas at periscope depth, and in fact we might make a bit better speed below the swells. On order, Dick eased *Tang* down to 80 feet, where we would cruise between observations.

Since the ship was following the slightly concave coast in this area, even a reversal of course would not take her out of view, and irregularly spaced trips to periscope depth provided tracking with all of the information needed. The ship was zigging at odd times and making 8 knots over the ground. It was sufficient to gain bearing on us in spite of her longer route along the coast. Frank plotted our two tracks ahead, and the enemy could indeed be out of reach before dark by heading into Taihoku. It was 1400, and as a compromise, we added turns to bring our speed up to 7 knots.

On the very next observation the bearing rate had decreased, but our extra turns were only in part responsible. Now coming to our aid were the seas kicked up by the opposing wind and current, for the enemy had cleared the lee of the shore and must now be bucking the waves from nearly dead ahead. Our tracks were converging slowly and another hour passed before we could truly make the ship out. Though identification might have been hastened by bringing the books to the conning tower on this one occasion, since not manning battle stations gave us plenty of room, the identification party preferred to work below from the details as they became available. The mast-funnel-mast silhouette had been furnished for an hour before the tall stack and forward superstructure were identified. Now we had the plumb bow and lower superstructure about the stack with apparent lifeboats atop. It was a game, but not until an hour before sunset could the OOD provide the clinching details of an after deckhouse and counter stern. They had the ship, an *Aden Maru* class freighter, constructed right after World War I, and one of about 50 in the class. Each member of the party took a look at the real ship and surely must have gained enthusiasm for his task.

A possible shot before sunset was foiled by planes apparently heading home from their daytime patrol, but such an attack had not been uppermost anyway, and we did not go to battle stations. At suppertime she passed directly overhead, her single screw beating out 70 turns through our hull, or at least that was the wardroom count. For the first time, *Tang* was trailing this ship; but there was no better way of determining course, speed, and zigzag plan when attack did not have to be immediate. Frank spoke of the similar situation in the Yellow Sea, perhaps for the benefit of those officers who had not then been in our ship, but this night I contemplated a variation in the attack.

The sun had set, and we trailed till the end of evening twilight. With lookouts ready in rain clothes in view of the threatening weather, three blasts sent us toward the surface. De Lapp did not save the high-pressure air, and a healthy blow had our decks well clear before the turbos roared. A spin of the SJ showed the enemy just over 4,000 yards dead ahead, but before we closed, the weighted sacks of trash and garbage came up through the conning tower and over the side, for the seas precluded opening the messroom hatch. With that done and sanitaries blown, we sheared out to pass the enemy 2,000 yards abeam. The stern chase would be a long one, especially since two mains were needed for battery charge. But that would hold only during the starting rate, and then the auxiliary could replace one of them. We had not rushed so far this day, and we would not do so now.

Our hope for another unescorted ship vanished when radar

raised two pips along with that of our target. They would undoubtedly be patrols escorting this freighter around Pakusa Point, or at least that was our wish. We came further left in order to pass the group at a more comfortable 4,000 yards, and since things could happen quickly when patrols were about, the Bells of St. Mary's chimed for the second time this day. The torpedomen had partially withdrawn four torpedoes from the forward and after tubes during the afternoon. The specific gravity had been checked, the batteries ventilated, and all were now in place waiting for the tubes to be readied. Frank gave the order immediately after Ballinger's "Battle stations manned."

It was good, for *Tang* was now abeam of the enemy, who was just visible through the spume on this dark night. We had used the SJ sparingly, but the information Caverly and Bergman provided was excellent. Especially the last report, that the escorts were falling astern. It was almost too good to be true, but such things could happen when ships were escorted only past extra dangerous areas. There could be no better opportunity, and Frank secured the charge and conned us in toward the enemy track as we had agreed. The seas rolled down our decks, but these were nothing *Tang* could not take in stride. Forward was John's business, and right now mine was on the after TBT. Through the spume, angles on the bow would be only a guess, but bearings of the enemy would satisfy TDC and plot. The shape of the enemy narrowed, and then came the expected report from Frank.

"We're on her track, Captain, and steadied on zero six zero."

"Slow to one-third, Frank, and come left when the range is two thousand."

The bow of the freighter showed up big and black, as if coming out of a squall, and I had to tell myself that she was still over a mile away. It was not much over the 2,000 yards, for almost immediately came the word that we were coming left with 5 degrees rudder. I would mark bearings on her bridge as soon as her angle opened, and Frank would keep our stern pointed right down that bearing. Getting off the track seemed interminably slow and must have appeared so on the true plot, for Frank went ahead two-thirds.

"The solution checks, Captain, still zero six zero and eight knots."

The angle on the bow was now opening rapidly, and I called port 45 with the next bearing. Our stern was now pulling ahead of the enemy's bow; Frank would be bringing *Tang* to a heading for minimum gyros with torpedoes to hit on a 75 track. Even after the first torpedo hit, a good setup for further firing would obtain. The 400-foot ship looked enormous as she started across our stern, mainly due to her proximity but perhaps amplified by this somewhat eerie, stormy night.

"Ten degrees to go, range five hundred, outer doors open."

Frank's words were like a starter finally raising his gun. One more bearing was buzzed, and then came the "Any time, Captain." The TBT was already trained on her foremast, waiting.

"Constant bearing—mark!"

"Set!" called Mel.

Her bridge came on the wire, followed by the open space, and then the tall stack dead amidships.

"Fire!" and a single torpedo raced from aft to intercept the enemy. Frank called up the time for the torpedo run of 450 yards, 30 seconds, 20 seconds to go. I marked a bearing on the ship's stack should this single torpedo not do the job, for we could still fire a spread of three more. A terrific explosion made this unnecessary. Her boilers had apparently exploded with the torpex, sending a pillar of fire and illuminated steam skyward. It was the fire control party's turn to come topside, but few of them saw much of the ship, for she sank almost immediately.

We now experienced something new in antisubmarine measures with the firing of 40-millimeter or similar automatic weapons from the beach. The fire was directed straight up, however, and we were quite content to let the enemy believe that our China-based planes were aloft. We did not laugh, however, and promptly headed down the coast to pass the two patrols between us and the area for the next day's operations. Night orders at this time would be out of date before the ink was dry; so I recorded our two sinkings, which we knew could not change:

Diesel freighter	7,500 *tons*	Lat.	*25° 12' N.*
		Long.	*121° 10' E.*
Medium freighter	5,824 *tons*	Lat.	*25° 08' N.*
(*Aden Maru class*)		Long.	*121° 08' E.*

It was 2115, only a quarter of an hour after the attack, and already SJ had made contact on the two expected patrols. As we moved in an arc on approaching Pakusa Point to give these patrols a wide berth, an unexpected third pip appeared on the PPI. It was slightly more distant than the others, to seaward, and was obviously another patrol joining in a search. Reluctantly we secured the battery charge again and moved up to full power in making a wider sweep around the enemy. The late-arriving patrol must have been equipped with radar, for tracking soon had her on an intercepting course that she could not have figured otherwise.

This patrol was turning out to be more than just a nuisance and from her advantageous point was closing on our port hand until we put her astern. Our new course, due west, opened the range, and tracking soon had the enemy turning back. The patrol had accomplished her mission in chasing us clear of the point and protecting her area. But we had business elsewhere and could get there almost as well by a jaunt toward the China coast and down to the middle of the strait.

We were still standing by for a specific lifeguard assignment for the next day, but if none came in on the Fox the choice of patrol stations was up to us. Already, Task Force 38 would be about 300 miles from Formosa, and though I did not know the details, air attacks on Kiirun, Taihoku, Takao, and the numerous airfield installations would certainly be made. We might do some good off the central coast, and I had left a selected position with Admiral Lockwood. Just the knowledge that a friendly submarine was waiting helped a pilot carry his bombs home. At least we were led to believe this after Truk, but it would be a much different problem here with no friendly air cover.

It was 2230 when the navigator recommended course 215, the route we would follow throughout the remainder of the night. The last 24 hours had been tiring, in part because we had not completely recovered from the typhoon, but mostly due to the duration of the last approach and attack. Every section had been involved in the tracking, and of course all hands in the attack, and frankly if the troops felt the same as I did, we'd all just as soon call off the war games for a day. In view of what had been happening, the enemy might just cooperate.

The wardroom was still buzzing, but after passing the Night Order Book around, everyone followed Larry's lead in getting what sleep they could before we were into another day. Our ship was quiet, and even the chop had subsided, adding to the stillness. But it was all broken with "SJ contact bearing one zero, range nineteen thousand." That would put it westward of *Tang*, 225 true, and I flipped the eavesdropping switch for any further information while locating my sand shoe. Topside, we already had masthead lights in view and came right to cross her bow and look her over from all around. First green and then green and red side lights came in view. Then halfway down her port side, a cargo light illuminated her white hull, a green stripe, and a large red cross.

We could find no fault with this properly identified hospital ship, and Larry, trying out his hand at navigating, recommended the course back to our track. Below, all was quiet again except for a conversation in control, which also reached my cabin since the special switch was still on. It probably expressed the sentiment of everyone embarked in *Tang* and was summarized in a single exclamation in Ballinger's unmistakable voice, "Aw, the bastard's probably transporting ten thousand troops, all with athlete's foot!"

Frank and Jones put our ship in the selected spot off Tsusho. The 15 miles from shore should permit surfacing periodically or at least poking our antenna out for possible messages concerning downed aviators, and with luck, to intercept the airmen's conversations. With first daylight, Basil's welcome blasts sent our ship below for another day of intense search. Volunteers for the scopes were no problem, for all hands knew that at this very moment our plans would be over the mountains. They would be fighters to gain and then maintain control of the air, and hot on their heels would come the dive-bombers. It was all easy to picture after Truk and then listening to the airmen for three weeks afterward, and we somewhat regretted being so distant. This was no

Truk, however, for the objectives were spread over 180 miles, and a combat air patrol to facilitate our surface operations would be impossible.

To seaward, especially, there remained a fair possibility of ship contacts, and we alternated the search sectors between the two scopes. Only enemy planes, mostly heading west, and an occasional surface patrol came in view. They interfered somewhat with our attempts to catch carrier plane transmissions, and nothing intelligible could be heard on the occasions when our VHF-UHF antennas were high in the air. The jammed transmissions and smoke rising from over the horizon left no doubt about the strike being in progress, however, and a general feeling of elation quickly went through the boat. The southern tip of Kyushu was only another 700 miles to the north, and certainly knowledgeable Japanese were aware that this attack was the beginning of the end.

Frank and Chief Jones were standing by with sextant and watch when three blasts sent *Tang* toward the surface. The order to start the turbos normally signified that the submarine would not be diving immediately, enemy willing, and the navigators bounded topside to get their round of stars on the fading horizon. An accurate position was always important but especially so this evening, for our destination was the focal point of two probable shipping routes from Formosa to China.

With a day for consideration, we had searched *Sailing Directions*, even an atlas, so the point for tomorrow's patrol was not selected by ticktacktoe. The seas, the currents, and the shoals are just the same for all seafarers, and we considered Foochow a logical haven for enemy ships during Task Force 38's continuing air strikes on Formosa. The routes we had worked out led from Takao and Kiirun, and there could be enemy ships along either one of them this moment, and more after dark. We were confident of finding the enemy, at least some stragglers, where the two routes converged, in the waters east of Turnabout Island. A single diesel was already pushing us along due north while the others charged the batteries. After Frank had his star fix he would plot it on the chart and then advance the point due north at our present speed. I'd see the chart in the wardroom when he was ready with the position accurate to the moment.

Remembering a captain who liked to lean over my shoulder, point with his finger, and utter sounds of disapproval, I went quickly below. The chart would follow just that much sooner, and we saved Frank's place at the supper table accordingly. Rest is a relative thing, or so it appeared with our young officers, for this night a jollier bunch would be hard to find anywhere. Perhaps they had checked the menu or dropped by the galley, for Adams arrived with a platter of rare roast beef surrounded by roast potatoes. Whatever Walker had in the serving dishes was of little importance, and the same would undoubtedly be true aft, for we all had the same meals, the best.

Frank had changed course 4 degrees to 356, and reported that our one engine would suffice. As had become the custom when there was no urgency, he placed the chart atop the sideboard and enjoyed his beef while it was still hot. That taken care of, we considered our position, and Walker brought the Night Order Book. With the chart spread out, those around the wardroom table could read at a glance just where we were going and gain a fair appreciation of the prospects. For all, including Walker, our first visit to China since the Shantung Promontory would be another intriguing adventure.

Early in the midwatch, Paul reported the wind drawing to the east, and about an hour later, passing rain squalls. Our periodic sweeps with the SJ were increased, and toward the end of the watch an indistinct pip appeared on the screen. Tracked at the estimated speed and in the direction of the wind, its dark shape was soon identified by Hank as a particularly black, dense squall, almost the first one to so show since Saipan.

The morning watch relieved. Frank and Jones were waiting, hoping for a round of stars, when SJ reported a forest out ahead. Such numerous returns could only come from a fishing fleet, but especially on the A-scope their pips seemed too good. Two more engines closed the 14,000 yards to 5,000 before the gray of dawn sent us down, and we moved on in with a hand on the general alarm. Now in good daylight I spotted the first shape, a patrol passing from one squall to another. The steersman pulled the handle and the Bells of St. Mary's held reveille this Friday the 13th.

It was 0530, ten minutes into the run to close the enemy, when we slowed for an observation. Our 6 knots should have reduced the range to about 3,000 yards, but Caverly had only light high-speed screws ahead, though they spread from bow to bow. At my four-finger sign, four tubes forward and aft were readied, and we sneaked a look into nothing but squalls. Two-thirds speed for five minutes should have the range down to 2,000 yards, and we slowed again. Sound now had light screws on various bearings, and it seemed that someone must be loose with the shaving brush in the forward torpedo room. Jones had the scope ready at deck level, however, and when Welch called 4 knots, I rode it on up for a water-lapping low-power sweep.

Seven different marks caused some confusion within the fire control party, and that is exactly what we had topside, a confusion of patrols. Our destination had been a possible focal point for enemy shipping, and by all appearance the enemy had chosen that very location for his patrols to wait out the strike. The bearings were on those that were fairly close, but there were others in view to the west and possibly several more beyond the squalls.

This was no target for any submarine, and we sneaked off to the east to a safe position for periodic radar sweeps. The patrols remained in a large, scattered group with no other pips coming into view, and after an hour we decided that our appraisal that they were waiting out the strike was indeed correct. Some of our searches had been with decks awash, and on the last occasion three blasts completed the surfacing. Frank gave 150 degrees as the course for Taihoku, or more accurately the mouth of the river leading to the city, and two engines drove *Tang* back toward Formosa.

Tamsui Mountain, rising 3,675 feet and located about ten miles inland from the northern tip of Formosa, rose above the horizon at midmorning. The coast was still 30 miles distant, but in clearing weather we could no longer be caught by a plane out of the clouds so we continued the run on the surface. It took but another hour to reach a reasonable search position and, prompted by smoke and flames ashore from the continuing strike, we pulled the plug. It seemed prudent on two accounts: We would likely be detected if we continued on the surface, and with no positive identification, we could be surprised by one of our own planes.

No planes of any sort, or ships, even sampans, came in view of the scopes as we closed the island and turned right to follow the shoreline to the south. When we surfaced at dusk, the fires ashore seemed to cover the airfields, or at least the general areas where we had observed planes landing. There could be little doubt about the thoroughness of the strike, but it had also cleared the seas. Our searchers along enemy retirement tracks remained futile but offered a gratifying display, for fires burned furiously day and night.

We spoke of the stagnant areas west of Palau following that strike, but knew that here it would be different. The enemy would have to resupply Formosa and his forces in the Philippines, too. It was just a matter of time, and any submarine could outwait the enemy. Task Force 38 had departed after the morning strike of the 14th, and *Tang* headed west. The enemy would surely seek the extra protection of remote shipping lanes along the China coast.

8

It was with some disappointment that Formosa was left astern, for we should have been able to contribute in some way to the success of the strike. During the three days of the operation many airmen must have been shot down, for we knew by our observations of enemy air activity before the 12th that he was not going to be surprised. It now appeared that our first two attacks were on merchantmen hustled out of Takao, on the southwest coast of the island; this port had over 2,000 departures a year and was the shipping point for almost all of the rice and sugar. We had gathered this and other information about Formosa before leaving Pearl. The *Monograph of the Japanese Empire*, which was on the allowance of large ships and staffs, was one source, but Thomas Philip Terry's *Guide to the Japanese Empire*, 1933 edition, had the facts we really needed—Formosa's seasonal weather, her history as a group of feudal states, her subjugation by the Chinese, Dutch, Spanish, French, and then Chinese again. The high point as far as we were concerned was the acquisition of the island by the Japanese as a part of the settlement of the Sino-Japanese War in 1895, marking the first venture of the Japanese as an imperial power. As of the date of our reference material, the Japanese had more or less contained the head-hunting tribes that still lived in remote areas in the mountains but had not subjugated them, and we wondered if these savages might not stand in our stead and befriend some of our airmen who could be escaping to the mountains.

Frank had taken a departure on Taiko Point and recommended a course of 316. It would take *Tang* diagonally across the strait to a position well south of Turnabout Island. We believed there was good logic behind this selection, for we would be able to move slowly with the current during a good part of our submerged patrol and would be in an excellent position to intercept any shipping from the north that rounded the island. And round Turnabout it must, for the shallow waters to shoreward would only accommodate ships of 5,000 tons or less, and that surely with a local pilot.

The strait was calm for a change, and we surfaced with a quarter of our voyage behind us and only 60 miles to go. If I had dared to dream, I might have considered this area a somewhat shorter though wider Long Island Sound, and lest others might be lulled by similar thoughts, I penned specific night orders covering our patrol in the middle of the strait until 0300, and then moving on to the mainland.

The night passed quietly and so did the day, though even the diehards in the engineers came to the conning tower for a squint at China. Frank and Jones kept busy identifying islands and correcting the chart; backed up by an occasional sounding, they were confident that we could lie close to this treacherous area throughout the coming darkness. They were right, but it did not make for a restful night, since no navigational lights were burning not even dimmed ones.

Only an occasional sampan had come in view of our scopes during daylight, and surely the enemy merchantmen would require some navigational aids at night. These considerations and blustering weather dictated moving away from the dangerous shoals, and Pakusa Point lay only a few hours to the east. We would have moved in another day or so anyway, for it was just our guess that the Japanese would hug the China coast. There was also the possibility that they had interpreted the three-day strike as a prelude to a further assault and landing. Even we had been fooled by our forces' previously unannounced island-hopping, and the Japanese might be bolstering Formosa for such an attack. If so, their ships would undoubtedly follow the more direct routes to the island.

Tang moved slowly east after surfacing just in case some

unconventional convoy commander decided to take his ships right down the middle of the strait. We were in no hurry, for the total run was only 60 miles. John reported our status in accordance with the night orders, and the smell of freshly baked bread made further dozing off impossible. It was not bread but hot rolls, and Adams was just taking them out of the oven. Hank and Paul, who had just come off the evening watch, were ahead of me, but there were enough for everyone. A moment later the duty chief's messenger came to the wardroom.

"We've got an Ultra, Captain," he reported. "It's still coming in." And then he hustled forward to wake the coding officer. A minute later Basil raced aft still buttoning up his pants, and I wondered if other's hearts had picked up a beat, too.

Waiting for the decoding of an Ultra was akin to waiting for the torpedoes to hit, and on this early morning the minutes dragged. That the decoding took longer was no one's fault, for Basil and Mel, who had gone aft to help, were using the old-fashioned strip cipher. There was nothing unusual about this, since boats operating in salvageable waters were frequently ordered to leave the electric coding machines at their bases. No one else went aft or otherwise interfered, so after a few minutes Basil came forward with the message printed out in continuous block letters. Vertical lines separated them into words, and the first group spelled CARRIER. The following words threw a sizable monkey wrench into the possibilities, for the complete message, less the padding, read quite simply:

CARRIER ANCHORED APPROXIMATE
CENTER FORMOSA BANKS

Frank was standing by with the chart spread out on the wardroom table and with parallel rulers read our new course, 230. Flank speed put four engines on the line. *Tang* was on her way, but just how she was supposed to reach the enemy remained a big question mark. In fact the padding, or additional random words to make the message more difficult to break, could well have included GOOD LUCK, for the banks run 60 miles from northeast to southwest and average 30 miles across. In some inlets we could dive, but elsewhere approach, attack, and evasion would all have to be on the surface.

The mission seemed a bit taut, but Ultras were not sent out

lightly, and *Tang* was the only and the action addressee. There was little use in fussing over it, for the center of the banks still lay 180 miles to the southwest. Even with an all-day submerged run at our best sustained speed, it would be on toward midnight before we could attack, and the remaining dark hours of this night were meant for rest.

Sleep was impossible; the roar of seas racing by, and a harmonic of our diesels, setting up a pulsing throb, were *Tang*'s war drums, or so it seemed to me. But others heard it, too, if the congregation in the wardroom was an indicator. Ed and John had raided the great, wide file drawers under the sideboard and had another chart of the Pescadores area spread out on the table. Dick had joined them, and the three were plotting out the possible routes for penetrating the banks. Unfortunately the deepest was only 12 fathoms, but it was five miles wide and extended like a crooked finger in for ten miles. Reaching it would require another 60 miles, however, since it led up from the south, but it might well be the route of the carrier or where she was actually anchored. We weighed this against a surface dash and the strong likelihood that we would get away with it unsighted but reached no decision before Jones came forward to call Frank for the morning stars.

When a situation is suddenly thrust upon you, finding the courage to see it through comes automatically. This operation was entirely different, for we still had three-quarters of a day to plan and also think about the enemy. Of one thing I am sure, without men like those in *Tang*, finding the courage would have been impossible.

Frank and Jones got their stars and I followed them below. The horizon was clear, but a sighting would spoil the whole effort. Paul's "Clear the bridge!" and two blasts initiated the dive, and 40 seconds later we were leveled off at periscope depth. Our heading remained 230, but now our speed was down to 5 knots.

The morning watch remained uneventful, but air patrolling commenced shortly after they had been relieved. The planes were almost welcome, for at least they signified that *Tang* was no longer patrolling a dead sea. The forenoon watch, with Larry in the conning tower, did an excellent job of establishing the enemy's air search pattern. It definitely showed that we were not the object and increased our hope that a practical commander might indeed make a run straight up the slot. Surface patrols in the afternoon added to the likelihood of coming shipping, and in all truthfulness, such a ship or convoy would give us a legitimate reason not to try penetrating the banks, the way the appearance of the *Yamaoka Maru* in the Yellow Sea had got us out of a pending inshore predicament.

Before the first scheduled Fox after we surfaced, another Ultra came in. Any Ultra had its own highest priority, but this message contained an operational emergency procedure sign in its heading. The last such use I could recall concerned the *Tambor-Triton* incident. Ed and Mel set up the strip cipher on the control room chart table, and never had a watch been quieter as the strips were inserted in the prescribed order for the date. Ed called the five-letter groups as Mel set the strips and then read down the prescribed column. The first four words were padding, but the next six letters spelled CANCEL. The remainder of the message would be academic, and right 15 degrees rudder brought us to 050, right back toward Pakusa Point.

We could only surmise that at headquarters a well-meaning duty commander had released the first Ultra without prior reference to the chief of staff or Admiral Lockwood. Very probably the admiral had taken one look at the dispatch board and, seeing the concise message containing no "for information" or other modifying words, immediately knew the action *Tang* would take. The message just decoded would be his countermand. We were still curious about the original information, however, and wondered if it was derived from a sighting or, as the word Ultra signified, from a broken dispatch. And of course, in the latter case, was it a ruse to sucker us into another type of typhoon.

That it might be a ruse became more than just a possibility when a bloodcurdling "Clear the bridge!" and two blasts took us down. Frank questioned the lookouts, and even those who were supposed to be guarding the after sectors confirmed the roar and blue exhaust crossing our bow. We considered this for a half hour, for only radar-equipped planes or those directed by other radar could come so close. Our SJ had detected nothing, so we tried another surface run, reluctantly at reduced speed since our wake at higher speed could be a telltale. Our nondirectional APR-1 had radar signals on the usual frequencies as before, but they could originate in the Pescadores, Formosa, or anywhere at sea. Only the intensity of the signal was significant, but the log showed no marked increase in any signal strength.

The slower speed seemed to have solved the immediate problem, but just before midnight two blasts took us down again. The blue exhaust was aft this time, and we rested below for another half hour, now quite convinced that the enemy did indeed posesss a radar-equipped bomber. Just as our SJ was unable to detect planes at any appreciable elevation, so his radar lost us when the down-angle increased during his approach. This was our theory anyway, but we had no desire to put it to further test. Three blasts and four engines pulled us clear, and we dived within striking distance of Pakusa Point at dawn.

We still considered this our lucky point, but only two patrols came in view of our scope during the day, and even they seemed to retire for the night. We stuck it out another day, perhaps becoming too impatient and completely forgetting the 26 days of our first patrol without a contact. Still, over a week had gone by since our last attack here, and this should be a concentrated area for shipping. The Japanese could be shuttling supplies to Kiirun for rail transportation farther to the south. It would be the hard way, but we would have to admit that it would be safer.

It was pitch dark on the evening of October 18 when we followed the contour of the island to the northeast. Rounding Fuki Point, our bow rose to great swells rolling in from another Pacific storm. In anticipation, Caverly with the SJ watch was already wearing his trademark, and as our bow commenced plunging downward others might need one, too. Our new course of 110 would keep our head into the seas as we skirted the dark northern coast, and the troops could at least be thankful that these seas were not on our quarter. Our immediate destination was a point three miles off Keelung To, a small, tall island that sits just inside the ten-fathom curve off Kiirun.

According to our information, Kiirun was the best port of Formosa, being completely sheltered and of recent years dredged to accommodate ships of all drafts. The city's ancient structures were built by the Spanish, but it had modern railway connection to Taihoku, the capital, only 18 miles away. An additional note that Frank had added made us all chuckle. The city boasted three gold mines, discovered by a Chinese miner from California.

The bits of information might not seem important, but those concerning the port and the railhead were responsible for our present course, and the rest added a bit of interest for all hands. The yearly average of over 200 rainy days and 200 inches of rain at Kiirun might discourage some of us from ever visiting the port, but we would see it from a distance at daylight.

Frank picked up the phone to his right. It was Dick reporting that SJ had Keelung To at 12,000 yards, and the navigator went topside to pilot *Tang* to the selected position off the island. We slowed and moved in cautiously; there was no hurry. The wavy interference of 10-centimeter radar appeared on the SJ, probably from one of our wolf packs, and it served to remind us that we were not alone in this endeavor. If they could make it too hot on the Pacific side of Formosa, ships would come our way. They, of course, were even more dependent on *Tang*'s actions within the strait.

At 2330 we turned left to the least uncomfortable course and slowed to steerageway. The run had been only 45 miles, but it could be an important one. We did not have long to wait before the after lookouts spotted a patrol moving out from the harbor across the open roadstead. We discreetly moved to the west as the patrol passed east of Keelung To. At least the enemy was patrolling, and we followed him out to the northeast, as this would give us the distance and time for predawn tracking of any inbound ships. Only an inbound patrol disturbed the night, and Frank piloted us back to our original position before dawn.

Larry took us down to trim our ship for these unusual conditions lest the great swells push up our bow, causing us to broach. It was 30 minutes before he reported, "Satisfied with the trim." He quickly modified the standard statement by reporting that depth control would be difficult. A few of us were in a position to appreciate the task that faced our diving officers this day, but all of us would share the results of any misjudgments. So Larry came off the regular watch list and stood by to assist the diving officer or take over if he saw fit.

Only patrols came in view in a long, tiring day. The swells made it necessary on occasion to run below periscope depth. Larry would then ease *Tang* up while holding appreciable down-angle, exaggerating the attitude I preferred when firing torpedoes. After a periscope sweep, he could call for speed as necessary and swim our boat down if she were tending to rise. Of course we could still flood negative, but during an attack phase the submarine might not then recover in time for constant bearings.

Darkness was welcome this night, especially to the planesmen and the diving officers, who could now relax as three blasts sent us to the surface. It was unnecessary to ask for a healthy blow, and our decks were high by the time we reached the bridge. Astern were Keelung To, the outer harbor, and then the harbor of Kiirun. The strong currents had made it inadvisable for us to poke very far into the roadstead, and we could not determine the actual presence of shipping at Kiirun. Certainly none would be leaving or entering now, for there were no patrols about. We could spend an easier night in the channel, southeastward toward Sakishima Gunto, and return prior to dawn.

Jones brought the chart to the wardroom, and Frank laid out a track for the night for one-engine speed. We'd need that at times for good steerageway. Frank relayed my instructions to the OOD, and *Tang* was just picking up a new roll from the change in course when Bergman came to the wardroom.

"We have a priority dispatch, Captain," he anonunced. Then turning to Dick and Mel, he continued, "It's all ready for breaking."

9

Dick beat Mel to the passageway, but only because he was seated at the end of the transom. The race aft was not all pure dedication, for the words forming the message coming clear one at a time added a suspense that could never be duplicated elsewhere. Then, being the first -to know, even ahead of the captain for a short time, put the members of the coding board in an exclusive position.

It was 2200, and while Dick and Mel worked on the dispatch we came left to west, put on the spare engine, and then stole another from Larry's battery charge. Aside from the content of the message, we could control anything in our immediate area, even from many miles away. A race toward China seemed obvious; *Tang* was on her way, and while waiting Frank and I spoke of peacetime communications training, which revolved around a so-called communications competition. Tests were conducted with stopwatches held by the observers, and time became almost as big a factor as accuracy. The result was a thoroughly boring affair, but there was nothing dull about the message Mel and Dick brought to the wardroom and placed on the table:

TASK FORCE PROCEEDING NORTH
ALONG CHINA COAST

Larry pleaded for his last main engine, and we compromised on another half hour since a fully charged battery would surely be required. The timing fitted in well, since the nearly ten miles we would travel should bring us to calmer seas. Now we considered the message itself. It had not contained the Ultra designation, and this removed a bit of the apprehension we would have felt in view of our last two experiences. On further thought, I personally believed that Admiral Lockwood himself had dictated the message form, since the Ultra prefix would have again been demanding. Tackling a task force was quite an undertaking, even for a submarine, and doing so in 20 fathoms might well be on the border of those taut demands of our *Articles for the Government of the Navy*. But *Tang* would do all that I felt she could reasonably get away with, and I kept all of these thoughts to myself, including my doubt that an enemy task force would be steaming north, away from pending action.

The increased speed, the change in the motion of our ship, and changes within the watch section quickly alerted the ship's company. One would think that we already had the enemy in hand, for an unusually large number of men had gathered in the crew's mess, and on second thought, the same had been true of the wardroom when I left to go topside.

Our course remained due west for Turnabout Island, as this should insure intercepting the enemy. As soon as the SJ presentation was sufficiently detailed to show that no ships were getting by, we would turn down the coast to gain contact and attack in darkness. The plan was logical and flexible, and I went on topside, for only the weather could cause a change. The seas had continued to moderate on this black night, and with complete confidence in Hank with the deck, I went below.

The midwatch relieved and then came the 0230 call in time for the first possible SJ contact on ships or the island. Within minutes the return from Turnabout appeared on the screen, followed by the pips of the smaller islands. No major ships could pass unnoticed, and we came left 30 degrees to 240 so as to close the coast of China obliquely.

An hour passed with no contacts other than the islands, though our SJ was turning in its peak performance as each new pip was tracked at zero speed. Ed came to the conning tower; Caverly switched on the old A-scope, said nothing as he cranked the range step, then calmly announced, "Ship bearing four zero, range thirty thousand." That would be 280 true.

The A-scope now had two dancing pips where there had been only one island pip moments before. One of them was a ship, moving away from the island, but determining which would take a minute. We crossed our fingers that the ship might be the one to the right, for that would mean she was heading northeast, putting us on her bow. Successive ranges would tell, for radar could not immediately determine the small bearing change. No change in range on the left-hand pip told the story: We had a fast ship heading southwest at approximately *Tang's* speed, and we were already well abaft her beam.

Culp conjured up a few more turns and *Tang* commenced closing the range slowly, too slowly. We would never be able to draw ahead to an attack position before dawn. Two more pips, obviously escorts, most surely marked the enemy as a warship and added to the urgency of getting in to attack. Plot now had the approximate track of the enemy, with frequent zigs, and therein lay our only chance. The Bells of St. Mary's held reveille for those few hands not already at their battle stations, and we came right to converge on the enemy's track.

With the decision, I accepted the loss of bearing. Plot already had an initial speed estimate of 20 knots, and we could not otherwise close the range. There would be refinements in our course as more accurate information came from plot and TDC, but only the very remote possibility that the enemy would assist by changing his base course to the left could really help our taut situation. The range was closing however, and I went topside to join Jones and Leibold, who had now spotted the blurps broad on our starboard bow.

Though indistinct, the aspect was broad and confirmed what I had just seen on plot; *Tang* was holding her own, losing little bearing, and literally walking in on the enemy's quarter.

Details of the silhouettes sharpened as we moved inside of 10,000 yards; we had a cruiser type and two destroyers, not exactly a task force and heading in the wrong direction as far as our priority dispatch was concerned, but SubPac's message was responsible for this contact. The cruiser would be radar-equipped, and we hoped that her operators would search ahead, in the sectors where a surfaced enemy submarine was supposed to be, at least until *Tang* had gained a position astern of the widely spaced destroyers. Then our pip could be lost amid the confusion of sea, wake, and own ship's returns, which would build up an incandescent hub about the center of the enemy's PPI screen.

The range decreased slowly past 5,000 yards, and now I could call the enemy's frequent zigs with some accuracy. Though they often left *Tang* practically astern, Frank reported that we were still holding bearing relative to the enemy's advance along the base course. No doubt with others, I found myself taking shallow breaths as we passed astern of the port destroyer, which plot had at 2,000 yards on the cruiser's bow. We occupied an identical position on the port quarter, and now at a glance identified her as a *Katori* class cruiser, one of the enemy's best.

Jones kept his eyes glued on the destroyer's stern and Leibold on the cruiser to instantly detect any change in either's attitude. Frank reported all tubes ready for firing, and I called angles as we continued to slide diagonally toward the cruiser. The range was 1,650 yards, and with steam torpedoes we could have opened the outer doors and fired. Our poor Mark 18-1s at 27 knots offered only a maximum of 7 knots speed differential; it was probably closer to 6 knots. Once launched, they were strictly on their own and could not reach the enemy for eight minutes. Not only was this almost three minutes beyond their best endurance, but the cruiser, with zigs every three to four minutes, would be off on another course long before then.

We would not leave the whole task to our torpedoes but would count on the cruiser's reducing the torpedo run with her first zig in our direction. Even then we would have one additional problem, for these torpedoes were known to tumble and otherwise run erratic if fired with submarine speeds above 12 knots. Backing full and firing would coincide, and so as not to add another detail at that time, I ordered the outer doors opened forward.

We rehearsed the procedure, all back full on the zig, my single estimate of her angle, followed instantly by firing. It would be a somewhat more complicated firing than that on the freighter of the two ship and destroyer convoy west of Saipan. But we'd fired once backing down and aground; this would not be too complicated. Perhaps the thoughts were to build up my courage a bit, for though this cruiser was no more lethal than the two escorts off Nagasaki, she looked big, mean, and more forbidding as we slowly crept toward her port beam. The zig could come at any instant. Frank called up the range, 1,400; it seemed closer.

"She's zigging, Captain!" It was Boats, whose sole job was to spot just this. I did not slow; the cruiser was zigging away and we needed all the speed we could muster to regain position, for she had put us nearly astern. Boats chuckled; we needed something to break the tension, and with encouragement he explained what he thought was so funny. "I just never expected to be maneuvering with enemy warships," he said, and I guess it's well to have someone around who can see the lighter side.

Zig plans do not simply meander back and forth along a base course at odd intervals, at least good ones don't. The Japanese commander had selected the best, with several changes of course in the same direction and then an indeterminate number back. On top of this, he would likely throw in a change of base course, so we could not afford to head on down the line hoping for his return. The fight to stay with the cruiser continued every minute, and three legs later came another chance, with *Tang* again well up on her port quarter. The torpedo tube outer doors were opened for the second time, and we waited with 7×50s to catch the enemy's first movement.

"She's turning, Captain," called Jones, who had swapped positions with Leibold, and again we continued on at full power as the enemy turned away.

A series of zigs definitely indicated a change of base course straight for Amoy. Frank stepped off the distance, and the enemy would be off the wide bay leading to the harbor at dawn. I had dropped down for a quick look and agreed. We commenced working up on the cruiser's starboard quarter, and two legs later the doors were again opened, but the enemy zigged away. A fourth attempt convinced us that the slant toward Amoy was just a part of the enemy's zig plan or a ruse. There was nothing unusual about this plan, at least from our point of view, and from a submerged position ahead that was anywhere near the enemy's base course, we would have been able to gain an attack position and hit no matter which way he zigged. Here, able to fire from one end only, and with the equivalent of 7-knot torpedoes, we had to guess which way he would zig and do so before gaining position for the firing. We guessed port, and were again rolling at something over 23 knots to reach the required position on the cruiser's port quarter. This would have to be the last such maneuver, since the start of morning twilight was but 20 minutes away, and the situation was further complicated by the fast-approaching Formosa Banks.

The range remained nearly constant as we moved from 1,500 yards nearly astern toward the quarter, but the speed differential of only 3 knots made our movement seem aggravatingly slow. The sharpest eyes *Tang* possessed had 7 × 50s steady on the destroyer well ahead and on the *Katori,* but having gained this position four times during the past two hours quite unnoticed, we expected to do so once again. The bridge was quiet, and no one would speak other than to report an enemy movement. Frank reported the outer doors open a bit ahead of time. It was good, for we would fire on an early zig even from our present position.

I continued to call bearings and an occasional angle as we passed the cruiser's quarter and continued on toward the beam. Her zig was late, but it came suddenly—away!

"Right twenty degrees rudder. Steady us on this true bearing, Frank." I marked a bearing ahead of the cruiser. "Keep the outer doors open. We'll try an up-the-kilt shot."

Frank replied with a ready "Aye, aye, Captain," but then added a caution; the crack of dawn would come in five minutes.

We were still a good 20 degrees on the cruiser's port quarter, and as *Tang* slid diagonally toward the enemy's stern the range dropped to 1,200 yards, then 1,100 as con commenced calling up the ranges regularly. The enemy's angle was 180, and Frank steadied us dead on. I glanced to the east, no tattletale gray; the range was 900 and I ordered, "All back full," for firing.

"They won't reach him, Captain. I've held up the maneuvering order." Frank was right on two counts, our torpedoes would be closing at only 200 yards a minute, and the enemy would be opening the range while we killed our way.

"What range, Frank?"

"Six hundred yards, Captain."

My thoughts escaped, and I heard my own muffled "Jesus Christ" as I slid my right hand along the bridge cowl to the diving alarm. The range was 800 yards and seconds seemed like minutes. Seven hundred yards was a minute away and then one more minute would put us at the firing point.

A blinding flash hit us; it was a battery of enemy searchlights. My two blasts sounded before some lights had completely struck their arcs, and no one could have missed my "Clear the bridge!" for I had years of training in hooking them up in series. Leibold and Jones cleared first, four lookouts raced by, and I rode John's shoulders down the hatch while hanging onto the hatch lanyard. Welch gave the wheel a twirl, setting the dogs, and *Tang* was below before the first bullets landed. There were still two orders to complete this evolution: "Rig ship for depth charge. Rig for silent running."

10

If the *Katori* detached one of her destroyers to work *Tang* over, our best defense in these 20 fathoms after daylight might well be a salvo of wakeless Mark 18-1s. We remained at battle stations, waiting, while Caverly followed the enemy's screws. Loud and on a broad band, their intensity was nonetheless decreasing as the cruiser hightailed to the southwest. An all-around search found no separate set of props nor echo-ranging, and the enemy commander had been smart in all respects, figuring that we might still be in a mood to shoot, no doubt.

After the first periscope search at daylight, we assumed normal submerged cruising, except that the smoking lamp, which was doused automatically at battle stations, remained

out. Now defense called for distance, and normally we would
be heading up for a dash on the surface. With the aid of the
current, however, *Tang* had run five miles from the diving
position; we were near enemy bases, and a sighting would
throw away our advantage. With another five miles the enemy
would have 150 square miles to search in the northeast
semicircle alone, an almost impossible task. We'd leave well
enough strictly alone, and chow went down for all hands.

Frank and I paused in control to brief Ballinger concerning
the expected plans. It took but a minute, and then the chief
pointed with a turn of his thumb toward the messroom.
Frank stepped over by the door and listened a minute before
returning.

"I was tempted to go on in and learn what really went on
topside," he commented and then explained that the lookouts
were holding forth, cutting their shipmates in on the details.
It was their moment; few adjectives would be needed, and at
least the troops would have a hot topic for conversation this
day.

We found it little different in the wardroom, with John
giving his impressions. Frank took my customary chair, but
only so I could prop up my foot on one of the chart drawers,
and then the discussion continued in the cheeriest of moods. I
had expected the opposite, for cruisers were of tremendous
importance to the enemy. Since the early days of the war,
Japanese cruisers had shown their mettle. And now this
Katori was free and racing to help oppose our imminent
landings at Leyte, in the Philippines. But we couldn't fight a
war if down in the mouth about a failure, and I was thankful
for these young men and their optimism. We had done our
very best and still had our torpedoes; to them that was
enough.

"I wonder what the *Katori*'s captain would do if he knew
that five times in a row he'd missed getting six pickles in the
side?" Dick asked. "And a half dozen up the fanny," Paul
added. This vein of conversation tapered off with the suggestion of adding bicyclist's spring metal pants clips to the
submarine allowance list, a set for each member of the topside
watch at battle stations. I trusted this included the captain.

Though the mood might not indicate it, we had serious
business. Our dead reckoning indicator could be somewhat in
error after the high-speed chase and early-morning gyrations,
and trying to run up our position from all of the entries in the

Quartermaster's Notebook would be almost impossible. But what we really needed to know could be found from a few soundings. If they were close to 30 fathoms, our course of 040 would be taking us across one of the deeper areas of the submerged plateau connecting Formosa to China. Ahead, halfway across the strait and due east of Amoy, would be a trench about 20 miles wide with a small area of 40 fathoms at its center. It was a logical place to hide, perhaps too obvious, for no sooner had the soundings shown us on course than air patrols commenced a persistent search. They were joined before noon by surface patrols, and it was at once apparent that they were paying little attention to all of the areas where we might have gone and were concentrating on the route toward the deeper water.

The enemy search succeeded only in making this October 20 seem a bit longer, and we were glad we had spent the initial two hours of the dive at standard speed, thus keeping out ahead of the enemy. There were no evening stars for Frank and Jones, for the enemy on the horizon kept us down until it was quite dark. Three patrols were still there when we surfaced and became more menacing when our radar started acting up. Before they made contact or called in night bombers, three engines started us north. The move was just in time, for Ed came to my cabin to report that the SJ had given up the ghost. A day north of the strait would give all hands some rest and permit uninterrupted repairs.

The night orders congratulated the troops on giving the *Katori* the scare of her life and did not contain any terse cautions; such were unneeded. Our course of 040, changing to 050 and slowing to standard at midnight, completed the entries. Frank would be about, trying his hand at celestial navigation on a truly black horizon.

The last 24 hours had been taut and tiring, but now with almost normal surface night cruising in pulling clear of the strait, I could consider the fortunes that had also accompanied our ship. The chase was far more dangerous than most any submerged approach and attack, but since it didn't pay off would receive no note. But we knew, and I believed the experience would further cement our ship's company. Frank interrupted my thoughts, bringing the chart and his plotting sheet to my cabin. His star lines had given him a triangle with about four-mile sides. He had conservatively drawn a circle about its center that encompassed all of the points. *Tang* was somewhere within this circle, near the middle of the strait and slightly southeast of Oksu Island, and that was all we needed to know.

We were greeted with rain and increasing seas before dawn. Such weather seemed a characteristic of the northern mouth of the strait, probably due to the warm current from the south emptying into the East China Sea. JK or JP would pick up the prop beats of any substantial ships long before they could be seen in the reduced visibility, so *Tang* dived during morning twilight. It was comforting to become a true submarine again, listening and searching as possible with the scopes for any ships; they were all enemy. Then too, Ed, Caverly, and Bergman could spread the SJ's parts out on the deck with no seasickness to interrupt their probing.

Others no doubt had tasks that had been pending, and we changed the Plan of the Day to make this October 21 a ropeyarn Sunday. It was a date I had been waiting for, since the luncheon menu called for a New England boiled dinner. The idea had surfaced with the discovery of two long-forgotten cases of S. S. Pierce canned clams. They had come aboard at San Francisco when supply had let us down during our provisioning for sea. I had readily signed a bunch of special purchase chits, and the whole commissary department, except for the duty cook, had left with a truck from Hunter's Point shipyard to fill out our allowance or procure reasonable substitutes. They must have had a grand spree, waving those chits and picking up whatever struck their fancy. Though most was substantial chow, San Francisco can supply weird items, too. The total was a bit staggering; I expected it to come to $1,000 or perhaps a bit more, but not to nearly $5,000. After each patrol a reminder would be waiting, a letter from the Bureau of Supplies and Accounts wanting to know by what authority these purchases had been made. The answers just added more references to be listed in succeeding letters until the whole thing became quite ridiculous.

But we had our clams, and I had provided security for those two cases that would match the radiomen and their Welch's grape juice. It was midmorning when I sauntered aft, for New England clam chowder, not any adulterated Manhattan stuff with tomatoes, would introduce the main course. Now for some reason, ship's cooks insist on opening cans with a cleaver. In the galley 46 cans were lined up in ranks, each with a deep cleaver cut in the top, right next to the edge.

The duty cook had the final two cans in hand, pouring the last of the clam juice down the drain!

I found it difficult to say good morning, but one can't saw sawdust, and I continued my turn aft. Everything was in fine shape, and no number of reports could ever replace the complete knowledge that could be gained from a few minutes' walk and brief exchanges with the watch. Back in the messroom, the aroma of the dinner was already attracting a number of troops, most of whom would be eating early prior to relieving the watch, but there was nothing about a boiled dinner that any one of us could filch ahead of the serving. Surprising to some, the meal did turn out well, as frankly does any chow that has meat and potatoes as the main ingredients. The clam chowder was something else, rather resembling corn chowder mixed with chewy nodules, but it was probably preferred that way by our lads from the Midwest.

Tang had been moving steadily due west throughout the day, for we anticipated that with the sum total of their experience, our radar gang would have the SJ back on its feet by dark. They did not disappoint us, and though we surfaced with no reflections but sea return, the waves presented a mottled, luminous disk spreading out from the center of the tube and not completely disappearing for some miles. The SJ was hot, and Turnabout Island should come on the screen early in the evening watch. A single tall pip on the A-scope preceded the expected island contact.

The time was exactly 2000, and we were off on another chase to the southwest but in a dark, stormy night. Our predawn experience of the day before immediately conjured up expectations of another cruiser, but additional pips of escorts did not appear, though the enemy was similarly zigging and heading down the coast. Closing the range this time offered no real problem, for section tracking showed us forward of the enemy's beam and gave a speed estimate of 15 knots. Ours was a wet bridge as three engines drove our ship through the rough seas, some waves breaking high on the conning tower fairwater and threatening to come solidly aboard.

At our 2115 position, the true plot showed an enemy angle of 20 degrees port, assuming that the ship was at the moment on the base course. It was time to slow and let her come on, and battle stations sounded. The enemy became visible for the first time at 2,500 yards; it was a warship but making much too heavy weather to be a cruiser. Frank reported the tubes ready forward and aft, and at the same time through our 7 × 50s we could see the waves crashing white on her forecastle. She was a DE-PC type patrol, well armed, but she could not possibly man her guns in these seas. We were in little better shape, for torpedoes set to run shallow enough to hit her would surely tumble and run erratic. It was a standoff, but the range continued to close as neither of us gave ground.

We were not this hard up for targets so early in the patrol, especially one that stumped us like this. We came left to put her astern and went ahead full. As if by mutual consent, the enemy reversed course and hightailed it, probably as happy as we were to get out of a nasty situation. When clear we slowed to a comfortable two-engine speed and at the same time gave Larry the engines he needed to continue the battery charge. The regular watch section was posted, and since our evasion course had taken us toward Formosa, we continued on toward where the lee of her mountains would provide some shelter from the Pacific's fall gales.

Tang was still pounding into head seas when I took a turn topside at midnight. We would not reach the coast anyway, so dropped to one-engine speed for the remainder of the night. Scuddy weather at dawn let us continue on the surface with little likelihood of being sighted, but with the first distant plane, perhaps a bird, we dived without question. Aircraft activity increased throughout the day, the numbers and types indicating an influx of planes to replace those destroyed during the carrier air strike. This also meant a concentration to oppose U.S. fleet actions in support of the Leyte campaign, if not to disrupt the invasion of Leyte itself. Perhaps the invasion was already in progress this very Sunday the 22d; but this was just a guess, since only those who needed to know were privy to such information.

The planes gave us no trouble, but neither did any enemy ships come our way. By 1800 all of the patrols seemed to have gone on or returned to their fields, and three blasts took us up into a quiet night. It did not remain so, however, for following the report of a pip with a range rate that could only be a low-flying plane, our SJ, which had been performing so beautifully, became temperamental and quit again. We headed north, as we had found this area unhealthy after our aborted run for the anchored carrier. Without the SJ it could quickly become untenable. It did, with blue exhaust roaring overhead.

11

Navigators and radio repairmen can work at their own methodical speed, and any interference or insistence on faster solutions leads to errors and omissions that cause unnecessary delay. The two blasts that sent us down were perhaps disturbance enough, but the triumvirate continued on the SJ without interruption, pausing only to grab parts that were sliding forward due to our rather steep dive.

Except for the possibility of air-dropped torpedoes, and the enemy had proven himself good at that, sighting the exhaust meant that he had missed. Staying around for another pass without any radar tracking facilities would be warranted only if we had a ship in sight. We ran north an hour, and with the old SD warmed up and apparently working well according to the echo box, its mast went up to catch the enemy for the first time since our second patrol. The skies appeared clear on a five-second observation, and three blasts followed instantly.

Again we moved north at a modest two-engine speed so as not to churn up a luminous wake. The remainder of the evening watch was uneventful topside, and the first movie in some days played all the way through below. For all appearance, *Tang* could be on a peacetime interisland cruise. An encouraging report came down from Ed, but we'd continue our run out of the strait and give the radar a shakedown all its own. We had done this for our torpedoes off Honshu, and now Ed and his gang deserved the same.

The midwatch relieved with Larry the senior officer. I'd hate to lose him as an engineering officer, but he should be fleeting up to exec; someone would get a gold mine. These thoughts were interrupted by his report that they were firing off the revamped SJ. There was no "Fixit Book" in *Tang*, and these men had spent more hours than any others in staying with their gear until it worked. I flipped on the eavesdropping switch to hear the results, and in the background came Caverly's unmistakable report of good sea return. Switching off the Voycall, I considered a change in the night orders but decided to stick with the original plan to clear the strait. The decision was barely firm when the duty chief's messenger literally burst into my cabin.

"We've got a convoy, Captain!" he almost shouted, and then added to the official report in his enthusiasm, "The chief says it's the best one since the Yellow Sea."

I thanked the messenger while already tying up my sand shoes, and he continued on forward. That convoy was in the East China Sea, not the Yellow Sea, I thought, though most everyone in *Tang* called our third foray the Yellow Sea patrol. What a time for nitpicking. I raced aft and up the ladder to the conning tower. Caverly had reported the cluster of blops as an island group at 14,000 yards after the very first sweep of the SJ.

No such islands, other than the Pescadores, lie in the strait, and Larry's turning south to put the convoy on our quarter as soon as the range was shown to be closing was absolutely correct. We'd need time to think this one over, and not just the minutes that would be available had we continued to close the enemy. Fortune had not been with us since the first two attacks, for the carrier possibility might well have resulted in an attack, and surely no warship had ever given more than *Tang* in her effort to chase down a cruiser. But in each case, so unlike our last patrol, we still had the torpedoes, and this convoy offered another chance to really hurt the enemy.

We had two options. One would be to stay with the enemy for an always successful, as far as *Tang* was concerned, crack-of-dawn submerged attack. With a split salvo we could sink two ships and, if luck were on our side, possibly a third. The other would be night surface firing, though I shuddered at the thought of another penetration between trailing escorts. That might not be necessary, however, for the best count from Caverly had been ten ships, half of them probably escorts based on the height of their pips on the A-scope, or five escorts compared to the 12 south of Nagasaki. This night, time was on our side, too, for the convoy had no nearby port, and a night surface attack, which could be deliberate and devastating, would not preclude an additional submerged attack at dawn.

A smaller pip moving swiftly from the convoy directly

toward our position, now 12,000 yards on the enemy's bow, was to make the decision for me. It was now 0050, only 20 minutes after the initial contact, and two more engines pulled us away, but not before the enemy patrol had closed half the distance. She then turned back, according to our plot, and was proceeding on a parallel but opposite course to that of the main body. It appeared that she had a radar contact that she lost, or perhaps she had side lobe troubles, too. Then Frank thought of the blue exhaust; that plane could have reported our presence, and this escort could just be making a cautionary wide sweep.

Whatever the case, we turned to follow her, and the Bells of St. Mary's chimed for the sixth time on this patrol. First things first, and Walker preceded those coming up to their battle stations with my cup of coffee. He was fast indeed if the general alarm had turned him out of his bunk. Then I remembered the chief's messenger proceeding on forward. If Walker had a standing call every time I was called, it would account for his promptness in many things and on numerous occasions. I'd have to ask Ballinger—but on further thought, why inquire about a good thing and maybe spoil it.

The patrol had slowed, and we moved inside 5,000 yards for a good observation. Her narrow though tall sihouette positively marked her as an escort but larger than any we had previously encountered, perhaps close to the size of our DEs. Our business was not with her, and we came right 30 degrees so we could close the convoy and cross its bow. It was still a probing operation to size up the enemy and thus see how we could best attack. The SJ screen showed three ships in column flanked by two other large ships, one to port and the other to starboard. Four small pips, presumed to be escorts, surrounded the convoy. The fifth, which we had just observed, would probably make up a five-ship circular screen.

The frequent zigs, placing one or the other of the forward flanking escorts in the lead, made it impossible to tell from the SJ just what position if any had been left uncovered by the patrol that we had followed back halfway to the convoy. But finding out was our immediate task, and we would do so with the eyes the good Lord gave us, albeit with an assist from our 7 × 50s.

The range to the main body closed quickly with our combined speeds, and we came right to pass broadside to the enemy while still outside of possible visual sighting. Now with the convoy on our port quarter, we slowed to let the range close as we slid silently across its van. Leibold and Jones were to starboard and port as I marked bearings on the after TBT, and I felt the best of eyes and experience were searching out the enemy. The silhouettes loomed big as the range closed below 4,000 yards, and those ships in the center showed little freeboard. This and their protected position marked them as tankers, targets of highest priority among Japanese merchantmen, and second only to capital ships of the Imperial Navy.

They would receive our first salvo, split as necessary; but moving *Tang* into firing position undetected offered a problem. A possible solution appeared with a report from Frank during our second pass across the enemy's van. Larry, on the true plot, had the convoy now steaming on its base course of 210, and the fifth member of the screen was indeed absent from her leading position while making the precautionary sweep. If she continued around the convoy she would be gone for an hour. There was our hole, dead astern of *Tang* at a range just under 3,000 yards.

Rather than present a broadside silhouette in turning, we stopped and let the convoy overtake us. The range dropped quickly, now 2,300 yards, and the ships took on sharp outlines, all appearing big and black. The situation was developing more quickly than it had with the convoy in the East China Sea, and we had little time for apprehension. At the moment the enemy was zigging, and we zigged too, arriving at the new course by an angle on the bow. If any of the ships could see us, they did not challenge our presence, but for the moment we had to go ahead at convoy speed or lose our selected slot between the port freighter and the tankers.

Frank would report when the convoy was again on or near its base course, and in the meantime Boats had another chance to maneuver with the enemy. On the next three legs of the enemy's zig plan, we moved closer to the major ships till it was my estimate that we occupied the position of the wayward escort, and we now identified the starboard flanking ship as a transport. Frank reported all tubes ready and outer doors open, and then on the next zig that the enemy was close to the base course. Plot was surely correct, for our position was right on an extended line drawn between the tankers and the freighter.

"All stop." The ships came on quickly.

"Port ahead two-thirds, starboard back two-thirds." *Tang* twisted right for near zero gyro angles on the tankers and to get her stern in position for a subsequent attack on the freighter. It was our standard maneuver, but the first time for ships in two columns.

Our bow was nicely ahead of the leading tanker, and shifting the screws for a moment stopped our swing. The three lumbering ships were coming by on a modest line of bearing, slightly disadvantageous to us since only the after half of the second tanker protruded beyond the leader. Tankers were not sunk by hits in their forward section, however, and this vulnerable stern would be all that we needed.

To assist plot, I had been marking bearings on each of the three ships; Caverly would be supplying the corresponding radar range. Then came Frank's warning of ten degrees to go. All bearings up to firing would now be on the leading tanker's stack. I marked but two.

"Everything checks below. Any time now, Captain."

"Constant bearing—mark!" The reticle rested on her superstructure.

"Set!" came immediately. Her squat stack was coming on.

"Fire!"

"Constant bearing—mark!" The wire was on her after well deck.

"Set!" Her after superstructure was coming on.

"Fire!" We shifted targets in trying to get all torpedoes on their way before the first would hit, perhaps impossible, for the range on the leading ship was 300 yards.

The third torpedo went to the stack of the second tanker at a range of 500 yards. The fourth sped to the stack of the trailing oiler at 800 yards; the fifth, to the forward edge of her after superstructure, was delayed a few seconds by the first two detonations.

John, Leibold, and the lookouts would have to vouch for the other detonations, as I was racing to the after TBT, where Jones was keeping an eye on the freighter. She was still coming on in spite of the detonations beyond our bow and the eerie light of oil fires, which surely must make us stand out in silhouette. Perhaps she figured that the torpedoes had come in from the starboard flank and that the tankers had in fact formed a protective barrier for her. Between TBT bearings, Jones checked forward for me and was gone but seconds.

"They all hit as we aimed 'em, Captain. They're afire and sinking."

No one could have asked for a better report, but I did not have time to acknowledge, as Frank had asked for one more bearing. I gave a "Mark!" on the freighter's stack; her bow was about to cross our stern. Impatient, I called, "Constant bearing—mark!' with the reticle ahead of her midships super-structure, but Leibold literally collared me, physically drag-ging me forward. I would not have left the TBT otherwise.

The transport on the other side of the tankers had spotted us in the glow of the fires and, like a monstrous destroyer, was coming in to ram. She was close; there would not be time to dive, and never had flank speed been rung up twice with greater urgency. Frank must have phoned maneuvering about the emergency, for the black smoke that poured from our overloaded diesels rivaled a destroyer's smoke screen. The transport continued to hold the upper hand, however, with her bow becoming more menacing by the second.

I would doubt that more amperes had ever poured through the armatures of a submarine's four main motors; the fields limiting the current were near zero, for the props had now driven *Tang*'s bridge across the transport's bow. But she was dangerously close, inside 100 yards and still headed to strike us near amidships. The enemy now added to our precarious situation with a fusillade, apparently of anything that would shoot. The gunfire was cracking overhead as if we were in the butts at a rifle range pulling and marking targets.

At her 16 knots the transport would strike us in another 30 seconds. We had gained a little more, and in calculated des-peration I ordered, "Left full rudder." At least the blow would be oblique, perhaps glancing, and there would be ballast tanks and frames to crumple before her bow could slice to our pressure hull. For the moment we were protected from the transport's gunfire by the extreme down-angle; a rifleman standing on her deck would have to lean out and shoot down. But more important, our stern's swing to star-board was fast, now accelerating as if it were the end man on a snap-the-whip, as indeed it was, for a submarine pivots well forward.

Unbelievably, *Tang* was alongside the transport. If we had been mooring to a submarine tender it would have been a one-bell landing, passing the lines over by hand, but not at our combined speeds of 40 knots. In seconds, with the transport's continued swing and *Tang* pulling away, the gun-fire now above us could be brought to bear. I yelled, "Clear the bridge!" sounded two blasts, and counted seven men precede me down the hatch. Out of habit, I took a glance aft to be sure nobody was being left behind. What I saw changed my mind about diving. "Hold her up! Hold her up!" I shouted.

I was afraid to sound three blasts to keep *Tang* on the surface; someone might interpret them as a plea to take her down faster (Mush Morton had once used five blasts in *Wahoo* for that very purpose), and I had unfinished business on the after TBT. *Tang* barely got her decks wet—and who would have thought that our dunking dives would pay off on patrol? About a ship's length astern, the transport was continuing to turn in an attempt to avoid the freighter, which had apparently been coming in to ram us also. Collision was imminent; the freighter would strike the transport's stern. I yelled, "Stand by aft!" and marked three consecutive bearings for a speed check before Frank's call, "Set below." The two ships stretched from quarter to quarter; I marked a single constant bearing on their middle, nearly dead astern, and Larry directed the spread of four torpedoes with the TDC along their dual length. The departure from our usual firing procedure was for speed, since seconds would count in getting us clear.

The four fish left in a seeming single salvo. Small arms fire dropped astern, and larger calibers had obviously lost us in the night. I called for John, Jones, and Leibold, for there were PCs on our port bow and beam and a larger DE about 1,000 yards on our starboard quarter with a zero angle; *Tang* was far from being out of the woods. To put the DE astern we headed for the PC on our port bow. The Mark 18-1 torpedoes commenced hitting, four tremendous explosions in rapid sequence, and Jones called the results, the freighter going down almost instantly bow first and the transport hanging with a 30-degree up-angle.

For some reason the PC ahead turned left, probably to assist the last stricken ship, and *Tang* pulled steadily away from the pursuing DE, perhaps catching her with one boiler on the line. When we had opened the range to 4,500, she gave up the chase, and our radar tracked her back toward the scene of the transport. The battle stations lookouts now came topside since diving was not imminent. We followed the DE, however, for the bow of the transport still showed on radar and then became visible through our 7 × 50s as the range neared 6,000 yards. Suddenly a violent explosion lighted the skies for a moment, and then the transport's bow disappeared from sight and the radar screen. The detonation set off a gun duel between the DE and other escort vessels, who seemed to be firing at random, sometimes at each other and then out into the night. Their confusion was understandably complete.

12

As recorded in the Quartermaster's Notebook, only ten minutes had elapsed from the time of firing our first torpedo until the final explosion that marked the sinking of the transport's bow. Frank had questioned the multiple witnesses to each sinking, since too much was going on for any one of us to have observed everything. There was no doubt that all five major ships of the convoy had sunk. As a further practical check, we took a turn around the scene of the holocaust. Assuming that the best speed of any ship would be 16 knots, that of the transport, an escaping ship could have traveled only 5,300 yards till that final explosion and another 2,650 to the present moment five minutes later. Our SJ was hot, and there was nothing on the screen except the milling escorts; but to cover a remote possibility, we made a great horseshoe sweep about the scene to widen our search in all directions. Nothing else appeared on the screen or in our 7×50s, and we steadied on north to clear the strait.

The night orders contained our course of 000, the speed (now down to full), a line of congratulations to the troops, and a caution to those with the morning watch to get some rest before 0345. To mention sleep would have been meaningless, for surely there was no one in the ship's company who was not too keyed up for that. In fact, the rehash had already started by the time Frank and I reached the wardroom. Mel was extolling his torpedoes, already a jump ahead in taking over from Hank, which was tentatively in the works, while John was taking him down a peg by remarking that Ben Hogan with a driver could have bisected each ship except the second and third tankers, and even those on the second or third strokes. Dick was listening, but with Larry's order it was actually his hand on the spread knob of the angle solver that had directed a perfect divergent spread accounting for the last two ships. It would be difficult to single out any member of the ship's company this night, for all had obviously carried out their tasks without mistake.

We spoke of the enemy, too, of the apparent failure of the escorts and the brave attempt to retaliate. In the first instance, sending the leading patrol on a scouting mission without covering her station was an error. Most likely *Tang*'s camouflage, which was now dulled from 25,000 miles at sea and at its peak, had made the penetration possible, while the ensuing ineffectiveness of the escorts could be attributed to the very suddenness of the attack. The action of the transport led us to believe that she carried the convoy commander, who seized upon an opportunity that probably should have been assigned to an escort, though his effort had very nearly saved the freighter. So many times we had observed · ships staying together following an initial attack, when scattering would have saved most of them. "Perhaps the constant possibility of a wolf pack has influenced them," John injected, and this certainly could be one of the reasons. But attacking as had the transport was in the Japanese tradition. One thing we had clearly proved this night: Mark 18-1 torpedoes could be fired astern at any submarine speed.

The wardroom clock read 0350, and there was no indication that the session would fold in a hurry. The same was not true of me, but a last turn topside was in order on such a night. Tiny was in the conning tower supervising the watch, and ever dependable Hank was on the bridge. They had just relieved and would have the watch through our dawn dive. The Quartermaster's Notebook lay open on the chart desk, with its entries since the contact covering four pages. Our maneuvers until in position ahead of the convoy had taken an hour and 20 minutes. Dropping back and twisting to shoot required another ten minutes, while shooting and pulling clear added ten minutes more. Next came the 40-minute horseshoe sweep, and now a full hour's run northward. On topside the night was moonless, and our wake seemed brighter than the stars. It told of our rush, but where were we going in such a hurry when the deeper waters of the East China Sea were less than 50 miles ahead?

"Slow to standard speed, Hank. I'll see that the navigator has the word." *Tang* lost her excess way quickly and settled into the quiet, easy aspect of a submarine on the prowl.

Duty Chief Hudson had apparently taken my turn topside as an indication that the bull sessions should close for the night. At least all below decks was as quiet as the bridge and seas topside. Nearly two hours slipped by, and then Chief Jones came forward to get Frank. After their morning stars, Frank would have Tiny or Hank, whichever was topside as the OOD, dive our ship for the day, and not many minutes later two blasts followed by a modest angle took *Tang* under.

It would have been Hank with the deck and now with the dive, for he liked the smaller, steady angle. Not as spectacular as a steep one, but it never took our ship into a gallop and at least on the average was just as fast as dives with large angles and a lot more comfortable. The bacon had been fried before the dive so the hull ventilation would carry off any smoke. The odor invariably drove those on the bridge with the morning watch into near pains of hunger, and now with *Tang* submerged it lightly permeated the boat. No reveille was included in Frank's Plan of the Day, and it would not have been necessary anyway.

Just over one half of our torpedoes had been fired, and before our next attack all understudies would have exchanged places with those men scheduled for new-construction submarines. A drill at some time during the day seemed in order, specifically for the few who might not yet have stepped into their new roles. Frank brought me up to date on what had been going on below decks; our last four torpedoes had been fired by the party that would control *Tang*'s torpedoes on our next patrol, sometime after Christmas. With the results of last night, John's remarks notwithstanding, we'd leave well enough alone. Since our evenings seemed destined to be busy, scheduling an afternoon movie was our big decision.

The day provided good training of another sort, for shortly after daylight the first air patrol passed by, and breakfast was accompanied by the tune of distant echo-ranging. Frank returned to report that the search covered a very broad front, which showed that the enemy did not know our location or thought that there were several submarines. We would find out which, no doubt, before many hours could pass, and one scope concentrated on the broad arc off our starboard quarter.

Before lunch the first thin sticks, the topmasts of patrols, poked above the horizon. Larry would determine their track. Having him in our ship's company was almost like having the second exec we had enjoyed when Mort was with us on the Yellow Sea patrol. Larry soon had the patrols crossing well astern and heading for the China coast, and our meal proceeded without interruption. Neither was our afternoon movie delayed, and we recalled early patrol reports wherein submarines had remained at battle stations under identical circumstances. Our comments were not in derision, for only the experience gained on those patrols permitted *Tang*'s methods of operation.

With the enemy about to slip below the horizon and the movie going, I took a turn through the after compartments and did not attempt to conceal my pride in the men with whom I spoke and in our ship. The troops seemed to share my feelings, and I found further evidence in the messroom on returning forward, for *Tang*'s score had been brought up to date and underlined. As of the moment, she was undoubtedly leading the force in ships on the bottom, and the troops knew it. Also posted was a copy of the recommendations for awards covering our last patrol, which I had submitted at Pearl. The individuals knew, of course, but others, especially our new hands, might not. I glanced down the second page, where the men's names were listed. Ed, Mel, and Ballinger would receive Silver Star medals; Culp, Hudson, De Lapp, and Fraz were recommended for Bronze Star medals. Next came the Secretary of the Navy's Letter of Commendation with ribbon: Fire Controlman Brincken, Torpedoman's Mate Foster, Electrician's Mate Kanagy, Radioman Schroeder, Radioman Bergman, and finally Motor Machinist's Mate Zofcin. The subsequent sheets containing the individual citations were well-thumbed, and I thought of Fraz's requesting the lesser award so that another might receive a Silver Star. Frank, and probably Ballinger also, were of course responsible for the posting, which not only added to each man's prestige but also provided incentive for others. Since awards were pegged to ships on the bottom, *Tang* was very probably leading others in individual awards, too, but we would keep these things within the ship's company.

The sound screen returned in late afternoon, passing about the same distance astern, and pinged its way on toward Formosa. It was a curious maneuver the enemy had conducted, as if trying to sweep out the whole Formosa Strait well into the East China Sea, like sweeping out a barn. The patrols continued to lag well behind us, however, and we surfaced near the end of evening twilight onto a calm sea. Frank and Jones caught their round of stars, the evening routines upwind were completed, and then the quiet ended. The heat was still on, first with night air patrols and then air and surface patrols in combination, apparently the same surface patrols that had crossed eastward during the day. They were now on our starboard bow, however, and we bent on turns for deeper seas to avoid what at least had the appearance of a trap. It turned out to be a general harassment that lasted till near the end of the evening watch. With the action starting at 0030 on this October 23, it had been an exciting, long, and tiring day, but the hours till dawn brought needed rest. We were still not ready to seek out the enemy, though should he cross our path that would be another matter.

Dick's two blasts at 0600 took us down for a routine submerged patrol in a position 30 miles to the west of our last contact with the antisubmarine forces. It was not a likely spot for enemy shipping, but neither had we necessarily found the enemy in logical places. Low and high periscope searches lured no ships to this side of the horizon during the forenoon watch, but the hours were well used in routine ship's work and a mild field day.

After lunch Frank dropped by my cabin with the chart in hand so that I might decide on our patrol for the night. Before getting down to that business, we talked about our patrol to date. This quite understandably led to a discussion of command and specifically submarine command, for there was a difference. The surface ship commander in a task force operation had to await deployment orders and then even the order to commence firing on joining the enemy. Operating generally with others, his duty was to carry out orders even if they seemed to be in error, at least until they could be verified. And in battle, a confirmation became practically impossible. Such an incident had occurred in the Battle of Guadalcanal, when an inadvertent cease-fire was given while our ships were engaged. The respite permitted the enemy to inflict devastating destruction.

By contrast, our actions were guided only by the broad directives issued in our Operation Order, with rare exceptions such as our redeployment for lifeguard or to Davao Gulf, and the orders issued to Don Weiss in the East China Sea. Even in our wolf packs, though better designated as group patrols, the senior only assigned sectors. The freedom to devise our own strategy and employ the tactics best suited to the situation and the submarine's particular capability carried also a deep responsibility. For each attack, it approached the wing commander's action we had witnessed at Truk, when the bombers headed down through the hole in the clouds into the flak. But we had the advantage of being able to turn back and do it over if all was not going well, or even of using our weapons elsewhere when the odds became prohibitive.

We had each requested submarine duty, as have all submariners, and by that very request had probably, though unwittingly, marked ourselves as candidates for that category of men who would likely put aside humane and human considerations of an enemy in carrying out attacks. Evaluation of my abilities had continued during four years of peacetime submarine operations, through qualification and then qualification for command. Frank's qualification for command had come quickly, for he could be judged in the face of the enemy. Frank and I checked off the commanders of leading boats whom we knew personally, Slade Cutter, Dusty Dornin, Eli Reich, and the list went on. Not one of them, in our opinion, would waver, have doubts, or let the inevitable holocaust deter him from operating with the judicious daring that put the enemy on the bottom.

It was time to get on with our business, and we first reviewed the enemy's actions till just before midnight. We had considered previously that the patrols might be driving us toward the minefields detailed in the JICPOA supplement to our Operation Order, but I had discounted that, for no field could withstand a typhoon that even approached the intensity of the one we had encountered. Further, the sea, though shallow, was much too deep for magnetic mines. The patrolling did show that submarine presence was at least expected along this central shipping route. Surely enemy ships would avoid the area of our last attack and passage on down the strait, and that left only the shallow waters of the China coast for their transit. Move they must, for the Leyte campaign would surely bring out forces of the Imperial fleet, with their vast support requirements.

Frank drew a line from our present position to the south of Turnabout Island, directly to the location of our original patrol there, which still showed on the chart. Perhaps we had just been too early on our first visit. Frank read the course from the compass rose and at my nod picked up the phone and ordered the OOD to steer 257 degrees true.

13

The lookouts were in the conning tower, the vents were closed, and Paul had reported *Tang* ready for surfacing. A sweep with the search scope verified Jones's calculated time for the midpoint of evening twilight, but it also showed the top of a thin mast broad on our port bow. The next true bearing was slightly greater as the ship drew to the right, and while Paul and Frank tracked her movement, I attended to the night orders.

Again they were brief, couching in general terms what we might expect this night and concluding with a caution that was probably unnecessary. The tracking continued, and I turned back to the lefthand page where I had listed the sinkings of the last convoy. Identification had made a good attempt by questioning lookouts and others who had been topside during that flail. After recording details and narrowing the choices, they had confronted the individuals with the corresponding pictures from ONI-208J, similar to police with mug shots. It was a good approach but had proved inconclusive, and I read again their frank results as I had recorded them:

3 large tankers	30,000 tons	Lat.	24° 58' N.
		Long.	120° 31' E.
1 medium transport	7,500 tons	Lat.	24° 58' N.
		Long.	120° 31' E.
1 large freighter	7,500 tons	Lat.	24° 58' N.
		Long.	120° 31' E.

The patrol had continued slowly across our track and was lost in the night at the end of evening twilight. Her passage at this time was convenient, for otherwise we could well have intercepted her on the surface. Now with the SJ warmed up, we eased up for a sweep. The patrol was out at 9,000 yards on our starboard bow, and a few more ranges showed her continuing slowly on her way. We had lost the escort handily, but so had the navigator lost his sharp horizon when three blasts finally sent *Tang* up into a quiet night with the first-quarter moon to the west.

The battery charge came first, three engines for the initial rate, while the fourth drove us along the selected track at a satisfactory speed. We were not rushed, for our destination was but a few hours away even at this speed. With the charge now starting at 2015, we would regulate our advance so as to arrive off the coast on its completion in about four hours.

The SJ appeared hot, for Bergman continued to report the patrol, now back at 18,000 yards. An early contact on Turnabout would verify our position, but Jones and Frank came to the cigarette deck with sextant, stopwatch, and shielded penlight nonetheless. Apparently the challenge of obtaining position lines on a dark horizon had caught Frank's fancy, too.

The ballast tanks were dry, safety and negative flooded, and Hudson reported our ship ready for diving below. We were ready topside, but diving would be a purely defensive measure, for then our only means of attack on a night like this would be on broad sound bearings. But we would cross that bridge when we came to it. Our immediate task was to find the enemy, preferably after the engineers and electricians had stored away a goodly supply of juice. The lookouts—and, as I went below, the whole watch—seemed exceptionally intent.

Within the hour, SJ made contact at 50,000 yards on what was most likely a distant mountaintop giving a pesky second pulse return. Ed went to the conning tower to check it out and to try for the first time his private alteration to our SJ, which varied the pulse rate. In no more than a minute he had checked this contact as being real, and the navigator confirmed it as Turnabout. The radar performance augered well for *Tang* this night should the enemy dare to move, and show he might, for in courage the Japanese were not lacking.

Our track joined the China coast obliquely, with the prevailing current on our port bow. At our low speed, the component toward the coast was considerable and soon brought the lesser islands within range of the SJ. A bit at a time the land contours became clear as they might in an irregular facsimile transmission, but Frank was the navigator and insuring that our ship was heading for the spot was his task.

Below decks, the battery ventilation blowers had been speeded up as the charge progressed. Kanagy, emerging from the battery well through the oval hatch in the passageway, extended five fingers. Five more points in specific gravity would bring it to the finishing rate. All was going according to plan, and I followed my own instructions by trying to get some rest.

Only the report of reaching the finishing rate disturbed the following hour. The final gravity of each pilot cell was gratifying. It was the same as that which we had reached on our shakedown. I thought of the contrast to *Wahoo*'s battery on her fifth patrol, when we were sent to the Kurils and down to the main islands of the Empire with only half of our battery capacity remaining. It made for taut patrolling, as did the low fog bank slowly surrounding us in the Sea of Okhotsk that turned out to be floe ice. A rush in the passageway brought me back to the present.

"We've got another convoy, Captain, range thirty-five thousand, and the navigator says there's no hurry."

The messenger went forward as before, and for the first time my foot slipped into its own sand shoe. Maneuvering bells were followed by a phone call from Frank to report coming to course 260 and going ahead standard. The change would put our ship well ahead on the enemy's projected track. He had not only taken the correct action but knew where to reach me while I had my cup of coffee.

In the conning tower, the chart showed our DR positions marked out ahead at ten-minute intervals and the enemy's track extending from the northwest toward Turnabout Island. The convoy's present position lay near the inscribed routing from Foochow to this turning point and as close to the smaller islands as any prudent navigation would permit.

Gunner's Mate Rector was manning the SJ during his normal rotation of billets within the four-hour watch. The very exact spacing of the distant pips had been the key to his differentiating them from the numerous islands. Consequently, we would have ample time to plan an approach to the best possible scene for attack, and that was the thanks the Japanese captains would receive for their excellent station-keeping.

It was now only 2242 and we would close the range for an expanded SJ view before even guessing at the composition of the enemy convoy, but three things we already knew: The ships were enemy, they were coming our way, and there were lots of them. For the moment there might be nothing required that our section tracking could not handle adequately, and it was too early to call all the troops to battle stations. But a convoy such as now appeared on the radar screen deserved the best, and individual members of the battle stations tracking party were called quietly.

The time was 2300, and a third engine added its horses in accelerating *Tang*'s movement to the convoy's projected track. It was a move to counter the remote possibility of the enemy's turning shoreward after rounding the island to hole up in protected shallow waters during the remainder of the night and then to proceed southward inshore of the coastal islands during daylight.

Our tracks converged, reducing the range steadily until Caverly and Bergman were able to make their reports consistently on the same ship rather than the group. With the more accurate information, tracking had arrived at a definite convoy speed of 12 knots. It was an increase of 2 knots over the earlier estimate but would not appreciably affect our approach since the enemy was still ten miles away.

Of greater importance than the enemy's correct speed was the sighting of the first navigational aid, a dimmed occulting light on our port bow. My first inclination had been to pass the light off as the riding light of a sampan; but with better height and perhaps better eyes, the lookouts had spotted what it was, and they deserved congratulations. Jones called the periods of continuous light and the shorter periods of darkness to the conning tower for possible identification.

It had not seemed likely that the light's characteristics would have remained unchanged since the start of the war, but moments later Frank identified it as the light on Oksu Island, to the southwest of Turnabout. It had obviously been turned on to facilitate the passage of the convoy, and I dropped below to see what advantage this knowledge might afford us. Frank was a jump ahead, already having drawn the enemy's track past the island and spun in his favorite circle as he had northeast of Pakusa Point. There, off the island, *Tang* would attack.

The approach was developing well, with everything falling

in place, and I paused for a final glance at the SJ before returning to the bridge. The A-scope was on and Caverly trained left, bringing the reflector on the bearing of the enemy. A veritable forest of small and tall dancing pips sprang up to the right and left of the range step. Caverly twisted the handle on the separate cylindrical switch to bring the presentation to the PPI-scope. Strung out in a line were 14 large blops, presumed to be major ships, and 12 lesser pips to port and starboard of the column. These were undoubtedly escorts, and in addition, a single detached larger pip to shoreward could well be the ship carrying the convoy commander.

In total, it was an array such as we had not seen since Task Force 58 closed Truk, and though this was not a warship formation, at least a bit of the Imperial fleet might have trouble operating without the supplies this convoy could be carrying. For a moment I regretted the four torpedoes we had fired in sinking the first two ships. They were Empire-bound, and though their loss might cause some tightening of belts or use of substitute materials in war production, no nation is brought to its knees solely by interdicting the materials flowing to its shores.

But our task was ahead, on our starboard hand to be exact, and if Caverly's SJ presentation was planned for my benefit by the complete fire control party, which seemed likely since the steersman's hand was poised on the general alarm, it had the desired effect. I nodded to Seaman Vaughn on the wheel and his hand swung down. The Bells of St. Mary's rang out, and our battle stations would be manned to attack the greatest concentration of enemy ships *Tang* had yet joined.

The enemy was now rounding the northeast tip of Turnabout to seaward of the outer island, and we slowed to steerageway until the convoy had settled on its new course. It quickly became evident that the maneuver entailed more than the anticipated turn, for SJ reported the smaller pips appearing to seaward of the main column. It could be a defensive move while the convoy rounded the next two promontories of the island; but the final disposition, with the apparent flagship now out ahead to port, at least confirmed the convoy commander's intention of proceeding southwest close to or inside the ten-fathom curve. His choice would now make little difference, for *Tang* was in position to counter any move.

The range seemed to close slowly, though the convoy's 12

knots was bringing it 400 yards closer every minute, even a little more counting our steerageway. We searched the general bearing of the convoy with our 7 × 50s and finally had the fuzzy shapes of the leading ships, which had heretofore blended in with the island. Frank called up the time of sighting, 2347, and the current radar range on the flagship, now down to 8,700 yards. Our attack could come, in 20 minutes should we let the enemy come to us, one half of that if we closed at the 12-knot maximum firing speed for bow shots with these electric torpedoes.

Battle stations had been manned since five minutes after the alarm, and now the decision concerning the attack was imminent. For the moment, I only ordered all tubes made ready for firing; we were in the driver's seat, but four engines went on the line and temporary load to preclude any unwanted blotches of smoke at the coming shorter ranges. We waited as the shadows took shape and slowly became defined silhouettes. The only sound was the crisp "Mark!" for each TBT bearing on the flagship as she drew ever so slowly to the left.

I wondered about the enemy formation and why the commander had elected to string his ships out in such a long column when he could place dual screens about a compact formation. Perhaps the enemy's experience during our last attack was the answer, and he might anticipate that now only an attack on one ship would be possible. For a nonsubmariner, his thinking would be logical since all except the leading and trailing vessels could have bow, beam, and quarter escorts. They did pose a problem, but not one that was insurmountable.

These considerations were concurrent with continuous observation of the enemy's van, but then the angles on the leading ships began to open, revealing a two-stack transport and, immediately following, ships with silhouettes resembling raised floating dry docks. Further identification was unnecessary; our priority now was to insure that our torpedoes hit before the enemy became aware of us.

"All ahead standard" ended our brief period of imitating a trawler, and Welch steadied on course 330, the bearing that would take *Tang* close astern of the flagship. It would not be our final course, for we would pass keeping our bow on her stern, as we had done in the East China Sea, and without an inner screen to interfere, the maneuver should succeed. Jones had his 7 × 50s on the flagship as did I, while Boats kept track of the leading escort to starboard. It was like old times, up to a point, and then came Jones's whisper, still keeping his glasses glued on the flagship.

"Her angle is sharpening, Captain."

Until our last attack, we had considered it axiomatic that a merchantman turned away on sighting a submarine and an escort turned towards. One half of our axiom had been blasted by that charging transport, and I now called for quick SJ ranges on the bearing of the flagship, for neither Jones nor I could be sure which way she had turned. The passing seconds seemed like minutes, but Frank had guessed the urgency.

"Range constant at twenty-six fifty, Captain."

The flagship had for some reason turned toward the main column, and we breathed more easily for the moment, especially since the way promised to become clear for a slice directly toward the transport. Any complacence was short-lived, for two DEs pulled out of the column on our starboard hand and moved toward the main body, then paralleled it in an opposite direction firing bursts of antiaircraft tracers into the air.

As far as any secrecy was concerned, the jig was up, made further evident when the flagship commenced signaling to the ships in the long column. She used the equivalent of a 36- or 48-inch searchlight, however, illuminating the ships down the line. Thus Jones, Boats, and I were able to pick out the prospective targets for our bow tubes. The ship we were approaching was a three-deck, two-stack transport; the next was a two-deck one-stacker, followed by a large, modern tanker. All deck spaces were piled high with enormous crates, accounting for the floating dry dock silhouettes.

Having our presence discovered was no great surprise, for the APR-1 had been saturated with radar transmissions since shortly after the initial contact. But it had been our hope that the enemy's radar screens were as saturated as our own, and that *Tang*, in the middle of it all, would reflect just one more indistinguishable pip.

With the searchlight display, we had gone ahead full to bring on the attack while the path to our targets remained clear, and now came Frank's welcome advice to slow and come to course 300 for firing on a 70 port track at the two-stacker. It required only the satisfying order, "Make it so."

Equally satisfying were the range of 1,650 and then a few moments later, "Ten degrees to go, Captain. The outer doors are open forward."

I marked three well-spaced bearings between the transport's stacks, where all previous bearings had been taken. The time was 0005 on October 25.

"It all checks below, speed twelve, range fourteen hundred, course two two five. Any time, Captain." Frank's report was calm, as if he were reading off the football scores from the press news. But he could not see nor probably hear the gunfire now commencing on our starboard hand.

"Constant bearing—mark!" The reticle was again between the stacks, and I waited for the transport's mainmast to come into the field of the stationary binoculars. It moved quickly into view, twice the thickness of the vertical wire, and they suddenly became one.

"Fire!" The first torpedo left with the characteristic shudder, but only a slight semblance of the whine reached the bridge. It was enough to assure us that this Mark 18-1 was on its way, and five seconds later the second torpedo sped to hit under her foremast.

"Shift targets. Bearing—mark!"

Tang was running the gauntlet between the two columns, and as of the moment the enemy still did not know where. The solution to bringing our ship out in one piece lay in torpedo hits, for they would physically and mentally disrupt the enemy's counterattack.

"Set below, range eleven hundred." Frank's report came up in seconds.

"Constant bearing—mark!" The wire was on the midships stack of the second transport, with the mainmast already coming into the field. This time Dick's "Set!" was almost instantaneous. The mainmast touched the wire.

"Fire!" I could visualize Frank's palm hitting the firing plunger and then felt the slight shake forward as when our bow hit a cross sea; the third torpedo was on its way to hit under the point of aim. The fourth torpedo went to her foremast, and we turned to the business of the third ship in column, the tanker.

"Range nine hundred, all set below." Frank's call came in quick response to the initial bearing. She was a lumbering ship with her added deck cargo, and now seen in her true size at one-half the former sighting range, she was worthy of all our available forward torpedoes. We'd make all two of them count.

"Constant bearing—mark!" The wire lay amidships, waiting for her stack to come on. The explosion of the torpedo would flood her engine and fireroom spaces, the only substantial buoyancy of a loaded oiler.

"Set!" came quickly. Her squat stack lumbered into the field right to the steady wire.

"Fire!" Our fifth torpedo was on its own, a streak of phosphorescence showing that its initial course would lead the tanker properly. The sixth electric fish went to her midships to break the ship's back and set her afire.

"Right twenty degrees rudder. Frank, steady us on the reciprocal of the convoy's course and get me the range abeam to port." The reply was a cheery "Aye, aye, sir." No torpedoes had yet hit, for though con had called 73 seconds as the time for our first torpedo to complete its 1,100-yard run, only now came the warning, "Five seconds to go!"

There were other things on our minds topside. A holocaust of antiaircraft and horizontal gunfire was in progress about a thousand yards ahead. A medium freighter was passing some 500 yards on our port hand; we would skip her for the next two ships, and I ordered, "Right full rudder," to point *Tang*'s stern at their track. The order was smothered by the first detonation, but our stern, picking up a fast swing to port, told that con had the word.

The detonations continued, like a slow-motion string of monstrous firecrackers. All of the five remaining torpedoes hit, apparently as aimed, and *Tang* had a holocaust on either beam. Frank corrected my range estimate to 600 yards and reported the outer doors open aft; he forgot nothing. With such a torpedo run on near 90-degree tracks, verifying bearings were unnecessary, and neither was there time, for salvos from the escorts, perhaps by chance, were splashing uncomfortably close.

"Constant bearing—mark!" And the fourth target, another tanker, was crossing the field of my 7 × 50s.

"Set!" came from below. Her big stack was coming on as she unhesitatingly followed the freighter we had passed up, probably figuring that the attack was confined to the first three ships. Her stack touched the wire.

"Fire!" A single electric torpedo whined on its way, the whole task of sinking the ship depending on its 500 pounds of torpex. The run would take 40 seconds, and to preclude the detonation's serving as a warning, I swung the TBT immediately to the bow of the next ship, another transport, or passenger freighter with long superstructure.

"Constant bearing—mark!" Her foremast was in the field, coming on.

"Set!"

"Fire!" came instantly, and I left the TBT steady while marking another constant bearing to thus speed up the firing. It had the opposite effect, causing some confusion until I called, "This is to hit under the mainmast."

"Set!" came in time. I mentally kicked myself for having changed the routine of our firing sequence at such a time, but coming into my binoculars' field from the right was the bow of a large DE or perhaps a full-fledged destroyer. She very nearly took my mind away from the transport's mainmast, now about to reach the wire.

"Fire!" and "All ahead flank!" nearly coincided, as did the streak of our last after torpedo and the boil of our screws. There was but one priority, to get the hell out of here, and this time I blessed the great blotch of smoke from our four diesels, for it received a well-placed large-caliber salvo from the DE. Other escorts now directed their fire our way, and my inquiry revealed that Frank was pleading with Culp for more turns. Successive blotches of smoke told of the nature of Frank's request; I could almost hear the words, "To hell with the overload and smoke, pour on the coal!"

Only seconds had passed, but never had smoke taken a tougher beating from large- and small-caliber fire. We were grateful but not laughing, for the DE was still plowing toward us. The single torpedo had hit home in the tanker, and the fire changed the whole area to an evening twilight. I considered clearing the bridge since we now had no after torpedoes to shoot. The decision was made unnecessary by two tremendous explosions astern, one in the transport and the other completely obliterating the DE.

A path to seaward was clear if the enemy did not illuminate, and we slowed to full power to insure leaving no further smoke to mark our route. Behind us four ships of the convoy had sunk, a fifth, the last transport or passenger freighter, was at least stopped, and either enemy gunfire or our last after torpedo had finished off the DE. The utter finality of the explosion suggested our torpedo, but a good large-caliber hit into her magazine could have done the same. Frankly, we were so relieved by the DE's demise that sharing or even giving the enemy full credit seemed the least we could do.

Now 5,000 yards astern, occasional low fires on the sea were still accompanied by sporadic gunfire. Hank and Mel, with the forward gang, would be pulling our last two torpedoes, which had been hurriedly loaded during the melee. There were batteries to be ventilated and other routines to perform that had been bypassed during our battle, and as insurance against surprise with two tons of torpedoes loose, we doubled our distance to seaward.

The SJ was still hot and again useful now that the remainder of the convoy had cleared to the southwest. Tracking as we withdrew, Bergman kept the transport spotted and that was all of interest to us except, in a somewhat different way, the two escorts that were slowly maneuvering just to seaward of her. With luck she would sink in due course, but with the probability of one hit forward, this could not be a certainty.

There were no torpedoes ready for immediate firing, and we stood easy at battle stations so a few men at a time could get coffee and otherwise relax from a taut evening. For certain, there was plenty to talk about, and the 30 minutes required for checking and reloading each of the last torpedoes passed quickly. The bearing of the transport had remained due west as we were each, of course, affected by the same current, and on the navigator's recommendation Welch brought our bow to 270 degrees true.

It was 0125 on this morning of October 25, and turns for two-engine speed moved *Tang* briskly toward the enemy. With radar ranges on the transport and identified promontories, plot now had the ship located four miles northeast of Oksu Island. The deeper water was welcome, for escorts willing, we could attack from any quarter. When the range had closed to 5,000 yards, two more diesels shared the load, all quietly rumbling and ready for instant full power. We watched the patrolling of the two escorts, close to DE in size, as they effectively covered an arc around the transport's seaward exposure but avoided a smaller sector toward the coast. It had been effective until the current had set them out to sea, but now their patrolling pattern posed no problem. We withdrew a thousand yards and commenced the nine-mile run around the semicircle. The time was 0140.

When we were further clear of the escorts, the four engines moved *Tang* on up to 18 knots, and within the half hour we had slowed, turning toward the enemy's port beam. All was quiet as we moved in at two-thirds, the speed we used in a harbor. At 4,000 yards all hands were called back to their battle stations and the outer doors were opened on tubes 3 and 4. At 3,000 yards we slowed to steerageway and searched her over for any telltale sign that she was sinking. She was dark, and we could discern no sign of life, but that did not mean that frantic repairs were not going on below decks; we had been in that fix on our first patrol!

We kicked ahead at two-thirds again, slowing to steerageway when Bergman, on the SJ, called 1,500 yards. She was definitely lower in the water than we remembered upon firing, but that was a fleeting glimpse at best. I thought of a similar incident in *Wahoo,* though in daylight, when a torpedoed, stopped ship suddenly got way on and left us. What was I saving these two torpedoes for! If that ship was actually sinking, either of the escorts could have towed her aground and at least saved her cargo!

Tang slid quietly toward the enemy at 6 knots, with not a ripple coming from her hull or props. The transport lay athwart the projected track, as though she had been positioned with a T square on a war-game board. There would be no ship movements involved in the attack, and neither would there be any advance or transfer of the torpedoes; the gyros need only maintain straight courses. I bisected *Tang*'s bullnose with the reticle, then elevated the binoculars to the horizon, asking for a TBT check.

"Right on at zero," Frank replied. The 7 × 50s would not be touched again until after the firing, and neither would the TDC and its angle solver be required to set the gyro angles; they were zero and would remain zero. *Tang*'s true alignment under Welch's experienced hand, my quick "Fire!" when the wire steadied on, and the near simultaneous movement of Frank's palm against the firing plunger would constitute our total fire control. It would split a degree, and even the Mark 18-1s could use nothing more accurate.

The range was 1,100 yards as we continued toward the enemy. I had conned to the half degree, and now seldom did the wire even wander off the point of aim, the transport's mainmast. She had been hit forward, of this we were sure, but the coming detonation would flood vital spaces aft and send her on the way to the bottom. Three knots is 100 yards a minute, and at our speed a range of 900 yards was but one minute away. Before the approach, I had informed Frank that we would fire from just inside a thousand, and the firing point was now but 50 yards ahead.

"Stand by below!" alerted all hands. The time was 0230.

"Ready below, Captain," Frank replied. It merely signified that nothing had taken place to change our plan. The wire lay just a hair to starboard and then steadied on, like the wire in a hunter's scope.

"Fire!"

The luminous wake streaked out dead ahead. At 900 yards the torpedo would hit in just one minute. Welch was already bringing the lubber's line to the left, and I had but to call when the reticle reached the transport's foremast. The wire steadied as if *Tang* had eyes, and in truth she did.

"Stand by below!" brought Frank's expected reply.

"Fire!"

The torpedo, our very last, broached in a phosphorescent froth only yards ahead of *Tang*'s bow, turned sharply left, and commenced porpoising in an arc off our port bow.

"All ahead emergency! Right full rudder!" initiated a fishtail maneuver in a desperate attempt to move our ship outside of the speeding torpedo's turning circle. On our bow, and now coming abeam, the torpedo continued to porpoise as it heeled in the turn, causing the jammed vertical rudder to become momentarily horizontal. In less than ten seconds it had reached its maximum distance abeam, about 20 yards. It was now coming in. We had only seconds to get out of its way.

"Left full rudder!" to swing our stern clear of the warhead offered our only chance. The luminous wake from our screws, the black exhaust from four overloaded diesels, each told that our engineers were doing their damnedest. The problem was akin to moving a ship longer than a football field and proceeding at harbor speed clear of a suddenly careening speedboat. It would be close.

The torpedo hit abreast the after torpedo room, close to the maneuvering room bulkhead. The detonation was devastating, our stern going under before the topside watch could recover. One glance aft told me that there would be insufficient time to clear the bridge. My order, "Close the hatch," was automatic, and my heart went out to those below and to the young men topside who must now face the sea.

Our ship sank by the stern in seconds, the way a pendulum might swing down in a viscous liquid. The seas rolled in from aft, washing us from the bridge and shears, and of small consolation now was the detonation of our 23d torpedo as it hit home in the transport.

Tang's bow hung at a sharp angle above the surface, moving about in the current as does a buoy in a seaway. She appeared to be struggling like a great wounded animal, a leviathan, as indeed she was. I found myself orally cheering encouragement and striking out impulsively to reach her. Closing against the current was painfully slow and interrupted momentarily by a depth-charging patrol. Now close ahead, *Tang's* bow suddenly plunged on down to Davy Jones's locker, and the lonely seas seemed to share in my total grief.

EPILOGUE

Though the first paragraphs will be redundant, the brief, official "Report of the Loss of the U.S.S. TANG (SS306)" is recorded below exactly as I penned it at the U.S. Naval Hospital in Aiea, Oahu, in late September, 1945. It formed the closing pages of the "Report of War Patrol Number Five," and based on first evidence is considered the most accurate account.

This report is compiled from my observation and the stories of the eight other survivors as related to me at the first opportunity after capture.

The U.S.S. TANG took on board the twenty-four Mark 18 Mod 1 electric torpedoes prepared for the U.S.S. TAMBOR who was being delayed. All torpedo personnel in the TANG had attended electric torpedo school and it is assured these torpedoes were properly routined while on station. In fact, the performance of the first twenty-three in all running perfectly, with twenty-two hits, attests to this.

The last two torpedoes were loaded in tubes three and four during the final stern tube attack. After pulling clear of the enemy escorts opportunity was available to spend an hour checking these torpedoes before closing the enemy to sink a cripple. They were partially withdrawn from the tubes, batteries ventilated, gyro pots inspected and steering mechanism observed to be operating freely.

With the submarine speed checking at six knots and the ship conned for zero gyro, the twenty-third torpedo was fired. When its phosphorescent wake was observed heading for its point of aim on the stopped transport, the last torpedo was fired from tube number four. This torpedo curved sharply to the left, broaching during the first part of its turn and then porpoising during the remainder. Emergency speed was called for and answered immediately on firing, and a fishtail maneuver partially completed in an attempt to get clear of the torpedo's turning circle. This resulted only in the torpedo striking the stern abreast the after torpedo room instead of amidships.

The explosion was very violent, whipping the boat, breaking H. P. air lines, lifting deck plates, etc. Numerous personnel as far forward as the control room received broken limbs and other injuries. The immediate result to the ship was to flood the after three compartments together with number six and seven ballast tanks. No one escaped from these compartments and even the forward engine room was half flooded before the after door could be secured.

The ship, with no normal positive buoyancy aft and with three after flooded compartments, went down instantly by the stern. With personnel in the conning tower and to the bridge falling aft due to the angle, there was insufficient time to carry out the order to close the hatch.

Personnel in the control room succeeded in closing the conning tower lower hatch, but it had been jimmied in the explosion and leaked badly. They then leveled the boat off by flooding number two main ballast tank (opening the vent manually) and proceeded to the forward torpedo room carrying the injured in blankets.

When the survivors from the forward engine room and after battery compartments reached the messroom, they found water already above the eye-port in the door to the control room. On testing the bulkhead flappers in the ventilation piping they found the water not yet at this height. They therefore opened the door, letting the water race through, then proceeded on to the torpedo room. This made a total of about thirty men to reach an escape position.

During this time all secret and confidential publications were destroyed first by burning in the control room, and then in the forward battery compartment as the control room flooded. This latter seems unfortunate since a great deal of smoke entered the forward torpedo room.

Escaping was delayed by the presence of Japanese patrols which ran close by dropping occasional depth charges. This is unfortunate for an electrical fire in the forward battery was becoming severe. Commencing at about six o'clock, four parties left the ship, but only with difficulty as the pressure at one hundred and eighty feet made numerous returns to the torpedo room necessary to revive prostrate men.

At the time the last party escaped, the forward battery fire had reached such intensity that the paint on the forward torpedo room after bulkhead was scorching and running down. Considerable pressure had built up in the forward battery making it difficult to secure the after torpedo room door sufficiently tight to prevent acrid smoke from seeping by the gasket. It is felt that this gasket blew out, either due to the pressure or an ensuing battery explosion, and that the remaining personnel were asphyxiated.

Of the thirteen men who escaped, five were able to cling to the buoy until picked up. Three others reached the surface, but were unable to hang on or breathe and floated off and drowned. The other five were not seen after leaving the trunk.

Of the nine officers and men on the bridge, three were able to swim throughout the night and until picked up eight hours later. One officer escaped from the flooded conning tower and remained afloat until rescued with the aid of his trousers converted to a life belt.

The Destroyer Escort which picked up all nine survivors was one of four which were rescuing Japanese troops and personnel. When we realized that our clubbings and kickings were being administered by the burned, mutilated survivors of our own handiwork, we found we could take it with less prejudice.

The survivors from the forward torpedo room were motor machinist's mates Jesse Dasilva and Clayton Decker, Lieutenant (jg) Hank Flanagan, and torpedoman's mates Pete Narowanski and Hayes Trukke. All of them used Momsen lungs, and they are the only Americans ever to have escaped on their own from a sunken submarine and to have lived. After pulling these men into the lifeboat from a Japanese escort vessel, *P-34*, the oarsmen cut the life ring free from the ascending line, which was still attached to our submarine, and took the ring aboard as a souvenir. It was from the *Yamaoka Maru* and so may have spurred some wonderment within Japanese intelligence.

Escaping from the flooded conning tower after it was already about 50 feet under water and selflessly bringing a shipmate on toward the surface was Lieutenant Larry Savadkin. He did not see the shipmate after he reached the surface, but Larry resourcefully tied a knot in the bottom of each trouser leg and, swinging them above the sea, trapped air and used the inverted trousers as water wings, repeating the procedure as necessary when the air slowly leaked out. Besides me, the others swept from the bridge who were able to swim until picked up by the same pulling boat were Chief Boatswain's Mate William Leibold and First Class Radio Technician Floyd Caverly.

We were all taken aboard *P-34* and know the time was exactly 1030 since Caverly, without thinking, leaned down to read a Japanese petty officer's wristwatch and received his first "knuckle sandwich." He has never forgotten the time. Though bound on deck, we were able to see to port. Our hopes rose with each succeeding rescue, but they were all survivors from the Japanese ships.

At dusk we were stuffed into a privy-sized deckhouse fireroom used to heat the typical Japanese bath, and though only two could flake out at a time, it was a welcome change from our plight on deck. Here we exchanged accounts of the tragedy, and Narowanski's statement verified the short interval between the firing of our 24th torpedo and the explosion that sank our ship: "I finished venting the tube, about six seconds, then stepped from between them, hit my palm with my fist saying, 'Hot dog, course zero nine zero, head her for the Golden Gate!' and I was flat on the deck."

The *P-34* had speeded up and by a circuitous route reached Takao, Formosa, the following evening. Our reception included threats of beheading, as expected, but few more lumps. Far worse were the mosquitoes, described accurately in Terry's *Guide*, who had a field day since our wrists were tied to rings set high in the jail walls. The morning publicity parade rather backfired. Trukke had somehow managed to keep long blond hair, but now all of the slickum had washed away, and his hair bounded down all around to the level of his mouth, giving him the extra appearance of Hairless Joe in Al Capp's comic strip. The onlookers pointed and laughed till the whole affair took on—for them—the nature of a circus parade.

We were issued tattered whites before going north by train, along the same valley we had observed from sea. But the Cook's tour ended in a late medieval Spanish jail in the port city of Kiirun, and in our predicament we were truly taken back to the dark ages: The cells had great wooden bars complete with scuttle for food, a slit high on the wall for light, and another slit in the deck to serve as a head. At dusk, to our surprise, generous balls of hot rice and fish wrapped in cane husks were pushed through the scuttles for each of us. Within an hour everyone received a blanket, and after kindly dubbing our prison the Kiirun Clink, we got our first shut-eye since the tragedy.

Sometime before dawn, the guard at the Kiirun Clink brought us popsicles, saying simply, "I am a Christian." Within hours we were en route to Japan aboard two destroyers and a cruiser. The protocol as I boarded one of the destroyers was exact and complete with side boys. The captain, a lieutenant commander of my age, escorted me to his cabin, saying that he would be on the bridge most of the time but would be down to see me on occasion. An armed guard was stationed at the door open onto the main deck, and though my view was limited, watching ship's drills and activities made the time pass quickly. The gun crews were exceptional, their speed telling why we had suffered setbacks earlier in the war.

I had been provided shoes, warm clothes, and meals on time, but the captain's first visit did not come until after dark. The discussions that followed ranged from naval tactics to literature. He correctly did not believe that a battleship confrontation was now possible but then changed the subject, asking, "How is it, Commander, that you speak no Japanese but seem to understand my English?" I answered truthfully that when I was at the Naval Academy, Japanese language was not taught, but that had since changed. The captain turned his palms up and said with feeling, "How could we expect to understand each other's problems when you made no attempt to learn even a word of our language?" When discussing literature—and I wished I had been better read—he reached to his bookshelf and brought down a copy of *Gone with the Wind,* saying, "You recognize Mitchell's *Went with the Breeze,"* and expressed the opinion that if most influential adults had read this book, our nations might have found a solution to the problems and avoided this war. I could not disagree, but when he returned to his bridge, my thoughts returned to torpedoes.

The question that immediately arose was why submarine torpedoes were not fitted with anti-circular run devices, a relatively simple addition to send them into a dive should they turn beyond a specific limit. Erratic and even circular runs, though rare, did occur in peacetime torpedo exercises. In fact in wartime, then Commander Nesmith, V.C., had a circular run in the harbor of Constantinople back in 1915, but his submarine was submerged. Perhaps that was the answer. A submarine at periscope depth was well below the running depth of torpedoes set to hit a surface ship, and submarine surface operations as they evolved for certain circumstances during the war with Japan could not have been envisaged.

Still, in *Pruitt* the Mark 8s and in *Argonaut* the Mark 15s, which were also used by destroyers, had anti-circular run devices. And then I remembered: Early in the period of Limited Emergency, some members of ComSubPac's staff, after witnessing a demonstration of destroyer antisubmarine proficiency at the sound school, were convinced that once a submarine was detected it would have great difficulty in escaping. The submarine base was therefore directed to provide the boats with rudder clamps that could be used to make torpedoes circle as defensive weapons against destroyers that might be camped overhead. In *Argonaut* we had considered this to be silly, and they wouldn't work on our torpedoes with their anti-circular run devices anyway. But the staff obtained permission from the Bureau of Ordinance to deactivate the anti-circular run devices, thus doing away with this safety measure as a requirement in submarine torpedoes.

(*Tang* was not alone in such a disaster, for after repatriation Gunner's Mate C. W. Kuykendall, the lone survivor of *Tullibee,* confirmed her loss to a circular run. She had been to the northeast of *Tang* at Palau. Given our total submarine losses, another two may have had the same fate, quite possibly including *Wahoo*, for on her last patrol she carried Mark 18-1s with their lethal turning circle.)

As the destroyer approached Kobe, I returned the warm clothes and shoes, assured by the captain that we would be issued replacements ashore. On thanking him, I asked why our treatment on the *P-34* had been so rough and in contrast to the courtesies his ship had extended. "That ship and the escort force are not a part of the Imperial Navy," he answered as he saw me over the side.

It was a dreary day, and we were thoroughly soaked and chilled by rain and sleet as we marched to the naval training station. In another hour, a tall rear admiral looked us over, stopping in front of Chief Leibold, whose teeth were chattering with the cold. "Scared," he said, and when Boats replied that it was the cold and tried to ask for clothes, the admiral looked him up and down and said, "Of course you're cold, stupid, no shoes."

That finished the inspection, and we were off for Yokohama by train. The countryside may have been beautiful, but the fast, loaded trains, the hydoelectric lines coming down out of the mountains, and the buzzing industry were depressing to us indeed. This was particularly so at Nagoya, where we disembarked for a time. It was dark, but the factories were booming like Kaiser's shipyards, with the bluish light of arc-welding spread out through the city. Once before I had been discouraged, after Tarawa, when a stalemate in the Pacific had seemed a real possibility. And here I knew that Japan, with her routes to China quite defensible, could be defeated only by invasion.

From Yokohama, an hour by bus winding up into the hills brought us before dawn to the secret naval intelligence prison at Ofuna. There we were assigned to cells that contained grass mats and a blanket. Another prisoner brought us bowls of warm, lumpy rice, and compared to our brief experience at Kobe, the situation at Ofuna seemed good. At morning quarters we learned that we were captives, not prisoners, and as such could be put back into the sea; further, since this was not a work camp, our ration would be reduced by one-quarter. On the nicer side was word that we would start learning Japanese on the following day. Discounting the threats, the opportunity to learn a foreign language seemed a fair exchange. Please understand as I write further that neither I nor *Tang*'s other survivors were complaining about our lot, for we at least had a chance to live.

The titular head of the camp was a warrant officer called the Taichō. He was seldom seen except when he chose to make the nightly rounds. The real power lay in the Kangochō, or camp pharmacist, a sadistic, hulking man whose guards were misfits from the navy. Following morning quarters on our second day at Ofuna, the nine of us, who were the only prisoners on the west side of the divided compound, were marched through the gate to the other side. There, Lieutenant Commander J. A. Fitzgerald, skipper of our lost submarine *Grenadier,* and two others, all three walking skeletons, were called from the other prisoners' ranks. We watched the largest guards, three at a time in rotation, club these men into unconsciousness while other guards held them up so the beatings could continue. Caverly was as tough as they come and had even been a professional boxer, but this sight made him vomit. We were marched off while the Kangochō continued kicking the limp bodies; erroneously, we believed them dead.

On indeterminate nights, sometimes under orders but at other times on their own, gangs of guards would roam the corridors to beat prisoners who had been singled out for "special" treatment and others whom they apparently simply disliked. Typical of the daytime punishments for trumped-up charges, and sometimes involving all hands, was the "Ofuna crouch," in which prisoners were made to stand on the balls of their feet with knees half bent and arms raised above their heads while guards stood by to club individuals when they commenced falling after an hour or so.

The daily ration consisted of a bowl of barley in the morning and evening, about a cupful each, and soup at noon. This was made of hot water, a dash of soya sauce, and two or three slices of potatoes or some bean paste. Sometimes, for variety, leftovers would be combined to make "all dumpo" for supper. Fruit, meat, fish, or vegetables other than the potato slices were never provided. During the war crimes trials, this ration was adjudged to have averaged 300 calories per day, and this was actually a quarter less than the Japanese authorities had planned. From an inherently honest race, they did not even suspect that through bookkeeping and thievery, staples were being diverted before they reached the prisoners' larder.

The object of the starvation, beatings, and continuous threat of them was, of course, to compel prisoners to reveal useful information. Fortunately, we knew nothing about our forces' war plans. We from *Tang* were as well prepared as possible to endure this, in part because of the rigors we had had to surmount in surviving the sinking; but equally important was the layer of fat and the excellent health we brought from our ship. This led to our being given work assignments, even dipping privies, which gave us respite from the guards.

B-29

When the first B-29s flew over Ofuna we were digging caves, and appropriately it was Thanksgiving time. During the following weeks, five submariners from H.M.S. *Strategem* and several U.S. airmen joined us, and somehow the wonderful Red Cross delivered the first of three food packages at Christmas. January brought ever increasing flights of B-29s, but also scurvy ulcers that would not heal.

There was no further work, so still in our tattered whites

and with rags for shoes, although we were each allowed a blanket, we walked incessantly in the snow to keep warm and as an antidote for the creeping paralysis of beriberi.

Our conversations ranged from boyhood to shipboard just to keep our thoughts from our stomachs, and now having shared tasks we had never dreamed of, the barriers our differing ranks had imposed were steadily dropping away. I doubt that any skipper has ever learned more about his ship from the viewpoint of the troops than did I. The first disclosure, sort of a trial balloon, was the true depth reached while *Tang* was being hounded by the destroyer west of Saipan. In the pump room a sea-pressure gauge had actually passed 350 pounds per square inch, or 700 feet, before steadying, but the few who knew this decided to keep the information to themselves, and I believe they exercised good judgment.

Having taken that in stride, I next was informed that I had conducted too many inspections, but that is probably a complaint in any ship. Some time passed before I was privy to the most interesting information, the true source of the troops' alcohol at the Royal. As Caverly described the radio shack still, I clearly recalled each element: the small fan mounted low on the after bulkhead, the Silex coffee maker secured in line, and the metal ring to hold a coffee mug as a receptacle. Even the condenser now registered, the transmitter's output coil fitted with rubber stoppers and with pin jacks drilled. I had seen it in the transmitter on inspections but suspected nothing.

"Skipper, you officers must have been snoof," Caverly observed, borrowing that word from Dickens, I believe. "If you knew how many times we burned our fingers in getting that damned coil from the Silex to the wastebasket, always expecting you to smell the stuff!" he exclaimed.

With a ready source of denatured torpedo alcohol from the storage tanks, this had certainly been a neater solution than the home brew. The output must have been drop by drop, but I could see that a tin or so could readily have been accumulated on even a shortened patrol. Well, the troops had left sex behind when we passed through the Golden Gate, but that was just about all. If this product had helped in getting them back into fighting trim, then perhaps Secretary of the Navy Josephus Daniels had erred when he made our navy dry.

In February we witnessed the grandest show yet, a great

carrier air strike, which signified to us that the Philippines were secure, for otherwise our carriers could not be this far north. As before, a glance to the skies meant a beating from the guards, but the sight of torpedo bombers just yards away was worth it. Sadly, more airmen arrived, all of whom were kept in solitary confinement. Mess cooking at the time, I could only place the food inside the cell of an airman who had broken arms and could not feed himself. My request that one of us be allowed to feed him brought knuckle sandwiches; I was removed from mess cooking and do not know his fate.

In the spring those of us from *Tang* were still strong on our feet, though the beriberi was becoming very serious. Two prisoners on each side of the compound who could no longer walk had quickly died, and another three on our side were stumbling. Naval intelligence had obviously expected that the physical terror and the starvation diet would break men down, but that the food would be sufficient until the prisoners were transferred to registered camps. They had miscalculated and now took alarm, giving us all shots in an attempt to stop the continuing dysentery and substituting bread for the barley, for they would be unable to transfer prisoners who could not work. The remedies had no effect, so they sent Major Gregory (Pappy) Boyington, from across the wall, with a draft that included all of *Tang*'s enlisted men on to the large army POW camp on Omori, a causeway-connected island near Yokohama. Two months later Hank, Larry, and I joined them.

Mentally, the change to Omori was like surfacing after an all-day dive, for the 500 prisoners made it impossible for the guards to single out individuals. Rice was a welcome change, and so was the soup if we kept our eyes off its weird-looking contents. At least it provided sufficient nourishment for the reasonable work of stacking sheet metal and roof tiles in the area across the causeway, which was burned flat as far as we could see. The task had an unexpected benefit, for civilians would hide handfuls of roasted soybeans where we might find them. Once our guard caught a man doing this and brutally whipped him in the face with a pair of pliers. Only then did we realize the true depth of the civilians' kindness and their hate for the military.

With invasion apparently imminent, our work was changed to digging great caves for the storage of staples and as bomb shelters. Thirty of us had been detailed for this daylight-to-dark work, but by the end of the second week only ten of us could even walk the six miles to the site. Boats had hepatitis; gyp corn, which is normally a hog feed, had replaced the rice; but just when everything seemed its darkest, Emperor Hirohito's voice came over the 1MC at the work site. We understood one key expression—"The war is over." It was August 15, 1945.

On the news, the Japanese slaughtered an old horse at Omori and carted it with them as they went over the hill. But our resourceful cooks scrubbed out the intestines, chopped them up, and we had gyp corn-horse gut "all dumpo" to celebrate the victory. Within days B-29s started raining assorted canned goods till Omori looked like a giant salad.

Grumman TBF Avenger

Another change took place while we awaited evacuation; Boats was on the mend, but now I had his recent symptoms, and we suspected that the culprit was the single needle used for everyone at Ofuna. It was August 28, 1945, when Captain Harold Stassen's destroyer division anchored off Omori at dusk. He came ashore to make arrangements for the following day, but after taking one look he called away all boats, and evacuation started immediately. We all weighed in the 90s, but my high temperature sent me to isolation. For some of us it was a long and trying voyage home, but once there our recovery was complete. Best of all, our prayers had been answered and we found our families and loved ones fine.

Trukke and Dasilva settled in Los Angeles; Decker returned to Denver and Narowanski to New Jersey. Although there was no assurance that we would return to submarines, the rest of us chose continuing naval careers. But at sea or ashore, none of us would ever take our wonderful land with all of its freedoms for granted.

APPENDICES

Citations and Decorations

On January 24, 1946, President Harry Truman awarded *Tang* the Second Presidential Unit Citation, for her fourth and fifth patrols; all of her patrols had thus been cited by our presidents. *Tang* joined *Guardfish*, the only other submarine to receive two such citations, and became one of only three ships in the U.S. Navy so honored. Affecting me personally were orders to Washington in March of 1946. On a day most certainly filled with pride though tempered by sadness, I received the Congressional Medal of Honor from the president for my actions in attacking the last two convoys. Now I could recommend further awards.

An early inquiry at the Department of the Navy disclosed that all of the citations I had recommended at the end of our fourth patrol had been approved and forwarded to those individuals who had been transferred or to our next of kin. But not until the writing of this account did I learn that the recommendation that I receive the Medal of Honor was originally made in early March of 1945. It seems likely that intelligence had gleaned some information concerning *Tang*'s attacks in the Formosa Strait, but the Secretary of the Navy considered the citation too general and directed that it be resubmitted after the close of hostilities, when more specific information might be available. However, the subordinate awards based on this recommendation for the Medal of Honor had clear sailing at that time since they did not go via the secretary's office. I believe I see Fraz's hand in the selections of the men to receive these decorations, but knowing none of this at the time, I made my own selections in 1946. It seems that Fraz and I still made a good team; there were no duplications and all recommendations were honored.

Frank Springer and Larry Savadkin each received the Navy Cross. Silver Star medals were awarded to Ed Beaumont, Floyd Caverly, James Culp, Jesse Dasilva, Clayton Decker, Mel Enos, Lawrence Ericksen, Hank Flanagan, John Heubeck, Dick Kroth, Paul Larson, William Leibold, Pete Narowanski, John Parker, Basil Pearce, Hayes Trukke, Leland Weekley, James White, Paul Wines, and George Zofcin. A Bronze Star was awarded to Marvin De Lapp, and Charles Andriolo received the Secretary of the Navy's Letter of Commendation.

If there had been any possible doubt, these citations added to those of the previous patrols and the two Presidential Unit Citations moved *Tang* far to the front of the submarine force in total awards, and quite possibly ahead of all other ships. Sadly, so many of her men could not share in the accolade of their countrymen, but down through history this has so often been the case.

Postwar Comparison

In Washington, the Joint Army-Navy Assessment Committee (JANAC) of the Strategic Bombing Survey had already begun the thankless, and in many ways impossible task of trying to verify and assign to the rightful force and unit each ship sunk in the war against Japan. In so many cases, verification was quite impossible, for there were no survivors or Japanese witnesses. The Empire convoy system of point-to-point protection about promontories and along dangerous beaches required only landline and short-range tactical radio. This accounts for the complete lack of Ultras concerning any shipping about the Empire and for the meager Japanese records of other individual ship positions.

The JANAC report was finally published in 1947. From

that time on, ComSubPac had no option but to accept, at least publicly, the official findings. The reductions in accredited sinkings brought on official explanations pointing to the difficulties of identification, poor visibility, and night actions, which could affect the submarines' reports, but never questioning JANAC's infallibility. In simple truth, it was impossible to correlate and verify each attack and sinking without accurate records on both sides. Submarine data was exact. At the shorter ranges, the required visual evidence was positive and usually confirmed by many witnesses for all reported sinkings.

But the war was over, and boats that had sunk a goodly number of ships, now with new commanding officers, shrugged off the ships not credited. In the case of some boats who had joined the enemy but months before V-J Day, it was quite a different matter. Ships had become increasingly hard to find, and the high ratio of escorts made sinkings difficult. To have these submarines stricken entirely from the pages of history by a Washington report did not sit well, especially with their wartime crews.

Tang probably fared as well as any other submarine, but the committee seemed to delight in disallowing the very ships for which she had worked the hardest and for which she had been placed in the greatest jeopardy. On the first patrol all or similar ships were credited except the large naval tanker west of Saipan. In her stead was the 1,794-ton cargo ship *Choko Maru*, about the size of *Tang* herself. CinCPac intelligence certainly had information of the naval tanker, for it had supplied the information for the first Ultra and then again for the message concerning the dawn change of base course. Unfortunately, Ultras remained secret and could not be mentioned in confidential patrol reports. It seems likely that through clerical error a zero had been dropped from our estimate of tonnage, and the committee's staff then found obscurely listed in ONI-208J the *Choko Maru*, which fitted the figure and had been listed as missing by the Japanese. But surely *Tang* saw no such ship.

The JANAC report had no statistics for rescued naval aviators, so *Tang*'s rescues at Truk during her second patrol were not mentioned. But it is satisfying to know that every airman who survived the crash of his plane was rescued. History also shows that *Tang*'s contact report on the RO class submarine, which she nearly torpedoed and possibly vice versa, led to an attack by the destroyers *MacDonough* and *Stephen Potter* and aircraft from the *Monterey,* which were credited with sinking the *RO-45.*

On the fourth patrol, neither the gunboat at anchor in Owashi Wan nor the new engine-aft tanker so close inshore at Nigishima Saki was credited, and similarly the escort that blew to smithereens. There were no survivors or Japanese witnesses to the gunboat's demise, which undoubtedly accounts for her omission. In the case of the tanker and escort, a typographical error in the patrol report listed the longitude as 136° 18′ east instead of 136° 13′ east or five miles up the coast, and cost *Tang* this credit. Similar small errors undoubtedly affect the credits to other submarines as well.

In the last patrol, lacking specific latitudes and longitudes, which were lost with *Tang*'s records, the committee appears to have assigned ships to her at random. Perhaps it did not have a Terry's *Guide to the Japanese Empire* and its charts did not show the key positions of Puki Kaku, Pakusa Point, nor Turnabout and Oksu islands. In place of the first two major ships sunk near Pakusa Point, *Tang* was credited with sinking the *Joshu Go* of 1,658 tons and the *Oita Maru* of 711 tons in a location north of Formosa where *Tang* had never been. Since there were no survivors of either ship sunk by *Tang* nor symbols on the postwar hydrographic chart of the strait showing wrecks in these areas, it is presumed that the Japanese did not know where the ships were sunk.

Three ships of the convoy of October 23 were allowed, but only two ships of the last convoy. The antiaircraft fire from the escorts indicated that they believed planes were also involved in the latter attack. Since escorts continued to search for survivors throughout the night and most of the following day, there must certainly have been ample witnesses to the sinkings and to the bow section of the last ship, which remained sticking straight up some 40 or 50 feet into the air.

On the postwar hydrographic chart of the strait and lying north of the Pescadores are 44 symbols, each of them representing one or more sunken ships. It is interesting to note that the four submarines that made forays into the area before *Tang* and the three-submarine wolf pack that followed her in January of 1945 were credited with a grand total of only seven of the represented ships. Perhaps *Tang* is fortunate to have been credited with a like number, though we had once heard an official of Japanese naval intelligence describe October losses to submarines in the strait as "very many."

No other force was competing for the ships sunk on *Tang*'s third patrol. However, a controversy that arose between the Japanese and the committee perhaps demonstrates the impossibility of objectively piecing together at a later date what actually happened in the heat of battle. *Tang* reported sinking one freighter and one tanker in the first attack north of the Koshiki Strait, though Steward's Mate Walker had remained adamant that "there was more." After the war, the Japanese confirmed Walker's observation, reporting that they had indeed lost a tanker and three freighters. The committee disagreed with the Japanese, assessing their losses in this attack as two freighters and two passenger-cargomen. Needless to say, thus it was recorded. Now, however, it is clear why *Tang* could find nothing to chase other than a destroyer that turned out to be chasing her, and surely a convoy of four ships sunk by a single salvo of six torpedoes must rank as the most devastating submarine salvo in history.

With the extra two sinkings, bringing the total to ten ships, officially this patrol ranked first among U.S. submarine patrols in number of ships sent to Davy Jones's locker. On another pleasant note, *Wahoo* picked up another ship for her Yellow Sea patrol, the one following my 29 cribbage hand, which she had reported only damaged. She thus came in a close second, only one ship behind.

At the time of her loss, *Tang* was tied with *Tautog*, who sank her first ship in April of 1942 under J. H. Willingham's command and then continued her successful patrols with Barney Sieglaff and Tom Baskett as skippers. Tom's two ships in January, 1945, took *Tautog* out in front as the top ranking submarine with 26 ships officially credited, but *Tang* remained in second place with her official 24 sinkings. In tonnage, *Tang* placed fourth, next to Gene Fluckey's *Barb*, but in sinking rate—one enemy ship sunk every 11 days—she was second to none.

Victory

Tang was only one of more than 250 U.S. submarines participating in the overall war effort, many of whom have brave stories we will never know. But just as with boats who lived to see victory, *Tang*'s story can be complete only upon unveiling the results for which she and all other submarines fought.

Within the U.S. Navy and Marine Corps, the great battles and landings—Coral Sea, Midway, Savo Island, Guadalcanal, Tarawa, Saipan, the Philippine Sea—though some were far from victories, received the kudos of the time and occupied the prominent places in the news of the day and in the histories to follow. It is quite understandable that this should be the case, for each operation and most of the ensuing battles followed months of preparatory planning and buildup, and involved tens of thousands of men and hundreds of ships. Their exalted place in history is not disputed.

Months before the war began, however, submarines were already on patrol. The order on the night of Pearl Harbor to conduct unrestricted submarine warfare was merely a transition; now one could hit the plunger without first being attacked. Submarine warfare continued relentlessly as new submarines joined in the battle. There were no slack periods for planning and buildup, only the three weeks or so for refit, and then the departing submarine was on its way for two more months of seeking out the enemy in his own yard. Every man knew his boat would attack and that there would be counterattacks.

Our submarines sent millions of tons of shipping to the bottom, the effort reaching a crescendo in 1944. But publicity was avoided, for the boats' safety and the effectiveness of their patrols continued to demand secrecy. By the time of the last sinking, on August 14, 1945, the 288th U.S. submarine had been commissioned. Over 250 had made antishipping patrols or participated in 300 special missions, and at least 185 submarines had each sunk one or more enemy ships. The loss of over 1,100 merchant ships and over 200 warships to submarine torpedoes had been devastating to the Empire and the Imperial fleet. When questioned after the war, Japanese admirals and generals alike placed losses to U.S. submarines first in the factors leading to the fall of the Empire. Exclusive of the valiant effort by British submarines, our boats sank over 5 million tons of merchant shipping, or half again the tonnage of all other forces combined. In warships, U.S. submarine sinkings of over 600,000 tons were barely exceeded by U.S. naval air. Surely this was a remarkable achievement for a force manned by under two percent of the navy's personnel.

These results were not accomplished without penalty. From the four boats who grounded in operations against the enemy, all hands were miraculously saved. All but four survived the first *Sealion,* destroyed at Cavite in the Philippines. Twenty-four men were saved from the *R-12,* lost in training off Key West. Eight survivors from *Flier* were eventually rescued. Three survived the *S-26,* sunk en route to patrol from Panama. From seven other submarines, including *Tang,* a total of 168 hands were repatriated from prison after the war. Sadly, there were no survivors from 37 more boats, which brought our total losses to 52 submarines.

As submariners are wont to say, 3,505 shipmates are still on patrol. Our submariners thus suffered the highest casualty rate in the armed forces, six times that of the surface navy, and yet young men were in line hoping for a billet in the more daring boats. Surely this demonstrated the true mettle of our youth.

The total destruction and loss of life on both sides may seem appalling, but this was total war waged against a stalwart and equally dedicated enemy. I know of no submariner, however, who would not have gladly settled for half his sinkings or less if that number could only have sufficed in terminating the war. We are, after all, mariners first and submariners second, with a continuing love for all ships and the sea.

EX UNITED STATES SUBMARINES OPEN TO THE GENERAL PUBLIC

USS Drum   SS 228
   Mobile, Alabama

USS Marlin   SS 204
   Omaha, Neb.

USS Pampanito   SS 383
   San Francisco

USS Cod   SS 224
   Cleveland, Ohio.

USS Croaker   246
   Groton, Conn.

USS Batfish   SS 310
   Muskogee, Oklahoma.

USS Requin   SS 481
   Tampa, Florida

USS Becuna   319
   Philadelphia, PA.

USS Silversides   SS 236
   Chicago, Ill.

USS Cavalla   SS 244
   Galveston, Texas.

USS Torsk   SS 423
   Militia, Baltimore, Md.

USS Cobia   SS 245
   Manitowoc, Wis.

USS Lionfish   SS 298
   Fall River, Mass.

USS Ling   SS 297
   Hackensak, N. J.

USS Balao   SS 285
Naval Shipyard, Washington, D.C.

Since the writing of the second appendix, the JANAC report, recognized as being incomplete and partially inaccurate, has been superceded by the later Japanese IJN report and the compatible master list prepared by COMSUBPAC. Like other submarines, TANG'S official sinkings are once again credited by COMSUBPAC and appearing in this book (31) sinkings.

GLOSSARY

After trim. Variable ballast tank used to adjust submarine's weight and tilting movement.

Air banks. Groups of large air bottles located in midships ballast tanks to store high-pressure air for charging torpedoes, blowing tanks, and other services.

Angle on the bow. The angle formed by the longitudinal axis of a ship and the line of sight from the submarine intersecting her.

APR-1. Nondirectional radar detector.

A-scope. A viewing screen of the surface-search radar.

Auxiliary tanks. Variable ballast tanks located amidships and used to obtain neutral buoyancy and adjust trim; one tank generally segregated for storage of extra fresh water.

Ballast tanks. Sections of the space between pressure hull and outer hull, and saddle tanks within torpedo rooms; blown dry to provide positive buoyancy when submarine is surfaced and completely flooded to give neutral buoyancy when submerged.

Bathythermograph. A device to record sea temperature and submarine depth and to show any abrupt temperature change, or gradient.

Bendix log. An underwater device for measuring own ship's speed.

Betty. Japanese patrol bomber or torpedo plane.

Bow buoyancy. Additional ballast tank to give extra buoyancy forward on surfacing or in an emergency.

Bow planes. The pair of horizontal rudders at submarine's bow, rigged out on diving to help give initial down-angle, then used in coordination with stern planes to control depth.

Can. Storage batteries.

Cavitation. The formation of a partial vacuum about rotating propeller blades; the collapse of this vacuum creates propeller noises.

CinCPac. Commander-in-Chief, Pacific Fleet.

Clamp down. Go over the living space decks with a damp swab.

ComSubDiv. Commander Submarine Division.

ComSubPac. Commander Submarine Force, Pacific.

ComSubSoWesPac. Commander Submarines Southwest Pacific.

Con. The authority directing the steersman, or the act of directing and thus maneuvering the ship.

Conning tower. The small horizontal hull directly above the control room and below the bridge. Houses the normal steering stand, torpedo data computer, firing panel, surface-search radar, periscopes, sound receivers (except sonic JP), fathometer, navigational plot, and receivers from target bearing transmitters; the heart of both ship and torpedo fire control.

Control room. The midship compartment containing all diving controls, the ship's gyrocompass and its auxiliary, the air-search radar, an auxiliary steering stand, the interior communications switchboard, and the radio room.

CPO. Chief petty officer.

DE. A destroyer escort type warship.

DivCom. Division Commander.

Dogs. The pawls securing a watertight door or hatch.

Dog watch. Normally the 1600 to 1800 and 1800 to 2000 watches, though any four-hour watch may be halved, or dogged.

DR. Dead reckoning position, obtained by using ship's course, speed, and elapsed time.

DRI. Dead reckoning indicator; receives inputs from Bendix log and gyrocompass, and has dials showing latitude and longitude.

End-around. Submerged and surface maneuver to pass an enemy and gain position ahead.

Engine-air induction. Large mushroom valve to provide air for the diesels.

Fire control. The mechanics of directing torpedoes or gunfire.

Five by five. Loud and clear (based on system of indicating a radio signal's strength and clarity on a one-to-five scale).

Fix. An accurate ship's position obtained by star sights or bearings of known landmarks.

Forward trim. Variable ballast tank used to adjust submarine's weight and tilting moment.

Fox. Radio broadcast schedule of messages for U.S. submarines.

Front porch. *Wahoo's* and *Tang's* name for 20-millimeter gun platform just forward of bridge cowl.

Gaining bearing. Catching up or drawing ahead when pursuing a ship.

Gradient. A layer where the temperature of seawater, and to a lesser degree its density, changes abruptly, thus bending the sound wave of echo-ranging clear of a submarine below the layer.

Gyro angle. The angle set into each torpedo's gyro so that its steering mechanism will bring it to the proper course to hit the point of aim.

Hull down. Description of a ship beyond the horizon with only masts or superstructure in view.

IC switchboard. Interior communications switchboard; handles AC electricity for gyrocompasses, torpedo data computer, interior communications equipment, and other uses.

JICPOA. Joint Intelligence Center Pacific Ocean Area.

JK. A listening sound head for supersonic frequencies (too high for the unaided ear).

JP. An amplified sonic receiver.

Kuroshio. The Japanese current.

Limber holes. Scalloped openings where the superstructure joins the ballast tanks or pressure hull.

Losing bearing. Dropping behind when pursuing a ship.

LST. Landing ship, tank.

Mark 18. A series of electric-powered, wakeless torpedoes with a speed of 27 knots and a range of 4,000 yards.

Mark 14. A series of two-speed steam-powered torpedoes running at 46 knots with a range of 4,500 yards in high power or at 31½ knots with a range of 9,000 yards in low power.

Mark 23. A series of two-speed steam-powered torpedoes similar to the Mark 14s.

Maru. A suffix to the names of most Japanese merchant ships; hence, in submarine language, any Japanese ship except a warship.

Momsen lung. A breathing apparatus to permit an individual to breathe normally while escaping from a sunken submarine; also serves as a gas mask in the submarine and as a life-preserver on the surface.

Negative. A tank holding 14,000 pounds of negative ballast to accelerate.

Normal approach course. An approach course perpendicular to the bearing of the enemy.

Normal course. An approach course perpendicular to the track of the enemy.

One bell. A single order to maneuvering.

1MC. The submarine announcing system, includes the collision, diving, and general alarms.

ONI-208J. Identification manual used by U.S. submarines and aircraft to assist in classifying Japanese merchant ships.

PBM. A U.S. Martin patrol bomber.

PC. A patrol craft of about half the length of a destroyer escort.

PCO. Prospective commanding officer making a refresher patrol prior to commanding his own submarine.

Pit log. Pitometer log; the scientific name for the speed log manufactured by Bendix.

Point. A point of the compass, accurately 11¼ degrees; employed by lookouts to report direction of a sighting with each lookout's quadrant divided into eight points.

Poppet valve. Valve to vent residual torpedo firing impulse air back into the boat to reduce telltale bubble on the surface.

PPI. Plan position indicator of the surface-search radar, on which the image appears as viewed from above with submarine at its center.

Pressure hull. The submarine's inner hull and conning tower; built to withstand sea pressure at the stipulated test depth plus a generous safety factor.

QC. The echo-ranging portion of a sound head.

Relative bearing. Bearing in degrees measured clockwise from own ship's bow.

Safety. A special ballast tank with the strength of the pressure hull; blown and sealed off in emergency to compensate for some flooding within the pressure hull.

S-boat. A numbered class of post-World War I U.S. submarines still operating in World War II.

SC. Submarine-chaser.

SD. Nondirectional air-search radar.

Side lobe. False image appearing on a radar screen to right and left of a contact.

SJ. Surface-search radar; shows range and bearing of contact.

ST. Radar periscope.

Stadimeter. Periscope range-finder; target's height or length must be known to determine range or angle on the bow, respectively.

Stern planes. The pair of horizontal rudders at submarine's stern, used to control the angle on the boat and, in coordination with bow planes, to maintain or change depth.

TBT. Target bearing transmitter, one forward and one aft on bridge; receives binoculars for transmission of bearings to the conning tower.

TDC. Torpedo data computer. Keeps the range to the target current and displays the respective aspects of target and own ship; its angle-solver section computes the proper gyro angle and continuously sets the angle into all torpedoes readied for firing.

Torpedo gyro. The heart of the steering mechanism of a torpedo.

Torpex. The explosive in torpedo warheads; a combination of TNT and metal flakes.

Trim pump. A dual-piston pump for shifting ballast and for pumping to sea.

True bearing. Gyrocompass bearing, or bearing in degrees measured clockwise from earth's true north.

Ultra. A priority message with information derived from a decoded Japanese transmission.

Very star. Signal flare fired from a pistol.

Zeke. A Japanese fighter plane or bomber.

INDEX

ABOUT THE AUTHOR

Rear Admiral Richard O'Kane, a 1934 graduate of the U.S. Naval Academy, was on patrol in the submarine *Argonaut* when war broke out on December 7, 1941. After patrols in *Wahoo* as executive officer to the legendary Dudley W. (Mush) Morton, O'Kane received orders to command *Tang*. Following *Tang*'s loss, he and the other survivors spent the duration of the war imprisoned in Japanese camps. Later O'Kane commanded a submarine division, a tender, a squadron, and the Submarine School, rounding out 20 years with the boats. He and his wife, Ernestine, now own the Red Hill Horse Ranch in Sonoma County, California.

Admiral O'Kane is one of the most highly decorated naval officers, holding the Commendation Medal, the Legion of Merit, three Silver Stars, three Navy Crosses, and the Congressional Medal of Honor. Only the passage of 30 years has sufficiently dulled the pain of losing *Tang* and her crew to enable him to tell their story.

Join the Allies on the Road to Victory
BANTAM WAR BOOKS

These action-packed books recount the most important events of World War II. Specially commissioned maps, diagrams and illustrations allow you to follow these true stories of brave men and gallantry in action.

☐	22832	**D DAY: THE SIXTH OF JUNE, 1944** D. Howarth	$2.95
☐	22703	**LONDON CALLING NORTH POLE** H. J. Giskes	$2.50
☐	20904	**UNIT PRIDE** J. McAleer & B. Dickson	$3.95
☐	20748	**ENEMY AT THE GATES** W. Craig	$3.25
☐	20749	**BREAKOUT** J. Potter	$2.50
☐	20753	**COMPANY COMMANDER** C. MacDonald	$2.95
☐	20493	**A SENSE OF HONOR** J. Webb	$3.25
☐	20248	**ASSAULT ON NORWAY** T. Gallagher	$2.50
☐	14569	**U-BOAT 977** Schaeffer	$2.50
☐	22803	**WAR AS I KNEW IT** Patton, Jr.	$3.50

*Cannot be sold to Canadian Residents.
Buy them at your local bookstore or use this handy coupon: